THE CAPTIVE
IMAGINATION

THE CAPTIVE IMAGINATION

ADDICTION, REALITY, AND OUR SEARCH FOR MEANING

ELIAS DAKWAR

HARPER

An Imprint of HarperCollinsPublishers

THE CAPTIVE IMAGINATION. Copyright © 2024 by Elias Dakwar. All rights reserved. Printed in the United States of America. No part of this book may be used or reproduced in any manner whatsoever without written permission except in the case of brief quotations embodied in critical articles and reviews. For information, address HarperCollins Publishers, 195 Broadway, New York, NY 10007.

HarperCollins books may be purchased for educational, business, or sales promotional use. For information, please email the Special Markets Department at SPsales@harpercollins.com.

FIRST EDITION

Library of Congress Cataloging-in-Publication Data has been applied for.

ISBN 978-0-06-334048-0

24 25 26 27 28 LBC 5 4 3 2 1

Imagination is not a state, but the human existence itself.

—WILLIAM BLAKE

The Holy Land is everywhere.

—BLACK ELK

CONTENTS

PREFACE

This book began as a conversation with a friend several years ago. We were discussing the "psychedelic" (from the Greek *psyche delos*: mind/soul manifesting) research I had been conducting with ketamine, not typically considered a psychedelic substance but capable of comparable effects. The question was what role my research, by then spanning a decade, might be playing in the so-called psychedelic renaissance: the buzz phrase for this second wave of academic, commercial, medical, and popular interest in hallucinogenic compounds, notably psilocybin, mescaline analogues such as methylenedioxymethamphetamine (MDMA), and N,N-dimethyltryptamine (DMT).

Psychedelic and *renaissance* are not the words I would have chosen to use. I do not identify as a "psychedelic" researcher; I find the label more appropriate for Western products of a certain style, be they music or fashion, than for substances or experiences dating back millennia, maybe even to our origins. Nor do I see a renaissance in the recent surge of interest. *Business as usual* is the better phrase.

These are the words, however, that have the day, even for people outside of English-speaking countries such as my friend. A public health researcher based in Switzerland, she spoke about psychedelics, which she pronounced "sicky-delics" in her native French, as if they were as clear-cut as machine cogs, opining on what they do and how they might transform our medical and cultural systems. I had heard variations on these ideas before, but something clicked for me listening to this ordinarily cautious scientist speak so knowingly. I recognized just how pervasive the "psychedelic renaissance" had become. What I found especially striking was the incongruity between her casual mention of "psychedelics" and the dark, murky mysteries involved. If there is one area where we should tread lightly and suspend our preconceptions, then surely this would be it?

Then there was the apparent sea change whereby psychedelics had become the darlings of popular and academic media. It was only several years prior that I had faced substantial resistance in obtaining support from the National Institutes of Health (NIH) for studying the anti-addiction effects of ketamine, a legal medicine in common use for several decades. (Most other hallucinogenic compounds, by comparison, are illegal and clinically inaccessible.) I confronted many prejudices during this process, pertaining to drugs, to addiction, to consciousness, and to the place of disruptive experiences in our lives. It seemed doubtful to me that the pendulum would swing so precipitously to the other side without retaining much of the same blind momentum.

Our conversation ended up extending far beyond ketamine and psychedelics. What seemed most important to discuss weren't psychedelics as a unique drug-class but the babble of scientific and cultural currents attempting to comprehend them, demonizing them one moment only to celebrate them as a rising blockbuster antidepressant pharmaceutical the next: a paradigm-shifting Prozac, as psilocybin has been called, for the twenty-first century.

I left the conversation motivated to bear witness to another renaissance. These words are the result. They do not proclaim a psychedelic renaissance, nor, in fact, any other kind. They do not proclaim anything at all. This renaissance does not need our permission or proclamations. It has always happened, and it has always been resisted: an unending breakdown of our beliefs and systems in the face of an ever-shifting, inscrutable immensity we might call *existence*. But even this well-known word deserves a renaissance lest we grow captive to it. We might call the disorientations and revelations that come with being human by another word, just as difficult to pin down: *addiction*.

•

Not finding a word with adequate scope, I invented a new one, *pharmakolalia* (from the Greek *pharmakon lalia*: drug talk), to designate the many modes of language surrounding the complex substances we've called drugs. The word will appear occasionally as we examine a variety of *drug talk*, ranging from the words we bring to drugs, to the words that emerge during intoxication, to the shifts in personal narrative that might occur. Pharmakolalia is also intended to mean drugs as a language and language as a drug, calling attention to the ways the two often work on us with comparable poetry, yielding ambiguous intoxications that are equally liberating, illuminating, and enslaving.

Addiction is a word requiring no introduction, with a collection of familiar faces gathered around it: rail-thin heroin addicts, down-and-out compulsive gamblers, disheveled alcoholics wandering the streets. The truth, however, is that we know very little about addiction, about what causes it, how drugs might be involved, or how to best address it. And there are many other instances of pharmakolalia, beyond words such as *psychedelics, drugs,* and *addiction*, that will require attention as we work toward fuller understanding. This will include passages where our language itself might seem intoxicated.

Integration is another word meriting examination. It has been in heavy rotation recently, especially as its meanings have expanded beyond mathematics and post-segregation America. The word now refers as well to the work occurring after a person takes a psychedelic to harness its potential, as compared to the "preparation" that precedes the consumption. A person readies herself for a substance or practice with "transformation" in mind, and the process of integration serves to incorporate any shifts that might have occurred into daily life.

The assumption here is that there is a psychedelic pivot—an annunciation, a recognition, an unveiling—after which a fresh coherence may be cultivated from the fragments of the past. Some people do in fact report this kind of retrograde orientation around a single *life-changing* or *transformational* experience: carving it in stone, regularly revisiting it, or *integrating* it like a missing puzzle piece. Yet this is never the end of the matter. And it may even be the start of something else; I have heard addicted people speak about their drugs of choice in nearly identical ways, hearkening back to some fateful early encounter.

Let's consider another path, perhaps truer to the spirit of such experiences, where we embrace neither integration nor completeness, but a profound and inexhaustible *incompleteness*: recognizing the

limitless field of possibility that was disclosed, and moving perpetually toward more fruitful attunement with that (im)possibility. This is
not a linear path, moreover, with the orderly structure of something
like an exposition, climax, and closure. I cannot imagine "integration"
without ongoing "preparation" or "preparation" without simultaneous
"integration." And I cannot understand either without a good bit of
disintegration thrown in as well: the order of things broken, scrambled,
thrown out of joint.

Psychedelics and integration are important to this book. Yet they do
not make a proper appearance until its latter half. As is often the case
with such matters, these words take their time getting to where they
need to go, even as the moment of transition, when it arrives, might
seem abrupt, surprising, perhaps disorienting. What is coming can be
foreseen in the material presence of the words themselves, in their repetitive patterns rippling across the page. And it can also be recognized
in the emptiness within which each word finds its place: silence on one
side, silence on the other, and silence, of course, filling the spaces in
between.

THE CAPTIVE
IMAGINATION

WORDS AT THE THRESHOLD

Freedom, truth, justice, progress . . .

I grow concerned when everyone seems to be repeating the same thing, using identical language, gestures, even intonation. It is uncanny and unsettling, especially when it goes unnoticed. Were a disease to replicate itself with such precision, we would cry pandemic. But we have words instead, which seem to get a pass because we all say them.

The most captivating words are those inspiring the greatest sense of possibility: *love, goodness, peace, home*. Words that are inexhaustible and boundless, offering the open space for anything to happen. They might elevate us to new heights, exalt us with wondrous visions of the future. And they might also bewitch our minds, break our bodies.

It has become common knowledge that we are in the throes of a "global mental health crisis." Increased rates of depression, anxiety, addiction, isolation, suicide, overdose: these have all been linked to the fallout from COVID-19 and related challenges. But this crisis is not new. It has been building for decades, maybe even centuries. The same few words give it away.

•

I just want to be happy. Patients say these words to me, or something similar, at least once a week. Just wanting happiness: common words, uncommonly entrancing and elusive, with no conclusion on what we mean in sight. But we cannot help repeating ourselves, patients or not, in thrall to what the future might hold.

Just is a good starting point for making sense of things. The word is slight and unassuming, nearly automatic; we hardly register saying it.

And it is crucial to the confusion, signaling a modesty of intention and endeavor, as well as deep frustration: that what might be simple and natural should be so difficult. *I just want to be happy. Is that asking too much?*

Wanting happiness is many things. But easy or straightforward? I have witnessed entire fortunes disappear in pursuit, with little to show for it. Nor is it likely we have a natural claim. Wanting happiness might be central to existence and inescapable, yet the same might be said for wanting deep love or boundless freedom, which are far from assured.

"Happiness" itself is a riddle. Connection, pleasure, community, romance, success, power, control, enlightenment, wealth, self-mastery, acceptance, family, peace, fame, creative achievement, freedom from pain, or even freedom from pleasure. There are a thousand different futures from which to choose, a thousand ways to want to be happy. And we continue to wrangle with ourselves for what the best way might be.

A thousand different futures, and at the beginning is one inescapable word. *Happiness* has been regularly repeated, and with the same emphasis, since ancient times. Aristotle identified *eudaemonia*, often translated as happiness, as the primary purpose to which all human beings tend. Modern psychologists have called happiness *reward*, the main motivation behind decision making. Utilitarian and pragmatic philosophers regard the maximization of happiness, for oneself and others, the basis for ethical conduct. The pursuit of happiness is considered an inalienable right; the attainment of happiness the sure sign of a life lived well. We trust a happy face because it suggests a clear conscience: this is a good person, we conclude, who just wants to be happy.

Wanting happiness is essential, it seems, to being human. The United States has accordingly enshrined the pursuit of happiness as one of three basic rights in its founding documents, granting (some of) its inhabitants more opportunities to pursue happiness than have most other nations. Yet there is a significant problem. The US tops the world in mental health issues, suicide deaths, and opioid consumption; it is the world's most active purveyor of war; and it has 25 percent of the earth's prisoners incarcerated in its facilities. For a country founded on safeguarding the pursuit of happiness, the US is deeply unhappy and growing unhappier by the day.

Just wanting happiness means, of course, that we lack it—that we might be desperate for it. The phrasing also suggests we would do any-thing for it. We often do. And we provide our apology or rationaliza-tion—*we just want to be happy*—for whatever crimes we might commit in pursuit.

Then there is addiction, where the pursuit of happiness becomes particularly single-minded. Nothing is spared: our bodies, relation-ships, and resources might all be devastated under its influence. There are more extravagant failures at happiness, more remorse at the terri-ble things we have done to secure it. The misery intensifies the more we pursue our reward, the further entranced we become by *eudaemonia*. As does our guilt: we want people we hurt to know it's not personal, that we are *just trying to be happy*.

Addiction raises many questions beyond the disorder itself, extend-ing to the agonies ravaging what was intended to be the world's most cheerful democracy. Why do we persist in wanting, more than anything else, what has been so clearly devastating? Is it happiness we want or something else? Is happiness something we can even pursue?

As a scientist and psychiatrist specializing in addiction, I have en-deavored to bring understanding to its assaults. I have found no single explanation that can contain it. Nor does it respect our reason. Addic-tion undermines, with our apparent assent, everything that makes life worth living: our discernment, creativity, and compassion; our integ-rity, health, and freedom; our sense of truth and meaning. And all this destruction occurs with the person just wanting to be happy.

At the heart of these pursuits are unrealities that are unique neither to addicts nor to Americans. Everyone is vulnerable. Addiction con-denses our capacity for cataclysmic self-deception into a single per-son: addicted people speak our language, they use the same words, they bleed from wounds afflicting us all.

●

Addiction (from the Latin *ad-dicere*: to speak toward) has become an unpopular word due to the moralistic prejudices that surround it. But these prejudices do not vanish by renaming the condition a "substance use disorder." I prefer "addiction" precisely because it is uncomfort-able, fraught, and ultimately accurate. The word invites closer atten-tion to our blind spots, values, and preconceptions—to the nearly devotional *speaking toward*, the imposition of word after word, that "addiction" seems to invite, from everyone involved.

I entered my medical training well after the brain disease model had secured its place as the dominant framework by which to understand various expressions of suffering, including addiction. According to this model, addiction is a brain-based disease caused by the biological effects of drugs, alcohol, or certain activities such as gambling, and characterized by abnormal reward seeking—which means that a pleasure or reprieve is pursued compulsively, despite distressing consequences. This model has its merits, and it might be useful in some respects. But it mostly misses the point.

Every one of us has been besieged by pain and meaninglessness, and by an agitation to feel better. We might also fall into false solutions to our anguish. In this sense, we have all struggled with "addiction." We deceive ourselves, grow entangled with illusory comforts, flail in perplexity—we compound our suffering, in short, with more words, more wounds, more suffering.

It doesn't need to end there, of course. It often doesn't. We might choose to flourish instead, examining ourselves to root out any confusions and to reclaim the fullness of what life might be. "Addiction" is when we persist in obscuring things, desperate to avert the breakdown of the "reality" in which we've found a place. We stay with what we know, torturing ourselves in the dark while making the same stabs at a better life.

The same *meaningful* stabs. People become addicted because to do so has some personal purpose for them, despite its obvious problems. And the process often begins quietly, without any drugs or behaviors involved, in the names and roles with which we identify: agreeable employee, abandoned child, devoted partner, wretched of the earth. We may also approach our relationships—with people, other beings, things—in ways that seem real, honest, and meaningful, even if they might, in truth, be far off the mark. This is how our minds work. We *speak toward* existence, attending to it through a screen of words, meanings, images, and sometimes drugs, and we (mis)take this fiction for reality. To dispel this familiar world is a kind of death we might resist violently, even if it is killing us.

Addiction brings this confusion to a head. The unreality is palpable, conjured by some captivating activity we pursue and choose regularly, such as smoking cannabis, having sex, even working. Addicted people confer a variety of meanings, conscious and otherwise, onto their intoxications, sensations, and habits: that alcohol, for example, is a kind of sanctuary. The world grows unreal, even anti-real, as the suffering mounts, with alcohol continuing to be approached as a solution to the very problems it creates. And the dissociation grows more terrible with every drink.

Addiction is pain, deception, and fragmentation. But it is also the story of how this fissure might bring us to our senses, driving our confusions and violence to the surface for a reckoning. This can be a deeply disorienting process, more difficult in its own way than sustaining our complacencies and remaining addicted. At stake, after all, is "reality" itself.

Addressing addiction is therefore a far profounder, trickier endeavor than finding the right medication, accessing suitable psychotherapy, creating better policy, or even addressing iniquities—though all these have an important place. It is an inescapably existential challenge, touching on the most basic questions of being. Who are we? What is our purpose for existing? How do we come to know anything? And how do we make sense of our sufferings, convictions, and desires?

Immense anguish emerges from this "reality" or "self" in which we find ourselves, fixing our sense of things into place with a knife through the heart. We may be witnessing something similar with "psychedelics" and with the knowingness brought to them during this apparent renaissance. And these substances, as we will see, have interesting tricks to play when we approach them knowing exactly what's coming.

●

A calling to engage with the humanity of patients has been important to developing the perspective elaborated here. Just as important has been an attentiveness to our humanity as scientists, doctors, and politicians, regularly making pronouncements on reality and the human condition from positions of authority. We cannot forget that everything written or spoken, be it a sermon or scientific paper, comes from mortal hands. Our theories, our ways of life, and our diagnoses do not erupt fully formed from the head of God; they are the fallible products of fallible minds and deserve to be scrutinized accordingly. This is especially the case if they are presumed to be objective, absolute, and "scientific." As a scientist, I have been struck by the nonsense that passes unchallenged simply because it is presumed to be science. This type of intellectual browbeating has been called scientism: the conceit that "scientific fact," whatever that means, enjoys a privileged relationship to reality.

Such skepticism is more than nay-saying. Though it throws all beliefs into question, it does so evenly. Nothing is free from doubt; no authority can be presumed to give the final word. This also means that all modes of inquiry might just as well hit the mark, no system or approach inherently superior to others. A novel or religious text may be just as likely to shed light on things as would a scientific treatise. I have found as much insight into brain development, for instance, in the thoughtful reflections of a sixteenth-century French nobleman as in the celebrated research of a contemporary Nobel laureate. Contemplative practices from around the world—including hatha yoga, Zen, shamanism, Indigenous ritual—have further broadened my sense of what might constitute knowledge and the different ways that we may arrive at it. This approach to truth, both critical and expansive, is invariably restless, forever aiming to penetrate to the heart of the matter. There are many modes of knowing that might illuminate the way.

This book is not about what we ordinarily mean by addiction. Its main intention is to better understand why we inhabit imagined worlds divorced from what we really are, and why we refuse to relinquish these unrealities despite suffering immensely. It is about "addicts"—and it is about all of us.

We ought to be alarmed at where we are as a species, at what we do to one another and ourselves. Consider the many self-inflicted problems threatening our survival: war, social injustice, environmental spoliation, poverty, alienation, polarization, tribalism, overconsumption, to name a few. If addiction is a personal crisis, these are collective, concerning everyone. And they each involve falling into a mutilated version of the world that does not have to be the case. I suggest that we approach addiction as a magnifying glass on the "normal," nearly invisible vulnerabilities that are breaking us apart— and as an example of how we might confront our violence to awaken beyond self-destruction, as individuals and a community, before it is too late.

•

This is not the time for yet more words and more beliefs. Our trance of believing and knowing is what landed us here. What we need is neither more knowledge nor more pursuits of happiness. What is needed is what's coming: more disorientation, greater confusion, more of whatever might restore our babbling, burning world to a silent and honest perplexity. Perhaps we might heed this interruption to stop and finally listen to ourselves.

This book is not an argument. Instead, it is intended to be read as a work of imagination: a recognizable yet created world offering opportunity for a fruitful break from the forward march of the familiar one. There are some twists and turns, too, leading readers by the nose into tricks that play with the reality that has been created. Surrendering to this seduction offers a certain pleasure. Another is watching out for the inevitable surprise. We practice a paradoxical mode of engagement: captivated by these words while, at the same time, maintaining clear-eyed freedom from them.

This freedom is useful beyond navigating works of imagination. We are, after all, already immersed. Fictions, fables, and riddles form the reality in which we have made a home, entrancing, perplexing, and addicting us with each word. There are also the many tales we have heard all our lives, so familiar we have stopped listening to them. Perhaps we will listen again to these old stories of good and evil, and see through their fictions, for once, to the other side. We may awaken to a more expansive recognition in the process.

We return inevitably to our yearning for what might be called happiness. There is a great deal that addiction can teach us about the many ways we strive for a better world, while at the same time destroying one another, the earth, and ourselves. This striving at the core of addiction, and at the heart of countless other pursuits, deserves to be better understood. It may be the most primeval, most insatiable, and yet most exalted yearning possible to us. This book is an attempt, in the end, at attending to and nurturing this longing, and perhaps carrying it to liberation.

PART I

UNDER THE REGIME OF SIGNS

DRUGS AND OTHER FICTIONS

I.

It was once believed that the dreams of certain people could shed light on the whole of reality. They were called prophets, oracles, and seers, and they would experience extraordinary visions in solitude that were truer to them than anything else. Today we might call such people artists, visionaries, and the insane.

An addicted patient shared the following dream with me. It arrived unsolicited; I do not insist that my patients share their dreams, much less monitor them. This imparts a private and urgent meaningfulness to what they feel compelled to communicate. Yet, there is something universal about them too, touching everyone willing to listen.

It begins as an ordinary afternoon, rummaging through a bedroom closet for something misplaced. The day accelerates from there: propulsive rapid-fire flashes of talking, eating, taking care of errands. The frantic sense of running downhill without brakes. Then a booming siren. You freeze in place, at a precarious angle. You are now home, but it resembles a set in a wax museum. Queen Victoria is waving forever. She has your face.

But it is not your face. This is not your home. This is not your body. It is not even earth. You don't know what it is. Perhaps you are no longer alive, but something else. There are others. A homogenous crowd packed like mannikins into your store-display living room, all facing the same wall. On its surface flickers an image, casting a spectral glow over everything.

You walk closer. Hanging on the wall is an ornately framed portrait of the glorious future awaiting you outside, marriage and fame and wealth and anything else you can imagine. It grows more granular as you come nearer, a widening flat field of crude pixels in severe close-up, and into the empty dark space between pixels you fall and continue falling, the siren now sounding the monotone flat line of an EKG . . .

The dream ends the moment we realize we are not in it. It seems to happen in an instant: a simulation of everyday life, then its abrupt breakdown. A dream's power is in what it represents—and in this case, we find the passage of the night itself, from reality through unreality to reality again. It dramatizes the startling possibility we face every morning. We may be awakening from one dream only to find ourselves in another.

The Taoist sage Zhuangzi put the matter a different way. Dreaming he was a butterfly, he woke to propose his famous question: Am I now a butterfly's dream of being human?

Who is the dreamer, who the dream? Or maybe one dream metamorphoses into another? A riddle so ancient as to be nearly cliché. But the question remains, awaiting our answer. There is much about our lives indicating this diaphanous fluttering unreality. We know next to nothing. The little we know is often wrong. And we pass our lives in a cocoon of hunger and habit, floating into the uncertain future as if it were crystal clear. Asleep to what is before us, dreaming of what's to come.

This murkiness extends to our wants as well. We are endowed with desires we neither choose nor easily command. They lead us in sometimes baffling directions, and we are compelled to obey: an inescapable propulsion of wanting, clinging, striving toward a final fulfillment that never comes. Always more, without any real sense of where we're going or whether there will be enough. More of anything that makes us feel more, feel less, feeling nothing at all.

Sirens signal an end to the scramble. The imminent loss of what we know and want. The world crumbling away, dissolving into darkness. Panic might set in, the terror of a creeping extinction. We grasp at what we feel is ours, even as it is eroding, already lost, never really ours in the first place. An impossible situation: agitated for more, faced with the certainty of less. We prefer to pass over it, which is why we might dream about it. Or we might cease dreaming altogether, drifting instead into a blank somnambulism: the hope for more and the terror of less coming to rest in a trance of familiar fulfillments.

•

This book chronicles a series of simulations and breakdowns. These are human beings interrupted as in the dream, awakening from make-believe worlds. Forming the ground of each story is *addiction*.

No language we invent can convey what a person needs to say in exactly her own diction—in her own manner of *speaking toward*. Data and research are not the center of this narrative; nor are historical anecdotes or policy. At the heart of these words are the secrets and intimacies shared in private conversations with individuals. They have been given the opportunity, as much as possible, to speak for themselves.

I refer to my patients and research participants as "addicts" throughout this book not because I regard addiction as an essential or permanent aspect of their identities, nor because I think the label sums them up. Instead, I have endeavored to understand "addiction" as a mode of being with which the person identifies, at least for a time. Referring to individuals as "addicts" is meant to call attention to this identification.

Personal details have been disguised to protect their privacy, but their pain has not been. The fullness of it will be told. These are neither success stories nor stories of some final redemption, but stories of failure, unmistakable failure, with the failure transformed into something like Beckett's picture of progress: failing, failing again, failing better. What we will find are deeply vulnerable individuals endeavoring to remake themselves, working their way toward greater serenity and understanding. They develop humility, constant attentiveness: every second haunted by the violent undercurrent into which, with a single misstep, they can slip. Many do slip. And many wake up, fall asleep again, perhaps dream something else.

•

"I would like to go home today so I can get started on the rest of my life," Ahmed told me, pacing the white linoleum of the inpatient unit. I joined him as he made his way from one end of the enclosed hospital hallway to the other. There were half-open doors to patient rooms on either side.

"I don't need to stay here the entire time. I'm ready now."

He spoke with a tone of hope, resolve, and fresh beginnings. But I felt an ominous pall descending with each word. I looked at his thin track-marked arms and his emaciated, sallow face; I recalled his history of overdoses, the most recent, a year ago, resulting in an extended ICU stay. Leaving the hospital early, without achieving his reason for getting hospitalized, was unlikely to end well. It may even end his life.

Ahmed was a research participant in a clinical trial involving detoxification from opioids in the hospital. The final few days of inpatient detox can involve sudden reversals. Common sense would suggest that once they get to the home stretch, and the acute discomfort subsides, individuals in opioid withdrawal will settle down, focus on the future, and do what it takes to ensure all steps are taken to prevent a relapse.

But the reality is that their risk of leaving the hospital against medical advice and resuming use is greatest when the worst of it has passed. They may no longer be incapacitated with sweating, shivering, and diarrhea or vomiting, but the hunger remains. So do the restlessness and agitation. Such departures can put their life on the line. They are at elevated risk for overdose because their tolerance has been reduced, or their usual supply might be inaccessible, leading them to use powders of uncertain potency and purity. The usual amount is often too much.

I asked him what the rush was.

"I want to get started on working, getting my resumé out, doing what I can to feel productive," he said. "This place is making me restless. I can't move forward if I'm here. And that's one of the things that makes me use: not having a job, not doing anything."

I realized something as we hit a wall and turned around to set out toward the other end. He was careful to trace a path as close as possible to the wall on his right side, in either direction. Ahmed had turned the long rectangular hallway into a stretched-out oblong track and was walking not in a linear back and forth, but in circles.

●

Ahmed was an out-of-work curriculum developer for troubled youths, a reserved middle-aged man from Brooklyn. Born to Filipino parents, he had acquired, along the way, a Muslim name, tattoos of dense Hebrew characters covering both arms, and prominent rosary and mala beads around his right wrist: a melding of nations exotic even by New York City standards.

He trusted me, and we had good rapport. He felt that I had gone the mile for him because I had admitted him into one of our clinical trials despite his having missed multiple admission dates and showing up unannounced one day, deep in withdrawal, asking to be accepted into immediate treatment.

Ahmed had been in treatment before, but nothing helped. There were several efforts at maintenance treatment with methadone and buprenorphine. These are long-acting opioids that help people maintain more conventional, functional lives by acting on the same brain receptors that opioids like heroin, fentanyl, or painkillers do; they alleviate withdrawal and craving, addressing some of the vulnerabilities that compel a person to continue using.

But he had consistently stopped taking these medicines a week into each treatment attempt, relapsing on heroin, on a few occasions overdosing. The hope was that a different strategy might finally help him.

Ahmed was set to receive an injectable medicine the next day called extended-release naltrexone, effective at blocking the effects of opioids for a month at a time: a benefit for people who have trouble taking other maintenance medications consistently. It works to discourage use given that they wouldn't feel an effect, and if they do slip, it minimizes the risk of a lapse progressing into a relapse. By blocking opioid effects, naltrexone also prevents overdose. To leave without the shot, given his overdose history, could be deadly. But it is understandable that he, like many other users, would balk at the eleventh hour and refuse the shot: the prospect of being out in the world and denied the ability to access the one thing known to help would be terrifying to anyone.

"I really want to take care of things, and I feel that I'm ready to do that now."

I asked him what he might do here in the hospital to feel productive, and he said that he had already been working on his resumé and looking at job postings. But he really would much rather be at home, where he felt more comfortable and better able to get things done.

"It's good to hear you're making the most of this place. Working on your resumé and reviewing job postings are definitely a good start. And what's the hurry to run home and get started, if you've already started?"

He gave a soft laugh: a good sign. He was listening.

"And about the shot. If you leave now, it would defeat the purpose of you coming here in the first place. So, what are your thoughts about the injection?" I asked.

He hesitated a moment. We stopped walking for the first time that morning.

Okay, he said, he will stay for the shot. It was another step in the right direction. But I was far from ready to consider the matter closed. Clarity in such cases is a spark that requires constant stoking before it takes flame. I knew there were bound to be further conversations about staying or leaving, if not today, then tomorrow. It is like speaking to someone while he is in and out of sleep; your words may not get through, and if they do, there is a good chance they'll be translated into the texture of his dream. We think we're talking sense to a person, waking him up, but his sleep fattens on our words, and the night deepens.

●

I am commonly asked by patients whether I've struggled with addiction myself. Unlike other conditions psychiatrists commonly treat—depression, psychosis, mania, anxiety—addiction is thought to require an understanding and sympathy best derived from personal experience. In light of the unique stigma that attaches to addiction, it makes sense that people struggling with it want to ensure that they are not judged or misunderstood by those to whom they turn for help. There may also be something unique about treating addiction, which necessitates a certain hard-earned insight. Enduring addiction oneself is presumed to be the surest path toward acquiring it.

I was confused when I first encountered addiction as a doctor in training in Chicago's South Side, thousands of patients before Ahmed. It wasn't an issue of unfamiliarity; I had known several people, both friends and family, who were addicted prior to that point, and I had provided support as best I could.

My confusion had more to do with the diagnosis. I was treating various conditions, which provided a clear contrast. There were obvious psychiatric issues like entering into a manic episode or psychosis. I knew my place with them. Addiction was far more disorienting. Sure, I could help people through withdrawal and provide them support as they detoxify. There may also be an illness that might predispose them to addiction, such as bipolar disorder or severe anxiety, which I might psychiatrically manage. But where was the disease in addiction beyond that? In general, these were healthy people, with apparent insight and the ability to function mostly well while sober, repeatedly making poor choices because they felt drawn to what was destructive. It seemed that the crucial questions were not quite medical and more existential: Why don't they control themselves? Do they even want to control themselves? What possible role can I have in helping someone who wants what is destructive to him? And what flicker of satisfaction or happiness can be worth so much pain and loss?

There was a more fundamental question. What is addiction really? Is it a problem of the brain, a social problem, a problem of character, a "spiritual" or moral problem? Is it a problem at all? The dominant medical/scientific explanations were deeply unconvincing. Where was the evidence that drugs "hardwire" the brain to become progressively more compulsive and out of control? Nor was it clear to me that people with addiction were any more compulsive than I was.

Then there was the confusion surrounding drugs themselves. I had experimented enough to know that drugs alone could not be the culprit, that it was absurd to attribute an inherent addictive quality to them—some "abuse liability"—that compels repeated, problematic use. Many friends, a lot of acquaintances, and I too had put down highly "abusable" drugs—cocaine, opium, heroin, cannabis, speed, a variety of hallucinogens—as easily as we picked them up. There were those who couldn't moderate and who went on to suffer from drug problems, but they were the minority. Our professors in medical school had emphasized this well-established point: most people who use drugs don't develop a problem with them. The same applies to other things that may lead to getting psychiatrically stuck: trauma, loss, failure. Most people take these inevitabilities in stride and keep it moving.

I couldn't find fault in drugs, it made no sense to blame the brain, it was cruel to judge the person. But the addict was clearly suffering, deeply so, and suffering in a way that seemed to have a solution that was obvious, simple, and yet impossible: *just put the drug down.*

Maybe most baffling was that despite never having struggled this way myself, despite never having been addicted to anything, I saw myself in my patients. I recognized myself. And not knowing what it was I recognized, I became perplexed about who I am, about what might be lurking behind my own choices and desires. I felt within myself the same charged abyss that I saw in their dilated eyes.

•

Ahmed had transitioned to the injection successfully and left the hospital motivated to remain in psychotherapy and receive monthly injections for the duration of the three-month trial. But a few of his words have stayed with me: *I can't move forward if I'm here. And that's one of the things that makes me use: not having a job, not doing anything . . .*

This was the paradox of addiction laid bare. The addict suffers because of his use—he loses work, money, family, friends, his health—and yet feels compelled by the anguish and sorrow to continue using. He uses when it would be better to control himself, when he should really stop, when he needs to be doing something else. He uses, in other words, exactly when he shouldn't. A seemingly insoluble dilemma. It can appear like "self-sabotage," a favorite phrase of the recovery community.

But what is being sabotaged, and by whom? Ahmed gets his heart's desire, what he wants more than anything. But that's also his reason for coming in for help. He feels helpless against what he wants. He wants to keep using and wants to quit everything, both at the same time. It is less self-sabotage, more the willfulness and agitations of the self carried to their crisis. Not using is haunted by the specter of using, using is haunted by the dream of not using.

He knows the absurdity of his position: wanting most acutely what he would prefer not wanting. On all sides of him is the certainty of something better, for anything is better than this impossible situation. Yet there is no clear path ahead, because he seems doomed to start out from the insanity of where he is: *I can't move forward if I'm here.* And his thoughts return, once more, to heroin, the most familiar ground he knows.

Addiction may seem unthinkable to those on the outside. Why keep coming back to something destructive every time? Tobacco, alcohol, cocaine, sex, whatever the "reward," whatever problems it may have caused, intoxication continues to beckon to the addict with its promises. It is only the fool or madman, we think, who continues to believe the liar. But this is what must be ultimately confronted: our vulnerability to certain confusions and deceptions. The addict continues to be seduced by the false promise—to heroin resolving our anguish, for example, as opposed to providing a temporary respite from it, with worse to come. And we become even more receptive to these promises the more impossible, and painful, our lives become.

Addiction is not "a bad habit." Nor an intractably devastating one. At its heart is a malignant persistence of unreality: a dream that grows to dominate the person. Intoxication becomes necessary to our existence, an indispensable part of who we are. Or it becomes something entirely separate, a ritual realm we feel free to occupy without consequence, like theater or fiction. And the deepest dream of addiction, regardless of drug or activity, is that one might inhabit the boundless moment as if it were all there is: an existence beyond the progression of time, a reality greater than any fact, with an absolute freedom somehow emerging from the chains and compulsions.

A dream utterly impossible. Yet it is also, as will become clear, the truest dream possible to us: finding repose in every moment, no matter how nightmarish everything might seem.

"Addiction," in any case, is where Ahmed has found purpose, reality, even normalcy for the greater part of his life. It is where he has made his home, however destructive he recognizes it to be. This is why he returns to it, why most of us would. While various routines may have developed over its course, these habits are only window dressing. What keeps him transfixed is the prospect of a consoling, meaningful world—and wanting this world, despite suffering, time and again, its failures.

•

Wanting is a fraught situation for anyone. The word comes from *vanta*, Old Norse for *lack*. Wanting something is to lack it—that is, to be in pain over it. And the pain is more than temporary. It is lacking something even if we have taken it. We lack it because we want it, even if we have taken it.

Addiction reveals the impasse. Our insatiable sense of lack, our wanting, is focused *on that one thing* to such an extreme that the insanity and impossibility become undeniable. And what we want comes to torment us—a perpetual lacking, even amidst abundance. Getting what we want, especially for the addict, only worsens the wanting.

Addiction is a suffocating riddle. We want, as a thousand songs put it, what we can never have. Yet what we want is right here, always within reach, always lacking. A birthright, a dead end, a confusion so mundane we hardly notice it. *I just want to be happy,* on repeat.

The words give the game up, were we to stop and listen. Happiness is freedom from want: not some future freedom, but freedom now, with nothing wanting. So, how to want and lack our way to what is beyond wanting and lacking? How to want not wanting? We scream at ourselves for silence and respond to that scream for silence with louder screaming.

The injection might block the effect of heroin were Ahmed to lapse, compelling him to think twice before using, or discouraging him when nothing happens if he does. It will not, however, block his wanting, nor his confusion. These cannot be simply removed. Perhaps they are even essential to him, to all of us, like the demon dwarf of ignorance on whom the thousand-armed Shiva dances for eternity, subdued but kept alive to preserve a cosmic balance. It is believed that if this demon were to be killed, the entire universe would die with him.

Even the creator of all worlds, it seems, is bound to this primal ignorance. Shiva stands on the demon to subdue it, but it is also the indispensable foundation on which he dances the world into creation. There may be no cosmic dance without it.

No less a creator than Goethe recognized this diabolical kinship: "there is no crime I cannot imagine committing," he claimed. To be human is to be capable of anything. The same imagination that wrote *Faust* might also endeavor to destroy an entire race. Ignorance is our ground, our origin. Will we find our balance and create gracefully, like Shiva? Or will we be taken for a maniacal ride?

We don't need Goethe's imagination to recognize what is possible.

The enormity of our violence is in plain sight. Stumbling in a trance toward catastrophe, the horizon already black with it. And we haven't had enough, not yet. We neglect the crimes inflicted on one another, on ourselves. The earth itself cracking under our assaults. The inevitable conclusion upon us, the fracture lines of a new beginning. But we are hunched over and breathless under the excess, too encumbered to recognize what is before us. And at the heart of our suffering: the terrible suffocating smallness of ourselves. We yearn to be more, better than *this* but find ourselves immensely less.

We shun any resemblance. Or judge the addict as uniquely sick. This is, of course, what addicts themselves do for many years: they pretend. They avoid facing themselves or their violence, falling back on the same distortions and consolations. They will do anything to avoid breaking the trance, lying to themselves and others: *it is not so bad.*

These reassurances can hold up for only so long. Suffering cannot be obscured forever: we must all confront it eventually. There might even be transformation in that reckoning. In John Donne's words, broken and burned, and blown anew.

●

When we first met, Ahmed told me about an occurrence from a decade ago. He had kept it secret for many years out of shame, but he was at the point, he said, where it needed to come out.

He was provided some money by his workplace to purchase supplies for a class he was supervising. The kids would be learning how to build a radio. So, he bought kits from a neighborhood hobby store with the money provided by his job, and the day before the class was scheduled to occur, desperate to use and without money of his own, he returned them to the store to get some cash and score heroin. The next day, he told the class they would build the radios next week, improvised a class for the day based loosely on the following week's curriculum, and scrounged up money over the subsequent days to buy more kits. But he found himself in the same situation the day before class—intimations of the sickness making him clammy, and no money of his own. He returned the kits, apologized to the kids, and told them to hold tight for the following week. This happened one more time, before a foster parent complained because her child was coming home upset each week.

The school investigated. "I knew each time what I was doing was crazy. I thought I could somehow pull it off. And anyway, I needed to use, I wouldn't have been able to make it to class if I didn't find some. The only real solution to all of it was to continue using, knowing that the day would come when it might be possible to stop."

He lost his job. But heroin remained. He went on using and went on looking forward to the day when it might be possible to stop.

Such limbo is a core feature of addiction. A frozen possibility, a willful suspension of time and memory. It continued even during treatment. A few days in the hospital, and Ahmed remained lost in some future freedom, agitating for an early discharge to "get started on the rest of his life," as if life can be stopped, restarted, stopped again.

There was a lot more he could have done to attend to his life, of course, without jettisoning the treatment. He might also recognize the reality that he might get started at any time, without waiting for anything at all—that beginning again is as inescapable as this moment now, always beginning, and always offering to us the spacious moorings for beginning again.

●

Everything is possible. Nothing is possible. This is the murky stage on which addiction makes its appearance. It is not Ahmed's alone. Humans, butterflies, dreamers: we all inhabit it. And like other stages, there is something unreal about it.

The curtains lift, had lifted, will lift again. We find ourselves in a barren landscape, stumbling forward under the pounding sun. Just ahead is an oasis interrupting the harsh terrain, murmuring with a spring. We throw ourselves to its banks, drink deeply from the stream. The water comforts our thirst, softens our anguish.

But this turns quickly. The stream was nourishing for only a moment. We find ourselves more parched than when we began, with every mouthful deepening our thirst.

We take a closer look. The water is not quite a mirage. But it is not water either. It glows with a peculiar light. An illusion far more convincing than a mirage: a *dream* of water we can taste, feel, and take into ourselves.

And we can't stop drinking. It doesn't matter that the water is inflaming our thirst. The "water" captivates us with a promise of water, which carries its own kind of nourishment.

We dream as we drink. The water entices and nourishes us, disappoints and pains us. We want it, we do not want it. We might continue drinking from the stream even if real water were to become available. "Water" promises to quench a thirst that even water can no longer touch.

•

Psychoactive substances have likely been with us from the beginning. Relics and residues, including traces of alcohol and cannabis, have been found at Neolithic sites dating as far back as 12,000 BC. We continue to consume these substances for the same reasons that our prehistoric ancestors did: their capacity to create states of being beyond what is apparent, more meaningful than what is at hand. They answer a need essential to all of us.

An intoxicated state is, put simply, *materially different* than what came before—a deliberate, occasionally extraordinary, and yet somehow familiar transformation in perception, thought, affect, and physiology. Familiar because not entirely new: what drugs offer, among other things, is *a representation* of a state that is possible without drugs but which may not be readily at hand, such as contentment in an otherwise demoralizing situation. Intoxication can range from mild and subtle alterations, as with caffeine, to profound and otherworldly transformations, as occasioned by N,N-dimethyltryptamine (DMT) or other hallucinogens. Sometimes the same substance might run the range, depending on our relationship with it: modes of use, setting, and intentions.

In the Dionysian rites of ancient Greece, for example, grape wine would spark a sacred ecstasy that elevated devotees to an apparently divine realm, granting intimations of immortality and transcendence. Now, in modern times, wine provides more banal pleasures: as we settle into the warm glow and mild euphoria, we gaze at our empty apartments, or our dinner guests, or our romantic partner, and find everything slightly transformed, pleasant memories and hopes weaving a gauzy film that mellows and softens what's before us, lending it an atmosphere lighter and more affable.

Whether consumed for purposes of archaic worship or domestic consolation, wine is working a similar spell. It transports us to a state that is possible and meaningful but perhaps difficult to achieve on one's own. There is also opportunity for this different state to illuminate the familiar and sober one. Especially if we drink mindfully and responsibly, we might awaken to a day renewed somehow by echoes of last night's inebriation.

•

Drugs transform what we experience with intimate immediacy—we enter into a representation of another state, such as "empathy" or "insight" under the influence of MDMA, and we inhabit it, more or less, as if it were really the case. The possibilities for remaking oneself through such incarnations are endless, and for the majority of adults who proceed with using drugs responsibly, mostly harmless and often beneficial. We might enter into "optimism" after losing a job, "confidence" in conversation with someone who is usually intimidating, "comfort" while in pain, and "inspiration" while we are at a creative loss. It is akin to playing a part or fleshing out a role. But without the need for us to act; the drug itself sets the stage and does the work.

Using drugs is therefore a deeply human act—that is, a deeply unreal and imaginary one. A parallel experience might be attending a play, watching a film, or reading a novel. There is a short-term immersion in an imagined realm related in some manner to the world we share with one another: an *idealized* world. And different drugs represent different worlds for different people. One person might opt to feel enwombed in amniotic oblivion with heroin, while another enjoys the introspective ease that it affords him, while yet another is inclined toward the laser-focused perpetual motion machine of Dexedrine.

Drugs are at the same time the most *material* of fictions. We take them into ourselves, and they interact directly with our bodies. Especially if it is powerful, a drug has us in its grip until the effects subside, acting according to its own rules, and therefore altering us, through material means primarily yet also influenced profoundly by personal, relational, and environmental factors (so-called set and setting) in a manner beyond choice or will. We cannot take a proper dose of a sedative, for example, and not feel somehow affected. This is in clear contrast to other fictions. We might inhabit a play, for a moment. But intoxication inhabits us, as inescapably as our own nervous systems do.

Given that drug effects are experienced as states of being, or more properly as *representations* of states of being, some of us might find it compelling to identify with the effects of the drug—to regard the alterations as if they were oneself. We experience the murky material world moving closer toward a stable ideal, exalting us with the promise of some long-awaited synthesis. We might become, if only for a time, what we dream of being.

Our identification with these incarnations can be so total that we might attach to the intoxicated state as if that is who we really are: our "true self." Such identification may be particularly compelling if the sober world feels nearly uninhabitable—or if our ideals fail to correspond with what is apparently before us.

We are bound, however, to return to naked, shape-shifting reality. There may be something familiar about this rise and fall: exalted and nourished one moment, disillusioned and debased the next. It might be what we know, what we have come to expect.

•

Our desires overreach our capacity, wrote the Italian poet Eugenio Montale, which is why we created heaven. Heaven is the endpoint we imagine for our wants, where our ambitious desires might finally find some rest. What may also be created, but enjoyed within this life, is a heaven brought down to earth, a new world better suited to our oversized desires. Nothing needs to change, because this new earth may remain within our own minds. We will dream ourselves into another identity, another body, another earth altogether, even as we remain exactly where and what we are. Lucifer calls attention to this creativity in *Paradise Lost*, giving demonic praise to the freedom of our minds to make a heaven of hell. But we can also make, as Lucifer reminds us, a hell of heaven.

Paradise is at hand. Nothing needs to change, Satan says, except our minds. The dream of paradise might be experienced, with a certain perspective, at every moment we incorporate the bounty of the world into our beings: unconditional love and tenderness, deep friendship, a sublime landscape. But it doesn't need to end with experiences of such obvious beauty. Whatever we do or consume can bring with it this dream as well. We drink something as uneventful as water, and in most cases, we feel less parched—but there might be more. Our absolute hope for the world, and our dream of what is possible, may be echoed in even this most mundane of satisfactions. We yearn for our contingency, sense of incompleteness, and precarious dependence on things to be transformed into freedom, contentment, home: we ache to be fulfilled, for the water to cleanse and complete, with nothing wanting.

So even water may come to partake of this correspondence between our deepest yearnings and the prospect of absolute fulfillment. Even water, as in the harsh desert, might become its own mirage, glimmering with the consummation of what we seek in it. Purity, contentment, freedom, redemption, emptiness, whatever transports us beyond our painful strivings and circumstances. We dream as we drink, experiencing in water the deeper promise of water that water alone cannot keep.

●

There are words, and there is reality. Addicts reveal that abyss very clearly when telling lies. But the abyss grows even wider when they are telling the truth.

"I take heroin, and it's like being with a girlfriend," Ahmed told me when I first met him, a few weeks before he was admitted into the detox unit. "She comes in, I can feel her entering the room. Everything negative melts away. Not just the sickness. I mean, everything, a sweet girl taking you in both arms and squeezing all tension and negativity out of you. I feel normal again, I feel as I should be. Nothing to do, nothing to worry about. Until you remember, and you start to worry that this is not forever, and by that point the sickness has returned."

Girlfriend, sanctuary, oblivion, escape: there are many words that might double for intoxication. It is not even clear what intoxication is anymore, never mind what might be happening in the "real" world. Perhaps yet another transformation is occurring, where a drug-induced representation of an experience comes to be incarnated as yet another experience, another dream, another word.

●

There are many words, innumerable representations, and each stands to illuminate a different possibility of being, providing a sign toward what might be otherwise overlooked or forgotten. The temptation is to fix this fiction into place, freezing our relationship with the pharmakon into a familiar and meaningful stasis, be it comfort, inspiration, fulfillment, or forgetting.

This is the great contradiction of addiction: we intoxicate ourselves into heightened fluidity, deliberately conjuring a different way—and yet we fail to recognize that nothing is ever the same, allured by the impossible: going back, as the chase is often described, to that first time.

Transformation is inevitable. We are remade every several years, cells dying and re-forming daily. Circumstances and relationships are similarly mercurial, poised to transform beyond belief at any moment. The stream of experience offers perhaps the most intimate, direct window into the flux of things. We cannot step, Heraclitus might have said, into the same mind twice.

Yet we cannot say it is a different mind, either. Our existence is not simply in constant cycles of birth-death transformation. It is also fundamentally opaque. Consider as mundane an occurrence as *blue*. We point and say the word. Or we read or hear "blue" in the absence of anything to see. We assume that we each experience the same thing, and it seems we do. But your blue is private and accessible only to you, while mine is just as impenetrable. Then there is the unpredictable metamorphosis of nuances and associations cycling through each of us: the dusk blue of melancholia one moment, the vibrant blood blue throbbing through life the next.

Neuroscientists recognize that our sense perceptions are private, perhaps relational. Blue is not a thing-in-the-world we perceive identically. Instead, its reality rests in the cascade of events at the interface of our nervous systems and the environment: a specific wavelength of light (450–495 nm) reflects off a surface, impacts cones in the retinas of our eyes, and activates certain occipital brain regions, which go on to generate a cortically mediated percept recognized as the color. Scientists claim that this proves a clear mechanism to our perceptions: though "blue" might be different for each of us, it is still very much real, and traceable to the invariant laws of the objective world in which we live together.

There is no question that such empirical accounts can be precise, reliable, and predictive. Yet they also have inherent inadequacies. A neurobiological account of blue, for example, fails to consider our unique associations and the importance of contextual and personal factors; it also disregards the possibility of blue in the blind and the mysteries of subjectivity more generally. But these are surface criticisms. The more serious problem is its "objective" claim on the *being* of things, as if such accounts "correspond" to "reality" with mechanical precision.

Light, wavelengths, our retinas, the cones in our eyes, our brain regions, down to the analysis itself, our parsing of phenomena into cause-and-effect relationships: these "objective" facts are as molded by our senses and understanding as any other story we tell. They do not reflect some absolute vantage point on truth.

We remain subjective, in other words, even while endeavoring to be objective. What blue might be independent of us, on the other side of our minds, remains out of reach. It is incomprehensible, beyond our perceptions and knowledge. What I see as blue is therefore unknown not only to you. It is unknown to me too.

Certain philosophers have distinguished between *phenomena* and *noumena* to capture this inscrutability. Phenomena are the limits of our world: the unstable flux we experience and comprehend through our perception, understanding, and embodiment. Pure noumena, or what phenomena are "in-themselves" and beyond human mediation, are a mystery. They exist "behind the scenes," outside the limits of our senses and understanding.

This duality is one way to characterize the fluid darkness of experience. There may also be no noumena at all, no stable essences beyond our perceptions, but only surfaces, surface superimposed on surface. Or a single surface may be protean and immaterial, reflecting at one moment our fantasies, at another a monstrous manifestation of terror, at yet another the implacable interlocking rules of matter. A dialogue between a dreamer and her dream.

We cannot know what blue might "really" be or whether it is anything at all. We may be dreaming a reality, while entirely in the dark. And *dream* is one word for it. There are other words, just as cryptic: *being, consciousness, God, emptiness, order, chaos*. Our world may also be more nefarious, a manipulation. We might be brains in a vat, as in the writings of Descartes, tricked by demons into hallucinating existence and believing that it is real. Or we might not be brains in a vat at all, but something far less comprehensible. There is simply no way of knowing.

We all intuit this mystery. And we yearn to illuminate this darkness in which we dwell, to inhabit it fully and bring its depths to light. This is the mainspring of our most exalted pursuits: art, science, philosophy, religion. It may also be what feeds our addictions. We might sense something like a limitless possibility in the emptiness: the potential for something truer. It quickens the breath with the promise of otherworldly fulfillment, or perhaps with the immediacy of the most mundane consolations: lover, sanctuary, oblivion, escape . . .

●

To consume drugs is to invite a dream. A rupture is created in the earth through which a new world, and perhaps a glimpse of paradise, might enter. It promises to create a better state at will, offering us an apparent freedom to live more fully and deliberately.

This fulfillment—seemingly accessible, reliable, direct—is deeply alluring. But it is not fail-safe, as everyone knows. Drugs don't always do the trick. There also might be untoward effects, unpleasant consequences, hangovers.

Then there are the risks that come with drugs seeming to do exactly what we want. A truth so obvious it hardly needs stating: we tend to consume more of what works. Studies have shown that young adults who find alcohol stimulating as opposed to aversive, for instance, are more likely to binge drink—that is, they are more likely to take what they want in excess.

Further problems emerge when the gratification entices us to lose perspective, pursuing the fiction at the cost of other things. Not giving attention to this discordance can be clearly reckless, as when we drive while impaired. It might also be subtler and more covert than that: we ignore, deliberately or not, the fullness of existence, including our relationships, our well-being, and the larger world surrounding this evanescent one conjured up and cupped in our hands.

We might ignore another truth. Any freedom we might experience through intoxication is in fact bound up with a drug, as well as with its problems. Addiction consists in believing, even partially, in these incarnations as if they were true, or at least overlooking their transience and contingency, as well as their *anti-truth*, the fissure between "representation" and "reality." We remain just as enslaved as before, if not more so because we have deepened a fantasy of freedom while the manacles have grown tighter around our ankles and necks. Frederick Douglass wrote comparably about the "holidays" of drunkenness imposed on slaves: "the cunning slaveholder, knowing [the slave's] ignorance, cheats him with a dose of vicious dissipation, artfully labeled with the name of liberty." And exacerbating our slavery is not the worst of it. To make a paradise of bread, the Argentine poet Porchia wrote, is to make a hell of hunger.

Ahmed concealed his shackles under a veil of names. Oblivion, liberty, lover, solution to sickness—but where in all this is heroin, or Ahmed himself? The tyranny and confusion might come to be recognized with time. Ahmed might also come to better recognize himself. It often comes by way of inescapable suffering: a merciless fall, without reprieve or comfort, to unadorned earth. Ahmed had his vision clouded by an intoxicating haze; perhaps the harsh obduracy of pain might work to widen his eyes.

Yet we shouldn't forget Satan's praise. Our imaginations might transform even the greatest suffering into names as familiar and automatic as *dope sick*. Perhaps the surest way forward is to push our words past the threshold—to interrogate them so thoroughly that they cease making sense, becoming as dark, finally, as the world itself.

•

A philosopher might call addiction a confusion between noumena and phenomena, or between reality and representation, with our unrealities mistaken for truth and inflicted on the world. We might also, joining William S. Burroughs, diagnose language as a virus: contagious memes infecting our minds, restricting us to our concepts and making us sick with "knowledge." These confusions replicate rapidly, ultimately jaundicing everything they touch.

Burroughs's metaphor, while profound, has its problems. Viral infections are generally experienced as foreign and invasive. With words or ideas, however, we might have total identification with their deceptions, even ardent enthusiasm for them. An addict's lifelong romance with "heroin"—with its halo of illusions and deceptions—is just one example. How much destruction has been perpetrated in the name of peace? How many murders under the flag of brotherhood?

Language might play a role in this destruction, as might drugs, visions, relationships. But at the bottom of our confusion is a subtle seduction inherent to being human, beyond any word or drug we might identify as the primary contagion. We want to know, to survive, to find meaning. The world bends to our wants and wounds, offering to our minds the generous malleability of its substance. And instead of bending with the world in turn, we halt in place, and expect everything to halt with us.

A dream paves the way, molding everything in its image. If there is a virus behind our madness, then this would be it: the totalizing unreality by which "reality" might be dreamt up, colonizing our beings and convincing us it is realer than anything else. It can be collectively experienced, like religion or culture, or it can be more private, as in the closed labyrinth of Ahmed's addiction—the intoxicated moment that came to dominate everything else, including Ahmed himself.

Our attempts at certainty and domination are bound to falter. The ground grows shaky, the path ahead circling on itself. Things are more than they seem. The earth a mother and grim reaper, our children pure and fallen, drugs a gift and curse. The fictions we had attempted to impose on the earth, on ourselves, doubling back and shattering us into fragments: heroin, lover, sickness, animal, amnesia, keepsake, flashing like the breaking facets of an immense current. We are elevated to a god, and stumble mute, a moment later, like a wounded ape.

An interruption and disorientation, yet also a threshold of many beginnings. We are free to do what we will. And we might choose, this time, a more fluent freedom—a more graceful movement through our incarnations and contradictions, with the supple ease of water joining water.

II.

We are free to enter a word, a play, a drug. We might just as freely put them down, forgo another drink, save the novel for later. But the influence can persist for longer than intended. Perhaps we might suppose that this is less the case with words than with substances; we seem to enter and leave the fiction at will, without its productions gripping us as inescapably as a drug might.

But this is clearly wrong. Even bloodless abstractions can be deeply captivating. And words, as Burroughs suggested, might be the most virulent of all, articulating the "reality" we've defined as our world and forging the artifices—laws, ideas, roles—we've defined as ourselves, above and beyond our shared materiality, our bodies, even our own direct experience.

Don Quixote exemplifies this process of fictionalization, with his adventures constituting one of the most enduring fictions in European literature. Devouring tale after tale of chivalry, Quixote came to believe that these storybook worlds were his own: he anointed himself a knight, mistook his mangy horse for a handsome steed, and endeavored to restore justice and nobility to the land, most famously waging war on windmills, mistaking them for monsters, and rescuing peasants as if they were princesses.

Don Quixote is not about a person. The novel might be about all people, an idea of people, maybe about ideas themselves. The man Quixote, in any case, becomes fictional; the words he had temporarily inhabited had impressed him so deeply as to inhabit him, altering his sense of self entirely. And this was not mere play-acting: he would come to court danger as a real-life knight might. The fiction had captivated the fullness of his being, and this transformation becomes indistinguishable from himself.

Quixote's quest begins as a colorful comedy. But it ends in solitary tragedy. Quixote comes to recognize that the truth, or at least the larger world, was not what he believed it was, was in fact being written by others—that his crusade was a lie, that he was not a knight but a maniac, and that the most plausible story was not his own, but that of his shrewd observers. He becomes as incorporeal as the words that had exalted him. Heroism to humiliation in one stroke: the inevitable pain of pursuing a dream, however ennobling it seems, at odds with the world of flesh and blood.

Ahmed was similarly devastated. Captivated, he runs after heroin as if after his salvation, the realities of his life—poverty, ruined relation-

ships, illness—no longer given the care, let alone attention, they require. Intoxication becomes the central truth of his life: how to achieve
and maintain its illusions, maybe even how to supplant entire days and
nights with it. Meanwhile, he had come to require it: the sickness ready
to ravage him at the first missed fix, the specter of sobriety now an anguished and hellish hunger.

Both men had become entangled with the things of the world,
with drugs, wandering, or windmills, while seeing there what doesn't
exist—searching for fulfillment in sheer fiction. Agonies and confusions will arise, of course. But these may not be enough to break the
spell. Ahmed, for one, has too much to lose. It is far more than a
physiological crisis for him to be on his own, emerging dope sick into
a fiction-less world. The disorientation seems a threat to existence
itself, a matter of growing unmoored from what had become his most
essential coordinates.

●

How is it possible to become so deceived? In Quixote's case, it began
with an all-consuming enthusiasm for the novels of knighthood, which
he read insatiably; this led to Quixote first confusing these fictions with
reality and then regarding himself as one of the elect. Perhaps he had a
narcissistic need to occupy a triumphant role? Maybe he was mad from
the start and searching for his true delusion?

Cervantes, however, depicts Quixote as a decent, ordinary, and re-
tiring man. There were few vulnerabilities accounting for his madness
beyond being "at leisure, most of the time," whiling away the idle hours
of late middle age. His leisure seemingly provided ample opportunity
for distraction, first to read voraciously, then to concoct a grandiose
destiny for himself. Interestingly, Cervantes began *Quixote* while he
himself inhabited an oppressive leisure; he was held captive for several
years by Barbary pirates.

It is compelling to interpret Quixote's manic idealism as his response
to a perceived lack of purpose or meaning—in his own withdrawn life,
in his cynical culture, perhaps in the larger, indifferent universe. This
deepens the resemblance to addiction, which might represent a comparable solution. The rise of addiction in the impoverished American
hinterlands, for instance, and due to social isolation, death anxiety, and

unemployment during the COVID-19 pandemic, suggest a similar void, with a corresponding need for meaningful fictions.

Quixote is clearly an extraordinary man. Most people in Quixote's circumstances—bored, adrift, purposeless—never embark on, nor even consider, such extraordinary solutions. And few readers identify with their novels to the same lunatic extent, of course, even if they are also "at leisure, most of the time." But what is most extraordinary is not his lunatic idealism—an all-too-common affliction. Quixote is exceptional because he takes a solution characteristic of European civilization, an identification with a leather-bound higher ideal—and he elevates his chivalrous Magna Carta to a delirious extreme, beyond anything most of us can imagine.

Addicts are similarly unique. Intoxication is as ordinary as reading novels or respecting founding documents. But something clearly extraordinary emerges in their lives—a mode of being transcending the ambiguous effects of the substances themselves. Prevalence estimates offer an important perspective: drug addiction has been estimated to affect only 3.9 percent of the US population, while illicit drug use is far more common, with most of us having used at least once over the course of our lives. Granted that some of us might have been foolish, occasionally making poor decisions or getting into a bit of trouble; such risks come with the territory. Or there may be the social opprobrium, and perhaps legal consequences, that come with engaging in regular substance use, especially of the illegal or unusual sort. Substance use disorders, however, are something else entirely: the diagnosis requires continued use of the drug despite personal distress and mounting problematic consequences.

Something extraordinary is occurring in drug addiction—or more accurately, something ordinary taken to its crisis. There is no fixed story for how this comes to pass. The transition can be gradual or precipitous, with use occurring in a binge-type or chronic manner. The drug might be pursued for obtaining pleasure, distracting oneself, or avoiding pain. A variety of vulnerabilities appear to render addiction more likely: psychiatric disorders, stress, trauma, impoverished circumstances, social fragmentation, genetic or biological predispositions, psychological factors. Different substances, furthermore, might be variably associated with addiction.

Addiction might also not involve drugs at all. The field is currently moving toward a better characterization of "process" or behavioral addictions, which are oriented around state-shifting and potentially intoxicating activities, such as eating, gaming, working, exercising, socializing, even tanning. Social media addiction, for example, may involve suffering as severe as that associated with drug addiction, and may also include classic symptoms such as craving and withdrawal, even as it remains outside conventional diagnostic frameworks. As in other cases of addiction, the "process addict" ceases to give sufficient attention to problematic consequences and continues to pursue the activity despite escalating distress. It also becomes difficult to rein in the behavior were the person to want to stop. The pursuit of the activity becomes apparently uncontrollable, compulsive, and monopolistic over other dimensions of existence.

A recent meta-analysis estimated the global prevalence of behavioral addictions at between 11 percent and a staggering 33 percent. If drug and alcohol addictions were to be properly diagnosed and added to these estimates, we would find that the proportion of addicted people grows to nearly half of adults. Even with the caveats that this is an imperfect analysis and that behavioral addictions remain a controversial diagnosis (the only behavioral addiction recognized currently by mainstream psychiatry is problem gambling), this is a tremendous number. If a medical condition were estimated at this incidence, we would wonder if we might be overlooking a global pandemic.

Even global pandemic, however, might be too modest a description. The problem is so fundamental to us as to seem written into existence itself. Status, resources, genetics, temperament, relationships—all the accidents of life—may shape our reality into different forms, perhaps mitigate its agonies: some of us incurring an obvious addiction, others apparently untouched. Yet it is the same yearning, the same plight, whether we carry the diagnosis or not: scrambling to keep our heads while propelled by the promise of more, more of whatever might be meaningful, more of whatever we want—and with our lives forced irrevocably in one fatal direction.

Such is the power of the veil we've placed over ourselves: the basic truths of our mortality—confusion, fragility, discontentment, death—

have come to seem banal and yet unspeakable at the same time. It might seem dramatic, even perverse, to dwell on them, unless in relation to agonies beyond the ordinary: catastrophe, terminal illness, madness. But dramatic words may be precisely what's needed to reawaken a sense of what's at stake, raising to attention the drama too readily concealed.

Worsening the apparent problem are our apparent solutions. Ahmed knew what he needed to do: whatever it takes to keep withdrawal at bay, including stealing from his students. There was the slim hope that he might correct things in the end and buy the kits the kids needed. The route ahead was clear, even though he continued to find himself in the same quagmire: dope sick if he goes right, a liar and a thief if left. The stalemate had found its crisis when he lost his job. But Ahmed did not regard this as a failure worth heeding. There are always new variations on the solution that might keep him going.

An entanglement with the same sick solution might be addiction; it is also a rare achievement. Though they hadn't been propelled by conventional notions of happiness, such as wealth, family, or social status, Ahmed or Quixote might very easily have been, only to incarnate, through extraordinary force of will, a similar single-minded stasis.

Whether oriented around material accumulation, drugs, or knighthood, our ambitions are always a hair's breadth from falling into a dream-like solipsism. Yet we push on, despite the cracks that start to show. For Quixote and Ahmed, the tangle of convictions breaks the skin as visibly as knotted roots, pushing their madness into the open. Reality forces an interruption that cannot be refused.

●

"I think the reason I've had such trouble stopping," Ahmed said during his hospitalization, "is because I haven't hit rock bottom yet. I keep thinking that it is possible to turn it around without giving up dope, you know—that everything might still get worse. Perhaps things aren't bad enough yet. I am not sure if I'm ready now, because at least I still have my health, my brother still talks to me, and though I have to hustle, I can still drum up enough to get through the next day. But it scares me to think about how much worse it can get, so maybe I'm ready after all?"

I've heard this many times: people with addiction speculating that it could still get worse, that they haven't yet crashed against the rocks. They find a reason, as usual, to go on using, forgetting that their minds can always provide a worse picture than what they have now, and that rock bottom, even for those at the deepest depths, can always be fictionalized as worse. The challenge is to let go of these ideas and take a hard look around.

The failures of romantic love, the overwhelming weight of our ideals, rapturous breathless visions of a perfect future. We all rise and fall on waves of imagination. We cannot help filling our minds with compelling fictions, mostly to nourish an idea of ourselves. It is so banal as to be nearly inaudible: a constant story architecting our worlds, featuring ourselves as main character, under a limelight of our own making.

Self-deception is not simply a private matter. There are dreams so common that we awaken to them every morning while hardly recognizing the ruse. Our shared words come to serve as the lullabies that keep us entranced. This is how an entire world can descend into nightmare: we lose ourselves in a babble of unreality.

We point at a stranger, casting certain judgments in unison. Or we point at anything and narrow in, excluding everything outside our line of sight. With each conclusion, we grow more convinced we see what we have named, that we have before us exactly what we believe. Inhuman, subhuman, savage, evil. Our certainties obscure other possibilities, and we go on to perpetrate insane crimes on ourselves, on others, on the earth. We wage war for peace and freedom, pillage the earth for progress, kill our neighbors for God, and devastate ourselves for happiness.

Neither fact nor fiction is adequate to encompass this immense and enigmatic world. We must all bear witness, as did Quixote, to existence reclaiming itself. There is a word for this unveiling: apocalypse. It happens to individuals, to families, to entire civilizations. It is terrifying and ecstatic at once. Our illusions come to be razed to the ground, and our systems of knowledge stand revealed for the pain and senselessness they have permitted, regardless of how high-minded the foundations upon which we erected them.

•

Addicts scatter a trail of solutions behind them. Were we to sift through the refuse, we might recognize many of our own belief systems in that junk heap: idealism, religion, hedonism, nihilism, nationalism, authoritarianism, utilitarianism, capitalism, romanticism. All ideas show their grotesqueness if pushed far enough. This is one way to understand addiction: the striving to inhabit some theory of everything taken to its natural, claustrophobic conclusion.

It is neither an intellectual nor even a verbal matter. Our beliefs come to deform our movements with the density of bone, from an opaque, compacted silence inside. Even if we come to recognize the problem, we continue to fall into form, inhabiting some calcified idea of things. Addicts do what they do, and destroy everything doing it, because their reasons have become as unknown to them and as obdurate as reality itself.

In that violence, we might see our own. Our "realities" are bound to fall away, even if their final days might not occur with such destruction. If we are fortunate, we might realize their inadequacy as early as possible. In this respect, the addict carves a path we will all, with time, come to tread.

●

"I know I should be leaving heroin behind, closing the door on it when I leave the hospital. But I'm not going to lie, I'm thinking a lot more about that door opening right now. Maybe it's an improvement that I'm also thinking of how it'll mess me up if I slip, or that it's a waste given I won't feel anything. Maybe that'll be enough to keep me good. But if it happens, it happens."

This ambivalence right out of the gate is not uncommon. Though he hopes to not slip again, Ahmed also seems resigned to an inescapable downward spiral: stuck in a world bound to get worse. It may even seem like he has been *determined* to make things worse. The world may be burning down around him, and he may recognize that the broken relationships, destitution, and hepatitis worsen with continued use. He may also suffer what he had told himself, with great conviction, would be the final wake-up call. Yet all these things will only compel him to latch even more tightly. *And that's one of the things that makes me use: not having a job, not doing anything . . .*

Destruction might be inevitable in addiction. But it would be a mistake to see destruction as the primary intention. Even suicide has a deliverance in mind, a deep meaningfulness, with a total act of violence to oneself the way to get there. Ahmed turns to what promises deliverance and what has given him a foretaste of that deliverance for decades. Of course he would be ambivalent about closing the door to it.

Perhaps addiction might be most fruitfully understood not as self-destruction, but as compulsive *self-creation*: a creative act so extraordinary that it is beyond material bounds. Ahmed incarnates a total fiction, an existence entirely made up and self-sufficient; he remakes the entire world in this image, with even a slow, painful suicide doubling as salvation. And the mere moment of shooting up, a passing intoxication, comes to be inhabited as if it were his supreme truth, untouched by the world beyond its margins. A sense of the world more *his* than anything he has experienced before: the all-too-human impulse to create a world entirely our own, leaving scorched earth in our wake.

This self-destruction—or more accurately, destructive self-creation—has been seen by scientists as setting drug addiction apart from other conditions. It is a special example of people losing control over themselves. Drugs are consequently viewed as uncommonly harmful, drug addiction unique among other modes of suffering (even though process addictions present comparably).

The special danger of drugs might rest, according to neuroscientists, in their direct activity on the brain. The idea is that by virtue of activating the reward system, drugs modify the vulnerable brain to promote decision making oriented around drug use. These neural adaptations to drug use, the argument goes, make addictive behavior nearly inescapable because they "hardwire" the seat of consciousness, choice, and behavior. "Hijacked" is the common metaphor: repeated drug use warps our brains so that we no longer act in our best interest, instead making choices primarily serving the drug.

Drugs are unique in their ability to enter our brains and impact the neural circuits associated with pleasure, habit, and relief. Clearly the brain-drug interface is relevant and deserves investigation. But we cannot restrict ourselves to a strictly neurobiological framework for understanding our relationship to substances. Among other limitations, the so-called brain disease model does not address the ways that an addict's sense of self, fulfillment, and reality become confused—a process hardly unique to drugs, as we have seen, with fictions as seemingly innocuous as words and fables also involved in such confusion. Nor does it address the vulnerabilities and circumstances that might make such an agonizing choice so alluring and captivating. Instead, the model assigns primary responsibility to the drug: a toxin impairing our minds. It is worth remembering that *pharmakon* has three meanings in ancient Greek: medicine, poison—and scapegoat.

There are countless paths concluding in this wilderness. Even words and stories, as in the case of Quixote, might nourish insanity, often in groups at a time: adolescent suicides inspired by *The Sorrows of Young Werther*, zealots motivated by scripture to wage holy war, disaffected young men militarized online into White ethno-nationalism. Violence can accompany our words in ways as varied and unique as human speech itself.

History shows us the global horrors that might occur when facts, mythologies, and beliefs become indistinguishable from ourselves— when we allow "knowledge" and other fictions, no matter how seemingly benign, to distract us from our lived experience. The catastrophes stemming from such entanglements—whether with ethno-fascism, neoliberal democracy, or God the Father—are devastating, tragic, and far greater, of course, than what might be traced to drug use.

•

The injection we had given Ahmed might block the effects of heroin were he to shoot up, but it cannot, on its own, do anything about his addiction. He could decide to not take the next shot and resume use. Or he could simply disappear from treatment. The absence of the drug, or of drug effects, may only provide a window wherein the process of attending fruitfully to his addiction might occur—the work of addressing his reasons for choosing to use, repeatedly, despite self-destruction.

The shot might provide this window of opportunity, but it may not even do that. There is no assurance that being on the shot, and blocking the effects of heroin, will stop use. A person may still decide to shoot up even though no high occurs. This is unfortunately what happened with Ahmed. He began injecting heroin as soon as he left detox. He recognized that it was a waste of money given he wasn't feeling the customary intoxication, and yet he couldn't resist. He was quite eloquent about his reasons, and about his confusion.

"I don't know if it's the ritual of buying and preparing, or the feeling of the needle entering me, the warmth of the injection as it spreads through me. And I can't say I feel the heroin, but I can't say I don't feel it."

There is a simple behaviorist explanation for this. An addicted person comes to associate a certain ritual, like injecting, with a drug's subjective effects (a process called "conditioning") to such an extent that the ritual itself comes to yield these effects irrespective of whether the drug was taken. But Ahmed hinted at something less mechanical.

"Maybe what I feel is the expectation of something. Maybe I want to expect what I've always expected, and I want it so bad I feel what isn't really there, you know? It doesn't happen exactly as I want, but it never has, really, to be honest. Nothing can compare to those first few times. But I can continue expecting it, like I always have, even though I know that this is totally crazy, especially now that I'm blocked. And yet there's something, I can feel a small something, which might be entirely in my mind."

There was more going on than behavioral conditioning or reinforcement alone. And it was different than a needle fetish—a fascination with the ritual of injection beyond any drug delivered—which is one reason people might continue shooting up even while blocked. I offered an interpretation: "You can't let go of what you expect from shooting up. Perhaps you're not sure what else there is to expect, and what you would look forward to, were you to stop using."

He shrugged. "Maybe. Or maybe I just want to pretend I am still using because I don't want to be sober quite yet. Maybe I'm not bottom yet, and I want another run with this before calling it quits for good. And maybe I want everything to fail so that I have no excuse but to continue using."

Maybe I just want to pretend I am still using. I didn't bother to point out to him that he was far from pretending; he was actually using. But it struck me as significant and revelatory that he saw it in this way. The drug was not what motivated him. It was the act of using, irrespective of any actual effects, that exerted power over him now: a pretense that preserved the promise to which he had become enslaved. His addiction had completely moved beyond what the drug materially does; it was only expectation and imagination that gave the pantomime any substance. The fiction motivating his use from the start had culminated in a gesture of pure theater: entirely empty of reality, and yet just as capable of captivating him with its incarnations.

These representations of using, in any case, were just as destructive as "actual" using might be. He dropped out of treatment within weeks. I have not heard from him again.

•

It is difficult to trace the origins of such destructive confusion to ourselves. The more familiar route is to shift the blame elsewhere, looking for the problem in what has been given to us: the books we read, the religions in which we are raised, the drugs we use. But the crisis is not in our fictions. Behind our destructiveness is nothing but our own selves, agitated for some measure of release. We sleepwalk into dreams promising the world, and the curtains open, moments later, to an apocalypse of violence and anguish.

We cannot flee our ignorance or pretend it away. The truest way forward is to recognize it as the demonic foundation on which we choreograph our lives into existence. Indeed, our ignorance might be our most faithful companion, humbling us, alerting us to our inertia, and correcting our beliefs and bodies when we lose balance. And through this wakefulness we might transmute our "self" and "reality" from an agitated ignorance to an ecstatic not-knowing.

Everything is dreamt up and created from a perch of total darkness. Even passivity—*I will let things happen to me*—is a system we actively sustain. We might relinquish it just as freely as we took it up. We might relinquish anything. This is how we practice our freedom—in remembrance of what is possible, while extricating from what we've concluded. Addiction emerges when we deny ourselves this freedom and limit reality to the straits of what we've incarnated, with our most cherished words and conclusions—even "paradise" itself—bound to be dead ends.

The word becomes flesh, becomes heaven, becomes hell on earth. Ahmed has struggled to emerge from this purgatory for decades, without apparent progress. But it remains possible. Every moment carries that redemptive possibility—an existence no longer eviscerated by the confusions and identifications that, in some form, torment all of us.

It is our nature to pass over what is possible. We are more inclined to stay with the familiar, the habitual, the impossible, despite suffering for it. Addiction is one word for this. *Knowledge* is the more common entanglement: the facts constricting our existence into a fable with its ending already written. Our madness is to insist on living within these confines, walled off from the only reality we have: our mounting suffering is obscured, our yearning for meaningful relationship forfeited. Even access to our own experience becomes covered over. This is the confusion at the heart of suffering, deadening us with the conviction that we comprehend the world and hurtling life forward with all the locked-in zombie mechanisms of the "real world" we deem inescapable.

Our suffering, of course, does not disappear. It transforms into what might better communicate the scream roiling our depths. We develop amnesia, inertia, other maladies. We break relationships. We close doors through which we might have passed; we suffer until the suffering cracks the surface and we heed its scream. There might be further deception even when the self-destruction becomes apparent: we scapegoat the drug or other fiction for what it does to us, and to our brains, as if we are merely the soil in which these seeds bloom into violence. We relinquish one illusion, find ourselves in another.

2

THE PURSUIT OF KNOWLEDGE

Today we are trying to spread knowledge everywhere. Who knows if in centuries to come there will not be universities for re-establishing our former ignorance?

—GEORG CHRISTOPH LICHTENBERG

I.

"Physical" is shorthand for what is often called the "phenomenal" world, for what might be perceived, comprehended, manipulated. Drugs, for example, are physical. They exist in the physical world; they affect us physically. And we ourselves are physical, with brains, bodies, material entanglements. Yet we are also other than physical. Even the physical world itself, and the drugs existing in it, are other than physical.

This is not a matter of prejudice, reflecting a metaphysical insistence that there be something immaterial—soul, spirit, divine energy—mixed into the world. Instead, the issue is one of intellectual modesty. Like other representations, "physicality" has inherent limitations, despite its pretensions of settling the matter. We will find that it is no more comprehensible than is the "reality" it presumes to sum up—that we know far less about physicality than our ease with the word suggests.

We claim that drugs are physical because they exist in the physical world; we can touch them, consume them, be affected by them. They might even change our bodies with repeated use, leading to sustained "physical adaptations." In its most explicit form, this process is called the development of physiological or physical dependence. It encompasses tolerance (needing higher amounts to receive an intended effect) and withdrawal (developing physical or psychological distress with the absence of the drug). These might be only the most apparent physical changes compelling repeated use; other physical effects are hypothesized to occur on a neuronal level.

Withdrawal and tolerance are often taken to signify, with unmistakable physicality, the profound captivity—the addiction—that might follow drug use. The addict is imagined accordingly: he comes to pursue his drug with the inescapability of any other physiological act, his choice to drink or inject or smoke as predetermined as falling, once the supply dwindles, into severe sickness.

The addict is imagined, in other words, as more *physical* than are nonaddicted people. The physical world is bound by immutable laws—of electron gradients, chemistry, physiology—and to be addicted, to suffer from profound physical dependence, is to be enslaved to those laws just as immutably. It seems a nightmare: trapped inside the chemical machines of our bodies, our actions no longer our own but orchestrated by impersonal mechanisms. But is this absolute physicality distinct from our standard dream of reality? If not in our cells and chemicals, where are we?

We are physical; we are other than physical. Consider a chronic pain patient on a long-term morphine drip. This person would descend into withdrawal were the drip to be stopped. Yet we cannot call this person addicted simply because he is physically dependent. And someone may be using drugs addictively without having first developed tolerance or withdrawal. As indicated earlier, addiction involves pursuing something repetitively, even in the face of mounting problems and personal distress. Physical dependence—or even a physical compulsion to use—is not enough. There needs to be a consistent choice that deepens suffering.

Ahmed's addiction, alongside including tolerance and severe withdrawal, circled around a fixed relationship with the drug—an entanglement so profound that he wanted more even as it threatened to kill him. His use had persisted after serial overdoses, after losing friends, after ruining his reputation; it had even persisted when the effects of heroin were physically blocked. This suggests that crucial to Ahmed's addiction was not the "physical" substance itself. Rather, it was his *idea* of the drug: a fantasy so compelling it rendered reality irrelevant. A theatrical production of using was sufficient to keep Ahmed going—injecting what might as well have been nothing, staged in his labyrinth of mirrors into something.

Nothing into something, while that something becomes something else: sanctuary, numbness, physical dependence, nothingness again. Everything always other than it is, if only because we are in relationship with it—bringing ourselves invariably into the encounter, with all our imaginings, certainties, and also contradictions, for we are other than ourselves too: addicted to the thing and also free of it, physically dependent and dependent on nothing.

•

I maintain a private practice in downtown Manhattan, in addition to my academic position uptown at Columbia University. Shuffling between the two, I have encountered addiction to nearly everything: to alcohol, methamphetamine, sugar, sex, tobacco, cannabis, heroin, benzodiazepines, online poker, crack cocaine, video games, painkillers, kratom, psychedelics, to whatever alters the mind. And the supports to which my diverse and restless patients turn have been just as mind-boggling: weekly hourlong office visits with me, AA, medications, recovery communities, shamanic healing, silent retreats, acupuncture, sweat lodges, sober companions, exercise and nutrition programs, ayahuasca circles, methadone clinics, self-management and recovery training (SMART), harm reduction, macrobiotic lifestyles, sober living facilities, Ashtanga yoga, hot yoga, aerial yoga, biofeedback, art therapy, halfway houses, transcranial magnetic stimulation, residential rehab programs, sound healing, equestrian therapy, herbal supplements—I could continue for pages.

This staggering variety has compelled a regular reevaluation of what it means to be addicted, as well as what we might call treatment and recovery. Whatever viewpoints might help the patient are worth considering, even if they are disparate: the same person may benefit from the brain-based insights of addiction neuroscience, for example, alongside the spiritual community of 12-step programs.

This fluidity is not unique to addiction treatment. Our main aim in any health care setting is to attend to suffering and provide help. This necessitates a supple, circumspect mode of inquiry, with any knowledge we gain concerning a person only as useful as the well-being it promotes. And nothing is "objective": these are real people inhabiting their own experiences, suffering in ways that are invariably private, within a nearly impenetrable world of representations and interpretations all their own. Our role is to serve and support, with inquisitiveness and care, not to make firm pronouncements about truth and reality. Helping someone, in fact, often requires *relinquishing* our sense of reality, at least for the moment, so that we might better understand their own. We look beyond our "objectivity" to better attend to the people entrusting us with their inmost suffering.

Addiction work typifies the importance of remaining attentive to a person's private world. Everything can flip any moment, as one should expect with complex people making complex decisions. I have had patients leave my office doing well and thriving, only to end up in a hospital having overdosed within days. I have been humbled regularly—have endeavored to remain humble, keeping in mind just how little I know. I continue to be reminded.

Inflexibility is bound to fail in clinical settings. Addiction work is especially unforgiving. The anguish of our addicted patients will reemerge all at once; there may even be heartrending casualties. Theories and treatment protocols we learn to hold lightly, with a readiness to change course at any moment. If it sounds like maneuvering in the dark, that's because it is. Our diagnoses are best viewed as tentative artifices, our interventions the lesser evils deployed by a well-intentioned ignorance. We are forever faced with the impossible abyss separating one mind from another.

Dogma can be compelling in such waters. It addresses our thirst for certainty, mastery, and simplicity. Addiction, we might say, is simply neurochemistry or social iniquities, trauma or disconnection. Addiction is "physical"; it is "spiritual." We propose absolute, one-size-fits-all definitions. Or we may slant toward the other extreme: embracing the simplicity of inexhaustible relativism, where anything goes, and truth is a mere matter of personal interpretation. All this may limit our ability to provide treatment that works. We might also abandon empiricism altogether, resorting to whatever dubious quasi-magical cure captivates our imagination, whether it works or not.

Good intentions are not enough. Wanting to support someone does not protect against hallucinating various views on what might be wrong and how we might help. These ideas often become indistinguishable from fact. It took centuries before we realized that bloodletting, for instance, was hurting more than helping. Many of today's medical facts and practices might come to seem just as absurd and dangerous. Anticipating this inevitability, and imagining other possibilities, helps us maintain a healthy distance from our concepts and methods—we might acknowledge that much of what we know are useful falsities. The best we can do is practice the discernment to recognize what is helpful and the humility and courage to surrender what is not.

•

We exist as perceivable beings, and there is a *physical* or observable aspect to nearly everything we do, whether gleaned from actions, facial expressions, biological assessments, or sophisticated neuroimaging machines. Yet we are also beyond perception and comprehension, much like "blue" might be—mysterious to one another, and to ourselves.

A focus on biology—the study of physical life systems—might be crucial in some instances of disease, as when addressing, say, an enzyme abnormality. But in most cases of human suffering, such explanations fall short. Further, they may be completely irrelevant. In a critique of the dominance of so-called biological psychiatry, the psychiatrist Kenneth Kendler noted that there are many levels of abstraction by which to approach mental distress: synaptic, cellular, structural, psychological, relational, economic, and so forth. Biological explanations such as the brain model, despite their predominance, are only occasionally more applicable than others.

Faced with a despairing father who had lost his young daughter to cancer months ago, for instance, a competent psychiatrist doesn't concern herself with what regions of the brain are being activated, or what the man's serotonin levels might be, despite a biological dimension to his distress. The activity of the brain in this case is peripheral, the most relevant issue being grief. The patient is approached accordingly, with sensitivity to his mourning. Determining the appropriate level of explanation is critical for understanding a problem, as well as for addressing it. The challenge is to resist the inertia of bringing the same explanation, and solution, to everything.

Health workers have the person's complexity to remind them that a new perspective might be needed, though they may not always heed it. The situation grows thornier when it comes to how people proceed as scientists. In scientific inquiry, we are far more inclined to concern ourselves with precise and interpretable data than with the messy, unruly, and private lives of others. And data, of course, are not human beings.

Further, the data may not be as "objective" or "scientific" as we pretend. Even established data, as will become clear, might be implicated in the unempirical belief systems we perpetrate on addicted people—despite our knowledge being rigorously rooted, like all good science, in the "physical" world.

•

I have been privileged to receive funding from the National Institute on Drug Abuse (NIDA), a governmental agency based in the United States that is on the front line of research into drugs and their negative consequences, with an annual budget in excess of $1 billion. It sponsors many research projects around the world, ranging from laboratory work with animals to large-scale population studies, and is considered the premier drug research institute internationally. Many of its funded scientists have also drafted the standard diagnostic and treatment manuals in current use, and as experts in the addiction treatment field, have influenced how substance use disorders are approached medically: establishing the nomenclature, definitions, and treatment recommendations that are employed. Given its centrality in the global research endeavor, NIDA also serves a prominent role as gatekeeper, deciding who can embark on a research career, and through its funding decisions, influencing what it is they can study.

The main challenge NIDA faces is that drugs are highly politicized in the US and most other nations. NIDA, therefore, highlights better than other scientific institutes the many nonscientific forces that may impact on research: the US government, politicians, the Drug Enforcement Administration, taxpayers, lobbyists, the pharmaceutical industry, other biomedical corporations, researchers, academic centers. The socioeconomic context in which NIDA operates is highly significant, probably more salient, as we will see, than for organizations engaged in nondrug research, and should not be extricated from the data that NIDA delivers. It may be argued that research findings, in any setting, cannot be properly weighed and evaluated without giving mind to such institutional pressures and commitments.

Government-sponsored drug research is as much a political affair as a scientific one. This dilemma goes back to its founding: NIDA emerged and remained a powerful (and well-funded) research institute in lockstep with a government waging "the war on drugs." The effects of this war have been catastrophic: inflexible attitudes toward drug use, draconian drug policy, widened socioeconomic disparities, and mass incarceration for drug-related crimes, primarily of African American men. Historians and sociologists are unanimous in condemning this war as a human rights disaster. Yet it is well into its fourth decade. The political establishment has come to define itself in its refusal to dismantle this war, with even politicians identified with "change" such as President Barack Obama having disparaged efforts to decriminalize or legalize drugs as unimportant and irrelevant.

As a federal organization with a mission to maintain, NIDA continues to prosper today in quiet obedience to this ideology that, in addition to demonizing drugs and highlighting their negative consequences, threatens to deprive those who use them of their dignity, humanity, and autonomy. It is understandable and pragmatic that NIDA has toed the line given its reliance, as a governmental organization, on federal funds. But this has come at a cost: it puts into jeopardy the political neutrality and independence that are central to scientific progress.

This is not news to anyone. The current director of NIDA has also recognized the problem. A prominent neuroscientist, psychiatrist, and advocate for the humane treatment of addicted individuals, Dr. Nora Volkow is renowned scientifically for conducting research into the neural correlates of substance use and disordered use and has led NIDA for more than a decade. Though she was raised in the house where her great-grandfather, Leon Trotsky, was assassinated, she regards herself as apolitical: a scientist above all else. Yet, as a self-described "general in the drug war," Dr. Volkow acknowledges that "politics and science are intertwined [and] there is no way to escape it."

Dr. Volkow's candor regarding the impact of political pressures on drug research is commendable, as is her willingness to carry on with the scientific enterprise in the face of them. What remains uncertain, however, is the extent to which the alliance with a "war" effort may have compromised NIDA. There is an inevitable outcome whenever scientific endeavors are explicitly politicized: "science" is weaponized to legitimize and advance a specific ideology, with "data" and "evidence" becoming another form of propaganda.

•

The politicization of data may not be a deliberate manipulation. Bias bleeds in from the beginning: every perception, according to philosophers of science, is "theory laden" and molded by the systems in which we learn to speak, think, and observe. There are no facts, Nietzsche wrote, only interpretations—though it is unclear what, if anything, we are interpreting. A Sufi proverb goes even further: every word is a lie.

Scientists want answers. They therefore ask questions, proceeding by a steady process of "hypothesis testing" to get at "truth": they propose a story or analogy—that *water*, for instance, corresponds to H_2O—and evaluate if it holds. It is putting Nature on the rack, according to Francis Bacon, to make her confess. The real-world consequences of these confessions are of secondary concern. It is confession for its own sake.

The aim of "pure" science is neither progress nor well-being. The hope is a consistent system with apparent evidence to support it: a story that holds up. This is what is called theory, which is as close to truth as a fiction can get. Theory may go on to influence more practical endeavors and applications, such as the development of psychiatric medications, but the story need not be productive to be valuable. It is "pure" knowledge, and its value rests in its capacity to reveal and predict correspondences.

Scientific accomplishments need not be productive either. Discoveries don't occur because they're useful, said the architect of the atomic bomb, J. Robert Oppenheimer, but because they're possible. And they're possible because the theoretical framework is there. This is another way that theories are valuable: their capacity to propose and solve new problems, providing the foundation for more questions and therefore more answers and discoveries. Thomas Kuhn called this framework a *paradigm*. It orients us to the apparent terrain like a map, and allows us to find our way to new landmarks.

The yearning motivating modern science is ancient and profound. It reflects an aspiration dating back to our origins: the attainment of total understanding into and communion with the world, driven by an intuition of the unifying interrelationships between all things.

Most philosophers of science, however, are doubtful that theory provides the way. Paradigms, Kuhn argued, are arbitrary and fictive constructions, inseparable from their sociohistorical contexts. They are highly tendentious and partial imaginings, not the landscape itself—a map, as Korzybski wrote famously, not the territory. And even *territory* may be too circumscribed and mind-bound a plane, according to the philosopher Deleuze, to encompass this disorienting rhizomic immensity in which we find ourselves. Every territory is one of countless strata: a single translucent-thin surface in a library of surfaces, stacked to the skies like Babel.

A single map or surface is clearly inadequate and misleading on its own, as in the parable of the blind men and the elephant. But the hope of science is that our many maps, taken together, will cohere into an "accurate" picture of reality. The assumption here is that science is progressive, cumulative, and coherent. Kuhn showed, however, that two contemporaneous sets of maps—as in the case of quantum physics and relativity—can be incommensurable and contradictory, even though both are ostensibly grounded in the same "territory." The clash is due to their evidence emerging from distinct and incongruent paradigms. A map is not the territory; and a single territory might yield multiple maps, each tracing a disparate path over the "same" terrain.

Imagine superimposing all existing models, one semitransparent map on top of another. The figures begin to coalesce, with further accumulation, into the contours of a more comprehensive map—let's call this our master paradigm. Foucault, deferring to Aristotle, named this an *episteme*: "the dominant system," he wrote, "that defines the conditions of possibility of all knowledge." The episteme of the blind men, for example, is not the elephant, nor a theory of elephants, but the shared foundation on which their knowledge is established—which is to say, it is their groping blindness.

As Kuhn and Foucault recognized, an episteme is far from providing a blank foundation for understanding. Every episteme, while capacious and somewhat flexible, is grounded in schemes that reflect contemporary trends, myths, or power structures, be they atomism, monotheism, or antidrug politics. One can therefore imagine various epistemes for different ages—each *complete* and *total(izing)*, and yet necessarily constrained by unique epistemic orientations. Meanwhile, our maps continue piling up, their accretion leading to a metastasizing opaque chaos of aggregate abstractions. An episteme is no more a total picture of reality than are the maps it makes possible—and even darker, more sedimented, with its foundational (sub)stratum less visible to us.

We nonetheless come to something like truth through such fictions, even if it is far from complete. This is the great paradox of knowledge: the lie that tells the truth—or is at least *analogous* to it. As above, so below. The least comprehensible thing about the world, to paraphrase Einstein, is that we can comprehend it—and employ an outright artifice to find our way around it. This existence is so profoundly interrelated and rich with correspondence that even comprehension is incomprehensible, every fact also fiction.

•

"There are more things in heaven and earth," Hamlet advised his friend, "than are dreamt of in your philosophy." Philosophy, however, might be too narrow a term. More fitting is *"reality"*: a word Nabokov thought meaningless without quotation marks.

Even better, without need for scare quotes, is *(un)reality*. Blind feelers piecing together a babbling cascade of worlds neither real nor unreal, each with its vantage point on the order of things: objective-materialist, extractive-egoistic, compassionate-egoistic, idealist-nonmaterialist, altruistic-idealistic, victimized-entitled-survivor, benevolent-humanist-interventionist, critical-skeptical, mystical-critical, depressive-traumatized-fatalistic, et cetera. And there are also (un)realities more blatantly mythological: hero-journey; covenant with God; mycelial-collective; constant apocalypse; constant communion. These worlds help us make sense of things, as they do scientists; they shape our perspectives, provide interpretations, and organize the phenomena to which we attend, with everything subsumed into our (un)reality from the start.

The trap is forgetting that the world is more than the world. We confuse our walled-in simulation with what is the case, a heaven-and-earth fitting inside our comprehension—the United States, God's country, with liberty and justice for all. An epistemic knot, a circular reality, with the facts of our (un)reality imparting substance and gravity to the whole production.

This has been termed *confirmation bias*. It keeps the story going, substantiating it in even counterfactual ways. This bias happens in science and everywhere else: we pay selective attention to what confirms our schemes, and are prone to disregard, or fail to register entirely, the phenomena directly before us but beyond our maps. We're proficient, at least for now, at navigating the town square. So why should we doubt what's real?

Then something happens: a dissonant phenomenon intrudes on us, demanding our attention and threatening to overthrow everything. An illness of unidentified origin, technology carrying hidden costs, forces for good burning children alive. Our fragment of the world begins to crumble yet further. We struggle to adapt what we know to what emerges. Perhaps we find we don't know anything at all. The ground of things falls away.

Or perhaps we succeed at cordoning the phenomenon off. A freak finding. Not worth losing our heads over it. We consult the usual data and navigate the same apparent terrain, with this impish phantom now lurking in the gutters, poised to spring again at any moment. We carry on, holding our breath, tightening ourselves against the inevitable surprise.

●

Wanting knowledge puts us in a difficult position. "Reality" is already elusive enough, a shifting relationship between spectators, territories,

maps, mysteries. Fossilizing this fluid relationship into static paradigms creates further challenges.

It also threatens to deceive and blind us. In science, this self-
deception can be recalcitrant because it has data, predictive power,
technological progress, and the authority of institutions behind it.
Invariably there are societal, political, and financial forces, as Kuhn
recognized, that also prop paradigms up. The fiction of "objectivity,"
in any case, becomes set in stone, just as we imagine the fact that blue
has its own autonomous and material existence in the world. Facts
are passed off as self-sufficient truths existing "out there," with the
epistemic scheme shaping these phenomena vanishing from view, as
if these data were never interpretations or representations in the first
place.

Logic and reason solidify any confirmation bias. There is little room
for contradiction in this coherent structure. Any phenomenon that
does not fit cleanly into the story, or that contradicts the rules, might as
well not exist. We come to see, as Schopenhauer wrote, what we know.
This means not seeing very much, nor very well.

We can choose to stay in our paradigms. But knowledge is not the
only way, of course, to maneuver through existence. We might also flow
forward, as does an animal, with a silent immediacy, not presuming to
know what is moving us or where we are going. The body leads the way,
in all its corporeal awareness and fluid intuitions. And beyond that is
the immense confluence of currents in which we are both participant
and observer. Practicing attunement with a flow impossible to map out
or even comprehend: we become opaque and translucent all at once,
like existence itself.

•

My first research project was focused on meditation-based therapy.
Meditation has been an important part of my life since adolescence,
helping me navigate difficult situations more deliberately. I've also noticed gains in serenity and self-composure with consistent practice,
as well as freedom from old patterns. I reasoned meditation would be
helpful in a similar way for addicts.

This was far from being a new insight. I was extending an ancient
tool to a DSM-5 diagnosis. Nor was I particularly original in attempt-

ing a translation to clinical settings. Mindfulness training—a modern reinterpretation of the Buddhist practice of *Vipassana* (Pali for "seeing clearly without delusion")—had already been developed as a treatment for other psychiatric disorders. In Buddhism, this practice refers to a specific path toward enlightenment, centered around developing an understanding into reality and the nature of suffering in the service of achieving "absolute liberation." In clinical settings, mindfulness training was divested of these more theistic, or "spiritual," dimensions to make it more acceptable to secular society and to existing models of disease and treatment. Mindfulness has come to be defined clinically as a capacity for moment-to-moment attention, acceptance, stillness, intentionality, and compassion. The training manual is a codified set of techniques and perspectives that, with regular practice, might promote serene detachment from thoughts, sensations, desires, and feelings, thereby allowing for more freedom in how one perceives and responds to them.

When I started the project, I was aware that mindfulness training had been found helpful for stress and depression. Its relevance to addiction treatment seemed clear. An addicted person has a craving, or experiences stress, or argues himself into getting high, and this ordinarily "compels" use. The practice of mindfulness creates an opportunity for freedom from such apparent compulsions. Rather than react automatically and pursue the drug, the person learns to maintain an accepting, nonreactive, and attentive stance. The intention is to foster the capacity to respond deliberately to whatever comes up, making decisions with discernment and poise.

I conducted a small study with promising results. But there were some clinical challenges. The very same vulnerabilities that I hoped to target with mindfulness practice—such as restlessness, reactivity, an identification with thoughts and ideas, and a tendency to go on autopilot—also disrupted engagement with the training regimen, which was oriented around being still, maintaining attention, and engaging in different mind-body practices. Not everyone struggled, of course, but enough did as to suggest that additional support could be helpful, beyond what the regimen on its own could provide.

I suspected that a medication that could simulate or promote meditative states would provide support in a variety of ways. It might jump-start a consistent practice by providing a foretaste of what's possible: an experiential stepping-stone. It may also facilitate enduring changes conducive to a practice, such as openness, equanimity, and a quieter mind.

I considered testing different hallucinogens/psychedelics, which are recognized to alter consciousness in ways comparable to the changes associated with meditation. They may also be associated with per-sistent effects on openness and nonreactivity. I settled on ketamine, an inexpensive anesthetic in common use that when administered at doses low enough to preserve consciousness leads to dissociative or dream-like experiences that have been anecdotally compared to deep meditation, trance, and other altered states. Of hallucinogens, ketamine seemed the most likely to be accepted as a treatment for substance use disorders. Ketamine is legal (unlike psilocybin, for example), has a long history of clinical use, and was at that time just emerging as a potential treatment for depression. Thus, while it is unconventional to give hallucinogens as a treatment for substance use disorders, and though ketamine can lend itself to recreational use (as "special K"), I was reassured that the legality and safety profile of ketamine, as well as its ubiquity in clinical settings, would offset some of these concerns. This would allow for investigating a controversial treatment model—hallucinogen-assisted psychotherapy—with institutional and perhaps federal acceptance.

I devised a study to evaluate the benefits of ketamine in cocaine-dependent people in the human laboratory and obtained a small amount of money from an internal funding opportunity within the uni-versity, which was, in turn, supported by NIDA. At the same time, I also applied directly to NIDA for a competitive career-development grant that incorporated a clinical trial of ketamine-assisted mindfulness training for cocaine-dependent people. We will delve into this research in greater detail later.

I was surprised at how smoothly I was able to get the internally funded ketamine project off the ground. There was the expected amount of resistance from colleagues and mentors, who were con-cerned about giving a substance with abuse potential to people with addiction. But a few months of sustained dialogue and debate led to their concerns being assuaged and for institutional support being granted.

Several months into running participants for this study I was also heartened to receive notification that the application I had submitted to NIDA had received an exceptional score by the committee of scientists that represents the first phase of grant review; the next step was for the grant to receive the green light from the more administrative wing of scientists at the institute that makes funding decisions (the "Council"). Council's decision is usually ceremonial, and often already determined in advance by the score of the application and by institutional priorities. A career-development grant by a young investigator with an exceptional score, according to my mentors, will do just fine and should get funded without a hitch.

My dominant feeling at the time, in addition to great appreciation, was reassurance. My ideals regarding the sciences were being validated. Even unconventional projects might be institutionally supported so long as they're sound. The scientific method will take precedence over politics.

Over the course of a single week, however, the narrative flipped. The first sally of emails came from administrators at the university. I was asked to stop my ketamine research immediately. Though it was internally funded, the laboratory study was ultimately supported by funds provided by NIDA, and the institute had not known about it until a week or so prior, after receiving an annual report detailing the research that was underway. Almost immediately, the project officer at NIDA threatened to pull all money from this internal fund—amounting to millions of dollars annually—if the ketamine research continued. NIDA was clear on its reason: it did not want its federal money going toward testing ketamine as a potential medicine given its hallucinogenic effects.

The second set of emails, days later, pertained to the application awaiting a funding decision. It would not be funded, the project officer wrote, for the same reasons that the existing research needed to be stopped: ketamine is a hallucinogen. Over the course of a week, everything I had been pursuing, and with apparent support, was in jeopardy.

It was not resistance to the research that disturbed me. Resistance is par for the course in science; I had already become inured to the interminable quarrel that is academic life. What disconcerted me was the argument that was presented. *Ketamine is a hallucinogen.* It became clear what I was up against. Behind this argument was a series of tired assumptions, entirely unempirical, none of them evidence based.

This opened my eyes to some difficult truths. Dogma and prejudice were far from relics of the past. Even the most celebrated institutions of higher learning harbor them. This was not, moreover, a rarefied academic matter restricted to the halls of the university. There was a far more consequential conflict at work. I could feel its violence in our words. Here was the war on drugs, yet again, working to demonize certain drugs, as well as those who use them, as irredeemably dangerous.

●

Scientists want answers. But as with anything else we want, the answers are never enough. What remain are questions, a growing heap of them. This is the great redemption of science. The method contains its own solution. No idea, no matter how celebrated, will rest on its laurels for long. Everything continues be interrogated and revised. Even the master map itself must be called into question: burned regularly and redrawn as Zen monks do their holy books.

Stepping outside the bounds of knowledge, we return to our fundamental condition. We join the laughing animals, as Rilke wrote, in seeing clearly that we are not quite at home in our interpreted world. There is a world beyond our interpretations that is much better suited. The chaos of unmediated experience offers new maps, new libraries and worlds, a truer home, if we allow our minds to bend with the fiction-shattering laughter of things.

It need not be a disorienting or astonishing deluge of truth. The most minor observations that pass through the chinks of our interpretive filters may be sufficient to upend an entire worldview, assuming they land, to paraphrase Pasteur, on a prepared mind. The old paradigm might be replaced by another that tells a better story—until that paradigm, too, comes to be dismantled, swapped out, and so forth.

The Copernican revolution is a particularly dramatic story, with a few throwaway observations and mathematical irregularities ostensibly doing the trick. The apparently trivial impressions of a single scientist were adequate to overthrow an established idea supported by state and clergy alike, and to usher in a new theory more cogently explaining the cycles and epicycles of our solar system, with the sun and not the earth recognized, for the time being, as the center of our cosmos.

Paradigm shifts are not always so cataclysmic as to force us from our perch at the center of things. They are often subtler, more gradual, an accumulation of glacial revisions. The scientist occupies a half-way point between Quixote and skeptic: equal parts fiction-bound and fiction-less. She works within the dominant (un)reality, while also endeavoring to transcend its stasis, making discoveries that cast new light on what came before, and illuminate the path ahead.

Theory is gray, wrote Goethe, while the golden tree of life is green. Scientists are at their most creative when recognizing this verdant mystery much as an artist might; they work toward enlivening the theories they've inherited by revealing glimmers of the gold that had awakened their curiosity and imagination in the first place. There is also a playfulness, an inclination toward creative activity and invention for no other reason than to exercise the imagination. New constructs or paradigms might emerge, with the hard stone streaked at first with what appear to be pulsing veins of gold and green. And these new theories will ossify with time too, grow brittle, and come in their own way to demand toppling and replacement. The ideal scientist remains skeptical of her fictions and maintains an imaginative distance from them, regarding them as artifices and makeshift approximations that will come to be surrendered once they are no longer fruitful. And like Quixote, the scientist makes a home inside her myths, too, with its words and fictions perpetually refreshed to maintain harmony with the golden-green wilderness in which we live.

This suggests that scientists may be well poised to jump between levels of explanation with agility and playfulness, maybe even more so than someone concerned with practical application, like a clinician. But science is a shared project, involving a community of human beings. A scientist on her own might be capable of impressive epistemic flexibility, and may come to some startling insights, but there are others to convince. As with any process that involves changing minds, paradigm shifts are often arduous, delayed, highly resisted. And they are situated invariably within the battleground of human history, with cultural, political, financial, technological, and other forces having as much a role to play in scientific shifts, including the Copernican revolution, as they do in other societal changes. Further, certain prejudices, as I experienced with researching ketamine, might be entrenched and inflexible to such a degree that they compromise our capacity for free inquiry, potentially excluding some scientists from the club.

Science remains a human activity, despite its lofty intentions. It can be just as petty, ignorant, and dogmatic as we are. Addiction science is particularly beset by such entanglements. There is the war on drugs, of course, with its propaganda, allegiances, political inertia. And the "physicality" of drugs demands, it seems, a physicalist understanding, with reductive brain-based explanations constituting the dominant theory.

There are also more fundamental blind spots, touching on the scientific endeavor itself. The fantasy of "objectivity," for instance, is false and unachievable, with a subjective interpersonal body our inevitable condition. *Intersubjectivity* is the more accurate and humbler term for it: a consensus of subjective representations. The sooner we recognize that we remain human and blinkered, even as "objective" scientists, the less vulnerable we become to turning prejudices into facts or canonizing our interpretations as eternal truths. Otherwise, the scientist is at risk of becoming just as confused, and as tragic, as Quixote: isolated in his laboratory, he takes his instruments, books, and theories to be the measure of all things.

Motivating science is an ideal to work through these human errors, as well as rules and methods by which we might do so. It is not nature that is put on the rack; what are interrogated are our own minds and ideas. With the arrogance of objectivity behind us, we might carry on the humble work of sifting through our notions, keeping the reliable and coherent, discarding the rest. And if good data are not being acknowledged because they oppose entrenched prejudices and methods, or if the rules are otherwise violated, we must speak up, loudly and persistently, to protect science from scientists, and scientists from scientism.

•

The resistance my research with ketamine faced was not a complete surprise. One of my mentors, Dr. Carl Hart, was clear on the many ways that politics and drug-war ideology threaten the integrity of drug research. He had cautioned me, as I was starting my research with ketamine, that it would not be easy. "You want to study hallucinogens as a treatment? I hate to break this to you, but I have heard from Nora [Volkow] herself that NIDA will never fund any research of this sort. So I suggest you either get really creative, or think about something else."

I was learning: there are no final victories, just lulls in a generally stormy sea. The research had started well enough, but now it was time to confront the prejudices Carl had warned about. It was an ideal moment to do this. I had the support of one of the country's most distinguished (and politically connected) teams of drug researchers, eager to support a new faculty member. Also, I was a young researcher just starting out, and this gave me a certain license that might be lost once I became more established.

It may seem absurd now, in the wake of the so-called psychedelic renaissance, but simply calling something a hallucinogen was enough to discredit it. Ketamine was thus a problem because it is a hallucinogen: dangerous and unlikely to be medically helpful. Or so it was believed. And hallucinogens are dangerous because they exist outside mainstream sanctioned modes of intoxication and are likely to be used irresponsibly and harmfully. Most hallucinogens are Schedule I in the US, which is a class reserved for drugs without any known medical benefits and that are reputed to lend themselves to abuse and risk. Such drugs are "highly controlled," in the same way that we control access to anything that is highly sought after but allegedly dangerous: controlling a child's access to candy, for example.

Giving a hallucinogenic dose of ketamine to an addict, in light of these views, is like giving candy to a sugar-obsessed diabetic child. No, even crazier than that: giving candy to a diabetic child as if it were medicine. It is no wonder they wanted to pull the plug. Never mind that all the arguments are complete nonsense. It is nonsense that had attained institutional legitimacy, that had permeated the words and ideas of nearly everyone involved, and therefore nonsense masquerading as truth.

The only argument that was going to win was a surface-level one that worked within this paradigm. Calling attention to the potential utility of hallucinogens was unlikely to go anywhere, at least at that time, and it was similarly futile to cast doubt on the presumption that psychoactive substances with recreational appeal—especially of the "Schedule I" sort—should not be considered addiction treatment. The time for addressing these prejudices might come later.

I kept it safe, careful not to challenge any assumptions—such as "hallucinogens are bad"—that were off limits and entrenched. So, ketamine is not in fact a hallucinogen, I argued, but a dissociative anesthetic. It does not cause hallucinations, does not work by the serotonergic mechanisms of classical hallucinogens, has been in clinical use for decades, and is Schedule 3, not Schedule 1, unlike LSD or psilocybin. Further, I marshaled the data I had collected thus far, and also data from depression research, indicating that ketamine is safe, well tolerated, and does not lead to persistent problems, such as ketamine misuse or psychiatric problems, when administered responsibly. I also argued against the notion that for an intervention to be helpful it needed to be free of risk—consider surgery, which may be quite helpful and at the same time associated with certain manageable risks.

These arguments were pushed at the highest level. Thanks to the political influence of my mentors, I obtained an audience with the heads of medication development at NIDA, who as luck would have it had been closely following the development of ketamine as an antidepressant. I received a sympathetic hearing. They felt that our arguments and data were persuasive and expressed support for the project. A few weeks later, I obtained the go-ahead to resume the research, and within a month, I received notification that the grant would be funded.

It was an important breakthrough for me, and not simply because of the substantial grant support I received. I was given a clear view of the drug research landscape, its opportunities and challenges. I also received important lessons about how to proceed.

The prejudices of others require a gentle touch. We have to meet our fellow scientists where they are if we are going to make any real change; we can't speak a language they have no interest in or push an idea for which they are not ready. We may be able to move someone toward greater openness, I recognized, but only by giving proper attention to whatever fiction dominates their thinking. I had found the right words to say, and things moved forward, fortunately. Left largely intact, however, were the prejudices I had side-stepped to make my way, like land mines still buried in the field from a longstanding war.

II.

There are poetic fictions, like those captivating Quixote. There are also scientific, moral, and political fictions. Each has a syntax. Becoming fluent in these languages means learning to see through the words, not be swept away by them. This is the only way to tell our stories right.

Intoxication offers similar opportunities. We access possibilities—pertaining to others, the world, ourselves—otherwise elusive. This expands the limits of what we might experience: pain-free instead of distressed, illuminated instead of bored, free instead of stuck.

But inhabiting a representation, be it a map or intoxication, has its challenges. We might grow attached to certain fictions, such as the "sanctuary" of heroin, while ignoring the dark fluid ground of things, our own and that of the substance itself. This entanglement with one-sided (un)reality is at the origin of all addictions.

It is not unique to our relationship with drugs. The attachment might occur with most anything else. Getting stuck regularly happens, for instance, in our infatuations and relations with other human beings. It also happens, more fundamentally, in our entanglement with ideas and maps themselves.

The medical consensus is that addiction is a unique biological phenomenon, primarily caused by the effects on the brain of repeated drug use. This "brain disease model" is the main paradigm for all of psychiatry: studying the brain and regarding it as the "hardware" of human experience dovetails with the materialist orientation of modern medicine more generally, which emphasizes quantification, materialism, and mechanism. Drugs lend themselves to this model perfectly. Among other things, they exert a direct impact on the brain. The brain is also clearly involved in our suffering, whether we call our problems addiction, mental illness, or something else.

These correspondences support the model, but they are not the main reason we've baptized it as absolute truth. It dominates our minds for the same reasons that any (un)reality does. We have come to regard what we know as more real than what we do not, or cannot, know.

•

The philosopher A. N. Whitehead called science an empirical elaboration of imaginaries. At the heart of our *epistemes* is a covert act of creative imagination—the immaterial, mind-forged firmament on which we find our place and behold the world. It might endure for thousands of years without anyone recognizing the sedimented, compacted artifice.

It is imagination, for example, that decrees that the mind emerges from the brain or that the "physical" world is our source of truth. These are ideas closer to metaphysics or theology than they are to unbiased observation. Yet their empirical value is obvious. Resting underneath our biomedical sciences, these axioms and mythic structures generate our facts. An entire well-articulated world has spawned and grown from this imaginary foundation.

Imaginaries provide clear benefits. But they're not without risk. What we experience might be completely constrained by such fictions, with the immense world reduced to cranial proportions. And we may find ourselves burdened with cranial problems, problems of our own making, much like Ahmed chasing a substance that exists only in his imagination. *The traps of language*, as Wittgenstein called our epistemic entanglements.

We are not bound, however, to remain trapped. Instead, we might choose to find freedom from our (un)reality and its claustrophobic problems, like flies released from a bottle. Philosophy, contemplative traditions, art, even drugs: there are various ways that we might step outside the constraints of our epistemic containers. The intention is a nimble freedom from the "realities" against which we smash our heads. We might also find the freedom to call new imaginaries into being, offering greater space for our wings.

Every fact is an open question, including the ground of "reality" itself. Every fact might be fiction. We can't say we know, the Upanishads tells us, but we can't say we don't know. Perhaps we shouldn't say anything at all. Coming to know beyond knowing, beyond anything we might say. Learning instead to engage the whole of ourselves, including our limbs, our organs, our many senses, and extending the inquiry to the layered earth beneath our feet, bringing our wakefulness to bear on our deepest imaginaries. Any correspondence is recognized in intimate silence, our entire being registering the resonance. Intuition is the most common name given this inmost concordance with subtle truths, beyond discursive or computational comprehension. But perhaps we should leave it unnamed. An understanding, Gödel might have said, outside the rules of understanding.

●

The mind-body problem is the philosophical matter most relevant to neuroscience, including addiction science. It refers to the question of how "mind" relates to "matter." *Mind* has a very specific meaning here; it is not simply "mental" phenomena or capacities, such as induction/deduction, memory, attention, perceptions, fantasy. It also pertains to subjectivity (direct experience), the "hard" problem that has kept the question of mind-body metaphysics unresolved.

At the heart of this question is a dualistic imaginary. We will examine it shortly. But the first problem to note is the presumption that we can arrive at a final comprehension of anything. Even mundane facts like "the sky is blue" are made up and rooted in a mysterious communion, with the primordial darkness of experience ordered into various stories: that there is a blue thing out there, that this thing exists, and that we perceive it as it is. We don't know these facts; we imagine them. And if "blue" is ultimately unknowable, what do we make of experience itself, the obscure process by which we perceive and comprehend?

Our language will reach its limit with everything. With "consciousness," this limit comes straight away—though it is difficult to stop there and put our words to rest. As we will find, the mind-body problem originates in this resolution to comprehend the incomprehensible and represent what cannot be represented, while following our logical concatenation of words into a dutiful confusion. The mind-body problem may, therefore, not be a problem at all, beyond the traps set by the words themselves.

●

Patients vanishing is common in addiction treatment. I couldn't discount the impact that being a research participant might have had on Ahmed's disappearance. Our approach to him was necessarily restricted to the research protocol, with our procedures designed and executed with an eye toward generalizability—that is, toward identifying a one-size-fits-all treatment plan capable of being extended, relatively unchanged, to as many people as possible.

This meant committing to a preordained treatment protocol designed to attend to his "chief complaint" of heroin addiction, which requires peripheralizing some of his other challenges. Ahmed as a singular person-in-the-world was not the focus; most relevant was his "severe opioid use disorder," presumed to be a largely uniform disease transposable from one person to another and amenable to uniform care. This type of diagnosis-driven, protocol-based treatment is not much different from modern medicine more generally. Given that we were testing a specific treatment strategy in a rigorous clinical trial, however, we maintained a stricter adherence to the protocol than might be the case in clinical practice. I wondered if we lost Ahmed because of it.

An important challenge in human research settings is to maintain awareness of research participants as *subjects* rather than objects. This can be challenging within a positivist model. By constraining our being-in-the-world to "material" phenomena, whether it is in identifying a pathological mechanism or formulating a diagnosis, we invariably objectify what is before us: diseases, brains, addicts. And our tendency in the face of creeping objectification, every one of us, is to make a run for it, with all of Ahmed's pent-up restlessness.

What does it mean to study consciousness? The brain disease model suggests a particular path. Observing, in various ways, a study participant thinking or speaking. Or if we have a neuroimaging machine, examining the neural correlates of consciousness—imaging the brain of someone thinking, perceiving, calculating, or acting.

None of these occasions, however, involves apprehending consciousness. We are observing behavior or phenomena, which is to say we are observing *objects*. Consciousness, conversely, apprehends and cannot be apprehended; it is not an object that might be observed. Try to observe yourself observing to get closer to this impossibility: we find ourselves in the same subjectivity that was observing in the first place. Consciousness remains a subject, even when attending to itself as its own object.

"Materialism" is bound to fail us if we aspire toward truer engagement with other human beings. To describe a person as "matter," or more specifically as the brain, is inevitably inadequate. Our subjectivity does not lend itself to being described or represented as anything.

Though we are ultimately beyond the reach of objectification, there may be good reason to represent ourselves as physical bodies, brains, or diseases in some circumstances. For example, it may be helpful to understand the neuropathology of a dementing disease like Alzheimer's so that we might develop treatments for it. But as with the scientist, we need to remain fluid with our constructs, partly fiction-less—as befits the subject, any subject, and particularly if the subject is a living being.

Another relevant example is an emerging model of perception called prediction coding. It hypothesizes that brain activity is perpetually reorganizing itself to minimize the mismatch between predictions and sensory information. This ultimately constrains what we perceive and experience to what is most congruent with the brain's "model" or predictive map of the world: a private kind of scientific process, with the neural paradigm restricting "reality" to what facilitates prediction. This model is a good metaphor for understanding how perception becomes theory laden and epistemically organized in the anatomy and activity of the brain. It can also illuminate the brain's involvement in psychiatric disorders characterized by a pathological narrowing of perception, such as depression.

Where we run into problems is claiming that this model, or any model, sheds light on consciousness or reality. This account, as with all other positivist accounts, has as much to say about such things as Kuhn's history of the scientific process does about the human beings who carry it out. Our paradigms, scientific or private, are not the world. Nor are they ourselves. It is crucial to recognize these limitations; scientific paradigms are never the final word. And the limitations are even deeper than that. When it comes to the irreducible mysteries of being and experience, our models are not fit to speak *any words*. Maps are only useful when we stay within their borders.

Yet we insist on saying more, on investigating the matter further; we believe that consciousness is *something* and that like other things in the world it is *involved* in some phenomenal way. A "hard" materialist claims this something is actually nothing, and it is involved insofar as it is caused by the brain or constitutes a concomitant property of neural activity, existing in some form at the level of the most primitive sentient organism. A softer materialist may be interested in understanding the dualistic interplay between brain activity and consciousness.

One can fill volumes with words about what consciousness might be. Or one can write apophatically about it, as I do here, remarking on what it is not. Wittgenstein had clear counsel on such matters: that which cannot be talked about, he wrote, should be passed over in silence.

Experienced clinicians understand this intuitively. They learn to quiet the tendency to explain the person and situate her entirely within their constructs. Then there might be the space to engage the person in all her embodied, conscious, and relational immensity, as we might the silent inscrutability of our own beings.

●

Consciousness cannot be located. It is nowhere or, just as elusively, everywhere. Nor can it be reduced to machine-forged correlates of mental activity, as with neuroimaging. These correlates, further, are twice removed: consciousness is neither mental activity nor snapshots of this activity. A double confusion: confused about subjectivity, confused about what we observe. We might have tried similar experiments when we were children, staring directly and pointedly into our eyes in the mirror, trying to locate the origin of vision.

Hard materialists agree consciousness is beyond observation. They therefore refute its existence, representing it as a miasma of neuroelectric discharge: an "epiphenomenon" or illusion. But this physicalism is identical to the mode of thinking we might disparage as antirational in prehistoric human beings, explaining natural events in the magical terms they understand. "It is impossible that bodies should be minds," wrote Giambattista Vico in *The New Science*, "and yet it was believed that the thundering sky was Jove." Just as lightning was once God, the body has come to be mind.

It is compelling for these reasons to insist on the reality of mind, separate from the body. Consciousness, we might say, is the most existent aspect of ourselves. It deserves full recognition, distinct from matter.

We might think of Ahmed, in this spirit, as a brain *and* a mind. This is undoubtedly helpful for correcting the impression that he is primarily a brain hijacked by heroin. We might then consider how his experience—including his values, maps of meaning, epistemic structures, and imaginaries—might be implicated in his suffering, and how we might engage these aspects of his being in the service of finding freedom from addiction.

But this dualism does not go far enough. Arguing against the tenets of materialism and insisting on the reality of the mind independent of the brain is to remain stuck in the same bottle, buzzing clamorously against its walls.

Even saying that the mind exists is saying too much. "Real existence" is a determination we give to *things* for which there are meaningful, empirical modes of confirmation allowing us to make the statement. But this is not a description that can be extended empirically to experience itself, to the impenetrably enigmatic stage of Being on which "real existence" seems to occur. There is simply no way to draw the conclusion, no field of correlation or correspondence within which to confirm the statement, or deny it. We cannot know whether consciousness exists. Nor can we know whether it does not exist.

Ahmed, in this light, is not even Ahmed. He is beyond the reach of all words, including those most firmly attached to him: his name, his diagnosis. He is real and at the same time beyond reality.

Being is boundless. It evades our words, all words, including *real existence*. A matter of endless inquiry. Deepening the mystery is that this inarticulability is not restricted to what we might call consciousness. Everything else is incomprehensible too. Minds, our bodies, Ahmed, and all we observe as "existing," all of *this*, whatever we wish to call it: being, matter, suchness, reality, behavior. Whether *this* really exists, or *we* really exist, we cannot say.

The problem with materialism is not that it demotes consciousness as secondary to matter. Idealism, for instance, takes the opposite tack, *promoting* consciousness and designating it the fundamental reality, like God, from which everything emerges. Yet idealism is just as mistaken. The trap is the presumption that one can say anything of the sort at all. We are trespassing in both cases, overreaching with our maps and limiting our horizons in the process. Such confusions are inevitable if we begin with the notion that being can be partitioned: "mind" on one side, "matter" on the other.

The more we say, the less we understand. Even saying our experience exists or is real is saying too much. Providing silent witness offers the fullest mode of engagement, as with anything beyond our bounds:

> *The wind blows where it wills, and you hear the sound of it,*
> *but you do not know whence it comes or where it goes.*

It is difficult to heed these winds silently. We are restless to dissect being, prove it exists, demystify it. Then there are the temptations of dualism: bifurcating *this* into mind and matter, or consciousness and its objects, the world in here and the world out there. This systematizing, theorizing confusion is the heart of the mind-body problem. Being is beyond subject and object, beyond objectification and representation: like "consciousness," beyond all attributes and qualities. It *is* not in the sense that it is "real," "true," or "physical"; it is in-itself, in *being itself*.

This may be what Descartes was suggesting in his famous maxim that found in consciousness our proof of being: *Cogito, ergo sum*. I think, therefore I am. But no proof is needed. A truer way of expressing it returns us to the silence within silence: *being experience* in its boundless possibility, without an "I," "think," or "therefore" necessary.

●

We are certain to get lost in these language-games. But there may be benefit in experiencing such disorientations. We stand to recognize the confusion beneath what we know. There is also opportunity to consider other possibilities, perhaps more fruitful. How is "reality" working to eclipse what we are? How might we *be experience* more fully?

There are consequences to what we imagine and believe, as should be clear by now, whether we are scientists or drug users. Our word games might also become war games. We return to the war on drugs: a seemingly abstract and bloodless campaign, with the apparent target inert substances. But its casualties, as in any war, are real beings. Far from dampening the harms that might result from drug use, the drug war has only deepened them—violating individuals, ravaging communities, legitimizing prejudice, and rendering drug use *more* dangerous. It has also disproportionately affected Black, brown, and peripheralized human beings, exacerbating a host of social disparities to the extent that it might be more accurately called *a war on being vulnerable.* The magnitude of this humanitarian crisis is now well recognized. Scientists and humanists should be careful to partner with such a disaster, let alone be designated a general in its field of battle.

Fueling the drug war is the conviction that humans need to be reined in and controlled—ideally by the state before other things get a turn. The alternative is some drug serving as the despot, addicting us to its power instead. A preemptive tyranny has been therefore instituted. Rigid rules proliferate, ideology replaces thoughtful and nuanced dialogue, and basic freedoms are taken away, including our access to "problematic" altered states: what has been called a violation of "cognitive liberty," of our freedom to do with our minds whatever we like.

A deeper freedom than drug access is violated too. The system of control becomes our own, with our identities and words molded accordingly. We come to restrict ourselves with nobody else needed, a private cognitive program compelling us to shun realities as much our birthright as this one, whether they relate to intoxication, social organization, or ways of thinking. We become master and slave at once.

This tyranny also extends to the ways we imagine our communities. The drug war mandates a complacency with social and institutional brutality. The addict's problems are his own, whether due to bad decision making or a bad brain, with certain substances, such as methamphetamine or heroin, thought to possess a terrifying capacity for neural devastation. The conclusion is that heavy drug users represent a distinct category of mental illness if not person, their brains scrambled to such an extent that they are rendered unfit to live purposefully: barely free, hardly human. Classism, racism, social engineering, disproportionate policing, impoverished opportunity, economic disparity, fragmentation, moral injury, lack of meaning—these go largely unexamined much less addressed, despite their clear role in addiction-related suffering. And the war regime finds further justification for its dehumanizations on the evidence of these drug-damaged masses.

Meanwhile, the conquests of drug war science continue, each empirical victory pushing the bleeding edge of our knowledge a bit deeper into uncharted territory. Never mind the likelihood of total irrelevance, with our maps unfit to guide anyone. What we risk most acutely is to be immured in this evidence-based "reality," its prison cells mistaken for the whole of the world. What we risk is *addiction*: holding on to a made-up world—peopled by brains, poisons, addicts—that deepens our suffering. And this world is far more devastating than that of any drug-related addiction because it is held in common as the one true reality: scientific, physical, absolute.

These "facts" restrict the world. They also restrict us, in quite blatant ways. We must be protected, so we're told, from accessing certain drugs because this would mean venturing beyond acceptable limits, risking derangement, and potentially losing whatever humanity we might have. Military-grade arsenals have been locked and loaded in nearly every American town to enforce this humanitarian agenda. The correctional system is ready to contain offenders as well.

"You want to allow drugs to be freely available?" I once heard someone ask a speaker on drug legalization. "We know what'll happen. There will be more addiction, more drug problems, more crime. You can't expect to unleash drugs on the population and not have there be more casualties."

A despotic world is being propagated in these words: upholding it has devastated many lives, many minds. The drug war is one brief chapter in it. This is the war behind all wars: the dark bones of our (un)realities, of our moral and philosophical regimes, a twisted dream of what we are and what is possible for us. As we will find, it did not start with this war, nor will it end with it. There is a deeper reality with which to contend.

3

DARKNESS WITHIN DARKNESS

For technicians, nothing is possible.

—ANDRÉ DERAIN

It is clear right away if a family is unaccustomed to being together. They will sit in my office ill at ease, breath labored, their bodies stiffened as if preparing for bad news. It seems they had been avoiding one another for fear of some difficult truth coming to the surface and making a mess of everything. They brace themselves for the inevitable recognition.

Steve, the eldest son, was referred to me for a severe prescription painkiller addiction; he was snorting about $120 worth of crushed oxycodone pills daily. He was in his early twenties, unemployed, living at home after leaving college. He had failed his classes and floundered depressed and isolated before taking a medical leave extending for three years now. They were a working-class family living in Staten Island, ground zero at the time for New York City's opioid problem. I had called the family together because it was important to hear what everyone had to say and to better understand how life at home might be influencing Steve's problems, for better or worse. I also wanted to observe everyone interacting, get a sense of how they communicated and related with one another.

"We want to help him, but nothing is working," his mother said. "It is awful what happened to him. He was a great student, lots of potential. I know he doesn't want to do this. We've tried everything, detox, therapy. He can't stop himself."

I saw his father bite down hard on his trembling lower lip, struggling to stave off the sobbing. His sister, a petite woman a few years younger, seemed irritated. His mother was also frustrated, a single tear rolling down a stern face. She had come to my office from her job as an administrator in a downtown bank, wearing a sharp business suit. Everyone looked tired and washed out. The toll Steve's addiction was taking was obvious.

It wasn't clear that Steve wanted to stop, contrary to what his mother said. He had come with his family to my office; that was a good sign. But it didn't seem he had a choice in the matter. He had a certain passivity to him, as if he had learned to play along with whatever was asked of him so long as he got what he needed. He was tall and burly, sitting on his hands like a child, motionless and apparently imperturbable. His half-lidded glassy eyes were as inexpressive as wet stones. He seemed to be zoned out daydreaming. He was clearly high.

I felt the anger in the room, the family's helplessness and confusion. Everyone was hurt and frustrated because of Steve's choices. But they also weren't sure whether his addiction allowed Steve to choose anything other than drugs in the first place. Or maybe he was choosing; maybe he was getting exactly what he wanted and to hell with everyone else. Were they all just fooling themselves? Perhaps Steve had turned into every parent's nightmare: "a lying and conniving junkie," as his mother later put it.

Steve had come to a dead end, carrying his family with him. They wanted to shake some reason into him, wake him up to reality. But he was no longer a son, a brother, or even a human being: he had become "a junkie," a pill-fueled automaton impervious to moral or rational guidance. There was nowhere for the anger to go. This may be why they were so uncomfortable when compelled to sit with the situation: they resembled a hissing cauldron ready to explode.

I asked how things have been at home.

"I hide all my jewelry, my cards, we can't keep money around anymore," his mother said. "We don't know who is coming into the house when we are gone. I can't trust a thing he says. I open the door at the end of the day, and I'm holding my breath because he could be dead. A few friends of his have already OD'd due to some fake pills that were spreading around.

"It's too much for us. His sister cannot have a normal life. Everything is about him and his problem. We give him an allowance so that he wouldn't do anything crazy. Just enough to buy his poison. Last thing we want is for him to move on to heroin, like some of his buddies. We tried kicking him out before, but I couldn't sleep at night thinking about the world out there. We've tried making conditions. Nothing sticks.

"Maybe tough love is what we need. Maybe the only reasonable thing is to throw him out and lock the doors and windows. People are encouraging this all the time. But what good is it putting him on the streets if he continues using? He is stuck in this wherever he goes. At least with us he is less likely to get hurt. We're here because we have nowhere else to go. And he just sits there. We can barely get him to talk."

I had been observing Steve as she spoke. He remained in the same position, seemingly not registering anything she said, wearing a blank and distant expression.

"I don't recognize my son anymore," his father said. "I think about what I could have done wrong. We're just an average family, Doc. Problems like anyone else. There was no abuse, no psychiatric problems. Everything they wanted we gave them. Why would he turn to this stuff? What did we do to him?"

A young man anesthetizes his anguish and languishes within an opiated passivity, leaving mountains of pain in his wake. His father shoulders the burden of responsibility. A mother demoralized and depleted, inches away from severing the cord; a sister devastated by the sadness of seeing everything fall apart. The patient, to complicate matters, is not properly a patient at all. Steve seemed the least interested of everyone in receiving help. He was quiet, while everyone else was doing the talking.

Addiction is a problem of systems as much as of individuals. There is a structure that sustains the suffering. A gridlock places everyone into the same helplessness and captivity the addicted person is presumed to feel. The family seemed relieved when I told them that they may not have done anything wrong. Neither Steve nor anyone else, I reassured them, can be held responsible for the current impasse. The issue is that Steve has a disease of sorts.

This brain model can be a good entry point for some patients. It must be wielded strategically. It provided the wedge here that broke the system. "Disease" carries more possibility than does "junkie," a dehumanizing indictment offering little room for change. The model would also be useful at facilitating an important first step and moving his apparent passivity in a healthier direction: a "patient" acquiescing to a medically supervised detoxification to address his physiological dependence, while transitioning to sustained treatment of some kind in the aftermath. It took some work to motivate him, but he knew what was coming. There were ultimately few options given the situation. He was admitted to the hospital within a week of that meeting; he transitioned successfully, with only a few minor complications, to an injection of extended-release naltrexone, the same treatment that Ahmed had attempted and failed.

Steve had detoxed and transitioned to buprenorphine before, though he had relapsed in short order. He may fail again. I provided him information about the "course of disease," spoke with him about "opioid receptor normalization" and the importance of staying the path as his "brain chemistry found a new homeostasis." He remained "diseased" as he experienced persistent withdrawal after transitioning to the injection: "post-acute withdrawal symptoms," such as insomnia and anxiety, can last weeks to months. He was given medicines to "manage symptoms." I worked with his family to incentivize Steve sticking to treatment. Steve continued to inhabit the "sick" role in those early weeks and was guided toward maintaining the commitments that came with that identity.

This role of "brain disease patient" may be helpful for introducing some possibility to the situation and shepherding Steve toward maintenance treatment. But we cannot expect it to carry him through the more important challenges ahead: dispelling his passivity, making healthy decisions (including staying in treatment), navigating situations with an eye toward well-being. This was the difficult truth that his family could not easily assimilate. It could be felt in the anger, confusion, and powerlessness during the family meeting. There was no avoiding it: the onus was ultimately on Steve, despite his being the least interested in taking it on. Something needed to be done that only he could do. No biological vulnerability can explain that truth away.

Addiction is a disease, and it is not a disease. I would talk with Steve about his "abnormal neurochemistry" and "altered reward systems" and at the same time would refer to "his responsibility" and "his freedom to choose." We would explore his values and motivations, initially with great subtlety and care to not leave him feeling manipulated and steered toward making certain decisions. This would lead, later, toward conversations centered more explicitly on commitment making in the service of a fuller life.

The tension between addiction as disease and as a choice had been evident from the first conversation. It was felt in the room, in his family's anger that Steve was abdicating responsibility, in the uncertainty about whether, as an addict or junkie, Steve could be reasonably expected to be responsible at all. The possibilities before us were his to embrace—not his family's, nor mine. Another life is possible. It is up to Steve, ultimately, to work toward it.

This started with encouraging Steve to accept medical treatment, as a patient. It would evolve into more explicitly guiding him toward accepting responsibility, as a human being, for what might become of his life, beyond what anyone else, neither his family nor I, could do for him. Steve would ultimately need to move beyond "patient" and "addict" just as he had moved beyond "junkie," toward new possibilities, beyond what anyone can map out in advance, beyond even the mechanisms of his own brain.

•

The brain model is only partly about the brain. It is also indebted to behaviorism, and to a lesser extent cognitive science, for its account of human behavior. In all these frameworks, the enigma of consciousness is deemed meaningless, with subjectivity unsuitable to empirical exploration. What is important to addiction is what can be observed by scientists acting intersubjectively: behavior, brain activity, and quantifiable cognitive processes. This is not an entirely empirical stance. As we will see, there are also moral, philosophical, and even religious frameworks that play a role.

This model faces the same problem that any other does: the problem is with us. We have lost the lightness and agility that allows us to enter its abstractions without losing our footing. Wielding any model fruitfully means learning to see through its words and playing with them, as when helping Steve: one of many stories to tell, each with its proper time and place. It also means being vigilant against absolutism or scientism. Otherwise, we risk hardening our theories, and ourselves. Emerson called such calcifications *an excrescence of words*.

Behaviorism was first postulated by John Watson and B. F. Skinner in the early twentieth century, and has come to be the dominant model for understanding repetitive drug use. It hypothesizes that our behavior is primarily shaped by reward, punishment, and reinforcement. We seek and respond to something compelling, such as food or sex, and we want more of this *reward*. Similarly, we work to avoid unpleasant and aversive experiences: *punishment*. Through learning and conditioning, we learn to secure rewards, and to avoid punishments, while giving proper attention to risks and dangers. Our behavior is thereby *reinforced*—either "positively" by pursuing something compelling, or "negatively" by pursuing whatever gives us reprieve from our distress or punishments.

We learn, for example, to be kind and generous to a prospective sexual partner, even if we might be jealous or anxious, because such behavior is more likely to lead to a fulfillment of our desire. We might also learn to choose a sexual partner complementary to our other needs and desires, and who offers a respite from loneliness—with the intimacy enriching and nourishing as opposed to destructive. But we might also choose a highly destructive and abusive partner, if that is the sort of relationship we have found reinforcing.

Reward seeking is pragmatic, situational, and amoral: the pursuit of the reward or reprieve is balanced against the risks, costs, and punishments that might affect the person. The field of possibility is wide open, encompassing all sides of our nature. We learn to enjoy intimacy with a partner, maintain a career, or play a game in the same way that we learn to be cruel to animals, engage in identity theft, or pursue serial abusive relationships, if these are meaningful to us and we can manage the aversive consequences. This is also how we learn to be addicted: through reward and punishment, conditioning and habituation.

Addiction is therefore considered a reinforced pattern that emerges from the same learning processes that entrench us in other behaviors. The end result of addiction, however, is clearly more problematic than are typical cases of "reward seeking." The most salient difference, according to this model, is that the reward seeking persists in the face of pain and punishment directly attributable to it, with the drug reward (or reprieve) given outsized importance.

Ahmed and Steve had continued using, despite the loss of so many things, despite even the risk of death. It can be frustrating and tragic to witness. And we risk growing as demoralized as the addicts seem to be when all our efforts apparently go nowhere. We want to understand why they are being held captive and how we might intervene to disrupt a process the person apparently cannot.

The power of drugs to create addiction has been attributed, as mentioned previously, to their direct biological activity on the brain—and especially on the so-called reward center, the nucleus accumbens. By virtue of acute neural activation and dopamine effects, the drug produces a powerful, unmediated burst of reinforcing neurotransmission, which is hypothesized to confer on the drug a disproportionate value that drowns out most other considerations. We become conditioned, with repeated use, to pursue the drug to the exclusion of other rewards/ reprieves and despite the emergence of painful consequences. The brain becomes programmed, so to speak, to pursue the drug at the cost of everything else. This is why Steve and Ahmed had seemed so helpless. Their own brain was apparently working against them.

Cognitive science dissects this self-destructive programming at the level of mental activity. It clarifies the disruptions in information processing associated with addiction, such as changes in attention, value attribution, and memory. Though important for the brain model as a distinct discipline, cognitive science is fundamentally an extension of behaviorist determinism into the realm of cognition, with its theoretical framework rooted in a behaviorist conceptualization of addiction: compulsive drug seeking as a conditioned process that follows in a predictable manner from certain determinants. For example, cognitive scientists have argued that there are conditioned and unconscious attentional biases toward cocaine-related stimuli that complicate a cocaine-addicted person's ability to steer clear, and that directly guide his decision making. The sight of white sugar scattered across a table, for example, may not register to an addicted person as merely sugar—it may trigger him to consider finding a few lines of cocaine.

Consciousness and subjective experience remain untouched in cognitive science, as with any positivist paradigm. The focus is on understanding the ways that the mind collects stimuli, as well as reconfigures, encodes, and processes them. The brain-mind becomes a kind of computer that has been programmed to respond to sensory data, interpret them, store them away, or act on them in a manner that is as orderly and ineluctable as that of any operating system. What matters, in cognitivism as in behaviorism, is what can be observed.

In addiction neuroscience, these different determinisms—behaviorism, cognitive science, and neurobiology—are stitched together. The overall aim is to identify how drug-related conditioning might become "hardwired" in neural circuits so that addicted individuals lose the "choice" to control their use. Dr. Volkow has therefore called addiction a "disease of free will."

This gives a glimpse into the most foundational imaginaries supporting the brain model. Free will implies decision making transcending the influence of prior causes. It is not an empirical term; it traffics in philosophical and even metaphysical notions, beyond experimental testing. That a neuroscientist would invoke the term is therefore disorienting, comparable to speaking about a fictional character as if he were alive. Equally disorienting is situating free choice within the brain disease model, as if the two are reconcilable. What room is there for freedom in behaviorist-physicalist determinism?

It is a disorientation worth heeding. One reading of Dr. Volkow's statement is that it delineates new possibilities for addiction beyond the determinism of neuro-materialism—and restores to the person the (temporarily compromised) capacity for free choice. I had intended something similar with Steve, guiding him from "junkie" toward "patient" while also gesturing at a freedom beyond all restrictive identifications.

Yet if we are not careful, even "freedom" and "will" might lose their moorings in freedom and be conceptualized in a way that deepens the hold of our restrictive models. Calling addiction a disease of free will might not work to emancipate the addicted, in other words, but, instead, to further diminish freedom more generally, situating it within something like a two-dimensional technical drawing.

•

Most behaviorists have made up their minds. They consider freedom a fiction, though a compelling one satisfying our need for agency. Our choices follow from their antecedents, they would say, with as much finality as apples fall from trees. We are conditioned to act, neither freely choosing our reactions nor our impulses, much as Pavlov's dog cannot help but salivate at the ringing of a bell. We don't do things freely. Our behavior is the surface eruption of automatisms that might go on to be modified, learned, extinguished, or strengthened—but never freely chosen out of thin air.

Some behaviorists have designated themselves "compatibilists" in their attempt to reconcile freedom and behaviorism. *Cognitive control* is the fruit of this attempt; it refers to the capacity to make complex, adaptive, and higher-order decisions by allowing us to balance our pursuits—our drive, say, for a drug or other reward—with the risks and costs that might be associated with them. Though we are not completely free, we may still have the agency to choose between available options and make balanced decisions in line with our desires.

This capacity for purposeful decision making is thought to be compromised in addiction: the drug reward becomes exaggerated, adverse consequences are neglected, and the impulse to use nearly impossible to manage, to the detriment of balanced choices. This fits nicely into the brain model. Neural correlates are identified for each of these vulnerabilities in decision making, confirming how cognitive control might be compromised in the brain.

Neural correlates are often invoked in addiction neuroscience, their significance taken for granted. A correlate means an observation that accompanies another: "red," for example, is a correlate of sunset. A neural correlate specifically is a neuroimaging finding linked to some diagnostic label, such as "cocaine use disorder," or to some observed behavioral vulnerability, such as increased craving; these data generally take the form of statistically significant differences in fMRI (functional magnetic resonance imaging) or PET (positron emission tomography) signal between the brains of addicts and those of nonaddicts, assessed at rest or during various lab-based tasks (such as being shown a picture of cocaine). Positive findings indicate a deficit rooted in a brain-based disease.

The nature of a correspondence, however, cannot be determined through correlation alone. A neural signal deviation that might be correlated with depression, such as decreased serotonin receptor density, is not a glimpse into the brain pathology "underlying" the disorder. Yet "underlying mechanism" is a common phrase in the neurosciences, with the neural correlate thought to have primacy and therefore causative or explanatory importance. This fits into the materialist and individualist mythos of modern psychiatry, where the neural activity of the person is what matters. The problem with this becomes obvious when we consider comparable conditions in the same light. Imagine claiming that the physical correlates of obesity—high body mass index (BMI), insulin resistance, large fat cells—are what "underlie" or cause the disease. We would be effectively glancing over the behavioral, neurobiological, psychological, cultural, moral, communal, and sociopolitical contributors to this complex phenomenon, reducing it to an abstraction that misses the point entirely.

This kind of uncritical devotion to the brain disease model has led, even in the work of otherwise careful researchers, to cocksure conclusions based on tenuous or ambiguous data, with a quickness to regard any apparent neurophysiological deviation between addicted and nonaddicted people as proof that there is a brain dysfunction. These differences are proclaimed as indicative of a functional problem (for example, in cognitive capacities), even as there is no deficiency at all. This is confirmation bias in plain sight. It has been recognized and critiqued by multiple prominent scientists in their reviews of major neuroscience studies.

The subtle prefrontal fMRI changes associated with an addict seeing a drug cue during a neuroimaging task, for example, have been interpreted as indicative of her impaired ability to control herself due to heightened cue reactivity. These comparison data are then presented as evidence that the "addicted" brain is impaired. But what would the brain of someone who enjoys rich meals or who is wedded to his job show in similar experiments?

Essentially the same thing. This has been demonstrated in a recent study aggregating data from cue reactivity studies. The brain shows comparable activity, whether the person is pursuing drugs, food, or other compelling things. Yet there is a focus on the neural correlates of addicts as if they represent a special case. This is one glaring instance of our epistemic allegiances—that addiction stems from pathological neuroadaptations, or that the drug addict is constrained by physicality to a greater extent than are non-addicts—informing and even predetermining our interpretations. There are many other examples; enumerating them all would amount to a textbook. The point is that the brain disease model grows further entrenched, while countervailing data or perspectives go unnoticed or pushed to the margins.

Overinterpretation and confirmation bias are common challenges in all scientific research. They need to be confronted at every turn; scientific progress necessitates a laborious disentanglement from the interpretive inertia of the dominant model. Also requiring attention are our deeper constructs beyond the paradigm: our unexamined devotion to the core imaginaries undergirding our facts.

These imaginaries are at play, for example, in the idea that the main vulnerability in addiction is impaired cognitive control or that repeated drug use undermines decision making. The allusion to free will in addiction neuroscience, and the conflation of cognitive control with well-being, provide a window into what these devotions and imaginaries might be. We will find, not surprisingly, that they stem not from empirical observation but from a deeply moral, nearly theological foundation.

●

It is important to limit our empiricism with human beings to only what can be observed, be it behavior, cognition, environment-subject interaction, or neural activity. The problem is when we regard these data as our only path toward understanding. From a succinct critique in the *Dictionary of Untranslatables*:

Behaviorism is thus right insofar as it takes into consideration the limitation of our discourse on the mental. But it is wrong insofar as it

seeks to take behavior as the criterion and foundation for knowledge of
human nature.

We practice good science when we restrict our data to what is rooted in direct observation. But it is a profound error to restrict *a person* in the same way. This effectively excludes from consideration our interiority, relationality, and subjectivity, which constitute an integral dimension of our experience as human beings. This error becomes clearer as we examine the fictions informing the idea of "cognitive control," and the restricted notions of human freedom involved.

Properly understood, behaviorism construes cognitive control as a means, not an end. It can be put in the service of nearly anything, including both rational and irrational, "good" and "evil" pursuits. It is what Whitehead called "the reason of Ulysses or the fox": the practical reason aimed at accomplishing some objective, through whatever means it takes. Sinners and saints are equally capable of it. Far from indicating "wise," "free," or "reasonable" decision making, cognitive control is the set of complex higher-order functions by which our goal-directed behaviors are executed, whether we are in thrall to a drug or an ambitious career.

Ahmed was clearly stuck. He was paralyzed by his fraught desire for the drug, his difficulty with overcoming this desire, and the complicated and conflicted worldview that propels his habit: heroin as sanctuary, as sickness, as a solution to sickness. Is his use an impairment in cognitive control or choice? He was clearly unable to stop on his own. It is compelling to conclude he had lost the capacity to pursue more purposeful and difficult objectives, such as abstinence.

Any analysis of his predicament, however, is incomplete without considering his tangle of values, self-identity, and purpose. Overcoming his desire to use might be subordinated to his powerful interest in heroin or undercut by his resignation to a hopeless captivity. Purposeful activity, in fact, may mean something wholly different to Ahmed than controlling his cravings or impulses and maintaining abstinence: it more likely means pursuing his fractured fictions as far as they can take him, despite any hurdles, ambivalence, and problematic consequences. Cognitive control might mean wrangling with himself for one more round, so long as he steers clear of hitting rock bottom.

The party line is that drugs cause addiction by damaging neural circuits and undermining cognitive control. One can make an argument, however, that takes the exact opposite tack, with addictive behavior *exemplifying* cognitive control. Addiction, after all, puts the implacable machinery of our rationality and decision making into the strict service of a goal, as would happen in the exercise of cognitive control with anything else meaningful to us. But the control is so pervasive in addiction that everything is subordinated to its unrelenting purpose, including our being.

It is also important to remember that a great majority of people who use drugs do so mostly in a healthy manner and at little cost to other activities in their lives. It is difficult to understand how the same drug-related learning processes that are presumed to impair cognitive control might also lead, in the majority of cases, to responsible and controlled use. Either drug use leads inherently to problematic conditioning, heightened drug-related reward, and impaired cognitive control, or it does not. In most cases, drug use clearly ends up being fine, with most people who use drugs enjoying themselves and not going off the rails. The brain model has been amended to fit these data by invoking a genetic vulnerability (what is called a *diathesis*); the fraction of drug users who develop addiction do so because their genes have put their brains at heightened susceptibility to developing drug-related neuroadaptations. But this drug/diathesis model of addiction, while accommodating certain facts, doesn't address the more fundamental question. Is cognitive control compromised in the first place?

Behavioral economics is the field of study concerned with human choice, and many of its findings challenge the core presumption that cognitive control and rational decision-making are impaired in addiction. A consistent finding from drug self-administration studies, which involve studying drug use in laboratory settings, is that the decision to use substances in addicted people is influenced by the presence of competing rewards, with people adjusting their choices in a reasonable, predictable manner. If it pays well enough to not use their drug, addicted people will abstain, despite how heavily they might value the drug. The right pay will vary for different individuals and different drugs, of course, but researchers have shown that addicted people in laboratory settings will stop administering drugs to themselves in a reliable manner if they are rewarded adequately enough with "alternative or secondary reinforcers" such as money. Some studies have also calculated the exact cost threshold when drug self-administration stops for specific substances, like cocaine. This finding has been duplicated in clinical settings with contingency management strategies, where abstinence is similarly rewarded. These data indicate that rationality remains functional in addiction despite the increased salience conferred on drugs. A calculation is occurring that weighs the drug reward against other things, as expected in people with cognitive control intact.

The same might be said for Ahmed. If we rewarded him adequately for staying abstinent, and if it were clear to him that staying abstinent was not simply an abstract exercise in "self-care," then he might have been more likely to kick his habit. Importantly, one of the challenges that Ahmed faced was an "unenriched environment": he lacked options and opportunities for being naturally incentivized to stay abstinent, such as a rewarding job, relationship, community, and other resources. This was partly a result of the ravages of addiction, with heroin having taken a central place in his life and other paths toward fulfillment subverted. It also reflects social and institutional iniquities that have been observed to contribute to addiction. The presence of an enriched environment may not have been enough to help him—there are plenty of addicts who are deeply enslaved even while sitting in the lap of luxury and with endless optionality—but it is an important aspect of his case to consider.

An intriguing finding in population studies is that people will disrupt a long-standing addiction on their own, and even all at once, without any clinical support. Perhaps they undergo a harrowing experience, undergo a conversion, make a firm commitment, or simply decide that enough is enough. Does cognitive control reemerge overnight? Of course not. The more plausible explanation is that it was never subverted in the first place, as the work of behavioral economists indicates. What likely changed were the purpose, values, worldview, or circumstances motivating the person's choices. These became more aligned with what we might call *a more authentic way*, with the person pursuing more fruitful (un)realities and decisions.

There is a deeper problem, beyond overemphasizing drug effects on the brain, neglecting the rationality of the addict, or diminishing the importance of nonbiological factors. We have drawn a firm line distinguishing reward seeking related to addiction from pursuits viewed as "normal," such as maintaining a career. A person working a 9 to 5, for instance, and refusing to miss a single day despite illness, a sense of dissociation, problematic ethics, and terrible coworkers, is entangled with a certain reality and value system to the detriment of his well-being. But because his is the common (un)reality, it passes unnoticed. That we are more inclined to see the addict or drug user as mentally impaired and captive to his reward seeking, and this compulsive worker as high-functioning, even admirable, has more to do with our epistemic and moral inertia than with our data. And this inertia is even more foundational than are the values pertaining to drug use specifically.

Free will is one of many moral fictions that have been conflated with the construct of cognitive control. Here are some others: self-control, willpower, impulse regulation, rationality. Cognitive control is, on the one hand, an empirical concept, with some precision and explanatory power in addiction neuroscience; on the other, it is a mongrel concept of various unexamined devotions, all reflecting our dominant *moral* values—which place a premium on "reason" and "control."

The brain disease model of addiction, in other words, is an ethical parable as much as a conceptual system, offering a moral gold standard for human comportment, with neurobiology and behaviorism serving as the backdrop. Our most exalted value is "Reason": a good in itself, the high-water mark of our moral fiber. We go wrong when we fail to bring ourselves in line with it.

We also go wrong, of course, when we are exercising it. It takes only a moment's reflection to recognize how misguided this idealization of reason is—especially in light of the atrocities humans have perpetrated on one another, *with good reason*, for all of recorded history. The science of torture, of strategically unjust governance, and of building more effective killing machines should be indication enough that rationality can lend a hand to the most deranged sides of our nature. Rationality is only as good as the ends it aims to achieve, whether it be managing disease, bombing enemies, or sustaining a paranoid delusion. Whitehead's distinction between this promiscuous reason of the fox and the noble reason of Plato or the philosopher (speculative reason) reminds us that rationality need not be aligned with higher values, purposes, or means. But even this distinction remains captive to the prejudice that rationality, though of the *higher* sort, must be involved in guiding our most authentic way. In combining the "lower" reason of behaviorism with the "higher" reason of antiquated philosophy, the idea of cognitive control reveals its indebtedness to rationalism, from which it inherited a fixation on "reason," in one form or another, as foundational to a good life.

The Middle Ages contribute their own prejudices. Much of addiction neuroscience mirrors the Abrahamic tenet that we *fall into temptations* on the one hand, through a lapse in faith or in self-control, and *rise above our sinful tendencies* on the other. There are echoes of Puritanical self-reliance more generally in the brain disease parable: a distrust of "unproductive" pleasure and a view that right action is grounded in impulse regulation and self-control.

The structure and activity of the brain are so ambiguous as to be a kind of Rorschach test: we see what we know, organizing the amorphous spongey mass so that it makes sense to us. What we find is a tale as old as time: a conflict between good and evil, between order and disorder. The midbrain is the "base" aspect of ourselves, the serpents of temptation hissing within our bellies, groins, and limbic systems. The forebrain is our higher self, the steady hand of reason steering the chariot of our beings. Goodness comes from the conquest of our higher nature over the lower. God vanquishing Satan. Order subduing chaos. The evolved prefrontal brain modulating the mesolimbic reptilian proto-brain. Rational civilization reigning over the dark and primitive hordes. Cognitive control directing the impulses. One can go on and on.

These fictions of self-conquest have deep roots in Western morality. It begins with Plato's charioteer, harnessing and steering the wild horses of the self. Then there is the struggle against *yetzer hara* (evil inclinations) in Judaism, the *Jihad al-Nafs* (the resistance against our lower tendencies) in Islam, the daily battle with sinfulness in Christianity. Trafficking in these ancient tropes is also the modern contract to control our selfishness within a secular civic-minded morality.

We turn to the brain model with the intention of bringing an objective and morally neutral perspective—a pure empiricism—to a certain expression of suffering. Yet we end up going beyond empiricism to find ourselves repeating common tropes in self-conquest morality: lapses in good judgment are interpreted, without much examination or analysis, as a failure to subdue with Reason the beast snarling within the dark depths of our cerebrum. Perhaps a better way to name our brain-based addiction science is *prefrontal morality*.

We shouldn't, however, blame the addict, we are told. Their brain isn't working right. A disease, according to Dr. Volkow, of free will. Addicts are deemed so damaged that they are not only incapable of making good decisions *but also incapable of making bad ones*. The mesolimbic brain decides for them, a destructive default-mode hijacking their lives.

Addiction, as it is currently understood, is a chimera of neuro-scientism and secular self-help gospel: a learned behavior that, due to drug-induced brain hacking, is automatic, irrational, and ultimately anguished. A contradictory and confused behaviorism, tortured into accommodating antagonisms and myths consistent with Western ignorance, including Manicheanism, positivism, even colonialism. These are the dark undercurrents behind the label of "substance use disorder": a fiction spun by the medical establishment, meaningful, comprehensible, and yet deeply inadequate, offering little insight into the human being.

Missing is an understanding of psychoactive substance use as enriching, responsible, and therapeutic. Missing is an adequate accounting of the many unique contexts and larger systems in which our choices occur. Missing is an understanding of why addicted people stop abruptly on their own, after years of supposed neural adaptations, hardwiring, and reinforcement. Missing, as well, is subjectivity and our enduring capacity for freedom and meaning, even during addiction. Missing, most of all, is the human being who narrates, loves, chooses, and suffers.

We have, instead, brain parasites and the zombies who lack immunity to them, anorexic rats hitting the cocaine button, and other images from drug war agitprop. Behavior as mechanical and lifeless as an MRI shot of the skull: the mind replaced with a machine, a broken model, headed for collapse.

●

The problem is not that we have snuck morality into our facts. An amoral science of addiction, after all, is impossible. The diagnosis itself is an ethical pronouncement, predicated on the impression that a person is making maladaptive choices, as opposed to choices promoting well-being and freedom. Behaviorism in addiction science is more accurately *comportmentism*, inasmuch as it concerns itself with the right way. What are freedom, well-being, and suffering? These are necessarily moral questions, questions of proper *comportment*, not "objective" ones.

The main obstacle is that we have failed to recognize and examine the (un)realities at play. Some accounting of an addict's choices and purpose—his world building and meaning making—is inevitable. Equally important is an examination of our own. Otherwise, we remain in thrall to complacent notions of *eudaemonia,* bound to do more harm than good, despite how good we try to be.

The sooner we acknowledge the inescapability of *meaning* in addiction, the clearer everything becomes. Addiction is not a functional issue—not a "hardware" problem, to use a popular metaphor. It begins in an unreal relationship with something—in a worldview misaligned with what is at hand. But this "reality" is deeply meaningful, speaking to the person in the ways she knows. So, the person rests in it, despite the fragmentation and confusion. And she begins emerging from addiction when she heeds her suffering and attends to what needs attention. "Free will," "reason," or "cognitive control" are misleading fictions in this case, ultimately irrelevant to the person's lived experience.

Despite the best intentions of addiction scientists to divest their model of a moral system, the ghost of the human being invariably haunts their machine. Freedom, meaning, and desire are critical to the experience of addiction (and to that of being human). It is important that Dr. Volkow had returned our gaze to them.

Sneaking loaded moralistic constructs such as "free will" or "self-control" through the back door, however, and conflating cognitive control and other executive functions with them, are hardly adequate ways to attend to the matter. In fact, these subterfuges represent the crux of the problem: it is the shopworn façade of objectivity once again, pretending that scientific facts transcend our values, prejudices, and imaginaries, even though they are necessarily anchored in them.

Sifted science, Joyce wrote in *Finnegans Wake*, will do the arts good. Reconsidering our approach to addiction—sifting through what passes for hard truth and dreaming up more fruitful (un)realities—is bound to expose and disimpact the fictions stuck in our systems, opening us up to more expansive exercises of imagination. As mundane a situation as failure, for example, might be redrawn entirely: an inevitability we might learn to accept without blame, aversion, or shame, while also assuming responsibility for the freedom to proceed differently. A teacher and friend, obstacle and path. And so much else will come to be reimagined too, with comparable expansiveness: the earth, our worlds, ourselves. The work of science is inseparable from this imaginative elaboration of new relationships, realities, words.

•

The brain disease model has been fixed in place like a granite foundation: a bedrock theory intended to support a thousand others. But it is difficult to imagine making a home in it. There is no oxygen, little space for possibility.

Consider the world it offers. Addicts dwell in hopeless misery: doomed to compulsive enslavement, with loss of choice inscribed at the most fundamental neuronal level. Their lives are brute mechanisms of synaptic misfiring, neurocircuitry dysregulation, derailed cognitive processes, and automation. Mired, like the ignorant uncivilized of prior centuries, in the material darkness of their flesh, which only the enlightened application of reason might redeem. And we wonder why most addicted people spurn medical help, as they might fire-and-brimstone missionaries knocking at their doors?

There are other, more compelling ways to tell the same story. In fact, since Alan Leshner first reified the brain disease model of addiction in 1997, the paradigm has been considered a humanist victory. Most philosophers and scientists view the model as a clear call to treat addiction as a medical problem, as opposed to an ethical or moral one best met with time behind bars. Contrary to what was suggested above, this means that the brain disease paradigm has been helpful for the plight of addicted individuals by further removing stigma and social mistreatment. It also suggests a radical departure from the drug war: it is the diseased brain that acts, not the person, and so there is absolutely no place for punishment in addressing the disorder. The brain model has therefore been hailed as an enlightened bulwark against moralistic and punitive irrationality.

It is a step in the right direction, of course, to approach drug using and addicted individuals with greater sensitivity and compassion. But this shift toward less judgment and greater care began long before the brain model. This was at the turn of the twentieth century within faith-based healing programs more concerned with redeeming souls than treating brains; these programs went on to provide the framework for AA and were active several decades before neural etiologies became the dominant framework. The compassionate turn here has more to do with recognition and understanding than with any biological theory. Once addiction was accepted as a type of human suffering, and as suffering, moreover, requiring the care of others, it came to be approached with greater empathy and respect for the dignity of the person. It doesn't matter how it might be conceptualized, as a character flaw, soul sickness, mental illness, trauma response, or reasonable adaptation to an unreasonable world. The suffering of addicted individuals was *recognized*, and our compassion and humanity responded accordingly.

There is another problem with positioning the brain model as humanistic. The argument presupposes that a person must be unable to make free decisions due to a brain dysfunction for his behavior to be given compassion and care. This says more perhaps about what we believe the proper bounds of compassion should be than about whether or not "free will" exists in addiction. Lying, manipulation, selfishness, poor judgment, frivolity, hedonism, rule breaking—along with all the other transgressions that might come with drug use or addiction—only merit our compassion or graciousness, the argument suggests, if the person is unable to choose freely due to some derangement.

This is a conditional and myopic humanism. It limits the range of our compassion to those inflicting suffering on themselves or others due to some organic brain failure. It is a humanism, therefore, that excludes most human beings. Most of us sow the seeds of suffering, for ourselves and others, simply because we are human.

There are also clear dangers associated with casting doubt on the reason or autonomy of an addicted individual—even if the apparent intention is to underscore that he is struggling and in need of therapeutic support. Attributing to him a brain disturbance that impairs his mind and decision making is to call important aspects of his humanity into question. If history gives any indication, such characterizations set the stage for further dehumanization, as well as for deepening the problems of stigma and social disenfranchisement already affecting drug-using and addicted individuals. Further, this model neglects the systemic problems that might be exacerbating the suffering of the most vulnerable amongst us, thereby failing to account for important structural contributors to addiction, such as poverty, classism, and bigotry.

This gets at the major blind spot of the brain disease model—as well as its dangers, beginning with its potential to deepen social stasis and deny personal freedom. Addiction is a disease of what is most personal to us—our values, our choices, our realities—and yet its etiology is viewed as entirely impersonal, traceable to "objective" physical events or brain abnormalities. Social, moral, or existential aspects of the condition are less relevant, if at all. The conclusion is that drug-addicted individuals, and maybe also those who use drugs regularly, are biologically different than the rest of society, with distinct neural and behavioral vulnerabilities that impair fundamental dimensions of their humanity. The problem is a disrupted brain, perhaps reversible, perhaps permanent, involving at the very least episodic impairments in freedom and cognitive control. This is not the first time, of course, that the mind has been mechanized, or freedoms lobotomized, in the pursuit of psychiatry: historically, the most carceral of all medical disciplines. And an entire (subaltern) class is created and kept in line: the neurobiological Other.

Shifting the focus to something less biological and attributing the problem to environmental factors such as trauma, inequity, or disconnection does not resolve the issue. It is the same effort to explain addiction in terms that exculpate the addict, finding the etiology in problems foisted on the person, be it a damaged childhood, a broken society, or a toxic culture. These viewpoints assume the person, the Other person, needs to be exculpated in the first place. They miss the opportunity to embrace addiction fully, as it is, beyond notions of good and evil, and without judging the affected person as immoral or selfish, or excusing her as sick, traumatized, or otherwise unable to choose reasonably. Instead of *speaking toward* addiction and shrouding it with further moralistic fictions, we might heed the invitation to inhabit it from the inside, and to recognize the yearning and suffering, without turning away, as unmistakably our own.

●

Once a story lodges and hardens, it is difficult to tell a different one. We find ourselves repeating the same lines, the lines we know best. With repetition comes belief. We are like children who can be convinced of anything, even an overt lie, because it has been repeated too many times to count.

It is not verifiability alone that sustains a theory, but a seduction comparable to that of the most persuasive, creative, and viral works of fiction. The impact of cultural and psychological forces is weighty enough—especially those so familiar to us as to be invisible, such as our worldviews, values, and allegiances. There are far subtler narrative devices at work too, as in any compelling story.

Tales that leave us hanging with the inevitable conclusion just ahead, and yet capable of being developed indefinitely, without any foreseeable end, are the most likely to keep their audience captive. These fictions might be so fractal, elaborate, and mesmerizing that they might even come to be confused with the endless fork-tongued ramifications of existence itself. Few stories are as inexhaustible as those purporting to explain the brain, with their narrative ambitions as labyrinthine as the dense neural connections they attempt to untangle.

It doesn't matter that brain-based investigations hit an impasse in correlation: new questions can always be proposed and new stories told. There are endless ways that the brains, neurons, and neural activity of those with substance addiction, either sober or under the influence of a drug, might be compared to the brains of healthy controls. Whatever technology might be most current and precise is put to use.

And maybe the brains of some addicts might be compared to the brains of different addicts: on drugs, off drugs, on different drugs.

The opportunities for research are boundless. Animals across the evolutionary continuum—mice, rats, gerbils, monkeys—are recruited to help answer questions difficult to pose to a living human brain: questions of toxicity, but also questions of anatomy and neurotransmitter concentrations and neurogenesis that would require decapitation and dissection. Laboratory studies with species of all sorts, including humans, to test new medications; preclinical examinations of their neural mechanisms, followed by studies to reproduce these findings in the clinic; and clinical trials to confirm and replicate efficacy, in progressively larger and more diverse populations. Longitudinal studies to examine the effects of naturalistic cannabis use on the growing brains of adolescents, retrospective studies concerning cocaine-using pregnant women, and twin studies, using new data collected in Scandinavia, to understand the genetic determinants of regular MDMA use.

This list of possible and actual research only scratches the surface. This generativity is important to the scientific enterprise; it is also an indication of the fertility and sustainability of our main paradigm, and of the nascent state of the neurosciences generally. The story must go on.

Billions of taxpayer dollars are earmarked for sustaining this sometimes-helpful fiction, with various actors in the biomedical-industrial complex playing their part in the production: academic institutions, corporations, pharmaceutical companies, career scientists, government employees.

I have played my part too. To secure my funding from NIH and maintain my academic standing, I have needed to foreground this model in my grant applications and manuscripts, even as I have endeavored to maintain my freedom from it in the service of challenging and evolving it. This book, however, represents the first time I have subjected the model to such a public and unsparing critique.

I have been slow to do so because there are risks. The brain disease paradigm has shaped, supported, and maintained countless careers, including my own. Scientists and researchers, for their part, are pressured to accommodate this worldview for pragmatic reasons of self-preservation.

Thus, researchers remain attached to their paradigm because it can provide explanation, a window into what neurobiological issues might be driving the addict, a helpful framework for developing treatments—but also because it pays, it legitimizes them as scientists, it conforms with mainstream politics, it allows them to maintain credibility in academe, and so on. Just as other individuals might deepen their attachment to a drug because it can provide a pleasurable change in consciousness, a disruption in the painful patterns of the mind—and because it sustains them, it preserves a certain sense of self, it gives meaning and purpose to their wanting, and it fits into the world as they know it.

We aim for "reality," or at least a better life—and, like Ahmed or Steve, we find ourselves the worse for it. No fiction, map, nor theory can replace existence itself. Drugs and ideas can both become burdensome, and dangerous, if we think we require them as we do blood and breath. But we hold on to what needs letting go because to let go means losing the person we feel ourselves to be.

This is a dilemma common to scientists, to politicians, to addicts, to just about everyone: preservation of what we presume is ourselves. We grow attached to our minds, to our perspectives and ideas and the worlds we have constructed, and we do what we can to preserve our notions of what we are, with whatever sustaining them being our deepest truth, everything else false. We try to preserve our lies and incarnations, in some cases, even as they destroy us.

•

I offer this critique as a scientist. The work of science is to interrogate our notions: to hang not nature but our own minds on the rack, with even our most familiar and established constructs subjected to scrutiny. And we always return to the thread, in remembrance of what addiction is: a person yearning for understanding, relationship, freedom.

The science of addiction must be aligned with this truth. Not the science of interminable storytelling, one fiction feeding others. Nor the insipid science of careerism or incremental elaboration. It must be robust and nimble, a joyful science endeavoring to move us toward greater realization of our possibilities. In other words: a *human science*, honest with its origins, embracing both our ignorant foundations and

God-like creative imaginations—a science anchored in a total affirmation of being, harnessing knowledge to foster our most fruitful incarnations, our most authentic ways. Knowledge in the service of being, all being, our own and that of others.

In the case of the brain disease paradigm, its endless capacity for elaboration might make for long careers—but what about individual and collective flourishing? Our science is nearly identical to the feverish explorations and experiments that Hans Castorp pursued to fill his days while convalescing from tuberculosis in the sanitarium of *The Magic Mountain*: hyper-refined and insular, endless, ultimately inconsequential—a sick excrescence of theory. Hans entered the sanitarium a guest but stayed on for several years as a difficult-to-treat invalid.

Meanwhile, as in the war-torn landscape of *The Magic Mountain*, there is blood on the streets. Though governments continue to spend billions on drug research, the US is in the grip of one of the worst drug-related crises in modern history, with overdoses increasing in incidence; treatments for addiction remaining underutilized and barely effective; harm-reduction strategies, such as free drug testing, not being widely implemented; mass incarceration deepening. Yet the war on drugs rages on. And this is only one aspect of our (un)reality. One doesn't need to look far to find other fictions inflicting violence. The suffering deepens the louder the lies grow.

This is our crisis. It is deeper than the entrenchment of the brain disease model or the ways in which federal funding is allocated; it is even deeper than the failed war on drugs. The crisis is what we have become: the sick conclusions we have reached about ourselves and the world. It is not only the addicted who must reckon with their fictions; there are shades of the nightmare in all of us, including the scientists who presume themselves wide awake in their "objectivity."

Awakening from (un)reality has a common beginning. Seeing the lie, Emerson said, is to deal it a mortal blow. And it is a lie because it obscures our intimacy with what is most immediate, concealing our experience—our possibilities and agonies—under its veils. This is why suffering is so primary and crucial: it provides a clear signal that something is not right. We might startle from dreams into a consciousness of morning.

Thus the "rock bottom" narrative of recovery: it is no longer possible to hide our experience or hide from it. Our suffering must be confronted, as well as all that feeds it. The dream grows tattered, and we might glimpse through its torn skin the obsidian and sunless darkness underneath.

•

We are not alone in this. The suffering of others offers its own revelations and opportunities. Clinicians engage with such illuminating anguish on a regular basis. Care with words is a necessary starting point. One reason for this was already mentioned: every explanation in clinical work is weighed according to its value in promoting well-being, one person at a time. No word is final. There is another deeper reason for thoughtful discourse, beyond clinical pragmatism. Faced with often impenetrable suffering, the clinician endeavors to engage sensitively with its meanings, working to recognize its inmost and private significance to the person. The inwardness of it compels her careful silence, and she is mindful about obscuring its truth with her own words. She learns to listen deeply.

We also learn in the space of this intimate communion to speak deeply. Forged in such a fire, language finds a clearer form: translucent as glass—and as fragile. We approach our thoughts as windows, not foundations: looking through them instead of attempting to stand on their delicate surface. And we choose our constructs with discernment, recognizing that some might be more useful than others. This receptive and alert stance might extend to everything: a persistent attentiveness, listening with one's entire being, and exercising care with whatever we introduce into the space between us.

I notice this quality in many of my colleagues. I notice it in friends who aren't medical workers as well: a watchfulness with everything that is said and known, care with the bounds of our knowledge. This is the "morality" inherent to the work of knowledge: valuing persistent self-examination and humility, while also recognizing the importance of fearless, even scandalous transgression, breaking through whatever artifice might be threatening domination.

The temptation is to fall into dogmatic certainty, protecting our (un)realities from the slightest threat. This may involve, for those of us identifying as experts and authorities, setting up camp in higher places, while sparing ourselves the booming, buzzing confusion of the world beyond our walls. We spare ourselves the possibility of fuller engagement, too—alienated both from others and from ourselves. We might create an esteemed office in these citadels, but at a tremendous cost. Our lives become brittle as old paper, with echoes of the mausoleum.

Other possibilities exist for how we might understand. There is a kind of knowing that transcends theory or expertise. Anchored in silence, and yet quick with words, we learn to employ our categories more playfully, euphoniously, and even discordantly, without pretending a purchase on absolute truth. Honest clinicians, academics, and scientists meet at this recognition: the incompleteness of all knowledge, our call to constant humility and creativity. The truth of our situation is simple beyond words. So let us abide in it for a moment, on a plane of awestruck disorientation at the edge of the world, pregnant emptiness in all directions.

This is the darkness of consciousness. It is also the darkness of what is before us, with even the blue sky beyond comprehension. The *Tao Te Ching* might have been referring to precisely this in that obscure passage: *darkness within darkness—the gateway to all understanding*.

At the heart of our worlds is an immense mystery. Perhaps we might cease speaking altogether and invoke, instead of the word *mystery*, a boundless ( ). Words can get in the way in general. Gabbing our way into knowledge is bound to deepen our confusion. After all, we might be nowhere, and filling nowhere with what might be nothing. We come to better know our situation, and to know other knowable things, when we remain attentive to the double darkness of ( ).

It can be disorienting to regard *being experience* as beyond any attribute—incomprehensible in all ways, including whether or not it exists. We grow dizzy floating on the winds of a vast and sonorous silence. We want to brace ourselves, anchor in solid ground, or at least say something about our coordinates so that we are not entirely lost. We are brains, we are holograms, we are quanta, we are spirits, we are the void, we are God, we are souls, we are addicts, we are scientists, we are Americans, we are humans, we are nothing at all. All that I know, we should learn to repeat after Socrates, is that I know nothing.

The invitation is to embrace an unbounded understanding, without speaking out of turn. We do well to remain free not only from the brain model, therefore, but from all systems of knowledge—and with special skepticism toward any (un)realities endeavoring to objectify us. Such closed systems of comprehension might, in the end, be the most profound ignorance: a deadweight of representations, what Deleuze calls the regime of signs, with the boundlessness of things paved over by our facts, and our choices and horizons shackled by the simulacra doubling as ourselves. The same addictive confusion with neuroscience as with substance use: we restrict our experience, and our being, to a fixed and too-narrow representational world somewhere peripheral to ourselves. We lose our footing.

If we hope to address addiction, we cannot be snared by the same errors. An "objective" theory of addiction is not simply a scientific misstep. It is, more fundamentally, a human one. In failing to appreciate the depths of experience, a fixation on the brain model also fails to recognize our truest possibilities, turning to stone the lifeblood of our being. It is crippling to impose such shackles on ourselves; it is inhumane to do so to those already struggling, such as addicts. Their lives are already obscured by the accretion of too many fictions. We should take care to not place further veils.

4

ADDICTION/FREEDOM

Acting as both poison and remedy, [the pharmakon] introduces itself into the body of the discourse with all its ambivalence.

—JACQUES DERRIDA

Words, stories, intoxications: they might illuminate and enrich our lives. They might also cast us into further darkness. Yet we hold on even as they inflame our violence. To learn how to surrender our fictions is a constant practice. Diverse teachers provide guidance: other beings, medicines, even poison.

Psychoactive substances offer a relationship more intimate than anything else in nature. They enter our circulation, interact with our systems, make themselves known directly. We stand to recognize how readily thoughts, feelings, perceptions, and sensations—so much of what constitutes our sense of self—can be shaped, manipulated, blunted, heightened, removed, introduced, or otherwise altered by nothing more extraordinary than a plant, fungus, or chemical. They reveal to us our interrelatedness and permeability, as well as our fluidity.

Drugs might therefore lead us in a direction away from addiction, neither overidentifying with our states of inebriation ("heroin makes me feel like the real me") nor anchoring our well-being to some fixed representation ("life is impossible without having this to calm me down"). Instead, we might come to perceive the patterns of our minds with greater freedom, intoxication ceasing to be a transient identification or an opportunity to be something else for a moment. We also learn to be nobody at all. Something and nothing at once. "Euphoria" or "tranquility"—the varieties of intoxication—are not simply possible aspects of ourselves; they are also *not* ourselves.

This perspective might extend beyond intoxication to encompass the world. Lived existence more generally begins to resemble momentary flashes in agitated and rippling water, patterns that recur until they exhaust themselves, variations on a theme—with an origin elsewhere, like a stone thrown into still water. We learn to separate from our thoughts, feelings, and impressions just as the responsible drinker maintains the distinction between what is drunkenness and what is real. It comes down, ultimately, to learning how to hold our liquor—and it is all liquor. The mind and its intoxications over there; and we watch the show from nowhere.

The more conventional route is tolerance and habituation. We grow inured to a certain stratum of existence, and leave it at that, as what is simply the case. Uncoupling from our states of being, and engaging in such radical self-excavations and destratifications, are far less common ways to engage with the liquor of things, generally pursued by those interested in inhabiting rarer perspectives from which to attend to "reality," such as artists, philosophers, and mystics. Dōgen described the process with gnomic concision:

> Before Zen, mountains are mountains and waters are waters;
> during Zen, mountains are not mountains and waters are not waters;
> after Zen, mountains are again mountains and waters again waters.

Addiction rings the alarm, presenting urgent reasons for turning the (un)realities of our mountains and waters upside down. A sweeping reappraisal has become necessary. A matter, Dōgen would say, of birth and death. In having tethered ourselves to what we know or want, we risk losing it all: the currents of consciousness spiraling around a dream in accelerating descent, sucking our minds and bodies into the abyss. The only way out of the downward flow is to recognize that this agonizing world is not who we are, perhaps it never had been, and to relinquish it much as we took it up—with a yearning for *more*.

●

We begin to awaken from our dreams the moment we recognize we are not in them. Drugs compel us, given how salient their effects might be, to confront our self-deceptions more palpably. They kindle the imagination, and incarnate a certain dream of self, more intimately than other fictions in the world might—and because they provide more opportunity for inhabiting our (un)realities, they also create greater opportunity, in one way or another, for giving them awareness, understanding their unreal foundations, perhaps recognizing our freedom from them. We are not what we think.

This recognition might not be so available to us when it comes to attending to our thoughts alone. We generally think in words, a rushing stream of words and fragments, and new ideas will insert themselves insidiously into the rush of our chattering thoughts such that we hardly notice these additional forces of influence and persuasion. The insertion of a drug into our minds is, of course, a more discernable though mutable addition, transforming into something else, or many things at once, before we even touch it. It is this process of transformation—from heroin into lover, reprieve, sanctuary—that is so uniquely material with drugs, and that may motivate us, especially when the incarnation becomes destructive, to commit to scrutinizing the mind's many transmutations. We are invited to confront, ultimately, the hidden origins of our (un)reality—our wants, hopes, wounds—and to recognize our reality beyond them.

But we must pass through darkness first. Our dreams begin in the confusions of night, where things are not what they seem. Heroin is a lover one moment, hellfire the next, medicine a moment later. This entanglement with hydra-headed illusion accounts for the cognitive dissonance so often seen in addiction: one recognizes the drug and at the same time fails to recognize it. It becomes more than it is. And yet it remains itself. Both material and ideal, ungraspable and grasped too well, like everything else on earth.

There are few situations where self-deception seems so eagerly courted. It is obvious, to both the addict and everyone close to her, that if it were not for the binge drinking this past weekend, there would not have been the problems with her mental health, the neighbors, the law.

This is all recognized, even by the addict herself. How can it not be? But it would be a mistake to regard the problem as resolved because the addict has acknowledged the fallout from the most recent bender and vowed to not let that happen again. If that were the case, she would not find herself drinking the following night, and incurring similar or worse consequences.

The problem is that the addict has invested intoxication with, among other transcendent qualities, an infinite creativity and boundless transformative power. It can, like some trickster god, overcome all rules and facts, and deliver on the impossible. Never mind that it has always turned out a mess. A constant refrain plays in the head: *Maybe next time will be different, or at least the same as it once was . . .*

Getting intoxicated is only a small part of it. The person strives for a state of being to which only intoxication seems to provide access. And the agonies deepen with the addict's insistence that this be an impregnable sanctuary, self-sufficient and contained, protected from anything that might encroach on it, from facts and problems, from any commitments or responsibilities, protected even from the truths of the drug itself. A special zone beyond time and space: what may have happened then or there is not what is really the case. *My* reality cannot be so easily circumscribed, localized, temporalized: it exists *here*, in *this*, the immaterial and endless *now* of my intoxicated mind. It is no wonder that the events of the past weekend are cast aside so freely, and tomorrow evening entered with such abandon.

But something continues to call attention to our embodiment. The substance endures, maintaining its place as our sole access to a world that we wish were free of such contingencies, a world beyond cause and effect, beyond materiality itself. Often resignation settles in, a grim acceptance. Sometimes the addict grows spiteful. This may also confuse those of us who aren't addicted: How can addicts hate and resent their substance so much, and yet also love it with the whole of their beings?

A crisis of paradox: manacled to unreality for the reality it provides. We attach to a dream for its promise of what seems our truest possibilities: expansive fulfillment and freedom, freedom from pain, from conflict, freedom even from the substance itself. Existence, meanwhile, fades away ever more quickly, carrying us with it.

The crisis presents an urgent question. How to break free so that even this substance becomes irrelevant? How to exist without constraint, and completely untethered, in this fiction truer than most anything else?

And the fiction presents itself, with all its ambivalence, as the answer.

●

I first heard about Fred from his wife, a warm and concerned voice on the line. It would be another week after the conversation before I would hear from him. She wanted to let me know that she was worried about him, that his long history of drinking had finally come to a head and led to some public humiliations. His outrageous behavior at a recent party—including, as if out of a playbook for alcoholics, screaming at her in sudden rage and dancing rambunctiously until he passed out—had "raised eyebrows," and there was no longer any uncertainty about it: he needed help. "He has other issues that he can tell you about himself, but I wanted to make sure you understand that he really needs help for the drinking, which he does daily."

Her tone became exasperated, impatient: "And if he doesn't receive help, and he continues to drink as he has, it could cost him his job and family."

They lived a little more than an hour from Manhattan in an affluent town in Connecticut, and she found my name through a philanthropist friend of hers to whom I had provided help in the past: "She said that you were a psychiatrist who could be trusted to not indulge him."

I asked what led her to call me first, as opposed to provide my information to him so that he might initiate contact.

"He is definitely going to call you too. But I wanted to get a sense of you first and to make sure that you understand what's going on."

Hearing from a family member first is most often due to ambivalence on the patient's part; a partner, for example, calls because the patient is on the fence about it, and there is hope that contacting the therapist or psychiatrist will create some momentum for the patient calling too. The situation here was different. The patient was ready to make the call; he seemed motivated, from what his wife said, to begin seeing someone right away. But the reason his wife called first was that she had wanted to speak with me before giving him permission to start, just to make sure I wasn't a sucker. Perhaps something had gone wrong before, or maybe she worried about his manipulating the whole situation and felt that some preemptive involvement was in order. In any case, she "held the keys at home," as he would later tell me. "No doors," he said, "could be opened without her permission"—except perhaps those to the liquor cabinet.

Fred called me the next week. I ascertained straight away that he was motivated to get help and eager to meet. But he wanted me to understand something during that first phone call, much as his wife had tried to impart her own perspective: "I need to make sure that we can continue making time each week for this because I definitely need it."

For both husband and wife, there was a need to ensure that the space of therapy was safe—Fred was worried that it might be taken away, while his wife was concerned that it might be provided too freely. One would think they were talking as much about drinking as about medical support. Private spaces of any sort, including the space of a psychiatrist's office, had become fraught in their relationship. Perhaps this is because the years of furtive drinking now haunted all efforts at finding sanctuary. Or maybe this preceded the alcohol, with the idea of a refuge outside their relationship complicated from the start.

The situation was clarified further when I met with him later that week. Fred came to my office directly from his job in midtown, where he worked as VP at a prominent hedge fund, dressed in a business suit that had become slightly rumpled from the day's exertions and with a tie loosened around his unbuttoned collar. He had a crisp New England intonation and a polite, somewhat diffident manner. His mildness belied the high-powered position he occupied in a quite competitive sector of the New York finance world.

He grew up in a home of privilege; his great-grandfather had been a successful industrialist and left a large legacy that had had grown through smart investments. The patient's father had been especially fortunate, having predicted the rise of personal computers and multiplying his inheritance by investing capital in the microprocessor industry. Fred grew up under the shadow of these accomplishments and despaired of achieving the same level of success. Adding to his early insecurities were a mother who struggled with mental health issues sometimes bordering on psychosis, a shyness that was often debilitating and led to bullying and taunting from his peers, and a younger brother whom he regarded as his superior in every respect: more attractive, more sociable, more intelligent.

"I had every comfort I could have wanted growing up, except for comfort," he said flatly, as if repeating a line worn from overuse. "Even my mother couldn't be there for me, more a source of embarrassment than of support. I felt adrift, with no future, no purpose, and going to boarding school only brought more isolation."

He turned to a recollection that had come upon him before the appointment: "I remembered while waiting in the common area how reluctant my mother was regarding treatment. She needed it more than anyone I ever met. But I guess it's the craziest among us who refuse to get help. I can't think about her without feeling ashamed. I know my feelings toward her are a bit strange: not sadness, not anger, not even irritation. Just shame. But she wasn't really a mother to me, more of a liability. I couldn't stand to be in public places with her for fear that she would act crazy and call attention to all of us. At the supermarket, I would always tighten up, especially while checking out, ducking my head in case my mom would start harassing the cashier, questioning the price of everything, asking for the manager and then the owner, causing a scene. You could never tell when it would happen. She would snap just like that, and start screaming, interrogating, getting verbally abusive."

He began drinking in boarding school and continued to do so in college, binging on the weekends "but no more than anyone else." He also developed an interest in LSD while at college, finding it helpful for "getting into things about myself that were otherwise difficult to get into." By this point, he had developed symptoms consistent with pathological anxiety: constant fearful ruminations, a readiness for the sky to fall, a tendency to startle easily, restlessness, avoidance of difficult situations, and so on.

"I would have probably become a full-blown alcoholic much sooner if I didn't have LSD to take me out of myself. I would use it max a few times a month, but it was all I needed to get through each week. It wasn't about the tripped-out visuals or anything like that: the goal was to get to that empty place. It's like it interrupted the chatter for stretches at a time, allowed me the space of mind to function without needing to obliterate myself at the end of each day. This has been the struggle pretty much since I started working in my early twenties, and since I stopped taking LSD—needing to drink myself to black out because that was the only way to get rest from it all."

He had stopped using LSD, but the psychedelia persisted as a collector's interest in obscure German *kosmische* music from the 1970s, with a vinyl library that spanned an entire wall in his den. Until recently, he would retreat to his den at the end of each day, put on a Krautrock record, and take back a few shots of vodka. After some time to himself, he would emerge feeling "ready to deal with the wife and kids." He would continue drinking from a large mug of vodka mixed with orange juice as he attended to household responsibilities, of which he was delegated a fair share. "I'm not sure my wife knew that I was drinking a pint of vodka every night, or if she knew she didn't seem to care. Her main concern was that I took care of business at home. It seems that she only really cared when it threatened her image as Ms. Perfect. She couldn't stand to have a husband embarrass himself around the shiny people she took to be her friends."

I pointed out what appeared to be disdain for his wife, or at least frustration with her. His expression immediately softened, and he appeared nearly chastened: "Don't get me wrong. I love my wife; I would hate it if she were to leave me, or if the marriage were to fail."

A flicker of contempt resurfaced as he continued. "And at the same time there is no question about it: I drink because of her, because she bullies me, because I go home, and I feel nothing but suffocation and fear. Everyone who knows me sees it. Even my previous psychiatrist, the one she didn't want me seeing anymore, saw it, and he never even met my wife.

"All that being said, I know I need to stop, and that it is my responsibility. What happened was a wake-up call. I'm glad it was a wake-up call to her as well, because otherwise she would not have allowed me to go back into treatment."

The resentment was thick, nearly impenetrable: the spiteful layers of justifications and rationalizations that had hardened over his eyes like cataract. It is likely his wife had challenges of her own: problems with providing affection and support, and tendencies toward controlling and patrolling him. But it is one thing to recognize these issues in a partner and attempt to address them; another to drink in order to hide from them. He had acknowledged, however, that the drinking was not helping and had vowed to attempt stopping. This was an important start, with the work of removing these resentments, and preventing further accumulation, yet to come.

•

The other important challenge ahead was creating a meaningful space for himself. Everywhere he went—work, home, running errands—he felt that he was denied the opportunity. He was haunted by home at the office, at the market, on the road, and angry at the intrusiveness of his wife, allegedly texting him continuously throughout the day and recently asking him to text her whenever he changed locations as well. "It's annoying as hell, and I'm sure others in the office notice. She wants to keep a tab on me, wants to make sure I'm available to wait on her. I'm constantly having to step out to put out some fire or attend to something she is too disorganized to face. But in some sick way, I appreciate the attention. She texts me, and wants me to text back, to keep an eye on me, because she values me and cares about me; it's always good to see that."

As his commuter train approached town every evening, Fred would begin to feel trepidation and agitation, as if gearing up for a fight. "It didn't feel like I was coming home. It was more like landing in a battlefield. There is always something I have done wrong, always blame and criticism and meanness. A list of demands, no concern for whether I want time to myself or with friends. Not even a smile on most days. And I can't remember the last time she initiated any kind of affection. I'm the one constantly giving compliments, trying to hug her, and being kind, even as my stomach turns with sadness and rage. From her, nothing but insults. My only consolation comes from the children, who are sweet and loving and innocent. But they also look at me sympathetically, I can see it in their eyes, a sadness for Daddy because he is always getting beaten up."

The den, the Krautrock, and the OJ and vodka await him inside, providing the comfort that he cannot find otherwise. "My dream is to stride in, and the moment she opens her mouth, to cuss her out and slap her head hard with my briefcase. I haven't done this, I never will, but the thought gives me the strength to keep going. It's like a secret that I keep inside, covered with the sad smiles she doesn't even bother to notice. The drinking is the other secret. I remain myself, privately saying screw it all, and not totally defeated yet."

●

There are several stories running through this one. Each proposes a unique problem but the same solution.

Fred has pathological anxiety, probably diagnosable as generalized anxiety disorder and posttraumatic stress disorder, that he self-medicates with alcohol.

Fred was deprived of love throughout childhood and into his marriage, and alcohol has come to be a reliable source of consolation, support, and succor.

Fred is ravaged by guilt at not having achieved the success that his forebears have, at his white-collar conformism, and at the violent rage he feels toward his wife. He has learned to both soothe and punish himself by drinking to excess, finding some solace, and at the same time incurring all the negative consequences one might expect—the punishment he deserves—such as hangovers, conflict, and further guilt.

Fred drinks because it dramatizes his conflicted condition and distracts him from it.

Fred drinks because he has come to regard it as the only opportunity to enter into a space all his own.

Fred is a privileged White male who has made millions by treating life as a series of strategic business bets intended primarily to maximize his gains, with no attention given to their larger social and environmental implications, and this has contributed to a starkly utilitarian approach to all of life, with his self-centered capitalist ethos fueling a pattern of drinking where even his own body and mind are neglected in the pursuit of alcoholic excess.

Fred has attachment difficulties stemming from an insecure relationship with his mother that have carried over into his marriage, leading to an increased sense of fragility and fear of abandonment vis-à-vis his wife, and that have also contributed to the problematic attachment he has developed to alcohol, including the precarious security that he finds in it.

Fred was born with character defects, such as willfulness, avoidance, ingratitude, and a proud refusal to recognize and accept his limitations, that have driven him to drink.

Fred is oppressed by and resentful toward his wife, his sense of his own mediocrity, his weaknesses, and his conventional life, and finds in drinking a mode of rebellion, revenge, and freedom.

Fred turns to alcohol, finally, as an escape from the same oppressive premises and (un)realities that have compelled him to drink.

These explanations draw on what Fred has told us to understand his reasons for drinking, and why he continues to drink despite the suffering it causes. Each is a variation on the same theme: alcohol posing as a solution, even to the problem of addiction itself.

Missing from this survey of explanations, some of them more helpful than others, is the one that the brain model would propose. Fred has various genetic vulnerabilities affecting his brain, including a propensity for anxiety and a predisposition to problematic substance use, that have rendered him vulnerable to drinking regularly and ultimately developing neural adaptations to alcohol that heighten compulsive use, especially within the context of a stressful career and marriage.

All the prior explanations provide the reasons that had led Fred to drink, be it feeling unloved, a hunger for stimulation, sinfulness, attachment issues, yearning for sanctuary, capitalism, the need for comfort from internal pain. The brain model takes away the existential dimension that might be revealed through insight into his subjective world. This is appropriate given its grounding in a hard behaviorism that regards such things as irrelevant. There is also the positivist bias in modern science more generally that concerns itself only with "external" phenomena that might be quantified and measured from an "objective" vantage point. What is added is the language of biological determinism, with matter rendered devoid of mind: genetic vulnerability, stress diathesis, and neural adaptations to alcohol.

Some adherents to the brain model go further. They insist on the latter characterization to the subordination or even exclusion of others.

This risks obscuring the rich subjective world that the addict inhabits, replacing it with mechanisms more applicable to the behavior of rodents in a cage than to that of human beings. Studying rodents is not an entirely worthless endeavor; it helps us answer questions unethical to pose to a human being (and some would say to animals as well). But there are some uniquely human phenomena that no research with rodents or even monkeys can reproduce, such as our attachment to certain worldviews, values, and ideas. Unlike animals, we also aim to fix things that don't need fixing, to find solutions, to paraphrase Marcel Duchamp, when there isn't a problem.

•

The brain model imposes a fiction, a paradigm, on the behavior of the addict, ascribing it to the "brain," "drugs," "stress," and "genetic vulnerability." Addiction is reimagined, in other words, from the outside, by scientists. But what about the world of representations the addict inhabits? The story a person imposes on herself, even if it is obscure, is bound to be more helpful at getting at why she does what she does than anything we can invent. The first task for us is to understand what this confusion might be: to listen, to observe, to ask questions.

Addiction originates in our evaluating, representing, and purpose-driven minds; we arrive at addiction, as with most things, by dreaming our way into it. Though linked to the "physical" act of drug use, our relationship to the drug becomes much subtler than a sensation: it becomes the world, and as difficult to see clearly as the back of our heads. A different vantage point is necessary.

The fiction propelling addiction, in any case, is just as hidden to the addict herself as it might be to those on the outside. She doesn't fully recognize why she does what she does, which is one of the reasons she continues doing it. To teach her to say "It is my addicted brain that does it" is to further bury her dream beneath our own.

A fundamental process of representation is presupposed by all the explanations above. Intoxication comes to gain a value that is both fictional and deeply compelling—as hedonic self-interest, as consolation, as an impregnable private space, as freedom of mind, as punishment, as rebellion, as antidepressant, as spiritual/demonic fulfillment, as a stand-in for mother. A double representation: the alcohol-induced representation of a state of being coming to be represented as something else. It is easy to see how one might get lost in this labyrinth. Even the grayish whorls and webs of the brain start to seem clearer: at least they don't keep shifting and mutating as the mind might.

The fiction of addiction justifies the destruction it causes by becoming more certain of itself the worse things get. Thus, Fred's resentment grows more venomous as addiction takes its toll and his life becomes less manageable, and as the bitterness, self-pity, and spite come to provide further ground for drinking to oblivion. Fred's suffering is imagined, with insidious logic, in the same destructive terms that intoxication has been: as a reason to continue drinking.

What differentiates addiction from more benign use is this rigid fictionalization of suffering, whereby it is transformed into a problem for which intoxication is the solution. There is one direction. The attempt to flee suffering, and deceive ourselves about it, binds us to it more tightly, like prey knotting itself deeper into the trap the more it flails to escape.

Yet it is an ambivalent trap, offering us an out. The suffering intensifies its assault to such an extent that it might scream louder than the story in our heads. Or rather, the scream and our "reality" become inseparable, affording us opportunity, perhaps, to recognize and dismantle the fictions deepening our suffering. What had held us captive has now agitated us awake. The poison reveals its medicine.

We might propose yet another hypothesis for understanding addiction, summing up the stories earlier: *People with addiction fictionalize and attach to an experience to overcome suffering, and in doing so deepen their suffering because their suffering becomes fictionalized as well.* The failure here is universal: the ignorance of taking unreality for reality, poison for medicine. Addiction inflames its agonies. It might also break us open.

●

We might regard the difference between these two types of representation as Cartesian or dualistic: the first model about minds, the second about brains. But it is more accurate to characterize the distinction as experiential, with the epistemic framework of each model hinging on which mode of experience is represented, the addict's or the scientist's.

The former attempts to represent his existential, epistemological, and moral challenges; the latter stems from a "physical" or "objective" vantage point on him.

Even if the fictionalization process were to be rendered as a neural map, with altered dopamine signaling, for example, found to be implicated via prediction coding with the intense and idiosyncratic salience that an addict confers on intoxication, this would not mean that the brain disease model has swallowed up the other and rendered a representation of the addict's experience irrelevant. It remains important to enter into his perspective as best we can, and understand the place of the substance or intoxication within it. No amount of functional neuroimaging will allow us to do this. But that is not a problem or a sign that more scientific progress is needed. Both models have virtues, and are complementary, so it is possible to draw from the two to inform our understanding, without trying to find, as with addiction neuroscience, a single materially oriented mode of explanation offering the last word.

Yet that is not to say that they are equally important clinically. Fictionalization is not restricted to an entanglement with a single (un) reality; it is also involved in extricating ourselves and creating another. This imaginal process often begins from the first contact, when a reorientation occurs from one self-fiction to another: "junkie," as was the case with Steve, to "patient." By bringing greater attention to this process, we stand to participate more skillfully and intentionally in it, while making better sense of what may be already happening under our noses. A common practice in addiction treatment, for instance, is the open-ended dialogue, during which an exploration may occur into the dissonance between the person's lived experience—her agitation, losses, yearning, and hopes—and the fictions and habits inflaming her suffering: what motivational therapists call "developing discrepancy." This dialogue widens the chasm in the person's world, deepening the separation between her (un)reality and the lived experience it obscures. From this schism comes an opportunity to attend to our suffering more sensitively, as well as to dispel or reimagine the world holding us captive.

Thus while the two models are explanatory in different ways, the fictionalization model is more helpful for engaging with the core process behind both addiction and freedom from it: the imaginal transformation of reality. Both clinician and patient stand to gain greater understanding into the fictions at play, as well as the fears, struggles, and desires—the suffering—that the addiction has evolved to address. This also allows them to make full use of the dialectic inherent to their relationship, the words of the person received as "reality" and then given back as "representation," a mirroring offering opportunity for the (un)reality to be seen for what it is. And it might also allow the person, more importantly, to recognize what he is not.

We will examine various ways to support this process of people recognizing their (un)realities and extricating from them. Regardless of how this happens, there is one main purpose: learning to meet the moment more freely, tending to the suffering beneath our regime of self-deception with clarity and sensitivity. From reality through unreality to reality.

•

The brain model has clear clinical utility, too, though of a more auxiliary and supplemental sort. It has been instrumental at developing medications to manage withdrawal, as well as to reduce or outright block the "hedonic salience" of drugs (how good they feel) and diminish the intensity or frequency of craving. These are important vulnerabilities to target because doing so may ease the process of overcoming addiction, were the individual to consider no longer using.

But here is the rub: addressing these vulnerabilities does not amount to addressing addiction. This is because addiction is more than its apparent determinants. One can be reactive, experience withdrawal and craving, be beleaguered by stress, be vulnerable in countless other ways, and still be in remission from addiction—not be actively addicted—because one is not destructively chasing a fiction or captivated by unrealities. This is the crucial criterion of addiction, without which the diagnosis is meaningless. The person must be actively chasing and using whatever it is, having decided that despite the mounting suffering, it is meaningful and worth doing.

Absent these repeated decisions to use drugs, drink alcohol, or pursue anything else, and to confer a meaning to one's suffering that compels this behavior, addiction wouldn't exist. Nearly every person who has overcome addiction will refer to the early months after changing course as beset by these very difficulties—he or she may experience protracted withdrawal, craving, irritability, and mood problems. Yet such individuals are not actively addicted, having decided, on a regular basis, to not pursue the thing despite these challenges. The "reward" has lost its old meaning, as has the suffering that went along with it. The brain model may be helpful, in such circumstances, at biologically impacting the challenges that come with maintaining sobriety, such as persistent withdrawal or stress sensitivity. But it is not equipped to address what matters most: the person's decision to pursue an (un) reality, despite being violated by it.

This decision at the foundation of addiction can be addressed only by treating the addict as a *human being*—not as a "vulnerable brain" for which memory training, rewiring, or pharmacological manipulation, for example, will suffice. A socially embedded, suffering, confused, and yet purposeful being who decides to do what he does for the same reason any other fulfillment is pursued: it is a deeply meaningful consolation, and notwithstanding its problems, vastly preferred to suffering meaninglessly.

Addiction shows itself, yet again, as a uniquely human predicament, with parallels in the many other ways that we might attempt to address our pain, distract ourselves, or find fulfillment. Perhaps we have been prone to mythologize certain moments into what they can never be: a perfect and complete contentment. We might go on to ravage ourselves in pursuit: more relationships, more accomplishments, more possessions, more sensations, more gratifications, more oblivion, more of whatever sings to us its siren song of total consummation. Or perhaps we find in some incarnation of ourselves a deep and resonant meaningfulness, despite offering only a moment's respite, with greater anguish in its wake. We cling with all the tenacity of the addict because to give these up would mean being left *meaningless*, which is worse than the most painful wanting.

This is the shadow side, so to speak, of that much vaunted endeavor: *man's search for meaning*. The phrase has the ring of anachronism to it—and not simply because of that antiquated protagonist at its heart, Man. The words carry sepia traces of the pioneer, the explorer, the discoverer. Man searches and searches, a conquistador of meaning, subduing the wilderness in pursuit of his purpose. Any meaning will do so long as despair is diverted, the dark continent put in order.

We might find ourselves pining for a meaningful inauthenticity and servitude to the loss of meaning altogether. Desperate for an (un)reality to which we might belong. Our solutions may, indeed, be totally benighted and insane. But it is what we know. This gives us an entry point to addiction that is close to home. Our meanings and systems stem from the same inflamed wound, regardless of drug, regardless of attachment. Entire worlds solidify over the mutilated emptiness like scar tissue.

Drugs, alcohol, pleasure, fame, anything under the sun might dangle the lure. But we don't realize the deception even as we want more and more of it. And more painful than wanting, especially in addiction, is getting what we want, repeatedly. No one can be expected to carry such a burden without breaking. The bedrock of morning awaits the fall:

And they do not fall from a real height into a real abyss; it is only
From an imaginary height that they fall and they fall only to the
Ground.

●

Fred stopped drinking before he came to see me, shortly after his wife called, but he didn't know what to do next. He wanted to stop for good this time. There had been previous stints of abstinence, precipitated usually by some problem related to drinking. But none had lasted longer than a few weeks. He was fearful about relapsing again, terrified that he might lose his wife and family.

"But I know how my mind works. I get scared and stop drinking, vowing that this is it. A week later, I'm carrying the mug around again, sipping into the night. A few days is all it takes, and I'm tricking myself into thinking that the catastrophe has been overblown, that it will never come. I drink, and of course the wife doesn't leave, the job doesn't fall apart, the kids don't find out. Nothing happens, at least not right away. I get stupid and comfortable. I slip into the old groove, forgetting everything. I want to make sure that doesn't happen again."

Fred was asking for help, but of a certain sort. He wanted to continue making the decision to not drink; the problem, however, was that *he knows how his mind works*. He wanted help, putting it plainly, with his mind, with becoming free of his mind, so that he wasn't so helpless against its problematic workings. Overcoming addiction involves, at one point or another, cultivating this type of freedom.

But the brain model has little to say about this. It views addicted individuals as hostage to their broken brains, with "cognitive control" rendered unfit by genes, drugs, stress, and habit. What matters most for recovery is neural manipulation, reconditioning, behavioral modification. And if the illusion of freedom helps the person attain a healthier lifestyle, then fine, it'll be encouraged. The person might also be given "choice" as in contingency management approaches: Will it be "a dirty urine" or this money voucher? All in the service of changing the person from without, given that it is doubtful any good can come from the broken brain within.

We might approach all this from a very different angle. Or make explicit that we already do. No clinician is a pure adherent to the brain model. People in clinical work are too engaged with real life for that. Perhaps by stating the obvious and restoring addiction work to its proper dignity free of ideological neuro-materialism, we might declare our freedom from the scientism of the citadel and better engage addiction on the ground, with an honest, supple, and human science, as sensitive to the complexity of Fred's experience as to our own.

Fred's experience is not simply implicated in his decision to drink. It is also involved in the possibility of choosing something else. Inherent to *being experience* is a basic liberty: the freedom to witness, interpret, reimagine, conceal, fictionalize, obscure, transform, modify, distort, reconsider, and otherwise represent our experience however we like. But Fred had lost sight of this primordial freedom, its opportunities as well its snares, beginning with the transformation by which he found in the fumes of alcohol the hazy enchantment of dreams, or in his marital challenges a problem that oblivion is best suited to resolve.

In addiction, our imaginings and representations grow ossified: heroin or cocaine or sex, for instance, maintain the allure of something essential, the thing itself, and we lose sight of the creative freedom that conferred a special nimbus on to the thing, that sustains its ideality, and that might also transform the substance into something else. We restrict our field of possibility. The moral injury of the brain disease model is to deepen the captivity by further concealing the addict's freedom, imposing on him the fiction that he is preordained by his broken brain to act in the ways he does. This is, of course, exactly what the addict in recovery intends to overcome: no longer predetermined to enact the same fixed patterns, liberated from the slavery of his thoughts, reactions, and (un)realities. The addict has a sense that the cure—far from involving a manipulation of the brain, or a vaccine, or a medication—is quite straightforward and simple, though not necessarily easy. He must choose differently.

To choose differently, Fred must choose freely. This begins with reclaiming his freedom to consider other possibilities, other realities. This is the challenge before Fred: awakening to his inmost freedom from the "reality" that had propelled his choice to drink. He must awaken to consciousness.

●

To crave is more than to desire—it is to desire something simultaneously good and evil. The agitation of craving necessarily emerges at this impasse of quarreling illusions: the same thing is invested with a sense of the good, as well as with the forbidden, the toxic, the evil. There is little we want more than what we also do not want. And we want it and don't want it because we have lost sight of it, our fractured minds covering it over with a clamor of signs.

Our cravings bring to light the more fundamental challenges of *wanting*. Wanting something—in contrast to requiring it, as we do water or breath—pains us in a particular way: it pains us for no other reason than our apparently lacking it. It diminishes us; it promises to complete us. There are no further fictions to dramatize the process and engage the imagination: no recourse, as in craving, to good and evil. This contradiction at the heart of wanting is inescapable yet so subtle and familiar as to be generally hidden. Craving takes this agitation to its climax, driving a rift into the thing and fragmenting it into opposing worlds: medicine as well as poison, hope as well as anguish, heaven as well as hell. The representations become so detached from reality that they start to fight among themselves.

We might also become impulsive: interrupting our agitated wrangling with abrupt, unreflective action. Both impulsivity and craving emerge from the same good-evil dissonance; they both reflect a dualistic, conflict-riven existence. Craving has what we want just ahead, though we fear looking back with remorse after obtaining it. Impulsivity finds what we don't want behind us, though we fear wanting it all over again. And the actual moment, this moment now, is obscured by the twin phantoms of what might have been and what might be.

Impulsivity is that momentary reprieve from overthinking things, necessarily recognized after the deed is done and with regret: "I would wake up in the morning," Fred said, "and I can't believe I drank again, especially because I had been telling myself not to all day. I think back and it makes me sick. The sickest thing is that if I'm not telling myself not to drink, or beating myself up for what happened last night, I'm looking forward to it, I'm waiting with bated breath for the evening."

A recent study found that when addicted individuals approach a drug while deliberately appraising its consequences, their cravings are diminished. The authors interpret this to mean that craving might be modulated by tempering our eagerness with more caution. I see the turn as simpler than that: from agitated self-quarrelling to intentional awareness, from pharmakolalia to silence. We enter a clear-eyed relationship with the fullness of what is before us: past, present, and future given equal attention.

We recognize all that is possible. We may also recognize the fixations and confusions obscuring us. An opening is created. Our suffering comes from struggling headstrong at this threshold and resisting the current: clinging to our good-evil familiarities, intoxicated and anguished by the incarnations that need to be surrendered. This invitation into a vast clearing will continue without cease until our last breath. There is opportunity to enter into that final break in the earth having practiced choosing it, having learned to relinquish the cacophony of too many minds when the freedom to do so was still ours.

It is, in the end, the same invitation. Readers, addicts, patients—the same call to learn to die. We might start today.

●

The rupture between a person and what was presumed to be reality is crucial to overcoming many modes of suffering, including addiction.

With such severance comes yet another freedom: the opportunity to inhabit ways of being liberated from the contortions and deceptions of the apparent world.

A lifetime of learning begins. The same invitation, a similar direction, addicted or not, reaching an impasse and relinquishing what seemed the measure of our lives. Learning to dispel our self-deceptions, our certainties, our selves. Attending to what requires recognition: pain and possibility, the call to another way. Walking into emptiness, into earth. It is unfamiliar territory, and the first steps are disorienting, our old maps flickering over the ground like short-circuiting screens. The path grows clearer with each step. And emptier. Walking into that endless emptiness as into death, learning to find our foothold in the dark.

Fred was already learning. He made an encouraging impression on me that first visit: a desperate man who had reached a critical point in his suffering. But this desperation was reassuring for more than the reason that it might make him more docile or our work together easier.

"I've hit rock bottom," Fred said. "It may not seem like much. After all, I still have my job, wife, and kids. But I'm sure of it. I can't imagine feeling any worse. Everything seems so phony: a big scam. Only God knows what's true, what's a big fat lie. Is my wife really a bitch? Is my job really that punishing? Am I really just a good guy getting a bad hand again and again? I don't know up from down anymore. But I know that the drinking needs to stop. And it's bottom because I know I can't do it on my own, I know I can't rely on myself to save myself."

Rock bottom suggests an inescapable ground, a ground ready to catch our fall—unlike the (un)real rocks Ahmed imagined as *not yet*. A foothold that exists beyond the vagaries of the mind. Recognizing the vagaries in the first place. A sorrow unto death. There are few betrayals more devastating than this: recognizing our own trusted thoughts as seductive imposters. This was Fred's first move toward disentangling himself—he accepted that his mind has turned against him, regularly deceived and devastated him. He was left with no real choice but to throw up his hands in defeat. And put his feet on surer ground. Crashing through his brittle fictions to find that obsidian bedrock.

How to believe in one's own devices again with such deceit at our doorstep? Reality itself a trick, created by a malevolent demiurge to toy with us. Fred had caught the trickster; he pinned him to the hard ground. He tore off the mask to reveal the villain and was shocked to find not his wife, nor his mother, but himself.

Fred had stopped drinking, for the moment. Rather than turn to his own (un)reality for guidance, he was surrendering himself to that of another. A radical vulnerability, defenseless even against himself, the imposter of himself. Not an easy move for any of us, entrusting ourselves to the care of a stranger. It is much more difficult for the addict, who has been going it alone for so long. Fred revealed to me the sanctum of suffering that he had closely guarded for decades. The reliable reality machine humming behind the scenes. The dream logic, distortions, and secret schemes that had been choreographing his life for years, even decades: his "reality" was being exposed to the light.

A careless word, a sudden unexpected step, might feel lacerating. It is like ripping open a scab, the wound still raw. A mutable situation, a delicate limbo of possibility. The same pain, helplessness, and terror that brought Fred to medical attention may also lead him, at any moment, to shield himself in his customary ways, including recoiling from my support and returning to his familiar reality.

A great deal of work lay ahead, but an indispensable foundation had been set. The source of his suffering had been identified; Fred recognized its origins in his own mind. He now aimed to free himself from it.

•

A nightingale appears to us, sings its song, disappears. We recall it and reflect on it, molding the bird into something that might be very different from our initial impression: a private invention.

The nightingale in the immediacy of experience is more vital, of course, than any subsequent idea. But our imaginations do not necessarily diminish the experience. The living mystery can persist and deepen. This hinges on how intrusive our minds are, how much mental noise we put into it. We think most clearly about a nightingale, perhaps, when we remain silent before its traces, quietly receiving its song.

So much of addiction occurs when we aren't using but are instead thinking, soliloquizing, and imagining our way into (un)reality. Stendhal had a term for the way a lover in his passionate solitude reimagines his beloved into a perfect fiction: crystallization. The idea of drinking becomes progressively removed from immediate experience in a similarly private way, leading it to crystallize into something else entirely: a refuge, for instance, from the ills of the world. Consider the vast amount of time spent thinking about a cherished activity in addiction—such as drinking and enjoying intoxication—as compared to the relatively little time spent doing it and finding relief.

The thinking does not end even when the activity begins. It has been shown that even when drinking, heavy drinkers remain inattentive and continue to ruminate on the usual preoccupations. They are thinking about doing something, even while doing it. They had been dreaming their way to their loved one, or to their fantasy island, only to find that they would rather keep dreaming than attend to the disappointment of what is really before them.

Idle thoughts, in such cases, are far more than a bland procession of disembodied representations. They are also charged with desire and emotion. *Alcohol* or *sex* are not abstractions of minor personal importance. They are often deeply cherished crystallizations invested with limbic salience. We shape our fictions into whatever we want them to be, harden them into the image of our hopes and dreams. The bird no longer offers its music to accompany our stillness and silence. We invoke the word and it appears. The nightingale opens its beak, and what we hear are our own voices, a siren song screaming for more.

●

If Fred's mention of "rock bottom" suggests an acquaintance with Alcoholics Anonymous, or AA, that's because he had indeed decided to go to a meeting at the suggestion of a friend, in the week prior to our first appointment. He had resisted for many years, but with the same spirit of desperation and humility that he surrendered himself to my care, he decided to give AA a fair shot.

Since its inception more than seventy years ago by Bill Wilson (Bill W.), an alcoholic in recovery influenced by the Christian model of the Oxford Group, AA has come to be synonymous in popular culture with mutual aid, anonymous fellowship, and personal transformation, at best, and with cultish conformity and dogmatic obedience to Big Book platitudes, at worst. The truth, of course, is somewhere in between. For those drawn to the abstinence-based approach, the deistic dimension—

surrender to "a higher power" or "the God of our understanding" is a crucial component of the AA cure—or the highly ritualized and all-encompassing reprogramming, AA can give tremendous benefit. The service it provides is multifaceted and well suited to addressing the myriad issues that beleaguer addicted individuals: among the most immediate and easily accessible resources are the sanctuary of fellowship and peer support, an explicit moral system, and a group-based framework by which abstinence is reinforced through "counting days," social validation, and the achievement of milestones. Central to AA, moreover, are the 12 steps, intended to guide individuals toward a spiritual awakening by delineating the process along that path. The 12-step trajectory is a redemption story—a journey through sinfulness toward self-examination, contrition, and grace—and most likely to appeal to individuals with a spiritual or religious background, notwithstanding the attempts to reach out to atheists and agnostics via more secular conceptions of a higher power.

The success rates of AA are low, as with most other treatments for addiction. A majority of individuals drop out of AA and continue getting intoxicated within the first year; but those few who remain sober one year in generally remain abstinent thereafter, with some kind of continued engagement with "the rooms." In other words, available data suggest that AA works only for a minority of people; but for this minority, it works very well. The reason for this has not been rigorously studied, but it is likely related to sustained engagement with the less accessible and more demanding component of AA: the 12 steps, which generally require years to complete. Most treatments, for any disorder, are unsuccessful unless the person receives the full therapeutic dose. It is believed by senior AA members that going to groups, sharing with peers, and counting days, without doing the crucial and long-term work of the 12 steps, is to shortchange oneself and settle for only the accoutrements, without benefiting from the meat of the matter. This is echoed in the popular phrase to encourage "step work": *it only works if you work it.*

Let's put aside the important criticism that engagement with step work might be a proxy for motivation and other strengths; those who are likely to engage with persistent step work, it may be argued, would have stopped using drugs or alcohol anyway given that they were motivated to move forward and possessed the attributes, such as consistency, discipline, and perseverance, to make abstinence stick. The only way to draw conclusions regarding the efficacy of the 12 steps is to move beyond naturalistic data and conduct the appropriate studies. In the absence of these data, we have stories: narratives of personal transformations provided by legions of AA members, beginning with Bill W., who worked the steps and documented their recovery.

Sharing such stories is an integral part of AA involvement; one can hear them regularly by attending a group and listening to the back-and-forth. While exercising all the caution and restraint such anecdotal evidence requires, we might nonetheless find in these stories some insight into how AA might be effective. Further, it may give some direction for how the helpfulness of AA, and of step work in particular, might be generalized and optimized to be more beneficial for more people.

A striking feature of these narratives is their *uniformity*. They are all variations on the same theme: from turpitude to transcendence through the guidance and grace of a higher power. This may be expected given the boilerplate language of the steps and the highly immersive social context for developing the narrative, including a sponsor who personally assists the aspirant. What develops, in any case, is a shared story, with a common lexicon, nearly identical thematic content, and even recurring characters (the "using friend") and subplots. But this does more than facilitate group cohesion: the uniformity of these stories lends the arc of "recovery through redemption" a nearly archetypal force, as if one were directly incarnating an ageless myth. This works to elevate the core narrative into a universal tale beyond each person alone but uniquely relevant to everyone: a kind of hero epic that particularizes into the personalized script of each member's recovery. Reporting one's progress to the home group, at prescribed intervals, can therefore resemble catechism, with members coming to intone the words that have existed long before and that will endure well after. The narrative itself attains a kind of sanctity, irrespective of whether it is a Christian or an atheist 12 stepper doing the narrating: a talisman to be shared, empowered through repeated articulations, and cherished as a safeguard against the confusion that preceded it.

This rigidity of language and narrative can be disconcerting to first timers, resembling as it does the indoctrinated groupthink of a cult. A common objection I've heard from those who don't return to AA for a second visit: *I'd rather struggle on my own than be brainwashed into sobriety.* The Christian subtext doesn't help. The dominant culture of secular individualism renders AA, with all its emphasis on humility, surrender, fellowship, and other Christian values, somewhat anachronistic. The most likely person to embrace AA is someone with some overlap in worldview and sensibility: like Fred, a white Christian who is well adjusted to traditional American–Western European culture.

But working the steps isn't simply learning what words to say, of course. The narrative develops through painstaking shifts in perspective, consistent introspection, self-correction, and relationship with a mysterious presence, a higher power, a transpersonal source of meaning beyond one's hypertrophic ego—all while hewing close to the template of the 12 steps so as to not lose one's way. The narrative—its familiar arc and language—becomes a sure sign to oneself and to others, therefore, that one did it right. And certain words and phrases are repeated to the letter, with a theologian's scrupulousness, because they are more than the story that comes to be told; they constitute the very grammar of a new mind.

It is fitting that this most enduring treatment for addiction—now entering into its seventh decade and claiming several million members across the globe—endeavors to heal the mind by imprinting a new story onto it, one that involves, among other things, recognizing that the previous fictions one had been telling oneself are false and destructive. These distortions and self-deceptions come to be methodically abandoned in pursuit of a less ego-bound consciousness illuminated by fellowship and a transcendent mystery. This may be the most critical work of recovery: shifting toward a clearer perspective, dispelling the old lies, and finding an (un)reality to occupy oneself that is balanced, supple, and translucent.

AA has a particular way of pursuing this transformation, and a very specific narrative it intends to impart. The program does not resonate with everyone, of course, and the number of people who find it relevant has diminished as the dominant culture has grown less responsive to

Christian-inflected thought. But the wisdom of this cure remains undiminished, though perhaps not fully recognized. Its wisdom is this: AA aims to systematically deconstruct the perspectives, values, and sense of self that feed addiction and to cultivate a personal narrative and framework that supports sustained transformation, personal accountability, and engagement with the mystery at the heart of things. In its focus on the brain, addiction science has overlooked mechanisms of healing that are more existential and humanistic; it has been particularly derisive of the AA cure. But AA provides a clear example for how the incessant and destructive fictionalization at the root of substance use disorders might be targeted. Importantly, the spirit of the AA cure is one that we might work to optimize and update so that it could be rendered more accessible to those whom the fellowship does not reach. There might be many ways to surrender what seems our mind so that we might grow more conscious.

●

Individuals in AA recognize that one must undergo great suffering before awakening to a new path, though their phrasing might be too absolute: "It gets worse before it gets better. You must hit rock bottom."

Fred drank to not suffer, lulled into believing this to be the only way. This dream came to its conclusion in a kind of sleep terror, with sleep and sight confused. The visions of the day as tattered as dreams, while sleep was broken into the jagged edges of a lurking violence. Traces of the affliction appeared everywhere. Even intoxication came to cut deeper so that Fred's pain and mortality might be heightened: a merciless teacher. Then there is the gasp of anguish, the signal that morning is close. A lifetime of deathtime. The suffering of alcoholism coming to provide its own solution: tripping us up as we sleepwalk toward the cliff edge, awakening inches away from the black depths ready to devour us. A stumble with the steps already authored, set in stone.

Certain dreams, it seems, can only conclude in the panic of interrupted sleep. Fred was shocked at how deluded he had been, frightened by the ease with which he had stumbled toward his annihilation. "I can't believe how messed up I was. Hypnotized by the booze into thinking I was helping myself, until the scales fell from my eyes and I recognized that I was actually killing myself."

Awakening at the edge, however, may not be enough. The allure of the abyss remains. An imaginary height, an imaginary pit. There may be an impulse to leap across the divide and soar into the darkness, finding wings in that final descent. Exalted, as in the beginning, by dreams that promise to reconcile falling with flight, heaven with hell. Even if we manage to awaken to a new morning, the conclusion of the day might be exactly as the many nights before it: the same phantoms, the same darkness. One must begin again with a new ending in sight, a transformed dream to survive the dying of the light.

The despair of addiction is to believe that the fumes of intoxication are the only oxygen one has, the single fantasy with any reality. A presence one can hold, take in, drink up. "I wonder if it's possible," Fred said, "to be rid of the anxiety, clear of all the trouble that's always weighing on me. I don't know if I can: to be perfectly honest, I have never been able to. Not that I am unwilling to try. Do I just need to learn how to live with the pain and give up on ever feeling better? Do I need to resign myself to feeling bad most of the time? And you wonder why I drink?

"I know drinking is not helping, believe me. But when nothing else takes the pain away, I get to a point where it doesn't matter anymore. I need a break, and I go for what has worked, even as I know it hasn't. I mean, this is the problem. I know it only creates more problems, I know I have destroyed myself with booze a thousand times. But I can't help believing that it'll give some relief, even for a moment, and giving it another go. It's the fear, most of all, that there is nothing else."

Fred dreams as he drinks, finding there a promise that drinking alone cannot keep.

It is in this failure, in the shattered dream, that he might rise to the right questions. How to fulfill the promise but abandon the liquor? How might he come to find comfort while sober, to dream while awake? Alcohol provides a foretaste of that fulfillment, but also a stern lesson: *Abandon all hope.* This is not where our yearning will be fulfilled.

It is important that this yearning remains after the intoxication dies: a need for absolute contentment, so urgent as to lead us to look for everlasting joy behind any door. Taking the dream to its natural conclusion. Contentment must be absolute or nothing at all: heaven everywhere, not merely under some fragment of rock, pearly white as it might be.

THE RETURN TO SILENCE

I.

Addiction is so impossible as to be alchemical. An ancient dream of miraculous transformation, like converting lead into gold or intoning prayers to stone until it attains a precious luster. Desperate to wrest a rarer, more sublime condition from the muck and density beneath us: we refuse to accept that this is all there is and yearn for luminous transubstantiation. The addict takes it even further. The material he works with is himself, his own existence, and he combusts his body and mind in the crucible, burning everything away until only the dream remains. It radiates a flash of gold, smolders for a moment, and then disappears into total darkness.

A moment's intoxication will never be an enduring reality, no matter how ideal the prospect. But this is an impossibility that cannot, for good reason, admit defeat. There is a deeper dream that will always be with us. It haunts the darkness and continues to beckon to us no matter how many times it fails. The dream may not even be ours. The earth is "charged with the grandeur of God," wrote the Christian poet Gerard Manley Hopkins. A sublime dream of paradise gleams through the cracks and fissures. The least Christian of ecstasies might serve as a doorway to it.

We seem to suffer without meaning, without end, any reprieve we find fleeting and precarious. The only certainty seems to be more suffering.

Our expectations are bound to be frustrated, our vulnerability violated, our dreams denied and forgotten. But we continue to yearn, with insatiable hope, for an absolute liberation from our suffering, an enduring fulfillment that transcends these agonies, failures, disappointments. This is the single desire that unites us: to enjoy in every moment, however upsetting it might seem, a profound and everlasting consolation, much as the addict aims to alchemize a reliable fulfillment whatever the circumstance.

This is the deepest yearning of them all. Homeland, creative success, fame, pleasure, self-fulfillment, romance, religion, career, political power, wealth, addiction, even suicide: the promise of the absolute wears many masks. The masquerade, in fact, is endless. There will always be new dreams vying to convince us that we have found our dawn. When the flimsiness of the fiction reveals itself, we continue our search, liberated by our homelessness, for a moment, to recognize another direction.

Just ahead might be a reality that feels more like home, better corresponding to our ideas, dreams, and hopes. Our eagerness for it permeates everything. It also invites the confusion we've seen before, and to which everyone, addict and scientist alike, is vulnerable. Our fantasies not only become indistinguishable from existence; they come to possess *more* reality than it, with even direct evidence subordinated to our designs. The dream, the fiction, the paradigm not simply true, but transcendently, absolutely true. This is the apotheosis to which most of our fictions tend, before they fall, like Icarus, to earth. We dream our way into heaven, only to realize we have wandered far from home, into the wilderness, perhaps into hell.

●

I had heard of Marcus for some time before actually meeting him. His older brother Matthew had been a patient for many years: a successful real estate developer who had come to me with a substantial dependence on prescription painkillers. Matthew had done well. There was an uneventful detoxification, few persistent problems, minimal cravings, no lapses. Or more accurately: no lapses at the time of this writing.

Though Matthew's success had very little to do with anything unique I had done for him—sometimes patients respond to standard treatment and never look back—he maintained the belief that I had performed an extraordinary feat and began to recommend friends and family to me, including a sister and a cousin. Marcus was in the background of each of these encounters: mentioned at least once by everyone I met as the most addicted, the most recalcitrant, a family legend. "He thinks because he's in pain then he has an excuse," Matthew said. "And, yeah, the pain is legit, but so what. It doesn't mean he should be putting three hundred dollars' worth of cocaine up his nose every day and drinking himself shit-faced to numb himself even more. If there's a guy who needs to see you, then he is it. Problem is, he never will."

Marcus was in my office within the year. I hear his brother's words—*the problem is, he never will*—every time I see him. It reminds me of how precarious our certainties are, for better and for worse. We make fixed conclusions about ourselves and about others as if we are fit for the task; the problem is we never are. The only conclusion we can make is that change is coming.

What brought Marcus to treatment was an accident. He had been visiting Las Vegas for a tattoo convention and scored cocaine from a dealer he didn't know, touted as having the best product, with a client list that included celebrities and high rollers. "I had a taste of it at the club," he told me. "The stuff felt right, more than right. It did what it was supposed to. But there was more to it than that. The texture itself was totally on point. It had that right level of flakiness, softness, and weight: there was no question it was the real deal. I bought two eight balls [a quarter of an ounce, or several grams] to make sure I could get through the weekend."

He remembers doing a few bumps in the club bathroom, and feeling overcome with a warm and pleasant sedation, as if overcome by sleep. He woke up surrounded by medics, defibrillator pads on his chest. "The stuff was laced with fentanyl. I don't know why anyone would do something so criminal, passing off dope as cocaine. Just a few lines nearly killed me. If I hadn't made a crash in the stall as I fell, I'd be another overdose in Las Vegas, found on a toilet after it was too late."

Fentanyl is a highly potent synthetic opioid that has been adulterating drug supplies since the late 1970s, with a dramatic uptick over the past decade. It adds a punch, though an unexpected, occasionally deadly one. Even seasoned opioid users have overdosed because their heroin or prescription pills were cut with this more potent drug. They think they're getting their usual dose, when in fact it might be far stronger and deadlier. Even more alarming is when cocaine, molly (MDMA), or benzodiazepines, like Xanax, are cut with fentanyl; one can't help but suspect malice somewhere along the supply chain given that most users of these drugs, like Marcus, may not have any tolerance to opioids and will be far more likely to overdose.

"As soon as I realized what had happened, I cried and couldn't stop crying, thinking of the risk I was running, thinking of my wife and daughter. They had brought me back with a naloxone shot. But it may end any time. I can't keep doing this, it is absolutely crazy to keep using. And yet I don't want to stop. That is idiotic, but there it is. I nearly died. I need to stop. And I can't imagine stopping."

He was in that agitated impasse characteristic of addiction. Like Fred, like Ahmed, he had come to recognize that change was needed, and was seeking the support he couldn't provide for himself. And yet he was also recoiling from the possibilities ahead. *I can't imagine stopping.* Perhaps addiction might most properly be called a disease of imagination: the mind gets so overheated in one direction that it loses the capacity to imagine anything else.

●

As with the scientist, our challenge is to walk a razor's edge between Quixote and skeptic: a dream of luminous fulfillment on one side, the dark of deepest night on the other. We are called, whether we recognize it or not, to imagine a home for ourselves that reconciles the two. Otherwise, we risk despair and nihilism: an agonized grasping at whatever seems to puncture, if only for a hopeless moment, the absolute darkness.

Plato, one of the first mythologists in this tradition, offers a path particularly relevant to our story. Like other fictions, it can be both illuminating and blinding. Plato proposed that at the foundation of all things are what he called Forms: absolute and universal Ideas existing beyond space and time in a numinous realm. Plato meant by *Idea* something very different than the common meaning. Ideas are, like *noumena*, the sacred archetypes behind the veil of phenomena; they create the perceptible and "material" world much as the eternal shapes of a circle or triangle originate in geometry and find expression in the stones and designs of our homes. Plato regarded our experience, and the phenomenal world more generally, as an echo of these numinous Forms. Even what we take to be our own identities are reflections issuing from that more perfect and elusive dimension: wisps of shadow on the walls of a cave.

Plato tells a story that inverts the customary order. Experience is the representation; the idea is reality. And our access to the real world might be understood as a direct experience of these essential Forms: what he calls *noesis*, or higher understanding.

Whether this image of the world is true isn't the right question. Plato was endeavoring, unlike a scientist or theologian, to promote intuition and insight, not to articulate an absolute map that might be memorized like scripture. Further, his metaphysical fictions are beyond the true/false binaries of intersubjective verification; they point not toward facts, but toward perspectives that might enlarge us. Their value rests in their capacity to expand the possibilities of being.

This has meant troubling, confusing, and interrogating us as well, inviting us to attend more closely to the mystery at hand. Millenia after Plato's death, we remain haunted by the soul-body divide he had bequeathed to us, and by *the question of being* that its bifurcations and dualities bring to light, the question Heidegger, a later philosopher, believed it is our supreme task to engage, and to continue engaging: that there is *this* where there might be nothing.

Variations on these questions existed in the ancient world before Plato, in the philosophies of Empedocles and Parmenides, as well as in Vedanta. It is a core question of being human: What are the reasons for our conflict, confusion, and desire? What is *this* really? Is our existence one thing, many things, real or unreal, perhaps nothing at all?

Plato took this inquiry into "the being of being," as Aristotle expressed it later, in a specific direction, extending it to what might be *absolute*. He was the first thinker in the Western canon to attend to our yearning for it. We continue to wrangle with it in diverse ways. Many scientists, for instance, behave like covert Platonists, searching for an *absolute* and fixed world ("reality," "objectivity," "matter," "subatomic statistical distributions") apart from the *illusory* and unstable one of appearances and subjectivity.

We know neither where this yearning comes from, nor where it's going, but there it is, showing up as paradigms, ideologies, dogmas, addictions. We yearn for an absolute home, with eagerness, with desperation, with entitlement, with confusion, with all the agitations that come with experiencing any lack. This agitation for absolute reality, if left unexamined, compels us to fall readily into delusion, error, and ignorance—to see the unreal as real.

Plato recognized this agitation, perhaps did his part to further stoke it. He also suggested a solution, establishing a school to educate seekers to pass through the inevitable confusions that dualism produces. The Forms of reality may come to be directly intuited by the seeker in due time, without mediation. But until then, Plato advised a rigorous path of inquiry, self-analysis, and purification. Questioning everything, we excise each of our conceits, with Socratic not-knowing, until we arrive at the *noesis* of recognition. And here, Quixote and skeptic, darkness and dream, knowing and not-knowing, might finally find their peace.

●

Ahmed, Marcus, Fred, just about every person struggling with addiction speaks the same line. I want to feel better, I want to be better, I want to use, I want to not use, I want to feel as if I were using without using, I want to be better while using, I want to be better while not using, I want to be free, I want to use and be free, I want to be free without using, I want the impossible, I want everything, I want everything.

●

It is more than the hope for *noesis* that might compel us toward Plato. His promise appeals to our deepest yearnings. With entry into the transcendent world of Forms comes an absolute experience of the phenomena dearest to us: bliss and understanding at the numinous source itself. The rift between what we want and what is received is finally annealed in a perpetual sunrise of delight, with nothing lacking: the dream of heaven made flesh. We will find ourselves illuminated, Plato promises, by an otherworldly radiance of which our suns and stars, with their countless spinning worlds, are pale and flickering embers.

Even licentious beds, Baudelaire wrote, are touched by dawn and its Absolutes. The ambivalence of the line is worth noting. Are we to understand that the Absolute will cast its severe light on our depravities come morning? Or does it enrich them, endowing our sins with the luminous power of sunrise? The Absolute, Baudelaire suggests, is far from a stable ideal: it is murky and ambiguous, glinting with both the light of seduction, the light of accusation. And there are glimmers of dawn everywhere: in science, in religion, in intoxication.

Plato was not interested in exploring these ambiguities, glimmers, or twilights. Nor was he interested in constructing a system that might serve as a conceptual citadel. He aimed to make a home in the absolute, and to support others called to that endeavor, so as to engage in sustained noesis with its Forms. His philosophy is one of the many contemplative paths, like the system of yoga articulated by Patanjali, involving a method, discipline, and mode of inquiry for achieving this communion. Such a path may be helpful because it prepares its initiates for certain challenges and encourages principles, such as nonviolence, self-mastery, and dispassion, that can guide the journey. It is far from a straight or easy road: a greater world disrupts the flimsy forms of this interpreted one. The danger is comparable to that faced by an addict presented with the exuberant promises of his intoxication. A foretaste of the absolute, propelling a lifetime of mad pursuit.

We know what may happen after the initial inebriations of philosophy, or licentious beds, or God. Once our eyes are pierced by such extraordinary light, even if it flashes secondhand like moonlight from powder, ideas, or flesh, they might grow blind to anything else. Such fullness of presence—intoxicating in its overwhelming abundance—inflicts a gaping absence upon its abrupt retreat that nothing can possibly complete. It is the sum of all that is good, yet even more than that: our deepest hope for what this world might provide, and an acute remembrance of how profoundly we lack it, realized in a burst of luminous fulfillment.

It is no wonder why some of us will chase this radiance, or at least a shadow of it, to the very end of the night. Guidance through that darkness, whether the helmsman be Plato, Patanjali, or Bill W., might protect us from drowning in its infernal depths.

•

Marcus has had many incarnations. He had been a professional skateboarder, a bass player in a punk band, a snowboarder, a painter, an art teacher, and now a tattoo artist. Each of his roles he had inhabited completely, as if his life depended on it. But no role was inhabited completely enough: he would discard one and assume another eventually. "I did whatever I did to the extreme. Skateboarding I would jump stairways everyone else avoided. I would break bones barreling down slopes on my snowboard. The problem was I couldn't stay with anything for too long. My body would keep breaking, I would keep falling, no one would buy my paintings. It was always the long valley of failure at the end, every single time, and I didn't stay with anything long enough for things to turn."

There were certain constants through all of this: drugs, wild behavior, and tattoos. He was covered from the chin down in ink. Getting tattooed had been a passion since adolescence. During a stint as an art teacher, he began learning how to tattoo, gaining experience on his own in his free time initially, and later apprenticing under an artist he admired in the East Village. It was during this period that his use escalated.

"I have real pain from real accidents. A herniated disc in the lumbar region, a pinched cervical nerve, broken bones all over that still ache when I make the wrong move or when the weather is too cold. I was a jackass and did tricks on my board without thinking. Drunken brawls. Beating up knuckleheads, pummeling them against concrete outside bar gigs. Damaging myself as much as them. The result is pain, pain all the time, pain to the point I can barely function without needing something. There are certain positions in tattooing that I can't hold for too long without my entire left side freezing up, pain shooting everywhere, and I feel beaten up for days afterward. But that's exactly how I need to sit, sometimes for several hours, in order to get a piece done. The only way to get through it is to use something, and nothing has helped keep me going like cocaine. It pulls me in, I trance out on the work, and the pain disappears for a while. A few drinks at night brings me back to earth so that I can sleep until the next day, the next session."

Without tattooing, he can't make a living; without cocaine, he can't tattoo; the only logical conclusion, he felt, was he needs cocaine to live. An irrefutable syllogism worthy, perhaps, of science itself. The problem, of course, is that none of it makes sense. Even the incontrovertible rules of reason can't turn mistaken ideas into something real.

"I said a while because the pain always returns, with a vengeance. But that's what I need to bear to create, it's what I have to go through to make pieces that only I can make. It's all worth it in the end, and not just because the bills get paid. There is nothing more satisfying than seeing a finished piece that will last forever. But I don't know how much longer I can do this before my body completely breaks down under the strain."

Addiction is like a parasite, exploiting all the resources of its host to ensure its continuation. Finances, of course, are diverted to it. Satisfaction becomes monopolized by it. Work and relationships keep it going. But the exploitation can be even more insidious. Logic renders its conclusions nearly impossible to resist. The imagination becomes preoccupied with its fantasies. And a patina of idealism might serve to protect the whole show from scrutiny. The long-suffering artist. Pain as a pathway to creation. The eternal hope of art. The fierce courage to be an individual, and to contribute uniquely to the world, burning out in self-immolation, if need be, instead of fading away . . .

"I really don't know what to do right now. I know I need to live differently. I know my wife and daughter deserve better—that I deserve better. What I don't know is whether I can, or whether I really want to."

Marcus is approaching that inflection point at which one world grows more distant and another emerges, even as he doesn't fully recognize it. His hurdle is that this obsolete world is all he knows; it seems the only reality possible to him. He cannot imagine, as he had said before, a different one. This is his crisis, one shared by other addicts resolute on their mad pursuits. He knows the old world is dying, but he cannot imagine not dying with it.

•

We dimly remember, according to Plato, the absolute reality of Forms that is our origin and truth. Reclaiming it, however, does not require moving toward or discovering anything. It is already with us, though long buried and forgotten. What is needed is a profound remembrance.

Plato offers us a compelling myth, interpreting our complicated condition as a kind of exile and amnesia. We are impatient to return home, with nostalgic echoes of this numinous reality in our every thought and yearning. Our impressions carry traces of these perfect Forms; our hopes gesture toward them; our intoxications invite them. But it is a strange kind of homesickness because we haven't really been exiled from anything, except in our minds.

And in our minds we fabricate what seems home. We might be so eager for this absolute ground that we step onto air as if it were earth. Seductive fictions entice our step like traps. They might hold us captive, but at least there is a sense of reunion. To lose this home we have imagined for ourselves, as Marcus knew, seems the end of the world.

Lovers, poets, and madmen, Shakespeare wrote, are of imagination compact. They share an inescapable desire for dwelling in dream and imagination. Their experience is therefore extraordinary and exaggerated, perhaps terrifying. Heaven and hell might participate directly in their lives. Spheres so far removed from the familiar that they might as well be made up. Just around the corner might be a final fulfillment or a hellish abyss.

Their worlds crystallize until they compact into what our consensus calls facts. And they come to be even denser than facts because they seem *absolute*: the substratum of reality itself. William Blake, echoing Plato, gives voice to this certainty: Imagination is the real and eternal world, of which this vegetable universe is just a faint shadow.

Plato had his rigorous approach, but he also recognized the power of these modes. He called madness a gift from the gods, and the poet a light and winged thing, holy and inspired. The long path he advises is not the only way. It might be circumvented, God willing, by a sudden apocalypse of vision. The same sacred fire, it seems, purifies all seekers in the end: gradually, as in the patient exercises of philosophy, or all at once in the flames of a sacrificial pyre.

But such visions also share a kinship, as Shakespeare recognized, with a less exalted madness. The insularity may be nearly violent in its unintelligibility, the ideas so fixed as to seem delusional. The psychotic populating his isolation with a babble of voices, stories, and galaxies is one example.

Another is the addict burning himself up in the radiance of white powder.

•

Cocaine was considered a wonder drug at the turn of the twentieth century, comparable to the superfoods or botanical supplements of today. It increases the levels of certain neurotransmitters—dopamine and norepinephrine—that are associated with stimulation and pleasure, so its appeal is clear. Freud had famously hoped to make it the lynchpin of his academic career and sung its praises as a cure-all before moving on to other fantasies. Over-the-counter preparations were a dime a dozen; a variety of beverages and tonics included cocaine to increase energy, lift mood, suppress pain, regulate appetite, boost confidence, improve eyesight, alleviate sinus problems, and even cure morphine addiction.

Cocaine is now popularly represented as a drug of the moneyed class. But it is not its price or demographic that accounts for the image; it is consumed by people of all backgrounds, with the wealthy accounting for only a fraction of users. Stock it up to an accidental kind of branding. Since the 1970s and '80s, cocaine has been identified with the wild debauches of Wall Street, upper-crust disco hedonism, languorous penthouse parties. This has deepened the allure by giving cocaine a gloss of glamour, further fictionalizing its crystalline shimmer into something grander and allowing users to better disregard, for a moment, that they are inhaling powders of dubious provenance into their noses in cramped public bathrooms. The glamour is a recent invention, as befits a shape-shifter that has assumed many masks: from South American folk medicine, to panacea, to anesthetic, to an elite drug of conspicuous addiction.

It is not simply the user, of course, who is captivated by the fictions of intoxication. A shared story develops around a drug that has very little to do with what it is. This is another way that culture creates itself: by constructing myths around what it consumes.

There is one period in cocaine's history that often goes unmentioned. For most of its tenure in the US, cocaine was neither superfood nor superdrug. Cocaine was functionally criminalized in the second decade of the twentieth century after being denigrated as a toxin that depraves its users. This was not due, however, to careful data linking it to addiction or medical problems. If that were the case, alcohol would have been criminalized, too—that came later, of course, during Prohibition, which did not last long. This policy wasn't about science or facts. "A great many people think they are thinking,"

William James is reputed to have said, "when they are merely rearranging their prejudices." The same could be said about policy making: the enshrining of our prejudices into law and order.

In most cases, it is not a prejudice against things, but against people, that dictates unreasonable policy. This is true, as well, of drug laws. The modern history of drug criminalization is propelled by two antihumanist currents. The first is a moralistic scruple against unearned joy and pleasure, with the proper aim of human activity being productive labor in the service of "higher things." The second is the preservation of racial and class dominance. This latter force has been particularly important for understanding the uneven and arbitrary approach of drug policy, with some substances demonized while others, such as tobacco or alcohol, simply regulated for most of their history. Every criminalized drug has been strongly identified with an out-group, mostly racial but also cultural, during the campaign against it. Cocaine was an early example. Beginning in 1890, cocaine was blamed for the "fiendish" sexual appetites of Black men, with politicians and scientists claiming, absent any evidence, that cocaine fueled "Negro rapes and other crimes," gave them superhuman strength, and even rendered them bulletproof. The only truth to these claims was that Black people used cocaine. Or, rather, they were provided it: it had been regularly given to Black laborers to increase their energy, reduce their appetite, and improve work stamina. It went from a White tool promoting subservient labor to a dark, devilish drug inciting violence. The power of fiction: even white powder can be painted black. Such racist fearmongering provided the primary justification for cocaine being outlawed by 1915, which legalized further oppression against an already beleaguered population. This fable of cocaine-fueled Negro criminality died out for a while, only to be resurrected during the so-called crack epidemic of the 1980s, which depicted Black people as maddened by cocaine, this time as freebase, once again.

These representations leave echoes and traces that go on to influence more private fictions. Marcus sniffs cocaine and the drug is like compacted histories: he is a mail runner chewing coca to endure the steep and jagged trails of the Andes, a slave dripping sweat as he works the field, a plump banker sipping a few fireside glasses of coca-infused Vin Mariani for that perfect evening balance of rest and stimulation, before doing bumps between lap dances, between sets with his New York City hardcore band, to keep himself going after one too many Jägermeister shots at a frat house, on a yacht with VC friends who scored premium uncut direct from Colombia, at a private club with insomniac models, a cocktail lounge, a dive bar with downtown tattoo luminaries. Pulsing through the masquerade is the white heat of the catecholamine fire, cascading shadows brought together in a climax of identical sunburst, skin bursting open, blood rushing forth emblazoned with dense designs that will continue to throb with life, Marcus hopes, well after everything else is dead.

●

"There's a right way to do anything," Marcus told me, "and a wrong way; good art and bad art; you either land the trick, or you don't. This should be obvious, just try your best to do what's right, it's that simple. But even when you spell it out for people, like don't go out in the sun after I spent thirty hours hunched over them to give them the perfect piece, they still send you pictures of themselves literally at the beach as if it's all good, their fresh tattoo getting the full blast of the sun, I kid you not. It's enough to say screw it all, why even bother."

The tattooing isn't simply a job he does well, and which pays the bills. It is his most perfect form of self-expression: his great and essential contribution to the world, whether or not "knuckleheads" give it the right care. "The most we can do is to make a mark on things, leave a memory of ourselves that can't be erased."

This is a yearning common to many artists, transcending one's limits by creating a vision that will endure. There is nothing else to live for, he feels. He is nihilistic in every other respect but this one. Carving his truths onto the eternal skin of the earth. The fantasy is compelling, even in its obvious impossibility. Where is the legacy? What skin is eternal? Tattoos are only as alive as people are, whether on living skin, in museum displays, or in magazines. But this is true of everything else we take to be imperishable, be it carved on stone, paper, or flesh. So much of our world is permeated with a dream of permanence: our ideas, our property, our institutions, our names and bodies. The great temptation is to trade away our possibilities and freedom for what we take to be more essential.

Where is the exit from such madness? The prison seems airtight. Marcus needs the relief that cocaine provides him; he needs the anesthetized opportunity to make a special mark on the world. Nothing else matters. He seems destined to confuse want with necessity: he seems destined for addiction. Then there is the apparent permanence of habit that has carried him through each workweek: wake to cocaine, tattooing until broken, drunk at night, repeat. The first indication of how this system might be dismantled comes from his reason for seeing me: the accident that revealed the truth. Overdose, then awakening. He had recognized that his life has not been what it seems, hardly the pursuit of fulfillment he had hoped for—and that he is courting destruction with every line. This is the suffering that gives us access to what is most real in his life: the risks he runs; his shame and fear; the loss of freedom; the deteriorating relationship with his wife and child. Undergirding all is the tremendous pain, physical and otherwise, that worsens each day he remains captive to his addictions.

The pain may be enough to wake him to the deception. But is it enough to motivate change? How does he change when he has lost the capacity to imagine doing so?

•

Freedom exists as *possibility*. When a sense of what is possible is lost, then freedom has been forgotten too. To reclaim freedom means recognizing that everything can be otherwise. It also means maintaining the capacity to extricate oneself from whatever appears to be the case.

There are, of course, many possibilities available to Marcus. He can remain as he is, without changing anything. Or he can stop using cocaine and drinking, become more temperate with his tattooing, perhaps pursue other outlets for his creativity. Maybe he might abandon tattooing altogether for work that is less physically demanding, take up stretching and physical exercise, and more generally revise his sense of what is worth doing, what is meaningful.

The question of "reality" becomes particularly pressing. There are many (un)realities from which we might start out, each creating its own horizon of possibility. Which offers the truest and most expansive path? There are a few bedrock truths guiding the way. Marcus is suffering; and though he yearns to overcome his suffering, he has only managed to deepen it. This is the unadorned reality of his existence. The rest of his story might be entirely unreal: a masquerade of fictions.

Marcus has further complicated his situation by fixing on an idea of who he is and what he needs. The deception here, as in every case of addiction, is that life amounts to the trance of certain desires and fulfillments. He knows better, but the pull is visceral as much as it is epistemological. These lies have become his life, silently sustaining him. And his suffering has only deepened under their weight, as has his confusion of what is real and what is not.

Marcus's horizon of possibility has been forfeited, with only one world available to him, becoming more obsolete every day. Yet the horizon continues to glow with heightened reality, as if there were no better tomorrow of happiness. He pursues, with a narrow-eyed focus bordering on blindness, what seems the fulfillment of his responsibilities, as artist, family man, breadwinner—while failing, invariably, on all fronts. A dead end of total contradiction, charged with the spectral light of false possibility. The same warning that Fred received awaits us all at such an impasse: *abandon all hope.*

Abandoning all hope in false possibility: this might seem obvious to everyone. But few allow themselves the sweeping hopelessness required. Addicts are faced with this despair daily, even as they often opt to look away. They fail and continue failing, beyond hope and yet refusing to relinquish hope. From the wreckage might emerge a hope that is not quite hope because it points to the reality already before us. The primordial dream beckons through the rents and cracks. Our anguish also beckons, as always, but we might turn to it without self-deception or complacency this time, and endeavor to experience it wakefully, beyond the impulse to give it the old names and forms. It is neither craving nor despair, addiction nor slavery. It is the most meaningful and illuminating moment we might have: the opportunity to pass through our shattered hopes toward the ever-present ground of ( ).

This is our inmost possibility as we flail our way through the night. We might awaken to its fluid expanse at any moment. The accident led Marcus to recognize the problem: he is stuck in a seemingly impossible situation. He also knows that this recognition is not enough. The way forward remains dark because he is hard-pressed to find a solution different from the one he knows. He is like a scientist locked inside his system. But he feels the anguish of it, which is a start. It signals a breakdown in the paradigm, an invitation to step into the greater world. My role here is to support Marcus as he destabilizes the old deception and cultivates a more honest relationship with the pain of things. This requires, before all else, providing him a refreshed sense of possibility, as well as encouraging the commitment to embrace it.

But how to help someone regain something he has so thoroughly forgotten? The truest possibility: nothing has been lost as to be regained. He needs guidance now so that he might open his eyes to what is before him, and what has always been: his suffering, the instructive immensity of it, and the freedom and responsibility to engage with that pain differently, with the hope of an ecstatic *being experience* filling the hopeless silence.

II.

Ketamine has had many incarnations. It originated as an analogue of phencyclidine (PCP) in the 1960s, and binds to the same receptors that PCP does, but with a shorter half-life that allows for more practical, controllable administration. We know what has become of PCP: the scare stories, its reputation for causing people to become psychotic and violent. But this is also the demon that spawned ketamine, recognized by the World Health Organization (WHO) as one of the world's essential medicines. Perhaps the benefits of ketamine might challenge the rigidity with which PCP is viewed, if only to encourage a more balanced and nuanced understanding.

The main virtue of ketamine, and of PCP if used at the proper dose, is that it functions as an anesthetic, while preserving the patient's ability to breathe properly and maintain normal cardiovascular functioning. This gives patients the opportunity to receive surgical procedures without requiring intubation and ventilation, as would be needed in acute settings like accident sites and the battlefield. Ketamine has therefore permitted life-saving procedures to be effectively performed that had previously been impossible.

Ketamine is a dissociative, meaning that it fragments aspects of experience that are ordinarily integrated (e.g., the sense of space, time, self, body, reality). It is thought to work by disconnecting the feeling (mesolimbic) region of the brain from the thinking and appraising part (cortical prefrontal); this occurs through blockade of the neurotransmitter glutamate at neural circuits involved in communication between these regions. When given at anesthetic doses, ketamine blocks crosstalk between these regions to such a degree that loss of consciousness and anesthesia result.

When ketamine is given at doses that do not cause anesthesia—what is called the sub-anesthetic range—it behaves very differently. Snorted as a powder, taken orally, and injected intramuscularly or intravenously, sub-anesthetic ketamine produces a broad spectrum of effects similar to those of psychedelics: trance, insight, visions, mystical-type experiences, and other non-ordinary states of consciousness. These effects first came to public attention in the 1970s, shortly after ketamine was introduced as an anesthetic, with individuals as diverse as John Lilly, Salvador Roquet, Timothy Leary, and Genesis P-Orridge coming to celebrate the experience as unparalleled in intensity, otherworldliness, and psychoactive scope. It wasn't simply an interesting drug for some of them, but a portal to another dimension. Lilly believed that it provided him consistent access to an extraterrestrial source of higher consciousness, which he called ECCO; P-Orridge enjoyed interacting with the fluid androgynous spirit that seemed to inhabit it.

The experience spans the range from gentle and meditative free association, with small amounts, to a primordial unitive state beyond space, time, life, and death at higher doses. A unique property of ketamine is its propensity to cause intense states of disembodiment and depersonalization, whereby consciousness loses its moorings in the body and in a personal sense of self. The mind may also dissolve into a vast and unfathomable void: the "k-hole." This detachment from the ordinary coordinates of existence can be quite disorienting. Some people find the experience enjoyable and refreshing, with the absolute freedom of consciousness apparently restored. Ketamine is now one of the most popular "party drugs": sniffed at the same clubs and dance events where cocaine had once reigned supreme. In addition to having recreational appeal, ketamine holds interest for those drawn to using hallucinogens therapeutically.

Psychedelic therapy refers to psychotherapy aimed at harnessing the "transformative" potential of such substances. Psychedelic therapy has a variety of styles, and incorporates a wide array of hallucinogens, but there is a common approach: preparing individuals for a powerful "psychedelic" experience, guiding them through it, and working afterward toward consolidating any benefits, insights, or perspectival shifts that might have occurred. A more modest approach is "psycholytic" (mind dissolving) psychotherapy, whereby the medicine is intended to catalyze the psychotherapeutic process by heightening the person's capacity to engage fruitfully with it: inhibitions might be weakened, introspection enhanced, and a more "mindful" vantage point cultivated while the person is under the influence. Psychedelic therapy centralizes the substance; psycholytic therapy centralizes the broader therapeutic process. Both models emerged in the 1950s using LSD, mescaline, and psilocybin, with research suggesting they may be helpful for various conditions including depression, anxiety, and alcoholism.

Hallucinogen-assisted therapies became obsolete in legal settings after serotonergic hallucinogens were outlawed in 1973. The target of the criminalization campaign this time was not a racial but a political-cultural minority: hippies, yippies, Beats, pranksters, trippers, and other members of the counterculture. There was a special convergence between the spirit of the 1960s and the effects of hallucinogens; they each involved a revolt against the established order. The antiwar, anticonformist counterculture was of course much more threatening to the social fabric than the transient disruptions of hallucinogens, especially to a country embroiled in Vietnam and ravaged by internal divisions. But such is the logic of drug criminalization, focusing on a drug to diminish a people.

Interestingly, the most significant public health dangers of hallucinogens did not come from the counterculture, but from the establishment itself. Starting in the early 1950s, well before hallucinogens were used popularly, they were being researched by the US government in clandestine studies aimed at assessing their wartime potential, capacity for brainwashing or mind control, and propensity to elicit confessions.

This CIA research program, code-named "Bluebird," MK-NAOMI, and MK-ULTRA, remains shrouded in secrecy despite concluding decades ago. The little information that has survived sketches a harrowing picture of the scope of "research" conducted with taxpayer dollars: providing large doses of LSD to coerced prisoners on a daily basis for months at a time, training sex workers to administer LSD to clients to assess its impact on sexual behavior, and secretly spiking cocktails with LSD at parties in the West Village of Manhattan, while studying the reactions of these unwitting test subjects through a one-way mirror. Some of the casualties from these outrageous endeavors, which ultimately "failed to find clear military potential" according to their architect Sidney Gottlieb, have been documented, and include death, insanity, and severe trauma. But the full extent to which our citizens suffered at the hands of these far-reaching covert programs, nearly cartoonish in their madcap and diabolical inventiveness, remains unclear; all records pertaining to the investigations and findings of MK-ULTRA were destroyed by Dr. Gottlieb and the CIA.

The public health dangers ensuing from recreational use, the target of so much negative media attention, pale in comparison to what was perpetrated by the CIA. Any personal risk, it now seems, was associated with irresponsible use, as is the case with all other substances. The true "harms" were cultural and epistemological. Perhaps the greatest danger that recreational use posed was the irreducible *privacy* of the experience: this truth is mine, luminously mine, not theirs, not yours, not the priest's, certainly not the state's. Normal people were suddenly poets, lovers, and madmen, having gained apparent access to the deepest essence of things, unencumbered by the words of others. God, truth, eternity, and other elusive absolutes could now be glimpsed with as little as 100 micrograms. It doesn't matter whether such radical subjectivity led to reality or not; it challenged the monopoly on "truth" claimed by politicians, educators, clergy, and other guardians of "the system." It also threatened, more fundamentally, to restore reality to its humble origins in the vast wilderness of experience, where it might be cleansed of lies, cleansed of truth.

This revolutionary potential was proclaimed loudly in the streets. Hallucinogens were lauded by many popular figures, including Timothy

Leary and Allen Ginsberg, as powerful agents for disrupting convention, social submission, and received wisdom. The subversion extended to inspiring alternative modes of living, such as anarchism, pacifism, mysticism, anticonsumerism, and communal living, all of which challenged the fragile foundations of the American mainstream. This played right into the hands of antidrug politics. The counterculture, of course, was questioning the dominant systems anyway, whether they were using LSD or not. But the aim was to delegitimize the counterculture more fundamentally. The script was the same as that of "the Negro cocaine problem": sensationalized and largely untrue reports of young people going insane and engaging in destructive behavior while using LSD. Reason, civility, and good judgment destroyed, perhaps permanently, by a brain toxin.

The same properties that led hallucinogens to be feared (and to be studied by the CIA as a potential bioweapon) also account for their therapeutic potential. Their visionary effects might indeed lead to violating the illusions of polite society, but they might also lead to seeing through the more personal fictions that crowd our minds. The schemes that organize our experience come to be lifted, for better or worse, so that the sublime and devastating immensity of each moment might be unveiled. This interruption in the person's worldview might allow for concomitantly imprinting a different one, especially in tandem with their apparent promotion of hyper-suggestibility. (*Suggestogen* has been proposed as a possible name for these substances.) People might thus become psychedelicized into better killing machines or more obedient citizens, as in the MK-ULTRA experiments or LSD trials with soldiers and recidivist criminals. Or healthier habits and values might be imparted, as in LSD-assisted treatment trials for alcoholism.

No suggestogen or psychedelic was powerful enough, however, to persuade the keepers of law and order. These substances could not survive the multipronged clampdown on unrest and political dissent that bubbled through the 1960s and boiled over into the early '70s. Drug criminalization policy was implemented at the height of anti–Vietnam War sentiment, under the guise of protecting the public. The potential benefits to individuals in clinical settings, it was argued, were not worth the risks that recreational use posed to the status quo. Or so the status quo decreed. And anything threatening the status quo should be addressed with the full force of the law, beginning with the people—the peaceniks, the emerging youth counterculture—who consumed these toxic substances.

There was one exception to criminalization. Ketamine is the only potent hallucinogen that remains legal and which can be administered by a physician. Another incarnation: ketamine as Trojan horse, allowing the psychedelic model to maintain its place in the clinic. This has made it possible to provide psycholytic or psychedelic therapy legally in the face of drug criminalization, with various providers doing so since at least the 1980s. Research had even been conducted in the 1990s in St. Petersburg, Russia, suggesting so-called ketamine psychedelic therapy had promising effects on addiction—until, as primary investigator Evgeny Krupitsky told me, ketamine was reclassified by Russia as a "drug of abuse," and all research and sub-anesthetic use ceased.

Ketamine remains alive and well in the US and most other countries. But there was another incarnation waiting in the wings. In 2000, researchers at Yale discovered that a single forty-minute IV infusion of ketamine exerted powerful and fast-acting effects on depression in people resistant to other treatments, with benefits lasting on average seventy-two hours. This is in contrast to standard antidepressant medications, which typically take several weeks to work, if they work at all. Interestingly, Dr. Krupitsky had been visiting Yale as a fellow in the prior decade, working with the same team that would go on to conduct the research. But its antidepressant effects were not studied in a psychedelic or even psychotherapeutic framework. Instead, ketamine was administered as a stand-alone treatment—as a *biological* intervention, without therapy, without guidance, and without attention to its psychoactive effects. The closest comparison is ECT (electroconvulsive therapy): a procedure intended to jolt the brain into a more normal state. This finding has been replicated in depressed people in a number of international studies, with some early data showing that a single ketamine infusion may also help anxiety conditions, such as PTSD (posttraumatic stress disorder) and OCD (obsessive-compulsive disorder).

Ketamine was resurrected as a "novel antidepressant pharmacotherapy," with "unprecedented" effects on the brain and on psychiatric symptoms. Hundreds of studies have been conducted, in rodents and humans, to clarify what these brain effects might be: glutamate modulation, promotion of synaptic growth, neurogenesis, changes in neural connections, functional changes. Pharmaceutical companies have also entered the fray in the hope of capitalizing on these discoveries. Ketamine itself has no commercial potential: it is an old medicine dating back half a century with "adverse" psychoactive effects and, what is worse for business, a generic status precluding patent applications. The holy grail is a medicine that duplicates ketamine's putative mechanisms of action, while lending itself to conventional psychiatric treatment: no IVs, no unusual psychoactive properties, a preferably oral formulation. The pharmaceutical company Janssen, for example, has patented s-ketamine, which is one half of ketamine (the other, less potent half is r-ketamine), and managed to just barely secure FDA approval to provide an in-office intranasal formulation for treatment-resistant depression. At about $1,000 a dose, s-ketamine is half the bioequivalent antidepressant dose of ketamine, but neither more effective nor less psychoactive, and nearly 1,000 times more expensive. Ongoing efforts to "tame the ketamine tiger," as the inventor of ketamine, E. F. Domino, put it, include investigating a patented version of the other stereoisomer, r-ketamine; testing patented metabolites such as r,r-dihydroxynorketamine; and researching comparable glutamate modulators. This may be ketamine's final incarnation: a hydra-headed big pharma behemoth, spurring the next wave of blockbuster antidepressants.

It might have gone in another direction. Ketamine presents a possibility for mental illness and addiction to be approached differently in conventional settings. As a generic medicine with psychoactive effects that may be particularly helpful when combined with psychotherapy, it suggests a new paradigm in mainstream medicine: away from a medication-based approach that privileges neural mechanisms over everything else and toward a treatment model less beholden to profit-driven industry, better integrated with psychotherapy, more likely to promote persistent and independent well-being, and more attentive to the power of non-ordinary experience. But such a shift would have required overcoming prejudices and pressures that had been molding psychiatry for a long time. There are two options when reality intrudes: change our ideas to accommodate the disruption or change the disruption so that our fictions emerge unscathed. The latter is how we deepen our delusions; we tame the tiger, or kill it altogether, so that it might better reside in our dominant systems.

The potential disruption is not entirely tamed. Numerous providers continue to give ketamine, despite the availability of s-ketamine, due to its greater apparent effectiveness and versatility. Ketamine-assisted psychotherapy has gained in popularity, especially with more popular interest in psychedelic therapy over the past few years, even as issues of access remain unresolved, with most clinics offering it at high cost. Further, wellness-oriented clinics have emerged offering ketamine for improving overall well-being, commodifying the medicine into a trendy lifestyle product very much in line with the psychedelic zeitgeist.

Also emerging, however, are clinics focused on evidence-based use, fair access, and communal responsibility. Similarly, more researchers are concerning themselves with how ketamine might fit into new models of psychiatric care. Even as there are pressures to tame it or milk it, ketamine remains poised, in the spirit of its countercultural forebears, to create holes in various systems of thought, both public and personal.

●

When I started seeing Marcus in my private practice, I was working on a project in my clinical research lab testing the safety and feasibility of a new treatment framework involving ketamine for cocaine addiction. At that point, my team had already completed a few laboratory studies with ketamine, as well as a clinical trial combining a ketamine infusion with mindfulness training. For the laboratory studies, we recruited cocaine-addicted people who were not interested in stopping; the main aim was to test whether ketamine would shift them into no longer seeking out cocaine. We found that, in the days following an infusion, ketamine reduced craving, enhanced motivation to change, and led participants to turn down the choice to use cocaine in our laboratory. The most intriguing mechanism was the change in perspectives and values, with participants acquiring a strong sense that it was possible for them to stop, as well as the motivation to do so. This suggested a new way to intervene in addiction: helping people make better choices by creating an opportunity for refreshing their perspectives, values, and motivations.

These participants were not depressed, so none of the above benefits was an antidepressant effect. That said, however, one similarity between depressed and addicted people is relevant. Both disorders involve losing a sense of possibility, much as Marcus had, and resigning oneself to the way things seem to be. This is called "learned helplessness": it refers to the passivity that animals develop when they've been repeatedly shocked. The pain seems uncontrollable, it is relentless, and the animal gives up trying to overcome it, curls up instead into a quivering ball of fur. This is thought to occur through unhealthy learning processes implicating glutamate, which might be corrected by ketamine. "I've tried stopping so many times," Marcus told me when we first met, "that I no longer bother trying. I know how it's going to end up, so what's the point of setting myself up for disappointment?"

These repeated bouts of what seems uncontrollable anguish—trying to stop, failing, and failing again—can be demoralizing, even paralyzing. Then there is the impact of other problems that come with being in the world: mortality, social oppression, trauma, abusive relationships, medical issues, lack of resources, limited opportunities, moral injuries, and other types of persistent stress, all of which might feed the sense of futility as well. A destructive fiction fossilizes: existence is grim, with no possibility for a fuller existence than what one has. One way to interpret the effects on motivation observed in our studies, therefore, is that this undercurrent of despair is disrupted, with addicted individuals emerging from their stagnation and feeling galvanized to pursue another way forward. This might be due to the effects of ketamine on glutamate-related learning, as well as to mechanisms involving neural plasticity, where neurons that had been pruned as a result of chronic stress begin to bud new dendritic connections.

Our findings in the laboratory were recognized by NIH, which provided funding for the research, as important and potentially paradigm shifting. These data also gave hope that a long-elusive treatment for cocaine addiction might be near. There are currently no FDA-approved treatments for this disorder, despite billions of research dollars having been spent to this end in the US alone. We therefore set out to explore the benefits of ketamine in randomized controlled trials (RCTs), the "gold standard" for studying clinical efficacy. RCTs evaluate the efficacy of a generalizable treatment protocol—a manualized therapy, a medication, a procedure—by comparing it to a "control," or placebo, condition, to which usually half the study participants are randomly assigned in a double-blind manner. This helps us understand whether the protocol is truly effective for the target diagnosis by controlling for individual variation, bias, and the power of suggestion.

In a study with cocaine-dependent, non-depressed people, my lab found that a single forty-minute ketamine infusion combined with mindfulness-based and motivational therapy promoted abstinence. The percentage of people receiving ketamine who stopped using cocaine was around 50 percent, as compared to about 10 percent in the control arm (involving a benzodiazepine intended to maintain the blind by providing some psychoactive effects). This effect was highly promising. It also suggested that a single ketamine infusion can lead to enduring clinical benefits when integrated into a framework that harnesses its therapeutic potential. We have continued to explore this question in more sophisticated and larger RCTs, also supported by NIH.

This treatment model is also relevant to other addictions. Alcoholism, for example, remains difficult to disrupt for some people, despite a variety of pharmacological and behavioral options. In a separate RCT, we integrated a single infusion of ketamine into a framework of psychotherapy intended to harness the clinical potential of the medicine. As in the RCT with cocaine users, subjects with alcoholism received psychotherapy and behavioral support throughout the trial, with more behavioral sessions concentrated into the days following the infusion to take advantage of any window of opportunity that ketamine provided. The rates of success were high, with ketamine showing promise for this disorder as well.

I felt that Marcus would benefit from ketamine-assisted treatment, though it was too expensive for him. The trial I was running at the time was a safety study, with no placebo control. Therefore, all participants receive ketamine along with a novel framework of psychotherapy: a benefit for those otherwise unable to receive this promising medication, for financial or other reasons. I suggested that he contact the lab and look into it. I was heartened to be informed that he was deemed eligible and that he had consented to begin treatment.

●

Marcus ended up doing well, sustaining abstinence for most of the trial and making enduring changes. It remains a mystery, however, what ketamine actually did—or if it did anything at all.

Some of the neural mechanisms proposed for the benefits of ketamine were sketched out above. The brain model has made much of these effects and has tended to dismiss any psychoactive properties as irrelevant. But this may be missing an important feature of ketamine's activity. Our analyses have revealed that some of the most impactful mechanisms may reside in its psychoactive effects. Specifically, we observed that "mystical-type" experiences during the infusion, one set of many ketamine-induced effects, served to mediate the benefits of ketamine in addicted individuals, which means that these short-lived states specifically were *crucial* to efficacy in addiction settings. This relationship has been found in several of our studies and is beginning to be replicated by other groups.

This finding is consistent with the main rationale for the psychedelic and psycholytic models—that certain non-ordinary experiences can be deeply meaningful and catalytic for the psychotherapeutic process. These data raise doubts, as well, about the wisdom of creating ketamine-like compounds that do away with psychoactive effects. The most helpful strategy, according to our findings, might be the reverse: heightening specific modes of experience.

More than a century ago, William James devoted a series of lectures, collected in *The Varieties of Religious Experience,* to exploring the role of spontaneous mystical experiences in personal growth, moral awakening, and religiosity. This was the first time that a scientist gave such rigorous attention to experiences as ancient as humanity itself, reported throughout history by poets, philosophers, artists, mystics, drug enthusiasts, religious leaders, and everyday people. James believed that the importance of these "conversion" phenomena in human history argued for broadening the range of what should be considered normal experience, challenging the prejudice, which still exists today, that these experiences are aberrant, meaningless, or pathological. More recently, psychologists have analyzed the different components of a mystical experience and identified several core features: it is difficult to put into words; it suggests insight into truth and reality; there is a sense of the sacred or absolute; it produces intense emotional states; there are varying degrees of transcendence from space and time; and the self merges with or dissolves into being/nothingness. Experiences can be as variable as people are. They might be deeply personal, abstractly cosmic, or both at once. And they might involve a joyous revelation or a dark night of the soul, an engagement with a truer reality or a descent into total annihilation.

Anecdotal reports, and some data, confirm James's conjecture that these non-ordinary states might be helpful. There is a robust literature on alcoholics and other addicted individuals reporting that such experiences played an important role in their recovery. AA's own Bill W. may have experienced the inspiration for starting the fellowship during a mystical vision brought on by belladonna treatment; he went on to preach that a spiritual awakening from addiction requires radical humility, self-examination, and service to others, and he outlined a 12-step path to sobriety. People who have more generally reached an impasse—creative, existential, emotional—have also found in these experiences a catalyst for moving forward, whether they are occasioned by drugs or not. Research with classical psychedelics, including psilocybin, has been consistent with our findings with ketamine, and has linked the mystical-type experience that they occasion with enduring changes in well-being, in remission from end-of-life anxiety, and in changes in addiction severity for people dependent on alcohol or on tobacco.

Certain non-ordinary experiences seem to exert significant impact. The role of drugs in facilitating them seems clear too. But various questions remain. There are many ways to interpret these reports and findings, ranging from a reductive neurobiological framework to a hodgepodge of New Age ideas. On the one end, the brain enters into a heightened state of entropy, leveling neural communication into chaotic and potentially therapeutic hyper-connectedness, with the experience a mere epiphenomenon, irrelevant and arbitrary; on the other, there is energy healing, communion with "spirit," or guidance from otherworldly entities. Both extremes veer so far away from the experience itself as to get entangled in words. The challenge is to clarify the process experienced by the person herself, while resisting the tendency to turn it into something else.

My lab endeavored to examine the experience more granularly. We found that one aspect of the experience—its inability to be spoken about, its ineffability—is especially correlated with the efficacy of ketamine at disrupting addiction. Ineffability is an imperviousness to representation altogether. This goes beyond the difficulty of putting something profound into words, as with complex content or an awe-inspiring experience, and indicates a meaningfulness that cannot be rendered into words at all. We might call such an experience, using "mystical" language, a disclosure of the sacred, the transcendent, or absolute reality; but no name or meaning is adequate.

Disrupting addiction begins with a recognition of its inauthenticity, in that stark chasm between some (un)reality and ourselves. This inauthenticity is felt deeply, from the inside, as a kind of disorientation. With ketamine, this schism might be deepened for a moment, the "addiction" on the outside, the inarticulable "I" on the inside. We are granted fuller access to ourselves, beyond the familiar and meaningful coordinates that had been constraining us. A grounding in that ineffability, while perhaps disorienting, is our only real starting point.

Ketamine might therefore work to provide access to the ineffable "interior" of the world: the Alone, in theologian Henry Corbin's evocative phrase, to which we come alone. But the ineffable is profounder, of course, than a transient medication effect. It is the truth of things. Further, it is the truth we had obscured with "reality." Our engagement with this inarticulable immensity may flourish beyond the medicine, and beyond any infusion-dependent "mysticism," to encompass what our systems of signs had more generally covered over, beginning with our everyday pains, our bodies, our possibilities. We break open our mountains and waters to find mountains and waters.

The ineffable can therefore be ecstatic and disruptive, a disclosure of Being beyond all maps and territories. One develops with time an intuitive trust in that mystery. But this may involve thrashing in it first,

the familiar mechanisms of cognitive control unraveling and revealing the stage-prop flimsiness of "the world." This might then allow
for reclaiming a freedom from the constraints of all cartography. And
once we've experienced such silence, we cannot simply forfeit that deterritorialized vantage point or lose sight of its liberating disorientations.

This might be how "mystical" experiences work to quiet and dispel any regimes that come to seem indistinguishable from reality: they
deafen our over-certain and oppressive babble within an unbreakable
silence. This silence can remain salient, if properly nourished, for an
entire lifetime, allowing greater opportunity for deepening our relationship with the rich inscrutability of things. A sense of radical possibility may be refreshed, and a profound intimacy restored, deep within
our dark interiority, with the Alone.

These are hypotheses, and they continue to be explored. Neuroimaging data on neural correlates also continue to be gathered, particularly as they pertain to resting-state default-mode network activity
and connectivity. But the person's experience is where the process is
happening. Nothing compares to hearing from him directly.

Q. What were your expectations for the infusion?
A. *I was definitely skeptical. How was a drug I've used a number of times
going to help me kick an addiction lasting a decade? But I wanted to give
the treatment a shot. Anyway, it wasn't only ketamine. The therapy,
the mindfulness, the intentions and commitments, a lot of guidance for
approaching the experience in a certain way. This whole attitude was there
from the start. The medicine as support, not a silver bullet.*

Q. What was the treatment like before the infusion?
A. *There was a lot of talk geared toward helping me sit with myself, quieting
the noise in my head, the whole mindfulness thing. I was also given the
space to think about what I could do to better myself, to recognize my own
responsibility in this. The therapist and I cooked up a plan that was tailored
to my issues, a blueprint for making the changes ahead. Just putting those
words to paper, and coming up with a path forward for myself, was a huge
step in the right direction.*

Q. You were ready to be helped.

A. *I was still using basically twenty-four hours on the dot before the infusion and had my last few lines exactly on the hour they told me to stop using, not wanting to lose out on that last little bit. If I'd kept using after the infusion, I'm sure I'd be telling a different story. Another flash of hope that went nowhere. Same story I'd been telling forever. This was far from easy. But it no longer seemed impossible, and that was the missing piece. There was hope. It was new, cutting-edge, selected to participate out of who knows how many people. It was like winning the lottery or getting a gift. I was prepared to honor the whole thing. But I'd be lying if I said I was totally sold on sobriety. Part of me was still pining for the old life, and doubting whether anything would last, still scared of the next failure, still torn into two.*

Q. So, how was the infusion? Maybe you can take us through it?

A. *The experience itself was unlike anything I've done before, including ketamine. You have a sense now of the work that led up to it. This created a momentum that took everything to another level. It was an early appointment. Comfortable and low-key, just the therapist, a physician, and me. I was asked to review my reasons for being there, to bring to mind the vision of myself for the future, as well as the challenges and obstacles that had been getting in the way, that sort of thing. Putting me right in the thick of it, craving, ambivalence, a hope for better days, the whole struggle then and there. Then we moved into a breathing exercise that I had learned in prior sessions, and that helped me relax, my mind felt less cluttered, I started to find some peace and focus. I was thinking that I was exactly where I should be, that if I could maintain where I was, moving forward, then I would be all right. I was already thinking that I was fine as is, nothing more is needed, a really unusual thought for me, I need nothing, and the thought only became more intense, I need nothing, I need nothing, I was repeating it to myself, as if there was some secret in the words I needed to see. The medicine had snuck up on me. My body was changing, sinking into the bed, I felt like I weighed a thousand pounds. My circulation starting to stop, everything coming to a complete standstill, as if I was dying and my blood was slowing down, but it was a calm stillness, that sweet surrender feeling that makes you think, Well the end can't be so bad, what's the problem, and I was repeating I need nothing, I need nothing, nonstop, the message then morphed, I am nothing, I am nothing, I felt my breath it was nothing, I thought my thoughts they were nothing, my sensations were nothing, my feelings were nothing, everything was nothing, but it was a nothing that is also everything, an everything in nothing, I know this doesn't make much sense, but that's where my mind was, and it didn't feel like my mind was anywhere either, my mind nothing, my body nothing, and at the same time they were everything, everything was everything, but everything was nothing too. Nothing and everything at the same time, walking a fine line between one and the other, keeping balance, one foot in front of the other, breathing, one moment at a time, I could hear the therapist, one breath at a time, in that meditation voice he has, just as before, doing as I was told, but I was telling it to myself, a simple message, I need nothing, I am nothing, I am everything. My wife appearing, my daughter, this miraculous life where there was once nothing, the lines drawn into me where there was once nothing, my wife and my daughter a gift, the life that I have received a gift, there was nothing, this is everything, this is what I kept repeating, there is nothing to worry about, there is this, the everything, my everything, rambling like a madman but there it is, where there was once nothing, I have all this, my wife, my daughter, my life, my everything, I was sobbing with gratitude like it was a miracle, so much where there might be nothing at all. But from nothing it will return to nothing, everything might become nothing just like that, nearly dead in Vegas, throwing everything away for nothing, chasing nothing as if it were everything, until it is nothing, until everything is nothing. This was what changed everything, I know it doesn't make sense to hear it now, but I have been given everything, everything, the miracle of everything from absolutely nothing. I wanted what I wanted, killing myself for what was already there, turning everything to nothing because I couldn't see that it was everything. I am trying to put it into words now, but I know it barely makes sense. The mind is the thing, the mind I was in, even as it is silent, I realize it now. I've been practicing since, practicing to stay silent, I mean really silent, the silence of that fine line, the silence of nothing and everything. Meditation, mindfulness, time with the therapist of course. Staying away from garbage. But it's even deeper than that. Career, how I spend my energy, my family, what I prioritize, everything changing.*

Q. What has that looked like?

A. *It's a work in progress. Some days are easier than others. I'm always learning, always working at it. I quit the tattoo gig, started teaching art at a private school again. I don't want to be burning myself out anymore. I have a life to live. The major change has been paying attention to what I have, cherishing my wife and kid, seeing life for what it is. That has been the most important change for me, seeing life for what it is, making the most of it, and not messing it all up because I'm running after something it's not. It sounds simple, but this has required everything I have, my full attention and discipline. And I'm still a beginner, only a few months into it.*

●

If addiction at its root is a malady of fictions, then one solution is to disrupt the fiction. New stories might then be told that better serve the reality of things, as in AA or therapy. Or the person may come to surrender storytelling altogether.

For Marcus, the treatment created windows of silence, along with some guidance toward living differently. With this disruption came the freedom to find new stories, new possibilities. This freedom is ultimately the freedom of consciousness, unencumbered by attachments to what it witnesses, considers, chooses. Marcus might then appraise the situation more clearly and recognize what needs to be done. This will invariably bring greater alignment with his inmost yearning: a more lasting reprieve from needless suffering.

The window of silence extended to any semblance of a story that he developed about the infusion. The words Marcus found were so meaningful as to be nearly meaningless: the absolutes of "everything" and "nothing," which would not fully yield their secrets even as he continued to repeat them. This became his story, though it borders on the incomprehensible.

The experience is not his alone. It has been communicated before by many people, countless times, each occasion refusing to provide the final word, in its own way. There may be nothing gained, no new stories or transcendent consummations. Yet everything changes. In the words of novelist Péter Nádas: "I wanted something in the here and now, a revelation, a redemption I was waiting for, I can confess this now, but back then I hadn't yet realized that precise knowledge of nothingness should have sufficed."

Marcus had found his place on that edge between nothing and nothing, where the "miracle" occurs. There is nothing we can say, about his brain or anything else, that comes close to it. He will carry on his work in silence, everything that can be said only helping to point the way. In silence, he had found a freedom that will never leave him—even as it might be concealed again, obscured by the hard facts of reality, were he to cease attending to it, silently.

●

Marcus emphasized that the experience, remarkable as it was, did not occur in isolation. Its therapeutic power was inseparable from the preparation he received, the mind-set he cultivated, the circumstances motivating him to seek help, and his attitude toward the treatment team. It would not have been so impactful, he said, but for his readiness for change, and for the work and practices he pursued, under the guidance of a therapist, from the very beginning and well after the infusion ended. And yet the infusion was also somehow crucial.

We return to a familiar point. The ways we relate to something and represent it play a key role in how it impacts us. In this case, the relationship and representations began well before the experience itself, from the first treatment contact. There was a consistent message, conveyed directly to Marcus, and implicit, as well, in how the infusion was incorporated into the larger treatment framework. Receiving and assimilating this fiction is as important as receiving the medicine itself. This is because the experience, or ketamine, is not inherently antiaddictive: if it were, ketamine might stand to help people with cocaine addiction if they sniffed it at a party. Instead, it is only as effective as his relationship with it, and the representations that emerge in that mode of communion: catalyst, medicine, neurogenesis promoter, a practice, a turning point, a source of support, gift, an opportunity, a moment like any other. These fictions were inextricable from the process and crucial to the form his engagement took.

Marcus had been prepared to receive the moment in these fictional ways and to work toward incarnating its possibilities. This was the purpose of the therapeutic relationship: to instill a practice, facilitate shifts in perspective, provide fresh narratives, and enhance commitment. It is comparable to the process of providing a new story in AA, but with the difference that this was his own myth he was instantiating. A new dream—a new idea of what is possible—had incubated in his thoughts and behavior: a dream that he aimed to further embody in his thoughts and deeds, displacing the previous, addiction-related one.

The mystical-type experience was important for this because it "materialized" what would have been otherwise abstract; it provided a "real" springboard—a lived experience—from which Marcus could make his leap into the unknown. Perhaps it was intoxication, perhaps imagination, maybe a mere fantasy. But it was *experienced*, each exhale a miraculous emergence of something from nothing. And each moment offering an ecstatic reality, a cascade of secrets.

"It was like trying to drink from a firehose," he said. "Some of the insights will stay with me forever."

Everything and nothing with every breath. The many gifts in his life recognized for what they are, with even a single breath given the deep attention and gratitude reserved for the profoundest of mysteries.

The primordial dream had awakened. The ground charged with it. Incantations, stories, medicine, and personal guidance had done the conjuring. It was now up to Marcus to bring this inmost possibility to the daily work of living; he would work to realize this dream, breath to breath, ever more silently.

●

Placebo is Latin for "I shall be pleasing" and originally designated Vespers during prayers for the Office of the Dead, whereby souls in purgatory might come to supplicate the Lord and be more pleasing to Him. It also came to designate the inactive control condition in RCTs: the "sugar pill" compared to which an active medication is tested. One group gets the active medication, and another the placebo, in a random fashion, with neither investigators nor participants aware of what is administered. This design is intended to identify what the medicine is doing "materially," as opposed to what the person or investigator believes it might do by virtue of all the pleasing things that might heighten a therapeutic response, such as enthusiasm, positive expectations, the clinical setting, and a warm rapport between patient and treatment team.

The placebo response more generally refers to the benefits a treatment might exert that do not emerge from its biological effects, in both research and clinical settings. It is a very real phenomenon; in depression studies, for example, the strength of the placebo response is robust, with many participants receiving relief from the placebo equal to that obtained from antidepressants. It is also thought to account for a good proportion of the clinical benefits of even real medications, including psychiatric treatments. But it is also a very unreal phenomenon. It emerges from the representations that surround a substance, and that are conjured by the suggestive staging of its consumption: the set, setting, meaning making. The substance becomes more than it is, to good effect.

Even a non-substance, a sugar pill, might have real power based on these contextual, representational, and psychological forces. A sugar pill is administered in a clinical setting, and it alleviates depression, an infection, lower back pain. There might be a number of explanations for why an "unreal" treatment might address a "real" condition. The first is that the (un)reality of the placebo mobilizes resources of real well-being on the part of the person; the placebo tells a story of healing, so to speak, to which the person listens intently and with commitment, accelerating his healing in the process.

This appears to be the inverse of the fictionalization that occurs in addiction. Recall Ahmed and his compulsive pantomime of injecting heroin, even when its capacity to exert an effect was entirely abolished. Both representational modes turn to a substance to alleviate suffering, and in each case, the substance becomes other than it is: a sugar pill becomes medicine, cocaine becomes indispensable to a full life, heroin becomes a promise. But there is a clear difference between the two sets of representations. With the placebo response, the (non-)substance is represented in such a way as to marshal the person's own capacity for healing and overcoming suffering: "This will help me heal from my distress, administered responsibly under medical guidance." With addiction, the story surrounding a substance, mental state, or activity goes the opposite direction, cannibalizing and depleting the internal resources that allow for well-being and freedom: "I am incomplete on my own, and I need this to feel better, come what may."

The mode of storytelling is also different. With a placebo, the meanings surrounding the substance are introduced and mediated by the clinical milieu. The patient receives the intervention from a treatment team; there is a ready-made script; the person can surrender to the story, knowing he is not in it alone and that there is relative safety and security due to the responsible involvement of health professionals.

Addiction involves a more perilous path, with very little to mediate the unreality that traps a person beyond his own desperate grasping (as well as that, perhaps, of the subculture with which he associates). The unreality is far more chaotic, more personal and binding, with the person making up the story as he goes along. If the placebo response is a well-practiced troupe performing Shakespeare, addiction is a maniac believing himself to be Hamlet, paralyzed by an urgency to do the bidding of ghosts.

This suggests another way that the placebo response might be helpful. The madman believing himself to be Hamlet suffers because of his (un)reality, as do Quixote, Ahmed, Fred, Marcus. The suffering, in these cases, stems quite clearly from (un)realities that have seduced the person. These are particularly obvious examples of how fictions can wreak havoc. But there might be an (un)real component to *all* suffering—a thicket of representations, let's say—that might exacerbate, deepen, or even initiate unease, and which might be disrupted by the more creative and therapeutic (un)reality permeating a placebo.

A person may be "depressed," for example, because his thoughts and emotions seem overwhelming, leading to sleep and appetite issues, work difficulties, apathy, and lack of pleasure in previously enjoyable things. He seeks support in medications that might render his thoughts and emotions less cumbersome; and he finds relief in a placebo administered during a RCT testing a drug intended to normalize his neurochemistry and restore balance to his mind. The placebo apparently revives his capacity to appraise his inner world more dispassionately and serenely. But perhaps this capacity for equanimity and detached attentiveness had never been lost. The antidepressant effect of placebo, in this case, might be a therapeutic type of disillusionment. He is disabused of the fiction that his thoughts and feelings weigh heavily on his consciousness; he regains his inherent freedom from them, a capacity to experience them more fully and with greater suppleness. This comes through yet another fiction: that the "medicine" has changed his neurotransmitters and cured him of his depression. The story he had been telling himself about his suffering is replaced by another, truer to what is possible for him. Healing here is a procession of lies, progressively approximating the truth. Such lies might be inevitable for moving forward from some diseases; maladies of fiction might be best met by fictional remedies: that is, by remedies harnessing the profound power of storytelling, invention, and imagination.

Consider the other falsifications that a placebo might disrupt: This infection is going to last forever, there is no way out of my pain, I need heroin to live. There are many cases of suffering that might lend themselves to this. Indeed, a recent report found that half of German doctors prescribe deliberate placebos of various sorts—sham surgeries, inert substances, vitamin pills—to address diverse medical problems, with consistent improvements.

The two mechanisms by which a placebo works—mobilizing self-healing and disrupting a certain (un)reality—often work together. This might be exemplified by the effects of psychedelics. It is possible that ketamine and similar substances exert their benefits, at least in part, by facilitating a uniquely powerful placebo response, tapping into the same mechanisms that account for the benefits that sugar pills confer. First, the staging occurs for a certain therapeutic story to be told: that freedom and enduring contentment are possible, for example. A perspective is cultivated that allows the person to leverage whatever might appear to his subjectivity toward this end. The medicine is then administered in a manner that transforms this possibility, for a blessed moment, into what seems actual and real. With that possibility rendered more palpable and within reach, the person feels galvanized to continue the work under guidance and with commitment. He allows himself to heal while he deprives his addiction of the deceptions that diseased him.

This is at least what happened to Marcus. The (un)reality at the heart of the addiction came to be silenced. The story that emerged, and which helped facilitate this disruption, was that of "everything" and its miraculous emergence from "nothing." But there may be many possibilities or fictions that might have been helpful. The stage was set for whatever might come. The "mystical" experience lends itself to such polymorphous storytelling: it awakens the person to his fundamental freedom or allows for communion with the ever-present ( ); confronts him with the shadow that obscures everything or unveils the ecstatic mystery within each moment. The experience may take many directions, though there is a shared momentum that unites these separate dreams: an unveiling of the ineffable ground in which "reality" is a mere stratum. It is up to the therapist and the person to harness it. A truer fiction might take root, which mobilizes the person's resources to overcome the "disease" while also defanging it, divesting it of the power to deceive.

Does this mean addiction is a made-up disease? That it might be cured by nothing more than a sugar pill? Calling attention to the (un)reality of addiction, and to the way that a placebo or hallucinogen might be helpful, is not meant to minimize it. The suffering is not made up, nor is the tenacity of its self-deceptions, despite how "made up" the lies might be. Possibility is important to impart, irrespective of what corner it comes from. When the sense of possibility has been lost, then even a placebo might be treasured as real medicine—especially if it brings a pleasing song that redeems the moment from purgatory, creating opportunity for things to be more than they seem.

•

A few words about the placebo effect in psychedelic research. There is growing recognition that placebo-controlled trials are ill suited for ascertaining the "efficacy" of these potent psychoactive substances, and that we need to reimagine our empirical approach to understanding them.

The main reason is that it is usually obvious who received the active compound versus a placebo, thereby breaking the blind and creating opportunity for all kinds of confounding errors. Importantly, these issues may directly affect outcomes, with a heightened placebo response in the clearly "active" group and disappointment, disillusionment, or clinical worsening ("nocebo" effects) in the control arm. Preserving the integrity of an RCT requires minimizing these shortcomings as much as possible—by strengthening the blind, reducing expectancy effects, and ambiguating the distinction between the active and control arms of the trial. A common solution is to give a psychoactive comparator, such as a compound known to be ineffective but nonetheless associated with changes in consciousness (for example, the sedative midazolam [Versed] in the trials testing ketamine), or a lower but still psychoactive dose of whatever is being tested.

But these solutions do not address deeper challenges. Modern RCT methodology has certain commitments, including a universalizing protocol-based orientation and a diagnosis-driven focus on impacting discrete outcomes in a linear manner. It is unclear whether these commitments are reconcilable with therapeutic work with these substances, which tend to have transdiagnostic effects, might exert benefit in nonlinear, subtle ways, and require sensitivity to differences between individuals, as well as to the unique relational field nurtured between provider and patient.

Conceptualizing the placebo response as a kind of pollutant that needs to be purged or mitigated is another major issue. After all, the same processes involved in the placebo response—staging, storytelling, therapeutic representation, the sense that something meaningful is happening—may be critical for harnessing the potential of these compounds. Undercutting these factors, and minimizing their impact, to test efficacy more cleanly might be "good science"—but it might also work to neuter the ineffable power that Blake called the tiger's "fearful symmetry," depriving the pharmakon of its evocative spell. The challenge before RCT researchers is to harness imagination while simultaneously diminishing its relevance: an impossible double bind.

Psychedelic research makes clear the inadequacies of RCTs, our gold standard for testing medical interventions. Though I have endeavored to evaluate the efficacy of ketamine in a variety of trials and have done so with positive results, I remain concerned about the compromises that were made, and not simply to methodological rigor. The medicine itself was denied the full opportunity to provide support given that its psychoactive, relational, and imaginal properties—all probably involved in its efficacy—were systematically deemphasized. RCT methodology, after all, is rooted in a biomedical system focused on developing biological products: physicalist, universal, and scalable interventions intended to address a circumscribed medical condition thought to be homogenous across diverse populations. Personalized treatments that harness imagination to promote general well-being or that unshackle the imagination entirely represent a very different way of doing things—often dismissed out of hand as placebo, folk medicine, or charismatic healing.

The major problem is that RCTs are captive to the same false earth most biomedical scientists regard as entirely *physical*. This doesn't offer room for the imagination to take flight beyond materialism—on the contrary, it militates against it. The placebo response is accordingly dismissed as a quirk of human nature interfering with our capacity for objectivity, much like the miasma of subjectivity itself. Thus, the sterile methodology of RCTs: the double blind, randomization, active comparators, modulation of expectancy, and manualized researcher-subject interactions, all intended to minimize the power of suggestion and imagination.

Another viewpoint, also supported by biomedicine, is that the placebo response is a "valid" phenomenon recruiting "real" neural processes, with neuroimaging data, not surprisingly, indicating a distinct pattern associated with it. While it remains a source of interference in RCT design and something to curtail as much as possible, the placebo response is at least "real"—because associated with neural activity. Some researchers have gone so far as to suggest developing interventions that activate the brain in the same way. Perhaps these might be added to the countless other placebos already in medical use?

We return to our captivity in "matter." I suggest moving beyond a reflexive recourse to neuro-materialism and recognizing the placebo response for what it is: a window into the profound impact that imagination, myth, and (un)reality have on our lives. Blake and Plato would have encouraged a similar perspective given the power they recognized in what we would call imagination, and what they might also call vision, noesis, or soul. We stand to learn how to inhabit this subtle dimension with greater skillfulness and intentionality. This will invariably change the way we approach testing and employing psychedelics, suggestogens, "super-placebos"—really anything else with which a relationship is possible.

This is particularly relevant to drug addiction. Drug addiction emerges from an (un)real relationship with a substance comparable to the alchemical relationship one might have with a placebo. But with placebo, the relationship is healthier and "charged with greater grandeur." It allows the imagination to consider other possibilities that are associated with flourishing, such as "normal serotonin levels" when taking a sugar pill in an antidepressant trial, but it is no more "real" than the fictions that surround a drug in addiction. One might even say that addiction touches on more *reality* because it, at least, involves a drug or act materially doing something, a predictable change in mood, faculties, or energy, while a sugar pill does nothing *real* at all, despite its neural signature.

The truth of a placebo is not in any real physiological effect but in a more subtle power. Placebo works to address suffering by harnessing our powers of imagination, conjuring an imaginal world of greater well-being. This outcome is truer, of course, to our inmost possibilities than are the (un)real shackles of addiction. A more healing relationship with (un)reality is made possible. A truer myth is enacted.

It was suggested earlier that Marcus developed an addiction because his imagination had become impoverished: so overheated in one direction, with the cocaine exalted beyond all reason, that he had lost the capacity to imagine anything else. The treatment seemed to work because it allowed Marcus to recognize and work toward a different possibility for himself, restoring to his imagination the freedom and creative power to radically reconsider what seemed the case. The centrality of the ketamine infusion to this process involved its capacity to materialize a new imaginary, rendering it experiential and therefore actual. The dream of reality under which he labored was thrown into ineffability for a moment, and he found opportunity to inhabit a more imaginative, more authentic way.

An entire troupe of therapists, physicians, and assistants was helpful for creating this world. A placebo response of impeccable stagecraft, with the close attention, deliberate framing, and careful orchestration reserved usually for the theater of surgery. And at its center—captivating his imagination deeply, yet also just one of many key players—was a powerful psychoactive drug. Among other things, ketamine produced robust subjective effects that allowed Marcus to inhabit with meaningful private relevance this emerging reality. It was no longer a wellness platitude or fantasy that "the present moment is a perfect gift." An intimate truth was spun and experienced that was undeniable, even as he couldn't quite articulate it. It resonated to the very depths of his being, dislodging the illusions of addiction, for at least the hour, from their pride of place.

That it was a psychoactive substance to do the trick is fitting given that drug addiction is a condition uniquely attached to the incarnations made possible by intoxication. Ketamine—a drug commonly used recreationally—was approached here in ways very different from how Marcus had engaged with cocaine. There was guidance from the start toward passing through whatever emerged, cultivating a mindful moment-to-moment equanimity. Not every seed takes root, but for Marcus it did. He received ketamine with profound freedom and emerged motivated for the work of silence ahead. Ketamine—despite its "abuse liability"—helped lead away from addiction instead of toward it, liberating his imagination rather than holding it captive: a psychedelic, a placebo, a moment like any other.

The process is uncertain. We do our best, but for everything to come together is a gift. That Marcus approached the treatment itself as a blessing may have increased his chances, setting the groundwork for the humility, carefulness, and personal responsibility inherent to the changes ahead. Pivotal to disrupting addiction, and to addressing (un)real suffering more generally, is nurturing this kind of attention toward all that is given us, while evolving beyond the drive to dominate other beings and things, including substances. A lesson that doesn't require much imagination to understand. We are best served maintaining humility toward whatever might humble us.

PART II

INTO THE WILDERNESS

A certain story is being told. We are telling it together. Speaking toward addiction. It is in this speaking that we might find the problem. A crisis of our meaningful self-deceptions, one word after another. But in that speaking, we might also find better words, truer to our suffering: neither brain disease nor unique failing, but a human process, an invitation to freedom, a merciless teacher, an intrusion of reality into our trance, an apocalypse.

These words offer hope. They suggest that our homesickness for "reality" will find its resolution, that our cry for more solid ground will one day be answered. Even our most confusing, cruelest occasions of suffering, what we try to avoid most of all, might become a doorway toward that liberation and reunion.

Addiction is reimagined here as a human truth so universal as to be nearly invisible. Our ignorance laid bare: a captivating "reality" dissociated from experience, with the snare being a meaningful "unreality"—a paradigm, a regime, a canalized and navigable Absolute. And "recovery" from addiction, as from all suffering, is finding freedom from this painful (un)reality and engaging more deeply with the question of *being experience*. This hope of making a home in () is what has been driving us all along, of course—whether with the desperate urgency of an addict, the game plan of a businessman, or the God yearning of a mystic.

Finding what we seek. We've heard this before. The story here may be another fiction among many. It is possible, as well, that we have it all wrong. Why diminish the capacity of the brain to become so compromised—through addiction-related neuroadaptations, for example—as to effectively foreclose this freedom? Are we disregarding the unbreakable inertia that our embodiment can create? The realities of birth and death are inescapable and inscribed on our flesh; addiction might be similarly inscribed and enfleshed.

Suffering as a gift: this might be another fiction playing loose with our wounds. Consider the apparently senseless suffering of children, of the abused, of the vulnerable. It is absurd, of course, to greet such suffering with a conviction that they are inherently meaningful or an occasion for a studious kind of gratefulness.

It is also possible that, despite our best intentions, we will lead storm-tossed lives of meaningless assaults, genetic disease, inexorable decay, endless exile, right until our last breath. The suggestion that suffering serves a greater purpose might be mere wish fulfillment: another self-deception, as in addiction, to give meaning to what is meaningless, or to protect our fantasy that freedom and contentment might be found in an existence more often besieged by pain and humiliation.

I offer support for a more hopeful perspective. Suffering as instructive, revelatory, and illuminating—as a passage toward a more expansive, though hardly effortless or passive, engagement with (). But data, clinical examples, and argument, I admit, will only get us so far. A seduction may be necessary as well.

A preexisting trance provides the grammar. I've selected what to say, as well as what to leave out, to further sweeten the disruption, as might any storyteller. I've also been deliberate to give familiar actors a familiar role: Bill W., Blake, Burroughs, Cervantes, Deleuze, Derrida, Descartes, Donne, Duchamp, Emerson, Foucault, Ginsberg, Goethe, Heidegger, Hopkins, James, Joyce, Milton, Montale, Nietzsche, Oppenheimer, Plato, Porchia, Rilke, Schopenhauer, and, of course, Shakespeare. Consider the narrator himself, wielding his medical training, his fluency in the sciences, his Ivy League bona fides.

Arranging our players in this way makes it difficult to miss what has been missing. They have been mostly White European, male, almost entirely privileged, some of them so canonical as to inspire a reflexive respect. They speak, we listen. There have been a few women elsewhere in the story. But two were left unnamed, another so powerful as to be a general, and P-Orridge was also a man. This cast of characters imparts greater "authority" to these words, and better aligns this fiction with our Eurocentric, masculine-patriarchal, merit-obsessed culture. The staging and omissions might have passed unnoticed for precisely these reasons. Many of us have been so thoroughly hypnotized by the dreams of civilization, as addicts might be by their own fantasies, that we fail to recognize when we've been ensnared by further manipulation.

It is helpful to respect the fictions of others, as already said, if we hope to get something across to them. Perhaps the hallowed wisdom of dead White men has made this story more compelling. Maybe we are more inclined to question the lies of "Western Civilization" when the words of its architects and forebears are inviting us to do so. We have descended into a familiar sleep, perhaps to rise again with new dreams.

But the point is not another "paradigm shift." Replacing one paradigm or narrative with another is only one step on an endless journey. The more profound opportunity is to cultivate an agile playfulness with our many constructs, especially those so established and familiar as to be out of sight, engaging them when they might be fruitful, and seeing through their fictions to the very end. There is also opportunity to create anew, with startling visionary force—forging new worlds more sensitive to the moment, while maintaining a lucid silence before all the mind's machinations, be they "fact" or "fiction."

The Eurocentric framing might serve to substantiate another fiction. The vantage point of privilege is useful when engaging stories of "self-improvement." Vanquishing addiction at its root—dispelling the destructive fictions to which we grow attached—requires at least some freedom from systemic, domestic, or other abuse. Telling a story of addiction as self-inflicted suffering in a persuasive manner has therefore necessitated bracketing, for a moment, the ways that we might suffer, repeatedly and without support, from oppressive actions, systems, and regimes beyond our control. It has also meant going along with conventional notions regarding who is most capable of the work that freedom from addiction often involves—those who seem disciplined in other respects, who aren't compromised by severe psychiatric or societal vulnerabilities, and who have been able to enjoy some measure of achievement in the world, ostensibly due to their efforts, opportunities, and talents.

I have therefore discussed patients who are successful White men to make my case—even though anyone else, including the under-resourced, unconventional, or vulnerable, might be just as capable of pursuing radical self-examination and transformation. Fred and Marcus have the privilege to exemplify the suffering borne of self-deception, suffering that is largely inflicted on oneself. They also have the means to engage unencumbered in programs of self-improvement, be it ninety AA meetings in ninety days, addiction psychiatry, or experimental treatment. This is not possible for everyone. To pretend equal opportunity is to fall into a meritocratic blindness that claims everyone is master of his destiny, that we are all uniformly unbounded by limitations. This is particularly inexcusable when it comes to disregarding the chains that have been placed around a person's neck. We cannot pretend these afflictions and chains away, especially if we hope to properly address the alcohol people might apply on their wounds every night, as salve and antiseptic.

Ahmed, for example, is more vulnerable than Fred and Marcus to psychiatric distress and to the violence that inhumane, divisive, and exploitative systems—some of the primary systems that organize our "culture"—inflict on human beings. This violence cannot be separated from his relapse, even as it may not have been the immediate cause. His sense of freedom was restricted not only by "learned helplessness" but also by an actual powerlessness associated with, among other things, severe illness, precarious social status, low resources, an antidrug culture stigmatizing him, lack of access to treatment, and limited opportunity for engagement with others. We must not pretend these wounds and chains away.

Taking responsibility for one's suffering is critical for overcoming addiction, as it is for finding freedom from any other painful entanglement. But this does not justify abandoning those who are not yet in a position to engage with that responsibility fully or who require a more permissive, looser approach. This is the compassionate truth of harm reduction strategies, such as free drug testing, safe using spaces, and heroin replacement treatment, that work to mitigate the legal, medical, and social fallout associated with high-risk behavior or regular drug use in our current culture of drug criminalization. Many of us may not be in a position to vanquish our addictions entirely; but alleviating distress through implementing wiser policy and creating resources that allow for less harmful behavior might be the best we can do for the moment.

We might also aim to change culture from the ground up. Harm reduction strategies often go together with progressive politics aimed at dismantling systems that perpetuate suffering, such as the war on drugs, social iniquities, and the correctional-industrial complex. Inhumane people and structures inflict deep trauma on the vulnerable daily, through neglect, demonization, direct violence, and a range of other assaults. Addressing these challenges and better tending to the vulnerable will not vanquish, of course, our suffering and ignorance; we remain human and fallible even in the best of all possible worlds. But it will move us a good way in the right direction and create greater opportunity for individuals, from all social strata, to engage in the work that will emancipate them.

●

This is where we break the trance of Western culture. It has served its purpose in supporting this story, but there is no reason to remain in thrall to its illusions. Calling attention to the seduction, and recognizing our vulnerability to it, might also protect us from becoming further entrapped in the reigning (un)realities.

Knowledge, children are taught, is *power*. Facts are a show of mastery over the earth, others, ourselves. And this conflation of knowledge with power is reflected in the barriers to high-quality education that sustain the status quo, with the legacy of the powerful secured and the usual power structures reinforcing their grip. The powerless and unknowledgeable are denigrated, meanwhile, because they might lack the rugged self-reliance and command of the facts that are so prized in this civilization of imperialists, civilizers, and colonizers, wielding "knowledge" to dominate and control. One of our defining fictions is a merit-driven individualism, with everyone getting exactly what he deserves. The losers in that equation are deemed an inescapable aspect of progress: the weak and ignorant suffer so that the deserving and knowing might get their due.

We have fallen prey to that civilized habit of reimagining ourselves in line with certain power-intoxicated unrealities: "progress," "success," "wealth," "knowledge," among other fictions. There may come a day when we have reimagined the world so entirely there is nothing left but scorched earth and mirages—when what remains is a barren wasteland, with all the progress, wealth, and knowledge in the world incapable of sustaining a single living being.

This is not some future fantasy. A regime of (un)realities has been metastasizing its necrotic way steadily into everything: our water, our air, our flesh. We might register the violence, sickness, and perversity, even if we feel too powerless or personally embattled to do much about it. Where to start, what to even do. The wars deepen, the seas grow more clotted with plastic and isotopes. A resignation settles in, one epidemic after another: meth, opioids, social media, loneliness, suicide, fentanyl, extremism, forever chemicals, depression, overdose. We take our daily medicines, our poisons.

Material gain, technological attainment, power over others, power over ourselves, all the insipid fantasies and lullabies with which we consume ourselves—it should come as no surprise why so many of us will seek, with the same propulsive individualism, to make a home in our own minds, in our own addictions. The comforts on sale and permitted are tame in comparison to the private terrors and ecstasies of an imagination crystalline and compact, be it intoxicated, exalted, completely mad. At least we might find, with each intoxication, a glimmer of that blessed dawn and its Absolutes.

•

The story I've been telling might be as made up as anything else. I have also told it in ways that might ease its entry into our dominant trance. And so, we return by a commodious vicus of recirculation to where we started. Words, words, words.

Words, also the empty space in between, echoing with something. Suffering is our indication that there are other possibilities: other words, (un)realities, relationships. It indicates our confusions, the lies that concern us intimately. This begins with words, but it is not a matter of words. There is personal work to be done, in silence, in the wild.

The anguish of others can be just as urgent and revelatory. Suffering offers the same truth, everywhere, regardless of whom it is breaking open. The other, of course, must be given attention, each dream, every agony. But certain modes of suffering, such as addiction, are so well understood we no longer bother listening.

We might incline toward (un)realities that console or obscure our suffering, our confusion, our violence. These words move in another direction. Not palliation but *total amplification*, heightening attention to not only our most exalted possibilities but also the agonizing night-time into which we are thrown: the sorrow, bewilderment, and darkness that beset us as we stumble from dream to dream. This might reveal our sleep, agitating our eyes open to the unreality of the world we have imagined for ourselves.

Perhaps then we might wake up.

CRUCIFIXION DREAM

New York City is plastic in most every sense. Manhattan has been almost entirely remade, a concrete grid where there was once an island wilderness of marshes, craggy rocks, shore, and swamp. Even Central Park is manufactured. The underground system of subways, pipes, tunnels; the towering buildings carving the sky; the signs and lights constellating to keep us oriented to its imagined topography: the city emerges from the sea like its own creature, a phantasmagoria of materials that had never existed before. Sheetrock, concrete, plastic, corrugated metal, glass, and fluorescent tubes compacted into new forms. Ambition proliferating in all directions, digging into the earth, reaching toward the sky, agitating the air and ether, subordinating everything to human striving and desire.

The city is also plastic in its versatility. It molds itself to a variety of wants and dreams, allowing for a dizzying array of lifestyles to be pursued. One can eat, play, date, pray, create, exercise, get intoxicated, have sex, sleep, work, heal, relax, and be entertained in a seemingly inexhaustible number of ways. The city is frenzied with possibility. More money means more options. This seemingly infinite optionality is our idea of freedom: the American Dream of one day possessing the resources and capacity to desire, experience, and achieve whatever one imagines. It is one of the reasons New York City has been so attractive to dreamers from around the world. They bring their restlessness, adventurousness, and ambition to this most shape-shifting of all places to live, where everything is permitted, or at least available for a price, and where all options might be exhausted.

Robyn was born and raised in Miami, a vibrant and dynamic city in its own right, with a confluence of cultural influences. She is half-Cuban, on her mother's side, French Canadian on her father's, and hails from an established real estate family specializing in high-end property. Robyn had come to New York City several years prior to extend her family's nascent hotel business to a new location in Chelsea. That venture had since been sold to an international hotelier, where she continues to work as an executive.

I will set aside at least a few hours for my first session with a patient. Alongside allowing me to gain as much information as possible, I find that this gives the patient an opportunity to ease into a more open and unselfconscious state. Robyn filled that visit with multitudes. She was in her early thirties and seemed to be several people at once. She was refined and street-smart, witty, polished, yet occasionally crude; was a certified yoga teacher, an occasional vegan, and capable of drinking men twice her size under the table. Her appearance was striking and mercurial: svelte and elegant with long red hair, she wore at that first session Louboutin heels, an Italian business suit, and diamonds. But she also collected discreet stamp-sized tattoos and enjoyed dancing at all-night underground parties in an industrial part of town. Her most comfortable look, she said, was 1970s Lower East Side chic: leather miniskirt, torn fishnet stockings, distressed T-shirt.

Robyn's manner and lifestyle were similarly difficult to pin down. Sexually adventurous and polyamorous, she nonetheless yearned, above all else, to one day find her "soul mate" and settle down as a mother and doting partner. Robyn was a tenacious businesswoman, ruthless in the boardroom, with a bulldog approach to financial matters. But she was also shy and demure in relationships, inclined to defer to her sexual partners, male or female, and to occupy a traditional gender role. The incongruity extended to her habits of consumption: alternately carefree with her drinking and drugging, often unsafe with her late-night choice of drinking holes and coke dealers, and exacting when it came to hotels, social events, restaurants: "I cannot afford to spend less than a grand a night on a room. I have certain standards."

She would make the typical rounds with her high-income circle: Art Basel, summers in the Hamptons, skiing in Aspen, and Mykonos or Tulum or Biarritz if she really wanted to get away. Yet she also saw herself as a mystical and "attuned" person who would commune with friends over long distances telepathically, who could detect "spiritual energy" emanating from the earth, and who hoped to one day simplify her life, discarding "all unnecessary material things," much as she had a few summers ago at Burning Man.

"I'm here because I'm not happy."

She traced her suffering to an older married man, a chief vice president at her company, with whom she had become sexually involved. It was the third such relationship in the course of her life. She sees the pattern as emblematic of her difficulties with commitment. She can play the role of devoted paramour, dreaming of her man when she can't have him and dropping everything when he is in town to have that special night together. But the arrangement also allows for the distance and space she needs given the demands of her career and busy social life. She began the relationship as deliberate fantasy, a diversionary make-believe of wild romance, the sexy redhead on the side circa the 1950s, saucy and smart, with a tender, overbrimming heart. But it had lodged somehow, and she couldn't quite extricate herself from the red-hot mess, as she put it, that her life had become.

"I've always enjoyed playing a part," she confided. The play-acting came at a price. Her cocaine and alcohol use had intensified over the course of the relationship, as had her wild flings, some of which bordered on dangerous, such as waking up after blacking out naked next to a person she only dimly remembered meeting.

"I think I love him," she explained, referring to the executive. "Or at least, I don't want him out of my life. He is one of the few people I look forward to seeing."

When she was twelve, she learned for the first time what it is to burn for someone. Her father's friend, a prominent businessman nearly forty years her senior, had seduced her during a shared family vacation in Turks and Caicos, and maintained a secret relationship with her through her second year in high school. She had alternated, she said, between a feeling of privilege, proudly embracing her apparent role as his precocious mistress, and debasement, anger, and shame, resentful at forfeiting her adolescence for toxic consolations from a manipulator. He ended it suddenly when he feared she would expose the whole thing and continued to send her hush money for years. For several months after the breakup, she experienced an intensification of the pain that ran through the whole relationship: wanting him in a way that could never be possible. He would never leave his wife, never give her the full love that she wished to receive. She hung on, clinging to his every gesture of affection, until he let her go.

There have been a few relationships since that have fallen into the same pattern: an older man, married, of tremendous means, with an intense sexual appetite, who would partner with her to confect a fantasy of true love. She wondered if she is destined to remain in the "other woman" archetype, forever unfulfilled and in romantic limbo. Certain qualities, she felt, conspire to keep her there. Perhaps she is too ambitious to ever settle down, too restless and hungry. There has also been little time for a more serious and committed relationship. Her social life was demanding and tightly booked, her calendar packed with events and engagements weeks in advance. The drinking and cocaine were part of the scene, but they also played a more personal role, helping her maintain the vivacity and energy to play the part of tireless socialite, free spirit, and astute businesswoman, as well as of the ever-cheerful other woman. It had been an insidious acceleration over several years, with the tipping point having come when she realized how entrenched and all-consuming her partying, working, and traveling had become: "I came to see you," she told me, "because I have lost myself in something that was supposed to make me happy. I don't even know who I am anymore."

Robyn confessed readily that she has a penchant for drama and smoke screens: "I'd be an actor if I weren't in my career." She has learned, she said, to affect a show of vulnerability to throw people off and keep her true face hidden. This extended, I supposed, to how she represented herself to me. Commitment difficulties seemed far from being the primary reason for the relationships with married men, the focus on career, the scintillating and sleepless social life. There is also an ambitious side to it. She acknowledged that her overriding motivation, what informed nearly every decision, was to belong to a specific, rarefied world: a world of inexhaustible wealth and power where she might enjoy the absolute freedom to pursue whatever she wants. It is that same dream of unbridled enjoyment, novelty, and stimulation that brings so many seekers to New York. "I have known what I wanted since I was a girl: to be able to do whatever I wanted, without restriction, without anyone telling me what to do. There were several people I know who had clearly achieved it. I wanted to be like them."

She has known what to do since she was a teenager, granted her first view of power. There is one rule: do whatever it takes to gain an advantage. She was a beautiful and spirited young woman in a world that fetishizes them. This was her strength, the rare commodity that, if played right, might gain her the upper hand. Wealth and power are often, Robyn believed, a function of whom we know. The further entranced or indebted those at the top might become, the more she can exact personal favors from them: cozying up to them, perhaps sleeping with them. The logic of the banking system, with every relationship in her life parsed into creditor or debtor. It was about getting what was owed, even though she gave up quite a bit in the transaction.

The doors of the city had opened to her. But what she found inside was not what she hoped. Not freedom but a gilded slavery. It would do for now, despite the tedium. Alcohol and cocaine, the combination of them, allowed her to find pleasure or spontaneity in what had become a joyless routine, while also consoling a deep pain that had first appeared when she was a girl, anguished by the confusion and sorrow of falling in love with an older married man.

"I knew I had lost something, and that I would never get it back. I wanted him with my whole heart, wanted him to love me. I was insane with love. It ruined love for me."

The depths of vulnerability to which I am granted access as a psychiatrist can often feel like trespassing. There are some wounds that are so private that to be complacent or inattentive in their presence, to do anything but observe a careful silence, would be comparable to a violation. It also risks closing the gates for good.

"My heart was the animal that got fooled into a trap, that was bled and skinned. Imagine a young girl steeling herself against love, swearing to protect herself against love. No girl should be in that position. But I was crying every night, banishing love from my life, as if it can ever be banished. Even the shadow of it rips into my chest. Resist love, refuse it or avoid it, and you will be torn open with heartache.

"I try to pretend that it's business, a hookup, a new adventure, whatever, but the pain is always there, a hole that only gets deeper the more I try to fill it. It's not just the drugs, the partying, the meaningless sex, the working too much. Everywhere I look I am reminded of the emptiness that is consuming me, that seems to feed exactly on the life I am living. The more I try to get on with things, the more painful it becomes. Perhaps it's the cocaine and alcohol, perhaps the relationship, perhaps it's more. I can't do this anymore."

Robyn had suspected that her addictions were contributing to her unhappiness, and she had tried to reduce on her own, without success. But she was ambivalent about breaking the spell. To give them up would be to give up the intoxications and consolations that sustain the life she had created, which means that she might need to find a new life altogether: a transformation for which she might not be prepared. It would also mean giving up the dream itself, the hope of what she had come to the city to find: an even deeper disruption than finding a new life, because it involves returning to the darkness and emptiness from which her vision of the city emerged. It is like razing everything to ground zero and building again, with materials and structures worlds different from what came before.

Her hope was that we might work with where she was and move toward reducing the drinking and cocaine use to more manageable levels. She was not prepared to give up on the life she had created, saw it as necessary to who she was. But perhaps fewer messy nights and hangovers, no extravagant cocaine binges, would lead to feeling better overall and would give her a greater sense of control over the runaway train her life had become. This approach is consistent with the harm reduction model, where the ills associated with substance use might be managed, as opposed to stopping the substance use itself. She was particularly motivated to drink and use cocaine more selectively, restricting her use to evenings when they were less likely to cause sexual indiscretions, irresponsible behavior, and other problematic consequences. Other aspects of her life that might be creating pain—her romantic relationships, the careerism, the unremitting social engagements, the limited opportunity for personal time and reflection—she was less interested in addressing now; she would entertain the possibility of addressing these other things, maybe later, if she could be assured she would come out happier on the other side. "But there is already a lot going on in my life, and it doesn't make sense to take on too much." She saw these changes through the lens of her current trajectory: as work that placed yet another burden on her, that involved taking on more in a life already encumbered with too much.

Robyn recognized the path ahead did not end with cultivating new ways; it also involved letting go of what had become obsolete and agonizing. I suspected that her deepest fear pertained to this prospect of disencumbering herself. Even heavy burdens might come to seem necessary to who we are. This is why we dread relinquishing what has seemed vital to us but which needs letting go: it always seems an amputation, terrible to give up, and threatening to terrorize us with phantom pain well after it is cut away.

But removing anything from our systems might be a profound challenge, even if it had not been wanted. A patient once told me, referring to the sexual trauma she experienced growing up: "It's like a knife lodged in your back. It becomes normal, part of you. The knife only hurts when it's coming out."

•

Robyn was eager to discuss treatment options. She asked for something that would help her abstain from drinking and using at will. On Fridays and Saturdays, yes. The rest of the week, no. She had heard that naltrexone targets the reward centers in the brain. Could she get a prescription?

Naltrexone, the opioid blocker given to Ahmed and Steve, is indeed one of the few FDA-approved medicines for alcohol use disorder. Presumed to modulate the reinforcing effects of alcohol by blocking the effects of endogenous opioids, it may be helpful at reducing how much people drink. But I also informed Robyn that while naltrexone may

help reduce amount of use, it has not been shown to promote abstinence or reduce the days per week she drinks. Nor can it, of course,
make the choice for her.

She balked at the prospect of diminished pleasure, as well as daily
medication. Was there anything else?

I suggested disulfiram. Disulfiram disrupts the metabolism of alcohol and leads to the buildup of a noxious by-product if alcohol is
consumed, which creates severe discomfort. If a person takes the medicine, therefore, she will think twice before drinking, because even a
small amount of alcohol will throw the person into a highly unpleasant
state. It is a way of girding oneself against consuming alcohol, even as
the choice remains, every time, whether to take the pill or not.

Disulfiram seemed a good strategy for Robyn on various fronts, including disrupting her cocaine use: she was unlikely to use, she said, if
she wasn't drinking. She simply needs to take the pill in the evenings
when she doesn't intend to drink or use to further dissuade herself. It
tends to work for a few days at a time, so it will protect her for subsequent days as well.

I also recommended that she pursue therapy alongside receiving the
medication. But she was disinclined. "I want to keep this as stream-
lined as possible. I know it's important to get into the past, explore
myself, figure things out, et cetera, but I really just need to make things
a bit more stable right now. I can't afford to feel any more vulnerable
than I already do."

I reassured her that the therapy was intended to help with charting
out a plan, adhering to it, and working out any issues. We wouldn't go
anywhere she wasn't comfortable going. And if she felt amenable to
more, then we would introduce other things. She cautiously agreed to
a trial of disulfiram and weekly therapy.

Robyn came to see me that first visit wanting to preserve a certain illusion of control and resistant to investigating this idea too
closely, much less ceding it. She was certain of what she needed and
approached the treatment with the same armor and shrewdness that
characterized many of her other relationships. But as in her romantic affairs, she couldn't help revealing moments of deep vulnerability
and confusion as well. I could see that she appreciated the safety I

provided her. It allowed her to let her guard down and speak with a candor and rawness that were hard to achieve elsewhere, even with her closest friends.

As I began to conclude the session, which had already lasted three hours, Robyn grew restless, wanting to ensure that she got one more thing across to me.

"There's also a dream I've been having, which started maybe two months ago. It's a bit embarrassing how cliché it is, to be honest, and I wasn't going to tell you. But it will not leave me alone. It is always the same: I'm walking around the city, it's a cool, sunny day. Everywhere I look are dolls, you know the horror movie kind with apple cheeks and saucer eyes. But they're bruised up and broken, some of them are missing hair or eyes. And they're all crucified, pinned to crosses. Thousands of them, in all sizes, all colors, sometimes solitary, sometimes crowded together. The crosses are everywhere, on billboards, street signs, marquees, windows. The streets are totally empty otherwise, not a single person. I always end up in Columbus Circle. But instead of the Columbus memorial, at the center is the largest crucifix of them all, with a huge bleeding woman hanging there, she must be more than ten feet tall and maybe still alive, and I start walking in circles around it, at first almost ceremonially, and then faster and faster until the world starts spinning, I feel my heart beating and breath quickening, and I wake up gasping for air, as if I was really running and it wasn't a dream at all."

This was another example of how vulnerable she allowed herself to be despite an apparent disinterest in therapy. Further, it was a substantial disclosure to make as we were wrapping up; she seemed to be playing with the emerging frame of our therapy, refusing to be contained and pushing against its boundaries. She went on:

"Growing up I stayed away from make-believe stuff like tea time and dress-up, all the other things you associate with little girls. So, toys were never really my thing, and especially not dolls. God, they're something that you would find in a schlocky midnight movie. And here is my subconscious creating this image of wounded innocence, or victimized girlhood, or whatever. My pain had been transformed into a cliché, a grotesque and ridiculous one at that, something out of a psychopath's bedroom. This just rubs it in. Even my dream world has been kidnapped, no longer my own. It's like I've been bought and sold to some snot-nosed lunatic boys who crucify their sister's toys, and I have nothing of myself anymore, nothing but this absurd dream to torment me."

And what about the end, walking circles around the bleeding crucified woman where the statue of Columbus had been?

"That is what makes the dream so disturbing. Part of me always laughs a little bit at the mutilated dolls, it's hard to take that hokey imagery too seriously. But the crucifix at the end had some kind of demonic power. I saw the murder for what it was. The dead center of everything. Not just of the city, but of the entire world. It put all the crucified girls I had seen into perspective. They orbited around it, as if they weren't simply victims but accomplices. Those words still creep me out: Columbus Circle. I get the uncanny sense that there is some secret code behind it. Walking into the circle is precisely when it all gets terrifying, when I realize that I'm inside something like a coven. I was becoming bewitched myself, performing the ritual, praying to the demon, circling the crucified woman, destined to end up just like everyone else. I would be the last person in the city to be crucified."

Cocaine and alcohol, as usual, were only the surface details. Her depths were roiled by a more persistent intrusion. I hoped she would continue to take opportunity in our work together for exploring what lurked beneath. But I would not press her, instead letting her take the lead. My role was to provide the safety and silence for her words to come, whenever she felt comfortable unveiling them. For now, disulfiram and other supports would be central to her treatment, though I had several concerns, which I conveyed to her as we finally concluded the session. I explained that it can be nearly impossible to transition, overnight, from a toxic entrenched relationship with substances, as was clearly the case with her drinking and using cocaine, to the kind of use she hoped to achieve: moderate, respectful, and controlled. I suggested that she compare her addictions to a broken relationship. It may take tremendous work and time, and it is a good idea to separate for a while, if there is to be any hope for a healthier relationship, free from the destructive patterns and attitudes that might have existed before. Expecting everything to change all at once is unrealistic. She understood the challenges, but she wanted to take her chances and attempt to moderate her use right away.

The next several months were tumultuous. Her reckless judgment and unstable mental state remained problems. I encouraged her to try a variety of low-risk strategies to improve her mood and decision making: mindfulness training, diet adjustments, sleep hygiene, high-intensity cardio, a regular hot yoga practice. She found them all helpful and incorporated many of these practices into her daily life. But she took disulfiram maybe four times over that several-month period. Her original intention was a few times a week. There never seemed to be a good evening for it.

"You don't understand," she would tell me. "I can't just go out and not drink. There are certain expectations. It isn't partying, or just a frivolous good time. This is my career we're talking about. I need to be on at all times, and while I could definitely be more responsible, I can't just stop mixing it up, and stop being the person people want to see."

The treatment shifted away from attempting to abstain entirely on certain nights. The focus was now on healthier habits: eating better, extricating herself from harmful relationships, attending to her emotions, moderating her use. She felt her life improving; she particularly enjoyed her meditation practice and her regular alone time, even as very little changed come evening. She continued to drink and go on occasional cocaine binges. She was still partying and socializing intensely. Sexual entanglements continued to occur, though slightly less frequently. And her primary relationship remained the married executive, who was revealing himself to be emotionally abusive and dishonest.

There were further disclosures, some of them difficult for her. Though physically attractive and slender, she regarded herself as "horse-faced" and overweight, which she took as reasons to fast for a few days each week to control her size. Her features were soft and delicate, and she had an ingratiating bright smile, but she saw her teeth, perfectly white and petite, as far too large for her face. She attributed her sexual appeal not to any inherent charm in her person, but to the powers of "hypnosis": she knows how to walk into a room, she said, and immediately command attention as beautiful and ravishing through "mind control" and "carefully controlled suggestion."

This power to control the room is clearly an exaggeration, or at least nothing that she can sustain through the night, especially once the debauches begin. She suspects she may have been raped a few times, in her early twenties, but her memory is fuzzy because she was deeply intoxicated on both occasions. Sometimes a certain physiognomy or expression fills her with inexplicable fear, "a lazy eye sort of pudginess and creepiness," and she wonders if her "subconscious registers something." She also acknowledged that she had mythologized her childhood, left a few important details out. Her father was far from a successful businessman. He was deep in debt for most of her childhood. The business that brought her to New York was not her father's; it belonged to a man with whom she had been sleeping in Miami. The wealthy family friend who seduced her when she was a teen? He was not a family friend at all, but an investor to whom her father owed money.

"I can't shake the feeling that he knew what was happening, perhaps even encouraged it. Or at the very least he turned a blind eye, suggesting everyone else in the family do the same. I mean, it strikes me as unbelievable that nobody knew what we were up to. Christ, I would travel alone with him, fourteen years old with a fifty-plus-year-old man. Just that possibility alone—my own dad letting this happen—makes me sick. Maybe he hoped to get a break or seal a deal. A secret agreement, man to man. The most horrible thing is that I can't pretend he is beyond that. I've seen people just like him do the same, or worse. Sell their daughters, sell their family and friends, ruin themselves, just to feed the beast. There is no question that nothing mattered to him like money, power, property, connections. Especially not me. I'm sure of that. I learned early on nobody was going to take care of me, I needed to take care of myself. It was better to sell myself than have someone else sell me. At least then I could barricade myself behind my own protection, my own money, the only thing that carries any power in this world."

Around the time that she divulged this, several months after we first met, she developed sleep issues, for which I prescribed a mild sleep aid. She also had more difficulty maintaining her customary coolness with the married executive, becoming much more sensitive to any hint of being taken for granted and uncharacteristically fearful of being discarded by him. A thoughtless word or gesture on his part, no matter how subtle, and she would dig into him. The relationship became severely strained, and any consolation she had previously found in his presence had become impossible, so alert had she grown to slights or negligent treatment. The situation was intensified by his complacency with her, having become habituated over the years to treating her any way he liked with impunity, including abruptly canceling dates and making extravagant sexual requests.

The relationship had deteriorated rapidly, with intense arguments at every meeting. She began to withhold sexual intimacy; he visited less often, which he ascribed to work, with greater lengths of time between their dates. They were both playing their hands. Her sleep continued to grow more difficult, and she found her mood worsening. She maintained her meditation routine, as well as her yoga practice, and these were helpful, she felt, at keeping her drinking and cocaine use in check and at ensuring that she continued to take care of herself. Her use remained stable, perhaps she even began drinking slightly less, but unusual things began happening.

Her sensitivity to alcohol changed dramatically. After only a few drinks she would cry inconsolably, feel waves of deep fear and terror, and experience long stretches of blank tape, sometimes losing hours at a time. She would startle awake in her own bed the next day, unable to remember how she got home, often covered in vomit and feeling beaten up. And these were the good nights. There were a few mornings where she would find herself bruised or bleeding on a friend's sofa, and on one occasion in an emergency department, having been escorted away from an event because she had alarmed people with her violent, provocative, and incoherent behavior.

"I want to believe these nights are the exception, but the blackouts continue to happen. I have embarrassed myself completely, I always hear about it from someone else. It always seems a totally different person. I don't know what is happening to me. It's like I completely forget who I am. I notice people observing me now from afar as the night begins, wondering if I will be drinking and getting themselves ready, I imagine, for a wild ride. I am now identified as the person with the drinking problem, I'm sure of it, the one everyone talks about be-hind her back. I know I am not that person, I know in my heart that something else is going on. I need to prove to everyone that nothing has changed, that I am who I have always been, and that I can still keep it together like anyone else."

She said she tried everything, nursing a single cocktail for an hour, restricting herself to wine, chasing her drinks with water, but the unrav-eling eventually happens, in one form or another. She learned to leave as soon as the crying starts, and it sometimes emerges after only one drink. This has saved her some uncomfortable evenings around others, but she still ends up suffering on her own once she returns home, with the discomfort quite intense; invariably, she vomits, grows dizzy, and feels gripped by an intense terror.

"I know you want me to stop drinking, everyone wants me to stop. And I would stop, believe me, if it didn't feel like a colossal defeat, if it didn't mean publicly conceding that I have a problem. I know what you're thinking. Perhaps I do have a problem, I mean I'm seeing you, right? But that's not their business. And this is something else. This is my wanting to curb things, privately, working with you, so that I can be happy for a change. They, on the other hand, could care less about me: I can see them now, smug and satisfied that I have lost control, that I'm batshit crazy, not worth their respect and best kicked to the curb. I can't let that happen. I need you to help me to figure out how I might get back to drinking normally, or at least how I was drinking before all this insanity started. That wasn't great, I know, but it is still better than this."

I was at a loss regarding what was going on. This type of precipitous intolerance to alcohol was very unusual. There may have been phys-ical or psychiatric problems that had emerged—depression, anxiety, somatic issues, and inflammatory or autoimmune conditions might all lead to challenges with tolerating alcohol. But I had never seen any-thing quite like this, with such a rapid onset and with no abnormalities according to her bloodwork. The problem was intensified by her un-willingness to take it seriously and put her drinking to rest.

Denial is most stubborn when there is a certain sense of self to up-hold. She could not consider that this was a problem, because to do so would mean supporting the viewpoint that she is crazy or out of control, thereby losing whatever social capital she believed she had. So she will continue drinking, she decided, doggedly determined to find a healthy relationship to alcohol reminiscent of the unhealthy relationship she had before. This is because she is not the person who lost it last night. She is actually a successful businessperson who could hypnotize entire rooms of people into submission while still managing to drink them under the table. They will come to recognize this sooner or later.

It would do no good to challenge this chain of reasoning head-on, despite how flawed it is. At its core was a deep-seated fear of vulnerability and weakness. I recognized echoes of that abused little girl clenching her fists, vowing to break others before they break her. It wasn't the time to enter into that pain too directly. She was too resistant and armored, the wound of molested vulnerability too fresh. Denial must be touched lightly, or better yet, left untouched altogether, as with an electrified fence, while gently probing for another way to get across. Otherwise, the electric charge grows more acute and lacerating.

"What do you suppose would happen," I asked, "if you tried to prove your point, and demonstrate how self-possessed you are, by not drinking? This might be a less risky way of going about things given that we don't yet know why you've been responding so intensely and uncharacteristically to alcohol lately."

"I understand your perspective," she said, "but it is past the point where I can just go to an event and not drink. Too much has already happened: going out and not drinking would be the same as messing up again in dramatic fashion. It would be an admission that I've failed, that I've lost control. It's better to drink a little bit, and retire early, believe me, than to not drink, field questions about why I'm not drinking, and appear to everyone like I'm pretending I'm not an alcoholic. And let's look at the positives. I'm drinking less than I ever have, even though it is far from pleasant for me, and I haven't used cocaine in God knows how long, never getting to the point in the night where that might be an enjoyable bonus. So, mission accomplished, in some sense."

I smiled at her ingenuity, spinning her intransigent suffering into a sign of progress. "Mission accomplished, in some sense," I said, "but in another sense, we haven't even started. You came to see me because you want freedom. But who's in charge here? You think you're flexing your power, proving to everyone who is in control, but we become their slaves the moment we decide we have to prove ourselves to them in the first place."

"I hear you," she said. "I realize it doesn't sound totally rational. But this is what I need to do. I need them to understand. It's not about approval; it's strategy."

Thus, she embarked on several more weeks of self-assertion, attempting to regain what she believed was herself. But it was more of the same. Parties entered into cautiously, tearful initiations, breakdowns in total darkness, embarrassing amnesia. Propulsive rapid-fire flashes of want, striving, intoxication, frustration . . .

•

She called me crying on a Sunday morning, an unusual urgency to her voice, as if she had just survived a terrible accident or awakened from a nightmare.

"I know what happened," she said. "I know why this has been happening. It was the pills. I switched them up. I realized it last night. I had put all my medicines into little canisters, unmarked, the sleeping pills, the Antabuse [disulfiram]. Everything got screwed up. I thought I was taking the sleeping pills, I was really taking the other one, the pill not to sleep, but to make myself sick. This has probably been going on for weeks. I've been poisoning myself, literally poisoning myself with alcohol, not caring, not even noticing, just focused on proving I'm not sick, to people who probably don't even give a shit. I'm the one who has to go to sleep crying and vomiting every night, I'm doing this to myself, nobody else, and I didn't care.

"I need help, I understand this more than ever. Thank you for all you've done, but I need to get away, away from all this."

She had found her explanation. Accidental and repeated ingestion of disulfiram, with consequent alcohol toxicity. This reaction can occur for a few days after a single pill, and she seemed to have been taking it nightly, which likely led to a buildup of medicine in her system and accounted for the toxic aversion she experienced toward a single sip.

She surprised me with her response. Rather than resolve the mix-up, stop the disulfiram, and resume the party, she was going in another direction. She would not turn her eyes from what was shown her. It had reached that point where her pain could no longer be covered over: "sick and tired," as she would later write me in AA speak, "of being sick and tired."

She had never seen more clearly, she said. She conveyed her realizations with the same breathless rush of urgent and disjointed phrases with which she began the call.

"This didn't start with the pills getting confused. It has been happening since I was a girl. Taking poison, praying for a miracle. I hadn't told you, I should have. I'm constantly praying, it's what I repeat to myself more than anything. My mom taught me this, a secret advantage, took me along with her to church sometimes. It was a power thing, if God rules everything, then God rules money and history too, God rules over the night, God can transform whatever fucked-up situation into its exact opposite. So, prayer, constantly. Please God, help me God, please, always under my breath, first as I looked for my way in, and then as I poured poison into myself, poisonous men, poisonous deals, poisonous drugs, poison in nearly everything.

"I prayed so that I might get what I wanted. But you remember the dream. A plastic doll nailed into place. Crucifixes covering every block, centering around the slaughter in Columbus Circle. I can pray, but poison is poison, being fucked up is being fucked up, not even God can change that. I saw the world I wanted, prayed that the city would show itself. But they say it to all children. Be careful of the face you make. You might just end up looking like that forever."

She began to speak more rapidly, the pathos bleeding her words together into a nearly incoherent current. I transcribe the words here as they emerged to best convey their chaotic power.

"I did it to myself. The same fucked-up dream every night. Copies of that reflection, thousands of them. Behind the façade was the system that runs everything. It was in my blood. Everything boils down to the same violence, the same exploitation and prostitution. Sell it before it gets taken away, take it before someone else does. An old story. Everybody knows the deal, nobody cares. The trap has been around forever.

We all know it, we all fall for it. I was forgetting entire nights, forgetting myself, waking up bruised and messed up. Then it was on to the next breakdown. You were right, God knows what's really in control, it definitely isn't me."

The start of a sob broke her words, then a deep breath, and she continued speaking, even more rapidly, the words coming so quickly as to seem no longer her own, as if propelled by some external pressure.

"I was taught to call it love, everyone looking the other way. You know how many people go through this. You've seen the worst of it, I'm sure: the abuse, the manipulation and damage and trauma. It seems to be everyone. An Indian curse, what else could it be. Generation after generation. Destroy everything destroy yourself. I am only the next person pushing her way to center stage. You want it, here it is, now drink up until there's nothing left.

"I know what it means to want to take. From debt to greater debt. Nothing is free. An endless circle of payback. I must have been hallucinating. The play of light on liquid who knows. Something in the glass was beckoning. They call it spirits for a reason. Wanting to show me something, come closer so that you can find what you need. Or not find it, the loss and debt of it. Drinking myself to sleep to sickness and insanity and blackout. Repeat every night every year. Only seeing what's to come, nothing else. Eyes on the horizon, the love of your life, anything you could want. Then it all bleeds into a blood-red sunset. Sick of everything. Darkness falls every night the same sickness. Stranded in a world upside-down, looking into the empty glass. Still hallucinating, still drinking. But I know it can be giddy too. Squint your eyes the whole thing looks like love. Maybe it is."

Robyn was babbling and sobbing. "You can't just stop loving. I feel like such a cliché: love rules everything. Even getting messed up night after night: love. We can't help but fall into it. But take it up gently. You can't want him too bad. Grasped too tightly the whole thing burns a hole in the head. But refuse love, deny it, it will torment you with sickness and heartbreak."

An upsurge of words, signaling something like total upheaval. Understanding it required stretching my own thoughts to their limits. Wild visions are a regular part of the work; language may reach its breaking point at any moment, though rarely with this level of apocalyptic fluency.

I recognized the revolt in her words. And the remembrance. She was overthrowing one world in order to return to something more fundamental. Though we forget the vastness that had been paved over, the silent wilderness layered with signs upon signs, there is a more ancient and perfect memory that registers when even the smallest stone is out of place. It can be felt in the soil, in the trees supplicating the sky, in the river glistening next to the asphalt and buildings like an open wound. But also in the depths of every cocaine binge, sorrow, moment of love: an inescapable yearning. It had found the words that needed to be said.

Her words brought a hope of freedom too. This man-made system will never run everything. No system will. She saw its power, its hollowness. The wilderness will reclaim its dominion in due time, birthing new life in the open air, breeching the cracks in the concrete, green tendrils creeping in gaps and worming into the monuments and structures. Robyn had created this teetering system herself, from a dream that may not even be hers, inherited like a curse. Her mind splintering into a thousand words, her hopes shattered, she watched everything dissolve into ground zero.

There was further crying, a few more words of confession, but this softened until she was quiet, her words having become softer until they stopped, too, and there was nothing left, neither words nor tears, simply silence and a growing calm. She was resolved. It was time to leave the city, she felt, or she might lose it all. She acted decisively. Within days of the phone call, she checked in to a well-regarded rehab facility in Connecticut for a several-months' stay. After rehab, she quit her job, moved back to Miami, became involved in a Christian recovery group. She remained in touch, sending me notes every few months. I heard from her when she got engaged, when she married, at the birth of each of her two children. She resumed work in real estate, at a relatively modest position. Alcohol and cocaine were left behind in New York City, she said, along with the other excesses she claimed to have renounced.

•

Her life became so wildly different from what I had known that it seemed to belong to someone else. The Robyn I had known had vanished; all that remained of her were intermittent emails, from more than a thousand miles away, reporting in a generic voice on her quiet life.

There was something uncanny about her transformation. She had been contradictory and mercurial from the first visit; her greatest paradox was that she seemed even more fluid and elusive now that she had settled into suburban life. She had reinvented herself to such an extraordinary (or rather, hyper-ordinary) extent that she seemed unreal: a ghost peering through the mask of a "normal" person. Not witnessing this new life directly, and only hearing about it in matter-of-fact notes haunted by a glaring absence of her customary intensity and energy, deepened my impression of a spectral shape-shifter.

I remembered the disdain with which she would say *cliché*, whether she was speaking of her dreams or of her emotions, as if the worst fate is to direct toward things the same tired words as everyone else. I sensed something performative, in fact, in that final conversation; she seemed to be staging the most spectacular rock bottom the world had ever known. And she surely recognized how "ordinary" her new life must seem to others—complete with a turn to Jesus and other standard recovery tropes. This only made her transformation appear more honest and singular.

I would also reflect on the anguish that preceded this extraordinary anonymity. The boundary-breaking multitudes that had filled my office over the course of our work together, the Chanel alternating with goth punk, the vigilant poise giving way to raw vulnerability, now seemed the defiant convulsions of a trapped animal, squirming and maneuvering and parrying to find release. Robyn had felt crippled but had not known the cause, and only realized later that the burden she carried was exactly what she refused to relinquish: the delirious masquerade that had become herself. She repudiated this persona in forswearing the drugs and alcohol and high society. She also seemed to disown a deeper entanglement: that she needed to be a person at all.

A real estate agent, married with two children, engaged in a Christian recovery program—as good a mask as any, especially if the intention is an unruffled sobriety. "Robyn" seemed less her identity now, less a person even, and more a deliberate device for upholding the main virtues, such as humility, simplicity, and surrender to a higher power, inculcated by the program. A strategy, a path, a costume, a cliché even, but not who she is, nothing to which she tethers herself. She had seemed to renounce, among other things pertaining to her life in New York, the binds that compel us to only see ourselves through the eyes of others, or assume roles at odds with ourselves, or become petrified monuments in our likeness that might, like God murdered on a cross, rise above the crowd. She had become what she would have called "a nobody"—and was freer, more fulfilled and fluid, than ever.

•

This is how I imagined Robyn from a distance, through the course of our intermittent correspondence: a free spirit finding rest in a plain-clothes persona. I had not seen her since she left, but I imagined a sly twinkle in her eyes, the hint of a conspiratorial smile, as if she had accomplished that rare trick aspired to by people as varied as artists, con men, and good Christians: to be in the world, but not of it. A nobody, in the most ecstatic and disruptive way. In her recovery, I sensed a new birth of that iconoclastic vitality I had come to regard as her hallmark, playing with her masks as opposed to suffocating beneath them.

But this interpretation—Robyn transcending a monolithic sense of self and trying on an identity conducive to well-being—may be false. The reality may be very different. In leaving New York, she might have remained a prisoner, one system replacing another. And what she found in Miami may not be a lightly embraced persona at all, but how she came to see herself, an identity as binding as the masquerade in New York. Far from playfully independent from it all, Robyn might have still been stuck in someone else's script, and performing much as she always had: with an overidentification with the stranger she was staging. This would not have been surprising given the catechism, the ritual, and the programming inherent to AA, the tradition to which her Christian recovery group belonged.

Forging a certain self through the pages of the Big Book and maintaining it through committed step work and community involvement are important parts of the path. It made sense that she would fit that mold, despite how incongruent it seemed with her prior act. This underscored my impression of Robyn as shape-shifter, this time with greater care being given to the mask she slipped on. Her AA self was obviously a ready-made production, its 12-step diction and worldview lending the identity a quality of self-conscious contrivance and deepening that secret distance between Robyn and "Robyn" that she seemed to be hinting to me from thousands of miles away. And I found myself wanting to believe in "Robyn" as if she were the hero in a story: I had become her main audience, captive to her character while rooting for a successful finish. The question of authenticity seemed moot, which was itself a kind of victory on her part. A remarkable performance: incarnating the freedom of someone in the program, working the steps and emancipated through recovery, and yet preserving the wild-hearted unclassifiable core of someone entirely other, revealing her command of the AA performance by intimating its artifice. In the rooms but not of them.

Robyn seemed to have achieved a rare freedom, a freedom simultaneously authentic and performed. I interpreted her simple, seemingly straightforward letters to me in this spirit—as ultimately uninterpretable, unable to be fixed into place, with their author neither clearly Robyn nor "Robyn" and yet undeniably a flourishing human being.

In other words, I was in the dark. It might have all been a dream on my part. But I had evidence of a sort. Compelling my hope for her revitalized freedom was the nightly crucifixion. The dolls on crosses had haunted her into awakening and might do so again. I read the dream as a cautionary tale, a warning she seemed to treat seriously: be careful of the ideal that you envision for yourself because you might end up nailed to it. Crucifixion as a deadly apotheosis of the fictional self; as a final conquest of angles and geometry over the fluid forms of our beings. This was a powerful symbol of her surrender to that greater power, the "system that runs everything": it indicated just how much her self-sacrificing striving for that golden ideal of the 1 percent was motivated by forces much larger than she, perhaps by a momentum predating her birth, by the relentless machinery of imperialism and capitalism, by the curse of 1492. Maybe it was even deeper and touched on a more genetic slavery.

Crucifixion, however, is ambiguous and intersectional, especially for someone raised in the church. Blood orgy, torture, and human sacrifice, and yet also sacrifice of the most exalted kind, pointing toward heaven with the hope of life everlasting. Robyn had maintained constant skyward prayer as she knotted herself more deeply into a system that came to seem ever more diabolical and destructive: aspiring for transcendence even in her prayers to the gutter. I addict myself to you O Lord. Whoever aspires ever upwards, as Goethe said of Faust, alone can be saved.

Even the sewer gates of hell might open onto grace and freedom, so long as one remains propelled by that exalted longing. Robyn found her way to AA and came to embrace many of its principles. Her upward longing found a focus, beyond drugs or alcohol. Waiting in the wings, the Big Book says, is a transcendent master promising deliverance as opposed to further tyranny and anguish. Turning to this "higher power"—in her case, Jesus Christ—brought Robyn greater ease and comfort. But it was not a passive stance. She wrote to me that recovery often seemed a tightrope walk, a balancing act of reconciling such apparent opposites as surrender and sovereignty, acceptance and change. Another paradox, she came to realize, is maintaining the transcendent focus of her longings, despite how earthbound and murky they feel.

"I direct everything to Him," she wrote. "If I have any desire to drink or party, which is becoming less and less frequent, I think of Him, surrender to Him, and the moment I ask for peace and wisdom, I receive it. Everything is an offering to Him, my work, my sobriety, even my cravings."

The serenity prayer was often invoked: changing what she could, accepting what she couldn't, discerning between the two. And regardless of what was going on, Robyn remembered that she retained the choice to surrender to her higher power, to offer her suffering and violence to Him. "Everything else is illusion. There is no other freedom. I am only free in turning toward Him, in thought, word, and deed."

It sounds simple, she wrote, and "the path forward is as clear as day. But it is constant work."

The gutter beckons. Haunting recovery, and complicating her acquiescence to a higher power, are the hungry ghosts of "lower" powers. They tempt with promises of immense and ancient fulfillments. One must therefore pause at every threshold and reflect thoughtfully on whether this is a door worth opening—it may lead us, once again, into the shadow lands of suffering. Family and faith were where she now turned her devotion, with distractions at every turn. She was busier in some ways than she had been in New York, an endless challenge of vigilance and discernment.

AA has its own horde of hungry ghosts too. Surrender to a higher power is not simply a personal matter, limited to the relationship between oneself and the transcendent. The process is mediated entirely by systematized, Big Book–based Recovery. This can lead to being mired in a variety of follies: conformity, validation by others, hierarchical progression, cults of personality, communal quasi-religious ritual, and other (un)real entanglements. There are many ways to misdirect one's devotions.

This is a common setback in the rooms, something to which experienced counselors and sponsors are attentive. The greatest danger is surrendering, once again, to what is too easily grasped—the groupthink, the text, the rituals—and falling away from ( ) into a static (un)reality. A related concern is maintaining a healthy expression of freedom, when freedom had so often meant a willful, heedless rush toward self-deception.

These are challenges that exist everywhere. AA is just as precarious as anything else constructed by human hands. And as ambivalent as the drugs themselves, giving a hand toward both support and folly with the same generosity. One might as well face these complexities in a setting that acknowledges the situation and that is practiced at helping people navigate it, with decades of collective wisdom.

Flourishing in recovery requires striking a paradoxical balance, sustaining a spirit of both surrender and vigilance, maintaining humility while exercising discernment at the door to every room. I felt that Robyn understood this somehow, given how she had been burned so thoroughly by the man-made. I trusted she would remain untethered to what might nail her into place, forgoing the alluring absolutes of crucifixion despite her newfound resolution to bear her cross, "one step at a time."

•

Robyn's recovery began in earnest in a single moment, with the recognition that she had been taking disulfiram instead of a sleeping pill, and therefore incurring aldehyde toxicity night after night, with even her natural instinct toward self-preservation derailed. But it was a moment that might have gone in another direction. She might have decided, for example, to stay where she was: to correct the mistake, discard the disulfiram, and run off to the next event to prove her self-control. Instead, the scales fell from her eyes, as Fred had described his own clarity and sense of redemption. She saw through the system that had seduced her, directly into its perverse core.

Such momentous transitions seem as orchestrated as a scene from cinema, with the touch of a miracle about them. But they happen all the time. Major shifts, so difficult to achieve for years, might occur suddenly, within the space of minutes. According to the National Epidemiological Survey on Alcohol and Related Conditions (NESARC), most people who recover from an addiction do so on their own, without seeking medical treatment. The shift may be gradual—a slow disentanglement—or it may be abrupt, but there is always the same emergence: a supple freedom from the old regime, with the person knowing what to do to maintain it.

This is not to say, of course, that treatment and support are not helpful for many people. But this finding raises questions about what is happening to a majority of addicted people who get better. It is possible that they experienced something like what happened to Robyn, with various factors harmonizing to create a profound disruption in what they take to be normal, or a more gradual and just as powerful disenchantment with the exalted gutter. The trap is recognized, and the person extricates herself while sustaining an adroitness with the snares ahead.

No treatment emerges from nothing. The examples of spontaneous healing in nature provide a model for our own inventions. The treatment provided Marcus, for example, had mobilized in a deliberate manner many of the key elements implicated in more "natural" turning points: the shifts in perspective, the self-examination, the commitment setting, the vigilance against being entrenched again. The 12-step program, in turn, approximates the spiritual journey that its architect Bill W. had undergone. These treatments and supports are providing what might happen anyway, but with greater "mastery" over the key processes that ripen the moment and bring it to fruition. This is the same civilizing spirit that we have brought to nature to enjoy its magic more methodically: moving to agriculture from hunting and gathering, for example, or creating durable works of art to preserve glimpses of spontaneous beauty. The 12 steps, medicine, and all our healing modalities are yet further ways we concentrate the bountiful miracle of existence into boxes, for better and for worse.

Most miraculous of all are not our inventions, though this capacity to channel the magic of nature toward fulfilling our desires is not a gift to be taken lightly or irresponsibly. The supreme gift—the great miracle, according to Marcus—is that the moment can be brought to fruition in the first place, despite all odds, despite how things have always gone. Whether it is due to a deliberate intervention or good fortune, or some unique combination, the shift in addiction toward refreshed possibility is comparable to inspirations, epiphanies, or other ecstatic experiences when the cellophane muting everything is ripped away. This moment, here and now, reveals its exuberant abundance: a contentment that had seemed impossible a moment ago is recognized to have been present all along. Clarity, better judgment, an improved perspective, whatever one might have been wishing for but failing to achieve—the ground for these realities is already our own. We allow ourselves *to be*, liberated from what we had tried to *become* in our mad search for fulfillment.

Simply being is already quite something. This is what is forgotten; it is why we become insensitive to the vital mystery, obscuring with "experience" our ineffable innocence. But remembering the present restores us to our senses. We are here, faced with the depths of being, as opposed to not being: there is something, as Marcus had repeated, instead of nothing. It is a mystery that deserves constant remembrance: in being, in being to our depths, we become what we are.

●

How to make sense of *becoming being* or *remembering the present*? I recognize that we risk losing the thread with such riddles. But viewing these words as riddles is an important start to breaking the stalemate. After all, they might instead be dismissed as *clichés*, their meanings taken for granted by everyone and passed over with complacent understanding.

This exact perplexity is the point, riddling and agitating the familiar surface of things. These are the same banalities that had confused Robyn and the others as they stood at the brink, with the usual maps and meanings ceasing to make sense. They were lost in a system of dead ends: looking for fulfillment in what deepened their dissatisfaction; entangled in an unreality that resonated with heightened reality; exalted by possibilities that were impossible. They were striving to become: euphoric, stimulated, free, consoled, successful, pacified, a variety of *conclusions*. But no conclusion, no matter how exalting, can capture the vastness of being. Even "happiness" is bound to disappoint. We are bound to become, but how to preserve our possibilities while still called to become certain incarnations? How to maintain our grounding in ( ) if we are dead set to conclude in one way or another? Death has now entered the conversation: the great riddle, the great banality, patiently awaiting an answer from each of us.

Death is not simply a distant prospect. Birth and death, being and becoming, are on either side of every day, darkness leading to darkness. Each incarnation suffering the dreary ooze of being into doing. And we court various conclusions—love, freedom, security, happiness—to suck from this cracked shell what seems the essence of life. The moments we secrete away like precious jewels, the joys we hold captive so that we might always have them.

What we think is life is death; death might be life; life and death might intertwine in one mortal thread, may indeed be the same thread from the start. Wanting things to be different, free of death, free even of life, is to knot oneself deeper into further disorientations: the Great Doubt of Zen; the dark night of the soul, as Christians call this passage through an illuminating confusion. The end reveals itself. Perhaps it is a beginning. Perhaps it is neither: a birth-death circularity expanding as one moment, samsara conjoined to nirvana, without beginning or end.

Consider death long enough, and the shadow of it will creep into everything. Life itself is no less opaque. Answering them separately is impossible enough before recognizing that the two make up the same inscrutable riddle. We are bound to be confused. We might practice our perplexity as we do stopping the breath, inviting disorientation, becoming acclimated to its inevitability. Death is most ferocious to those

clinging to breath, perplexity most galling when we cling to our certainties. But we will need to find a way to marry the two. Samsara and
nirvana: confusion and awakening, addiction and freedom, intertwined
in one endless circle.

These interruptions, whether created by questions, stories, medicines, or practices, can guide the way, especially if we have reached, as
has the addict, the painful gridlock. Koans and riddles are therefore another gift of nature we might box into the toolkits of medicine. These
confusions and paradoxes are not far from the surface anyway; they
need only be named and given attention to become more visible, as
happened with Robyn when she was aghast to recognize that she had
been poisoning herself while also praying for the miracle. The work
ahead is to support people as they answer their confusion appropri-
ately, not with fictions or drugs, as might be their habit, but with the
wakeful attention of true presence, a beginner's mind flowing beyond
whatever conclusion might deaden it.

A crucifixion dream might also be a dream of resurrection, with the
geometric conclusion giving way to our caves cracking open and a miraculous emergence. There were two riddles that compelled Robyn to
see me. The first was that she was striving for the very fulfillments that
deepened her dissatisfaction: the scintillating career, the pseudo relationship, the social currency. She aimed to become, it seemed, what
deepened her anguish, and yet this becoming had come to seem indistinguishable from who she felt herself to be. The second was that she
was dreaming the same dream, and awakening breathless from it, every
night: the plastic, torments, and banality of a thousand crucifixes. This
riddle seemed to haunt her as much as alcohol and cocaine had. Adding
to the mystery is that the two riddles might be the same, with the same
sphinx awaiting a response.

We might wake up every morning to the same day. Why do we grow
so unsettled when we fall asleep every night to the same dream? We recognize a problem in one that we are too well adjusted to recognize in
the other. Night and day are mysterious in equal measure, life conjoined
to death, darkness adjacent to darkness. But the alien ambiguity of the
night doesn't allow itself to be ordered as readily as the day might. The
night will alert us to the dream blinding us with too much light.

The content of a dream plays an important role, of course, in whether it pains us or not. The relevance of its story to Robyn's waking life, and the way that it reproduced her daily agony to torture her in sleep, were clarified by her in that final phone call. But rigidly organizing the darkness, with every night circling around an identical dream, creates its own trouble: the night itself comes to be nailed down and crucified. It doesn't matter what is being conveyed or what forms the chaos takes. Something in us registers that this is a wilderness that needs to remain wild. Dreaming is often the last refuge of freedom: even if the rest of one's life is predictable, overly familiar, and seemingly mechanical, at least here we might find a fresh and startling beginning. Inhabiting the same tired rerun in sleep, the same characters and stories, reveals to us that the flow of our lives has been interrupted in a fundamental way. We might recognize that something has lodged in us, like an apple in our throats.

Robyn had dreamed the same dream and startled from it nightly, yet always without closure. There may be something in the shadows that will not rest until it is revealed: a message, a wish, a presence, a darkness. The labor of day becomes the work of bringing to attention whatever requires recognition, much as we might learn to acknowledge the hard truth that fire scorches or that water drowns, despite their beauties and benefits. A necessary confusion, with everything more than it had seemed. She had paved over the spirits, utilizing liquor as an indispensable support, but came to realize later she was poisoning herself with each sip. A clear-cut path had yielded to one darker, more amorphous. Yet also more wakeful. Robyn's clarity crystallized, in fact, the moment she recognized the profound murkiness that led her to confuse one pharmakon with another, her medicines and poisons all jumbled together.

Robyn regained herself, similarly, by regaining darkness and invisibility, beyond the iridescent images that had flashed through her heedless nights. Residing in the liminal realm of possibility can go in many directions: it can be liberating, as it had been for Marcus or Robyn, offering opportunity for a nourishing silence and freedom from our incarnations, but its limbo might also be sleep-inducing, deadening. What keeps us asleep isn't simply our relationship to a dream—it is also, of course, our relationship to sleep, to formlessness and stasis, to death itself.

Waking up breathless, close to death, seems a true reflection of where we have ended up. Suspended face down in the mud bank, choking on earth, the current passing us by. Finding our breath, reentering that natural flow, seems the only answer to the riddle holding us captive. As we liberate ourselves from the suffocating stasis, other things will find freedom too. The wilderness will eventually creep its serpentine way through the cracks of our boarded-up brains, compacted and clamoring with dreams that might finally be liberated, given back, forgotten.

7

MOTHER'S MILK

Robyn isn't the only patient, of course, who has communicated with me from afar. Letters are often an important part of the process, with the correspondence initiated generally by patients themselves to maintain the conversation, receive support, remain otherwise tethered.

One of the most memorable letters I've received was emailed by a patient with whom I had only met three times over the course of a few weeks. It arrived months after he disappeared from treatment and went silent. Some history, told mostly in his own words, will set the stage. Then the email will be shared verbatim, edited minimally to maintain confidentiality.

My own words will be limited to moving things along.

●

A thirty-year-old man dividing his time between LA and NYC, Jermaine contacted me for support with, in his phrase, managing his medications—a puzzling request given that he also said he wasn't on any medications. "I'll tell you more when I see you."

Arriving late for his first appointment, he made a striking first impression. He wore cascading layers of various animal prints over his thin frame, his angular face peering at me from atop the pile of fabric, expressionless as a mask, with deep-set eyes and sharp cheekbones. Amplifying his eccentricity was a Boston accent so peculiar and mannered as to seem put-on.

He disclosed right away, as if to explain himself, that he had been adopted in infancy by a high-net-worth New England couple, both coming from what he called "old Boston Brahmin money." He grew up "as close to American aristocracy as one can get." Yet his parents were not "garden-variety billionaires"; he described them as "reluctantly wealthy" and "socialists to the core," interested in wealth redistribution, correcting resource iniquities, and other social justice issues.

It was far from an idyllic childhood, despite the tremendous resources. By the time he was twelve, there had been a suicide attempt followed by a psychiatric hospitalization, aborted attempts at treating what were diagnosed as ADHD and bipolar disorder, and a suspension from his elite school for smoking cannabis in the bathroom.

"I felt more like a charity case than a son," he said. His sense of alienation and status insecurity was deepened by racial differences; he is Black, his parents and older sibling are White. Adding to his angst as well was a deep terror of imminent upheaval: to be abandoned yet again, by his parents as well as the greater world, drifting on his own toward an inevitable wreckage.

"[After the suspension] my parents sat me down and said what they always say. Don't grow up to regret what you could have done. This time, for whatever reason, their words took. I felt the fire to make the most of myself. And also the threat of what would happen if I didn't."

He began to do well, rising to the top quarter of his class year after year. His psychiatric health stabilized as well, without medications or therapy. But he still felt beleaguered by the usual issues. "My brain didn't feel right. I came up with all sorts of stories—that my mother had smoked crack while pregnant, that my dad was messed up and schizophrenic . . .

"I worked hard, extra hard. But it's not like I really wanted what was on offer either. I did what I needed to do, top grades, killing the SATs, getting admitted into Harvard, all the boxes getting checked. Wearing my Magic Negro face, smiling big white teeth, good school, good grades, good diction, I knew what was next if I stayed in line, good college, good job, good White money in a good White neighborhood."

At Harvard, he found greater peace, enjoying the freedom to take whatever courses he wanted and find his own way. Drugs became a more regular pastime, "reading Erowid and keeping journals," with a particular interest in psychedelics: "They opened up different parts of my mind; and they also seemed to fix connections that were broken."

Getting involved in the jam-band circuit through his freshman roommate led to more access to "top-tier drugs, 5-MeO-DMT pens, Swiss lab-grade psilocybin, the best synthetics," and he began using psychedelics in greater amounts, "doing the Whitest possible drugs in the Whitest possible scene." This culminated in a monthlong binge of escalating daily LSD the summer after his junior year, capped off by a violent confrontation at a Phish show.

"It seemed some kind of alien civilization was involved, planning everything. The drugs, the parents I never knew, my super-sensitive receptivity, the one Black guy, again and again, at these shows. It felt like destiny. I recognized I might be an alien myself. And there was a message I needed to deliver. The bottom line to it is that everything is one. There's no real difference between any of us, no you, no me. It's all a lie."

A peaceful message of unity, however, was only half the story.

"I saw the con. We were basically cows at pasture in our religions, schools, nations, races. Everything was part of the manipulation, our agitation was what they needed, their food, that's why we they [sic] are constantly creating wars, division, and confusion. They had us where they want us, seeding agitation in us and then feeding on it. The message was there to set us free."

"They" were reptilian, shape-shifting beings who had secretly colonized earth long ago. And the message was from enlightened aliens who have been at war with these parasitic shape-shifters, battling for the fate of "true consciousness" in a war spanning many universes and millennia. "I also saw who was in on it, human collaborators, lizards in disguise. I got into it with someone at the show. But I still had enough sense to know that the last thing I needed to be doing as a Black man was getting into fights at Phish."

Jermaine committed to stop using LSD and other psychedelics so frequently, and to focus instead on setting the groundwork for communicating the message. He settled on making a movie, an action-adventure blockbuster "like a more spiritual *Matrix*," which he pursued during his free time as a senior at Harvard. Problems began almost immediately.

"The biggest issue was that there was really nothing I could say that hadn't been already said. The message was everywhere, in movies, books, religions, but also TV shows, comics, even in advertisements. And none of it had an effect anyway. Stupidity and cruelty were the rule. Even putting the message out there again would do nothing but drown it out further, adding to the glut of information already too much as it is. It amazed me how sophisticated the cabal was, always one step ahead."

After graduation, he lived off a trust fund in NYC, unwilling to work because he didn't want to support the system, now no longer alien or reptilian but something deeper, a "mind-disease of pure evil" ruling over everything and everyone. Demoralization and nihilism set in. "Nothing seemed to matter. I would see myself in the mirror and my pupils seemed soulless, like the light had been plucked out of them. Staring at the ceiling while spending hours in bed, too catatonic and listless to do anything."

He had restricted his LSD use to once a month "to keep [his] head." This only worsened his despair. "I would modulate, using just enough to sustain the vision without going too deep. But the emptiness would feel emptier, I always felt worse afterward, every fall back to earth more intense than the time before. I was depressed and getting worse, and not sure how to get out of it."

He decided to try ketamine to disrupt the cycle: a 100 mg shot into his deltoid. "I'd read about it being a good antidepressant, especially when injected, so I thought why not. It began as I knew it from having sniffed it at parties before. A synthetic elastic expansion. This time it kept going and going, expanding me so much I disappeared. All that was left was being itself. I no longer even existed as me, I was pure being, the infinite peace of pure being, before it gets whittled down into my body, myself, my problems."

His mood lifted. The second time, a few days later, was intended to deepen the improvement. And while he felt energized afterward, he was taken down a harrowing path to get there.

"I fell into a deep sleep, an awake sleep, like getting locked-in during surgery feeling everything but unable to scream. The pure being of things became a pure deadness. Then the deadness would flicker waking up here and there as solar systems, planets, people, before falling into darkness again. I started to feel that old terror again, the emptiness and meaninglessness. As the k faded, I woke up gradually into real life, and I remembered my name, I had gone so far out as to forget my name. I was grateful for its sound, grateful for everything, a speck of life emerging from the deadness against all odds."

Regular ketamine use worked to revive his engagement with life, improving his depression and propelling him to work on various projects, including starting the cannabis company that became his primary source of income.

"I had a system, mostly pretty good. This lasted years. The injections would reset things, bring me back to pure being, every time feeling refreshed, three times a week was the number I settled on. I would use daily bumps as well to maintain momentum, just enough to keep things fresh without going overboard, though there was the occasional deep dive when things got a bit out of hand . . ."

But this "DIY ketamine clinic," as he put it, did not last.

"I lost myself somewhere along the line. It may have been a dosing thing, a frequency issue, I don't know, but I went from feeling good to being tailed by a deadness every night and day."

His gaunt face, I remember, darkened with terror as he spoke.

"The k is still doing something, it helps more than anything else, but it also isn't helping. Where I've landed with all this is where I've been, the empty reality of things, struggling to find my way. At least I have k to help me through it, a moment of relief even if it is nothing in the end, I just need to get back to a system with it that works, the right dose, maybe not sniffing it so much, perhaps having someone take care of it who knows what he's doing. That's why I need your help, you know addiction and you know ketamine, I need you to help me get regular with it again. It wasn't easy to own up and come to you with this, so I'm hoping you can help me manage my medicine in a way that works."

Over the ensuing weeks, Jermaine remained committed to viewing ketamine as a necessary substance for him. Many of our conversations circled around other perspectives or strategies he might bring to the situation, though nothing landed. He grew frustrated, doubled down on his request for medication management. Then he ceased contact and stopped responding.

I know it has been a while since you and I talked, so I want you to know right away that I didn't disappear because you said ketamine was the wrong solution. It's true I didn't want to hear it, that your words made me angry. But I did what I did for no other reason than because I was instructed.

It started after our last meeting months ago. I was introduced to someone a close friend described as a powerful healer. We got to talking, and he cut to the chase. Would I be willing to only receive medicines from him and not take anything on my own? I agreed, surprised at my lack of hesitation. I was desperate, ready for anything that might help. He took my phone number and told me he would call in several days.

I felt something inside of me shift. They say that this happens when you've decided you're ready. I knew that I wouldn't be using ketamine again, at least not until he called, I can't describe what changed in me. I also wasn't scared to stop, and that sense of hope was a welcome change too.

He also asked me to start meditating, a suggestion I'd heard a hundred times. This time I went for it, taking a class at a Kundalini center in the East Village the next day.

Another shift was that I would consider working with a healer in the first place, especially someone who provides stuff like ayahuasca. The whole plant medicine scene seemed so corrupt to me, celebrity shamans, commodified spirituality, celebrities on CNN talking about finding God. But my friend reassured me this guy was the real deal: he wasn't selling anything or promoting himself, he was simply serving the plants.

I now realize I had been waiting for something like this, wanting at least one thing in this world to be sacred, outside the usual bs. It felt right as well that it would be happening in the city, as opposed to an expensive center in Peru or Costa Rica somewhere, sitting with a tribe that isn't mine and pretending everything was authentic. Doing it here

in the States with someone legit who speaks my language and recom-
mended by a close friend: this was more my speed.

He called within a week. We had a longer conversation. He asked
the kinds of questions you might ask, about my views on things, my
fears, my hopes, he asked about the dark presence haunting my steps,
about what ketamine does for me, some basic biographical stuff about
my parents, schooling, business. I felt as though he was asking me these
things that he wasn't paying attention to the conversation, that he was
listening to something beneath the words.

Then he asked a question out of nowhere.

Do you feel your mother's death? It was like he hit a release but-
ton. I was surprised by the intense grief welling up, swelling my chest.
The mother who raised me was alive and well in Boston, but my other
mother, the mother who carried me to birth, I knew nothing about. She
might in fact be dead. I was carrying these other parents inside who
might as well be dead, and refusing to mourn them, not even recogniz-
ing that they needed to be mourned.

Also, this idea of the other parents. You remember how much their
otherness haunted me, as brain damage, as bad genes, as insanity, even
as straight-up aliens.

You must be willing to feel the death around you and inside you,
he said. This begins with paying more attention to what feeds you. He
suggested that I eat only plant-based foods moving forward, to begin
eating at noon and stop at sunset, as well as to give thanks to every bite,
every sip of water. There is so much in your life. You have forgotten
how to be grateful.

He asked me to fast on the day of the next full moon. To live, he said,
we must be willing to no longer deaden ourselves, even to death, and to
be as vulnerable as we can, as naked and soft as frogs.

There was heaviness in the days following, a sick ball of nausea in
the stomach. The anxiety had also intensified. It was more than anxi-
ety, it was some kind of sickness, maybe delayed ketamine withdrawal.
He called me on the morning of the full moon. He asked me to enter
into silence with him. I didn't know what he was asking. He wanted me
to put my affairs in order and communicate to everyone that I would
not be able to meet with them for at least two months. I thought he was

crazy, I nearly told him to forget it, it seemed impossible to disappear for even a few days, let alone months. My anxiety was already bad enough without more stress.

But I hesitated. I remembered the help I had already received from simply getting to know him. Would I be able to talk to anyone? Email? He was firm. I would not be able to see anyone in person other than him, I would be able to talk to people by phone or by email for no more than an hour a day, and only for deliberate reasons. The aim is solitude and silence.

I was running through how to make plans for this, how to delegate responsibility to my CFO and cofounder for certain things, so many loose ends that needed to be tied up, you can see why I forgot to communicate with you. But scrambling on the spot to make it work revealed to me that it's possible. I could do this, was already preparing to do it. Yes, I will do it, I told him.

He texted me a location for the evening, suggested I drink lots of water. I showed up with flowers to a warehouse deep in Brooklyn: a large open space that was almost totally dark, with only a few candles flickering near two chairs, close to the entrance, and another dimmer candle much deeper in the room near what looked like flowers, an altar, and crystals.

There was a people living in the jungle, he said as we sat down, who had lost their way. A dark force had descended on them. Their medicine workers asked for help from the plant world, from the spirit world, from the water world. They were given many medicines, and these provided support and benefit. But the medicine men and women were concerned that the fear of their people had not been completely vanquished. Many of them would grow listless and afraid when it was night, afraid to hunt, afraid to pray. The head medicine man prayed for deeper healing and guidance, asking the spirits of the night to help him in better serving his people. He wanted them to face the darkness like mighty warriors, to hunt through the depths of the jungle with boldness and swiftness, to sing with strong powerful voices to the Creator. The prayer had been answered. A loud voice tore through the jungle, speaking directly to him. He followed the song to a riverbank, and the call continued on the other side. He swam across the river, maintaining a direct course despite the strong currents.

A small frog awaited him, groaning and singing in the night. It had been watching the suffering of the people and had become heavy with grief for them. But it was a grief that had transformed in the sacred heart of the frog into song and medicine. The frog taught the shaman how to receive its medicine and sing its song.

You must prepare yourself to be as watchful and sensitive as the frog. It is fearless because it is protected by the power of its softness and nakedness. It sings and pours medicine and finds freedom even in the jaws of hungry beasts. Learn from the frog. Receive whatever is coming, do not fear when the mouth of the night closes on you, do not fear when the claws and fangs of a hundred vicious beasts rip into you. You must allow yourself to be torn apart, to cry blood and water, to pour everything out of yourself, remembering that you are protected just as the frog is protected. May you find mercy and restoration, may you find grace, may you find courage and the taste of tears like nectar in your mouth.

He blew tobacco smoke over me, waved a burning sage bouquet toward me, asked me to continue breathing through my nose and maintaining attention to each breath as he led me to the altar. He told me to repeat after him. We ask permission to receive guidance and healing from our ancestors, from all beings, from the earth, from the water, from the stars and moon, from the spirits, from the Creator, from the source, from the night, from the silence. Then he started chanting as he gave me cup after cup of water to drink. He made several small burns on my left upper arm, asked me to not look at the wounds until the end of the evening. They are now as sacred as the sun, he said, and should be respected. So be mindful with your eyes, do not study your wounds too closely.

You may know about kambo. I'm sure other patients have mentioned it. It's basically venom released when this frog from the Amazon is stimulated or scared. I felt the ball of nausea in my chest pulsating as he prepared it. He rubbed spit on my arm, then very quickly applied several small dots of the venom, one on each burn. A warmth began immediately in the base of my spine, my burns stinging and radiating warmth, up my arm, into the center of my chest. My body began to throb, heart beating rapidly and head pounding. And I felt my face become numb and swell up. I was reminded for a moment of speed-balling, it was the

same complicated rush of warm numbing and swelling and euphoria, I
think I even started to enumerate the points of comparison as if this were
Erowid and I was characterizing the precise drug effects. Immediately
there was this revolt in myself, an intense fear growing along with nausea and sickness in every cell.

Give it up, you don't need it, he said very rapidly, you don't need it, so
it isn't yours, it isn't yours, so let it go, give it up, so it isn't yours, so you
don't need it, let it go, more and more rapidly, in a kind of chant, while
rattling something. I couldn't see anything, even my eyes were throbbing
as if about to burst. Then the ball of nausea that had been bothering me
all week intensified to a searing level of pain until it seemed to rupture.
An overwhelming slimy sickness began to crawl through my veins and
vessels. There were delirious flashes of disgusting ameboid things. I had
a crazy thought, I still remember it, that the slimy underbelly of the
world was going to take its revenge, everything we kill without thinking
twice. It seemed things were swimming and moving inside me, swarms
of tadpoles and maggots that had entered through the openings on my
arm, breeding into leeches and worms and frogs. The space itself seemed
slimy, the earth exuding wave after wave of venomous gelatinous ooze,
picking up and carrying everything to the surface.

I remember wanting to leave then and there, but there was no way
I could move. I remembered his words about courage and nectar, and
began to repeat them to myself, as well as giving thanks to the medicine,
remembering my purpose, asking for relief from the darkness and anxiety. I heard him chanting in the distance, and I continued breathing
through my nostrils as things deepened, it seemed there was no limit to
how sick this could make me, my throat had become so swollen I could
barely swallow, cramps were wrecking my abdomen, the taste of bile
at the back of my mouth, I was being taken as close as possible to total
shutdown. And right when I thought it would break or subside, the
sickness would ramp up a bit more, moving even closer to the agony of
something needing to leave, but not leaving, not yet, not leaving because
it needed to torment me a bit more. Then in a flash the medicine made
total sense to me, its healing power became clear. It was a total purification. The pain of painful things, heightening the agony they caused
me, and it was inviting me to give up all that needed to leave me, my

fears, my habits, my filth, my guilt, whatever it was. Life had been kind to me, too kind, allowing me to commit countless violations to myself and others with impunity. But this isn't kindness. Absolute impunity produces absolute corruption. I was grateful to be spared no longer.

I began to say thank you as I realized this, thank you, and yes, take it all, going through all the nauseating attachments I might have, and refusing them, starting with my need to feel lost, unwanted, a constant outsider. There was grief for my parents, my denial of them, my shame. My arrogance, my fear of silence, fear of death. There was also the tripping, the messing with my head, the idea that my head was messed up in the first place. I was running through everything, feeling the sickness throb more intensely by the second. And then the gates opened and fluid was pouring out of me, I was gushing snot, sweating, hurling bile and vomit into these plastic bins at my feet. I could feel it bursting out the other side too, but I couldn't even get up to walk to the bathroom. I asked for help, he walked me to the toilet, and it was like every door was open, what had come in was now coming out. Sweating, vomiting, crying, shitting, pissing, snot mixing with my tears, eyes burning under layers of mucous, a watery eruption carrying with it the accumulated discharge of a decade messing myself up.

I made my peace with the medicine. The calm expanded with every purge. I remembered his words, you must feel death in you and around you, and I understood. I understood how much I had been deadening myself to death, and I understood the nectar that comes with feeling the dead, mourning and releasing the dead.

The whole process took maybe an hour. I returned to normal quickly after the purge ended, made my way home feeling light and inspired. There was a profound peace that persisted for several days. Painful things continued to be more painful, with punishment arriving so swiftly and intensely there could be no doubt: I would be thrown into panic and disorientation the moment I fed into certain kinds of thinking or gave into resentments or allowed myself to let my guard down in any way. There was greater guidance the medicine gave in the other direction too, there was just as much clarity about what helped as what brought pain. This applied to everything, food, my thoughts, how I spoke, how I listened, the choice I had every waking second was being brought to light.

It was intense and sometimes overwhelming, but I saw that there was no other way if I wanted to live in alignment with everything. I can see why he wanted me in a practice like meditation. I needed to be able to observe and notice the patterns, I needed to pay constant attention to what followed what, or it would have felt like I was thrown into total chaos. Kundalini became crucial, it refreshed me and kept the light of awareness bright and clear.

He was also helpful at opening my eyes to certain things. He would refer to everything as the work. I had read Gurdjieff when I was in college, getting acquainted with mystical literature, and he used that word too. But this wasn't an esoteric or secret path. It was clear what the work was, and he would point it out repeatedly. You are being taught, he said, with the sticks and carrots of your own spirit. Your responsibility is to pay attention to the teacher. Give remembrance and give thanks. Give respect to the lessons that are received. Give yourself. In this way, you will grow in force and understanding until nothing, not even the Creator, can break you. But do not think, even if you live for 1,000 years, that you do not have more to learn, or that the Creator has stopped breaking you.

There were many conversations following that night of kambo, we would meet three to four times a week and would talk and walk around Lower Manhattan, starting near my place in TriBeCa. I was feeling much better than even a few weeks before, though still uneasy about certain things, still unclear about what was next. I was also beginning to doubt this path, so clearly spiritual and perhaps even religious. Maybe this healing was, I would sometimes fear, a bait and switch—he would support me, all while inculcating beliefs when I was at my most vulnerable. I didn't know what he wanted, as well, and I was considering what the catch might be. I was already bothered with the Yogi Bhajan thing, the revelations of exploitation, and it complicated my Kundalini practice, forced me to turn a blind eye to that stuff, creating a dissonance that hadn't been there before. I feared I was getting into a similar situation here, another guru type, especially as I was still processing my own alien Messiah thing.

I would get irritated whenever he said Creator. During one of our walks, I interrupted to ask him what exactly he meant by the word.

God, the universe, nature, what? We walked in silence for a while. I want you to consider some questions, he finally said with a smile, and don't answer too quickly. What does a dream mean? How do we know what its meaning might be? And can we substitute that meaning for the dream itself?

We continued walking. His silence intensified with each step. I understood his point after reflecting a moment—dreams are elusive, and explaining a dream is not the same as dreaming it. A dream also remains ambiguous, even after we give it meaning. But what does this have to do with the Creator? I contemplated his question further but felt stuck.

He stopped after walking in silence for several minutes. He stared into my eyes so piercingly I had to force myself to hold his gaze. You think you have understood a dream or a vision, you think you know what it means. But with every word you say, you know it less and less. So how do you expect to know the dreamer? This is a mystery far greater than any dream.

We resumed walking quietly until we arrived at his subway stop. If you continue this work, he said, there will be many things made clear to you. You may come, after years of practice, to understand the dream, and you might come to understand the dreamer, and you will no longer ask questions about the Creator. Yet even then you will not know the dream, the dreamer, or the Creator. Remember this. Remember this before you ask the meaning of such things. I will be sending you instructions for the next phase of things. Deepen your practice and commitments in the meantime.

It felt abrupt and strange leaving him, as if that was it and we would never meet again. The correspondence changed after that night, seemingly confirming my suspicions. No word from him. I began worrying, running that last conversation in my head incessantly. One thing he said stuck like a thorn: If you continue this work . . . I lingered on that if, the uncertainty of it, as if our work together might be over. Days, then weeks passed without hearing from him. He had not asked for anything but commitment. And instead of considering how I might support him, I had been doubting him, doubting his intentions, worried that I might be brainwashed, all while he continued to give. My careless words made me sick. The pain of painful things, ingratitude and pride, and this was a pain greater than what I felt before, it felt irreversible, the damage was done, everything seemed finished. I was back to where I started, deadness all around me.

The difference this time was that I was off drugs and there was a practice. I had made a commitment. What kept me going was remembering his final words: deepen your practice, he said, until the next contact. I remembered his smile when I had asked the question, his lightness about the whole thing, and that buoyed my spirits too, led me to consider that maybe my fears about him were in my head, that I was projecting my anger at myself onto him. I felt as well that there may have been a lesson in this—perhaps I was being taught to let go of certain agonizing patterns that went back to my earliest days, such as judging myself severely, or fearing being judged and abandoned. And with time, those ambiguous words—If you decide to continue the work—seemed less threatening and more empowering. He was encouraging me, I realized, to see that the work was my responsibility, my decision.

Weeks passed, and still nothing. I remained steadfast in my commitments, but it wasn't easy. I was tempted, of course, to give up on everything, my thoughts heavy with futility and self-loathing. The old despair would also come and go. There were many times where I was close to sending him a text thanking him and moving on. But I knew that I needed to see this through, that I was being shown yet another layer of what was holding me back. And even that would give way to doubt. A constant struggle back and forth, staying the course the hardest thing I'd ever done. I would always return to his encouragement to deepen the practice and honor my commitments, facing whatever comes up. In the background was a reassurance that so long as I did my part, it was far from over, reconnection would happen eventually.

It was still surprising, at the same time inevitable, receiving his text, a month or so after I left him at the subway. He wanted to meet in a week, asked that I begin to observe the sunrise and sunset until we do.

He shot a quick glance deep into my eyes when we met, and I felt his vision penetrating me to my bones. I knew what I had done, and I had nothing to fear. I felt a power in myself as I met his eyes.

I was looking for a particular leaf, he said, while I was walking through upstate last weekend. It was night, there was little to no light, and what helped was not looking for the leaf, but for an arrowhead. The leaf has a particular form and symmetry that are best recognized when we are looking for something else, something we might create ourselves.

Our conversation had started right away, as if we were picking up the thread from only minutes ago. We deepen our vision, he said, by practicing it at night, in total darkness. This is how we learn to trust our sight. But our vision may need some help so we can find our way. There are many arrowheads that might help light the way. I have called our work together work not because it is work. It is as much work as an arrowhead is a leaf. Work helps us find our way to something else, using what is our own creation to recognize what we cannot create.

He was quiet again as we made our way to the Hudson. I sensed a stillness in myself. I hadn't experienced it so clearly, but it had been there, slowly growing, the deep serenity a culmination of something that had been building for years, through all my challenges, and especially during the past month.

I told him that I understood. He raised a hand as if to stop me. Do not understand too much. That old serpent might appear, called to attention by your understanding. It is best to invite the sacrifice when we are ready. He spread his fingers wide and lowered his hand while emitting a soft whistle. It was uncanny and strange, his talk of sacrifice and serpents, and I felt an anxious flicker of what I experienced during the worst of kambo. A vague flashback of the reptilian conspiracy too, orchestrating everything. It was weird how easily disconcerted I still was—how the old unease could flare up so quickly.

We began walking again. We recognize the creation, he continued, through what we make, but we have not actually made anything, not even the arrowhead. The creation unfolds without rest, unfolds even in our imaginations. But these creations are offered so freely they seem uncreated. Even if we think of them as appearing from nothing, even if we fail to give thanks, the offerings continue. The leaf will be born again a thousand times. And we will see it as a thousand different things, as arrowheads, airplanes, buildings, perfect triangles, a thou-

sand new creations we take as our own. So much is given, both solid earth and empty illusion, so that we might find our way. He gestured toward the buildings across the West Side Highway, a dense thicket of windows and walls. Our greatest creation is to be created. This is the work, receiving the offerings deeply, letting them work on you and create you, in the same way that a breath creates music when it fills a pipe. Empty yourself to receive this breath and create its music. It is a great sacrifice that sustains the world. You come to life when you involve yourself in it.

We paused for a moment and looked out over the water. It was a clear day, and the sun was reflecting off the waves as striations and flashing pools of light. He pierced me with his gaze. Do you feel ready to sacrifice everything you have received and have become? I said Yes, startled at my quickness. He asked me to repeat myself, and I said more loudly, Yes. What he said next will stay with me forever. You will prepare yourself for the next new moon, when the night is darkest and our dreams most vivid. I will have medicine for your eyes, a thousand medicines for your thousand eyes. This is a medicine like an arrowhead is a leaf. See it as medicine, work, teacher, arrowhead. But know it is none of these things. Gifts will open onto further gifts, gifts upon gifts upon gifts, until we come to the inescapable sacrifice. He was whispering rapidly, as if a secret needed to be delivered while there was still an opening. Remember what is being given as you ready yourself. It is true that sacrifice is a giving. But the deepest sacrifice is a receiving. Ancient serpents will break the earth, rising from silence and secrecy to present you with their generosity. Prepare yourself for the great sacrifice. It is already here. We have been burning in its fires, blind to its light. Remember what is coming: the nourishment of a thousand medicines, a thousand mothers, a thousand nights. Receive as the sacrifice receives the fire, the broken earth a seed, the hollowed-out bone the breath. The offering you cannot refuse, the offering already given. Prepare to be nourished and created, regardless of what might emerge, what might burn away. The mother's milk of a serpent, he said, is its venom.

I had planned on writing you what happened that night. There is much to say, about the ayahuasca he gave me, the ceremony itself, the whole process. Now I'm not sure. I recognized during that new moon *and what followed that there are some things that must remain concealed. The dream that awakens us not to something else, but to itself. No words, no memories. It just is, nothing else capable of taking its place. That's where I am now, staying with what happened, not rushing to something else. Letting it unfold while doing my part.*

I am writing you from California where I am transforming the cannabis venture into something more honest, better honoring the plant, protecting the earth, supporting people and life. You will know more about this in the months to come, when I see you, I hope, in New York. I appreciate your receiving my words, giving them your time. I'll be clearer the next time we talk. There is more to say. Or we might sit together quietly. I am learning to do both.

8

PURGATORY

The words arrive through letters, through other people, through the person herself. But the distance is always difficult. A vast abyss must be crossed, whether the person is a continent away or sitting across the room. It is the work of a lifetime to discover who exists on the other side of it. And even then, we can't be sure.

Jamie came to me for habits that might seem innocuous and mundane to most people his age: cannabis and video games. The problem was that most hours of the day and night were consumed by them. Though an adult in his early twenties, Jamie was brought in by his mother, who also initiated the referral, a common enough occurrence with young adults smoking perhaps too much pot under the watch of their high-achieving parents. The patients themselves may not be as motivated on their own to do much about pot or their other diversions and may not even regard these habits as issues.

There are obvious problems with having the initial call come from someone other than the prospective patient. But as in Fred's case, this wasn't because Jamie was unwilling. Instead, he was too apathetic to do much about it on his own. His mother's main concern was to ensure I had some experience working with "quirky" people who go against the grain, and that I was sufficiently practiced at addressing his cannabis use, his gaming, and his tendency to procrastinate, which had led to failing grades the last semester. I asked his mother to have him call me, and Jamie sent me a text instead, in which he emphasized that, while he wanted help at getting his life back on track, he also wanted to explore the reason for his problematic habits, and examine why he took such pains to "escape" his life.

I found Jamie to be a pleasant and polite young man currently enrolled in a well-regarded art school in Manhattan where he was studying visual arts, with a focus on acrylic painting. His most striking feature was that he appeared remarkably younger than his age. Much about him seemed like a caricature of a teenage boy in incipient puberty. He had no facial hair and smooth, pale skin, spoke in a high-pitched voice, and seemed ill at ease in a lean boyish frame. He was wearing a baseball cap, a hoodie, and loose, baggy clothes at that first visit, as if his fashion sense had failed, much like his sexual maturity, to move beyond seventh grade. He was also timorous and anxious, with apparently limited and unpracticed social skills. The overall impression was stagnation, biologically, socially, academically—a young adult in arrested development in nearly every way.

There was one important domain, however, in which Jamie seemed older than his years. He was very articulate and apparently self-aware. He spoke about the flux of his mind—thoughts, associations, memories, and imaginings—with a precision and ease suggesting a long-standing familiarity with his inner world. I speculated on what this seemingly developed introspective capacity might indicate. One possibility is that his incessant gaming, his near-total solitude, and his regular cannabis use had afforded him many opportunities for solitude and inwardness.

But it seemed heightened inwardness *despite* his gaming and cannabis use. Every peculiarity usually has some particular suffering behind it. In Jamie's case, I sensed that his intense self-awareness was probably driven by anguish of a deeply private kind. Riven by pain or confusion not easily traceable to anything outside of himself, he had fixed his attention on his tormented inner world, wrestling with himself for answers. The cannabis and gaming, rather than deepening his introspection, were probably devices by which he found relief from it.

If there was indeed private anguish, it likely pertained to his transition to adulthood. He seemed to be struggling with issues of responsibility, with individuation, with independence—with all the challenges that come with being grown up. His boyishness and apparent immaturity, as if he had been frozen at early puberty, further reinforced the impression that he was at an impasse.

"It's hard to get motivated," he said. "Schoolwork, eating, cleaning up, it all seems pointless. So, I stay in my room, staring at the ceiling, waiting for time to pass, for sleep to come, for anything that might make time move faster. My mom thinks it's the pot, or my brain being fried from staring at the screen too much, but honestly they're what get me out of it, if it weren't for those things, if it weren't for the little bit of interaction I get from smoking and gaming, I wouldn't be doing anything at all."

He had been smoking and gaming, he said, since his late teens. But it has been even more intense recently, over the past few years. I asked him to clarify what he meant by "the little bit of interaction" he gets from smoking and gaming.

"When I smoke, my mind gets going, I feel less bored, better able to enjoy things. I game with people, eat, watch things online, have some creative ideas. I guess time passes more quickly, without the sense that I'm, like, wasting my time. And I'm less depressed and anxious and, like, more involved with things. I'm interacting with my life, you know, not stuck in bed, paralyzed, dreading everything, but actually doing something, even if it's, like, not much, even if the schoolwork doesn't always get done or the ideas don't go anywhere, at least I'm thinking about them, at least I'm not stuck in place listening to the traffic noises. But it can sometimes be unpredictable. I sometimes smoke a bit more than that sweet spot and I'm back in bed. It sometimes happens with just a few hits, like all I want to do is take a nap. So, my mom's right that it's not always perfect. But if I'm gaming, then I'm up."

What does gaming involve?

"The game I play most is called *League of Legends*. You're part of a team, you have a mission, one team pitted against another. It's a bit difficult to explain fully, there is a goal and you're working with your team, coordinating through a headset. You're also part of the *League* community, with every player assigned a ranking so that you know where you stand, how your skill level compares to that of others, what your progression has been. If you aren't playing regularly, you will get left in the dust, with more regular players leapfrogging over you. Each match is about forty-five minutes, and I try to do at least four matches a day to keep my rank from deteriorating. But the point is to do nothing. I don't think about anything. I'm just there, you know, like living my life, doing whatever I'm doing."

I asked him to expand on what he meant by "just there."

"I'm not thinking about what I need to do, or like who I am, or anything like that. I'm just me, and that's it, you know, nothing else needs to be done, no labels, work, grades, nothing messing with me. Just being here is good enough, like nothing else is needed. But, like, what else is there anyway? I forget about the world, the politicians messing everything up, all the people without homes or anything to eat, the plastic in the oceans, the pollution, global warming, people killing each other, all that stuff fades away to leave me right here, right now, it's like I can finally take a breath and relax, free from the noise for a moment."

The consolations of intoxicants might resemble anything, including the present-awareness of a meditative state. I asked him to expand a bit more on the way pot helps him not think about who he is. How does he ordinarily think of himself? He startled a bit when I asked, looked at me for a quiet moment as if mulling something over.

"It's the boy thing. Being a boy. It doesn't sit right with me, though it feels like it should. I'm wondering if I made a mistake."

Gender dysphoria is the medical term given the unease with one's apparent gender and sex assigned at birth. Jamie seemed to be articulating discomfort with being male; perhaps he yearned to be female. He was wrangling, in any case, with his assigned sex, interrogating his discomfort with being male, feeling that he is in the wrong somehow, and presuming that he ought to accept it. This may account for the conflict I had suspected was complicating his transition into a healthy, responsible adulthood.

The cannabis, gaming, and stagnation now seemed to have a deeper dimension—not only ways of alleviating general discomfort and stress, but strategies by which he protected himself from the tremendous difficulties presented by gender dysphoria: "being myself, no labels." They allowed him to remain in a limbo of possibility regarding his uncertain gender without committing to anything given the challenging path ahead. And alongside not committing to a gender, and denying himself the opportunity for authentic self-expression, Jamie was in a stalemate with most every other aspect of his life: a crisis of perpetual procrastination. But something he said didn't quite fit. What did he mean when he said he had made a mistake?

"I'm not sure I am a boy. But I know I'm not a girl either. It wasn't easy to do this, the hardest decision I ever made. Now I'm wondering if I made a mistake."

I asked him to clarify what the mistake was. He looked at me quizzically.

"Didn't my mom tell you? I thought you knew."

He took a deep breath, as if readying himself to disclose something still raw.

"I was born the wrong gender. I knew as soon as I knew anything. I transitioned to being male when I turned twenty. I thought it was clear at the time, I always knew I wasn't a girl. I'm still clear that I'm not. I'm sure you the know the process. I had seen doctors and psychiatrists, and we all came to the same conclusion. This wasn't some overnight thing. But I don't feel any better than I did when I was misgendered. The pain and confusion haven't really gone away."

Enshrined in the diagnosis of gender dysphoria is the construct of a binary gender, male or female. Jamie had been assigned the gender of female at birth, found it incongruent with who he is, and had transitioned to what seemed a more authentic gender. But being male turned out to not fit any better, and he had continued to agonize about what he is.

"I sometimes worry that I make too much of it. I mean, what does it really matter how people see me, how I dress, what my body is. It's all random anyway, like I could be anyone, I could have been born anyone, I didn't choose this life, didn't choose my parents, my face, it seems stupid to even try to choose anything. Male, female, as if there is any choice, it's one or the other, with us or against us, Democrat or Republican, it is the same system in the end forcing two choices on you. So, say I decide I'm not a boy after all, what does it matter? I'm still me, still stuck in this world, still stuck in what people call me, what I call myself. Maybe I should just accept that it doesn't really matter, settle into what I am now, neither this nor that, and stop trying to put myself into a choice that isn't really mine to begin with."

Jamie's transition from one gender to another was like moving from one prison cell to the next. The liberation he had hoped for had not occurred, because he remained trapped in a duality he found artificial and destructive. It seemed the same circumstances that led to the dysphoria, sense of inauthenticity, and incongruity when Jamie was "female" accounted for his unease while "male"—Jamie felt suffocated by a forked fiction of what is possible to us as sexual and social beings. He seemed to be agitating for emancipation again. But what would feel more liberating?

"I want to be released from all this. Neither male nor female, just whatever I am, without putting on an identity that isn't me. It bothers me to be seen as anything other than what I am, for people to hear *he* or *him*, *she* or *her*, to see, like, the familiar landmarks of gender, and assume an immediate stance toward me that has less to do with me, or even with them, and more with maintaining the power structure that throws people into two boxes, one against the another, male against female against male. So, it doesn't matter what I am—male, female, or anything in between—the categories are there, every move on my end reinforces things, and I am bound to lose myself even more while the system grows crazier and more fascist. So, I don't participate."

My initial impression of arrested puberty—with his androgynous appearance and unisex fashion sense—was consistent with remaining liminal, ungendered. It also proved his point. I had been so complacent with the gender binary myself that I had assumed he was stunted somehow because he hadn't cultivated the conventional markers of gender. But he was far from stunted. At least in this regard he was decisive. It didn't feel right to him to assume a binary gender, despite having transitioned, so he would rest in a willful limbo.

The limbo extended beyond gender. His apparent refusal to "grow up" was itself a conscious statement—a declaration of independence from systems, categories, and power structures he felt were artificial and inhumane. He was frozen in time by design, as a total strategy of paralysis that shuttered him in his room, away from this oppressive regime of signs. This was Jamie's quiet rebellion against a world that seemed monstrous and perverse.

There was a clear element of moral integrity and personal authenticity to his behavior. But it would be absurd to regard his stagnation in only these heroic terms. He was also deeply stuck, with his rebellion accomplishing little more than increasing his tolerance to cannabis and improving his ranking in the *League* community. He was still agonizing, still entangled with the system, still finding it difficult to inhabit himself fully. I noted that his cannabis use and gaming had seemed to intensify around the time that he came out as male, at age twenty. How did he understand that?

"It clearly wasn't the win I had been looking for. I had been thinking about this for years, no longer being female, being the wrong person. And there are some advantages to what I did. I don't think it was a total mistake. I would likely feel far worse if I had grown breasts and if my hips filled out and if I was menstruating every month. Plus, I think that the hormones, even if they haven't masculinized me that much, have definitely thrown my sexual development into chaos, living in a no-man's-land of gender all my own. But I'm still male. That's how I present myself, how my parents talk about me, how you and others see me, there is no escaping it. I sometimes imagine myself as intersex, a mix of things. Beard, small breasts, high voice, long thin legs, chest hair, I don't know. Some male-female hybrid to throw people off. Something that can't be pigeonholed. Or maybe staying as I am now, more of a blank slate. I realize now that it wasn't being a female that I was opposed to specifically. It was being a gender, any gender, and having such an important part of my identity inflicted on me. Being male, of course, will not fix that. I'm not sure anything will. Maybe I'm depressed, and I just want to figure things out while laying low and feeling better. But smoking pot is the only thing that helps me forget."

The treatment of gender dysphoria is accepted medically to be gender modification through hormones, social reconditioning, and surgery. But what if the gender dysphoria emerges, as in Jamie's case, not from a mismatch, but from a refusal of gender altogether? What if no gender is adequate at expressing the person's sense of self? Jamie was not able, as so many of us might be, to conform to this prefabricated mode of being. He felt its weight and unreality, and rebelled against the larger regime of which it was an important part.

"You have been burdened since birth with the weight of these received ideas," I observed to him. "You were gendered as female—with all the trappings that this entails—when you felt that you weren't. But having taken the step to become male, you suspect you have only entangled yourself further in a scheme that has never sat well with you. Your current discomfort comes, it seems, from having committed to being male, when you know that this label is just as inadequate and burdensome."

Jamie began to tear up while wringing his hands. I asked him to share his thoughts.

"This is what makes it feel like a mistake. It's one thing to be forced into something and to endure it, you know, with a realization that it's all artificial and not really who I am. Maybe that's what I should have done when I was a girl. You learn to cope while staying true to yourself. You find a freedom inside. The illusion doesn't totally penetrate you. But it feels like I've only fed into the lie by transitioning into being male, I've only reinforced the system and its gender binary and all that, and I'm more burdened by it than ever, because, like, I have now chosen it."

He had wanted freedom from gender and found himself more attached to it now that he "chose" to be male. Thus, his desperate and punishing efforts at extricating himself: the stagnation, the cannabis and gaming, the refusal to engage.

Gender, it seemed to me, was a particularly visible indication of a deeper captivity, operating at many levels. There was the gaming, of course, and the cannabis use, and various other modes of self-imprisonment, such as staying in bed and refusing most human contact. Then there was the "system that runs everything" that Robyn had also railed against—compromising his freedom with imposed yes/no choices and identities, perpetuating illusions of who he is and what he should do, all in the service of regimes that are cruel, shortsighted, and unjust. More fundamentally, there was the gaze of others: objectified, labeled, and categorized in ways that we know are reductive, even as we can't dispel the need to fit favorably into some consensus. And deeper than that are the strictures that come with entering the world as a suffering body, forced at birth into an all-encompassing web of limitations, names, wounds, and forms that feel arbitrary and often ill-fitting.

It didn't seem the cannabis merely helped him escape his anxiety and zone out. There was something positive it seemed to give as well: a richer sense of self. I returned to something he had said: How did cannabis help him be himself? What did he experience when he was high that felt so authentic?

"I didn't really begin smoking until I was seventeen or eighteen, my senior year in high school. I was a bit of a loner, did well in school, stayed out of trouble. Drugs weren't really on the radar for most of my life. It was a girlfriend who introduced me to weed—the only person I've been with in a romantic way. Eva was kind and warm, super comforting and beautiful. And she was just like me in so many ways, not really buying into society, not conforming. She kept to herself, did whatever she wanted to do. But she was a lot more adventurous. She told me that weed helped her explore herself, better understand things. I didn't need much convincing. The first time I smoked it felt like I entered into a different world, one where the usual stuff wasn't weighing me down. Everything was light and playful, less cookie cutter. Just being ourselves. We would smoke, watch movies, and game together, cuddle and hook up.

"The sense of being in the wrong body was gone. It's a bit hard to describe, but it was like everything became one thing. There was no real difference between anything because it was all connected, what each thing was by itself didn't matter because it was all the same. The same substance, the same magic. Eva and I were connected, but we were also connected to everyone else, and everyone else to the earth, and I would also think about the stars and the moon, the sun, the night, and all the galaxies, and it was the same beautiful magic everywhere. I was that magic, too, I felt it within myself, I felt the perfection of everything. It was all so beautiful and special. I didn't need to worry about what my body was, or what people thought, or what I had between my legs. Weed is actually what helped me realize that I could be different than what I was, that I didn't need to settle for being a girl. It planted the seed that I could move beyond these boundaries, like there were no real limits. I could be anyone, it didn't matter, I could be a boy, I could be a girl, whatever felt most free."

A dream of freedom and contentment. A dream of the wilderness too, the interconnected mystery of forms and fluid in which we make our home.

"Now when I smoke I remember who I am. It's not the boy I've become, it's not the girl I was. Yes, remembering is the right word, a memory of something past that is almost here again, so close I can almost touch it, kind of like nostalgia. The magic is here, but I have to remember it, too, bring it back from memory. It's a magic that wouldn't exist without the past, without Eva and the hope of what might happen. You know what it's like? A warm bed I don't want to leave. But it is like the bed you knew when you were a kid, really comfortable, fitting you just right, and taking care of you so that you might sleep without worry. I'm right back in my old room, in my old thoughts and feelings, and everything feels like it's going to be fine, the future seems bright, and there is no danger of losing what I usually feel has already been lost long ago."

I appreciated his capacity to articulate these elusive thoughts so clearly. Such patients cast a light that illuminates much more than their own problems. The nostalgia he described was relevant to many of us, and especially if we struggle with an explicit addition: a present burnished by the past but buried by the past too. The illusion of securing things that have already left us, grasping at experiences that concluded long ago. Sinking into our childhood beds, falling asleep to obsolete dreams of the future. Though we know their day is gone, we surrender to these fantasies anyway because we feel they are the only real future we have.

Cannabis may have served a helpful purpose at one point, awakening Jamie to a foretaste of freedom, with gender no longer an issue, and inspiring him to disentangle from the gender imposed at birth. There was recognition of the creative "magic" inherent to being alive. But coming out as male and transgender gave cannabis a different purpose. He felt he was stuck even more deeply now, having chosen his incarnation himself this time. Cannabis was his way of reconciling with this dead end. It allowed him to dwell in a timeless purgatory of prepubescence where he could enjoy a memory of that vital and emancipatory magic, swaddled within the unified field of formless everything. Why assume the hard labor of a more authentic embodiment if the cannabis was delivering it to him directly? He couldn't trust himself, in the end, to not make another mistake, especially because there were so few apparent options, both of them terrible.

"The pot has been clearly helpful at opening your eyes to what you are," I told him. "You had been inspired by it, after all, to move beyond female. And you have also recognized, perhaps also with the help of pot, that being male isn't right either. This time you're less hopeful. Being male has led to greater anxiety and powerlessness because you are not sure what your other choices might be. I can understand how trapped you feel. But turning to pot to remember who you are, and keeping it at that, needing to smoke to feel like yourself, is only making you feel worse, even less authentic and free. You have come to feel that the only way to be yourself resides in getting high, and not in your own choices and actions. This is a really painful, helpless place to be. I encourage you to consider—what can you choose, how can you act so that who you feel yourself to be might become a reality beyond being stoned?"

What might seem obvious to outsiders might be an impossible riddle to the person himself. But the riddle becomes less vexing when it is presented to the person plainly. In asking Jamie to consider how he might achieve what he wants, I was asking him to acknowledge, first of all, that he actually wants something.

Everything Jamie said suggested he would find greater well-being and authenticity as a nonbinary person. His difficulty in even acknowledging his expansive identity seemed to stem from feeling entrapped in typical conventions of gender, alongside fretful sensitivity toward the opinions of others. He could not see any options, it seemed, beyond refusing the binary, protecting himself from its apparent hegemony. It had not occurred to him that he might take a more active position: emerging from his embattled retreat and embracing the nonbinary as an authentic way of being on its own terms.

There were already precedents in place. The gender binary was losing its cultural dominance, with large segments of society more receptive to expressions of gender beyond the dualistic system. The emphasis on pronoun sensitivity at many institutions was a clear indication of this development. Coming out as nonbinary would not be a decision that would alienate him, as he might have feared, but would be welcomed and respected in many mainstream spaces.

Jamie came to realize, within the first month of our work together, that a nonbinary identity was most fitting for him. The recognition was swift and momentous, as were the changes Jamie initiated, as if he had been simply waiting for the word go. Without much hesitation, Jamie changed their pronouns to they/them, while retaining their name. There was also more playfulness with personal expression. They were more accepting of the full spectrum of their sexual characteristics, without feeling the pressure to censor or suppress themself because they did not conform to either end of the binary. There were also other ways of presenting themself that were uniquely their own, of course, beyond gender entirely. While not quite the hybrid creature they had once imagined themself to be, they began to experiment, with great creativity, blending different articles of clothing, makeup, ways of speaking, mannerisms, hairstyle, and jewelry to create a personal style and to approximate the embodiment that felt most representative. Jamie seemed revitalized, finding greater release from the shackles that had weighed so heavily on them. This showed in their schoolwork, their cannabis use and gaming, and their lethargy and tendency to procrastinate. Everything improved dramatically.

This was only the start. Alongside their sensitivity to the constraints of gender, Jamie remained troubled by what they couldn't control more generally. This is a tendency I've often observed in people who gravitate toward developing mastery in predictable and controllable spaces, such as video games, where progression might be orderly and airtight. Jamie's discomfort with the imposed constraints of gender, it seemed, had only been intensified and complicated by this temperament, one of many challenges in their life related to a heightened need for personal sovereignty. The failed solution was to assert their sovereignty by committing to only what seemed entirely within their control—which was, beyond perhaps *League*, precisely nothing.

Jamie had found themself, so to speak, but finding oneself does not conclude with choosing pronouns and a personal style. One must continue to find one's way through this unfolding, disorienting, and shape-shifting world—a world often indifferent to our notions and expectations. The temptation to assert their sovereignty through refusal—staying in bed, attempting to forget themself, and neglecting responsibilities—had diminished significantly, but it persisted in various ways. They were aggrieved by worries of what people thought of them, were anxious about being overdetermined by their circumstances, and were easily disconcerted by unexpected or disruptive events. They were, therefore, still contending with challenges beyond gender, which led them to occasionally choose apathy and disengagement as a solution to them. Cannabis had remained in the picture as well, occasionally contributing to intense inertia when their high exceeded that "sweet spot." Social interactions were also challenging, with ongoing worries that people would consider them "a freak." Intimacy with another person, something Jamie craved, seemed impossible. They remained frozen in certain respects, and felt the tremendous anxiety that comes with a life still placed on hold.

Cannabis had served as a gateway to something else: a radical acceptance of themself, which inspired Jamie to move beyond female, and then beyond male, to arrive at a sense of self that was entirely other, evading gendering fictions of what it means to exist. But there was more to it than that, which is why they continued to smoke. It also gave them a foretaste of boundless freedom, which intimated a path not solely beyond gender but beyond many of the other structures and demarcations that contain us. Even phenomena as apparently binding as one's thoughts, sensations, and emotions need not be so pressing and oppressive. Jamie was able to enjoy, while high, the serenity, acceptance, enchantment, and fluidity so comparable to the experiences, as mentioned before, associated with meditation. This is the gift of psychoactive substances: through their fictions, they allow us to inhabit what might be the case but which might seem inaccessible at the time. And the freedom they found in cannabis, Jamie learned, is a fiction worth taking seriously. It had pointed the way to emancipation from gender norms, and may do so from other things too.

We do well, in general, to give our full attention whenever the field of possibility is broadened. Our world stands to grow larger. In Jamie's case, what was revealed was truly extraordinary: the capacity for serenity and joyfulness independent of circumstances. They felt compelled, naturally enough, to seek this out as much as possible, and especially if the present moment seemed to preclude it. But the present moment does not really preclude it if cannabis can awaken us to it.

Cannabis can be a stimulant and soporific in equal measure, inspiring us to act and, sometimes at the very same moment, compelling passivity and inertia. This is one of its greatest teachings. It will not act for us. Nor will the dream come to fruition without our free and conscious participation. To hope otherwise is to fall into a terrible sleep. With every hit, Jamie would come to inhabit their experience, for a boundless moment, with that ancient primordial freedom newly intact, and with their being unrestricted to the ephemera and particularities with which every one of us is inclined to overidentify, such as what is resting between our legs or clamoring between our ears. Perhaps this representation of mindfulness might lead the way to enduring liberation, beyond cannabis. Much as they had come to find a sense of self free from the traps of gender, they might find freedom from the more fundamental bondage of "sense" and "self"—from the manner that we tether ourselves to our sensations and thoughts, or to what seems to be ourselves, or to the narrows of a certain self in the first place. Cannabis might, yet again, signal the way.

•

Jamie found in intoxication a sense of possibility as deadening as it was liberating. The stupor emerged most clearly when Jamie sought out this freedom as a refuge, as opposed to a goad to commitment and action. Life slowed to a creep, leaving them to seem a typical video game and cannabis addict, stuck in an endless adolescence of gaming and smoking to the detriment of "normal reward-seeking."

But there had been some steps toward liberation too. In addition to providing the reassurance to move beyond gender in a stepwise way, cannabis gave Jamie an intimation of the peace and freedom that might be possible in wakeful moment-to-moment experience. This served to jump-start the next phase of their attempts at "finding themself." Jamie and I recognized that this altered awareness, so comparable to the practice of mindful awareness, was the main motivator for their continued cannabis use. We realized, as well, that the "mindfulness" occasioned by smoking needed to be respected as a possibility that might be achieved without THC and pursued accordingly.

Jamie was inspired by the possibility of inhabiting this way of being on their own. But it required them to commit, and to put in consistent effort. This began with surrendering cannabis as their only access to it: instead, the craving for cannabis—or for anything—might invite Jamie to engage with that agitation in a new way, not as a compulsion to consume or avoid, but as an opportunity for seeing their suffering through, and seeing through it. This is our inmost possibility, even as few of us might come to see it so clearly, or with the same urgency. Jamie might now pursue the freedom that they sought in the outer reaches of intoxication to its conclusion—in the patient, deliberate, and sustained practice of *being experience*, through mindfulness training, self-examination, healthy habits of daily living, and other practices. I would support and guide them through this process. And together we will work toward the day when their dream of cannabis might come to a close, its teachings having been exhausted, its intoxications of possibility no longer merely possible, but completely awakened and realized.

9

QARRTSILUNI

How did it begin? In the intimacy of adolescent romance, Jamie allowed themself an opportunity to venture beyond their self-image as a misfit loner. Their introduction to cannabis further supported their expansion beyond the narrows of this self, inspiring them to inhabit, among other things, truer expressions of gender identity. But cannabis came to be narrowing and oppressive in its own way, with Jamie turning to the freedom and expansiveness made possible by it as if these benefits were impossible otherwise. This led to a cannabis addiction accompanied by compulsive video gaming. Identity expansion was monopolized, in the latter case, not by intoxication, but by the coordinated multiplication of simulations on a screen.

How did it begin? Eva introduced Jamie to cannabis during a developmental stage characterized primarily by accelerated individuation. The entry of cannabis into their life, while bringing Jamie's gender challenges to a head and inspiring them toward progressively richer gender expansiveness, also served to deepen a sense of limbo, halting their developmental trajectory at a particularly ambiguous place. Cannabis had become a permanent transitional object, with Jamie lost in a permanent transitional stage, protracted gender dysphoria only one of many frustrations that would come to shape this purgatory.

How did it begin? Before the prosthesis, there is a felt absence of what seems essential. The prosthesis simultaneously fills this vacancy and marks its presence, rendering the deficit more explicit. A prosthetic limb is clearly not a limb; in fact, it exists because there isn't a limb. Yet a prosthetic becomes as essential to us as the striving that created it, a calling out for completion from the mutilated emptiness. Before cannabis and *League*, there was a felt absence of what seems essential, a striving for completion that equipped the void with a simulation, a presence, a mark of mutilation.

How did it begin? Cannabis use has enduring effects on neurocircuitry related to "reward" and "appetitive pursuits" (e.g., the nucleus accumbens). These "neuroadaptations" promote addiction by increasing the reinforcing effects of drugs and diminishing the salience of healthier rewards. Jamie's "amotivational syndrome" is likely linked to these neuroadaptations as well, with their chronic cannabis use engendering apathy toward exercise, creativity, and academic progress. Further, cannabis may have functioned as a "gateway drug" to problems beyond drugs, setting Jamie up for a gaming addiction. It is critical that Jamie exercise care and restraint because their neurocircuitry remains vulnerable to not only the abuse liability of cannabis but the addictive potential of other things too, even worlds that are entirely virtual.

How did it begin? Cannabis can render people hyper-suggestible, like other substances in the hallucinogen class. This might lead in many directions: more deeply into the dominant culture, or further away from it, toward fringe groups or even cults. The cannabis-addicted person, in any case, may take up an entire world without evaluating how appropriate this ready-made existence might be for them. The role that cannabis had in Jamie's sexual awakening was not solely emancipatory. There may have been a dark side too. Cannabis might have heightened Jamie's susceptibility to distorting their gender expansiveness in deference to the binaries of the medical orthodoxy, as "trans-male gender dysphoria": a label that they came to find as ill-fitting and inauthentic as the prosthetic male genitalia they had declined.

How did it begin? There are designs on our children. They are being plied with manipulative social media, sexually suggestive entertainment, innumerable other distractions, a culture increasingly more tolerant of drug use, and some would say a systematic assault on traditional notions of family, gender, and sexual behavior. Perhaps the aim is the production of more exploitable consumers, people who will buy anything, with a reset function installed during childhood to allow a succession of market-based programs to be imprinted. Jamie occupies a drug-addled, gender-confused inertia, a blank slate on which the invisible hand inscribes its commandments directly, which is exactly what is encouraged in this toxic profit-driven culture, likely underwritten by self-serving sociopathic elites at the highest levels of finance, entertainment, and politics.

How did it begin? Cannabis is a *non-specific amplifier*, Stanislav Grof's term for psychedelics. In Jamie's case, it amplified the pain of being misgendered and heightened recognition of what a fuller life might look like. Cannabis also amplified the many ways in which Jamie hides from life by promoting what was termed "cannabis addiction" and bringing into sharp relief Jamie's vacillation, fearfulness, and challenges with intimacy. Their cannabis use disorder, in other words, was an amplification itself: their vulnerabilities pierced the surface and demanded attention with the same heightened force that Jamie's forward-looking gender expansiveness had. Cannabis highlighted both the "good" and the "bad," offering opportunity for attending to the two as an integrated self, beyond the usual divisions.

How did it begin? God has placed many temptations on our path. In His infinite wisdom, He introduced evil into the world to test and strengthen our devotion to Him. Cannabis is a poison plant that above all else *deceives*. It gives one false hope, false faith, and false creed. It weakens moral integrity, distorts reality, and renders a person more vulnerable to temptation. Jamie refused the good counsel of their parents and chose instead to smoke cannabis compulsively, descending into a despair that led them to doubt even their God-given bodies and minds. Unrepentant and insatiable, Jamie has endeavored to corrupt themselves beyond cannabis too, poisoning themselves with further "medicines" like man-made hormones and growing more distant from God in pursuit of some illusory drug-induced identity. But God is good, punishing with a divine rod those He loves, patiently awaiting the obedience of His prodigal children.

How did it begin? There is a distinct family history of what might be conceptualized as problematic substance use, dating back to at least the 1700s. Jamie also has many ancestors who were viewed as eccentric or odd in their day and who might now be considered neurodivergent, such as a cross-dressing laudanum-using great-aunt. Jamie is a product of their genes, as shaped by the forces of the moment. A contemporary harvest of seeds that have been steadily bearing idiosyncratic fruit for centuries, the most recent crop being a neuro-atypical, gender-expansive, cannabis-communing individual struggling to find their way in a world too rigid to accommodate their amorphousness.

How did it begin? Adolescence is a delicate time, despite its heedless rush toward novelty and risk taking. An insult to the growing brain, be it a drug or head trauma, may have enduring, even lifelong consequences. What might have seemed a helpful support for navigating those difficult teenage years was, in fact, working to undermine Jamie's neurobiological development. Emerging data suggest cannabis perturbs neocortical growth and white matter remodeling, thereby jeopardizing important aspects of higher-level adult functioning, such as purposeful goal setting, stress management, and emotion regulation. A terrible price to pay for an all-too-common adolescent diversion.

How did it begin? Stimuli arrive from every corner to keep the senses ensnared in compulsive finger rituals. The attention merchants vie for screen time. The bombardment can be equal parts intoxicating, agitating, deadening. Individuals of a certain sensitivity, such as Jamie, may opt to protect themselves by retreating from the multisensory assault, engaging whatever consolations, tools, or drugs might be available. Jamie diverts attention on their own comfortable terms: a preemptive individual addiction rather than the mass-produced one driven by dopamine-loop manipulations and consumer engineering. This deviation from the norm has led invariably to other refusals, including ambiguating or forestalling gender expression, pressing pause on conventional modes of productivity, and logging out of the system more generally, devoting themself instead to a cartoon-world gamification of endless social mobility.

How did it begin? From the indeterminate chaotic quantum flux structures or relationships coalesce that stabilize existing upsurges of form into apparently symbiotic alliances be they atomic or molecular or organismic that are lawful couplings of interlocking molecular chemical and ultimately geometric architectures impeccable in their goodness of fit but that may also perturb or undermine the larger matrix with THC in this case binding to receptors and modulating neurons to the extent that enduring relationships were created molecularly and then at the level of gray matter as stable relational neuroadaptations and further downstream in the domain of human striving and representational world building with these progressive emanations of more spectral totalities culminating in the coherences named *Jamie* and *cannabis* seemingly entangled as epiphenomenal accomplices to the biochemical interplay of building blocks locking into a firm edifice that might be called interspecies enmeshment or addiction or suffering or even consciousness but which may also be inhabited at the more fundamental level as the ineluctable ordering of these errant forms restless for a system in which everything might find its elemental place.

How did it begin? We have given this plant to you. You have been given it as a gift, just as it came to us as a gift. It must, therefore, be received as a gift. But you have no experience with giving or receiving gifts. You know only how to take. We give this plant to you as a gift so that you might learn what a gift means. We give this gift to you so that the gift might put you in your place.

How did it begin? Cannabis has been modified beyond recognition. Many strains are widely available that have been bred to unnatural potency to satisfy consumer demand, with the ratio of THC to other, less psychoactive alkaloids, such as CBD, now far higher than ever. This leads to more powerful intoxicating effects and more harms as well. The propensity of cannabis to exacerbate or even initiate certain mental health issues, like anxiety or addiction, has increased in proportion to its potency. Jamie was introduced at a precarious time in their development to a powerful sativa strain called Green Crack, which became their preferred flower. Consuming this modified strain regularly has thrown Jamie into a cascade of problematic behavioral and mental health consequences.

How did it begin? Jamie was raised in an atomized culture where a certain mode of individuation is given heightened emphasis, to the detriment of other aspects of human development, such as communal engagement, psychospiritual maturation, and relational well-being. Many modes of suffering have been viewed accordingly in that monochromatic light—as a failure of the self to find fuller independence and expression. Jamie was conditioned, due to this ego-oriented acculturation, to approach their challenges in highly individualistic terms: gender dysphoria, failure to launch, depression, cannabis addiction. Other challenges that are more relational and transpersonal go unrecognized, such as the deeper systemic, cultural, existential, psychospiritual, and ecological failures that beleaguer us all.

How did it begin? Our intricate web of interrelatedness has been fragmented. The yearning for closeness finds its fulfillment in a relationship with the ontic Other. Green Crack preserves a primal bond with the green earth in a consumer culture dead-set against transhuman modes of communion; it offers a private womb in which Jamie can find sustenance away from the agitated divisions that have torn the whole asunder.

How did it begin? Human existence is deeply iniquitous and traumatic. This begins at conception, with an unfair distribution of genetic inheritance; some are better endowed than are others. Then there are the variable circumstances, also iniquitous, into which one is born and struggles to erect a life. But even being born in the first place is an imposition to which no consent is given. Add to this primordial trauma the many ways that violence and injustice become written into law and order, and the situation seems nearly hopeless. One solution is to join the patriarchy while its reign of power still prevails. Jamie attempted a male form but found it a false solution; they opted out early, declining the phallic finale. Renunciation came to seem a better path, aided by a liminal gender and pot. Jamie made their home in a private sanctuary populated only by themself and the League of Legends, where the order is just, the rules clear and fair, the binaries of good and evil, privileged or poor, male or female, collapsing into a level battlefield where the most skillful team wins.

How did it begin? Cannabis is a powerful plant teacher intended by Great Spirit to guide us through this in-between dimension. It must be approached with respect and ceremony. It will punish and humble those who approach it heedlessly. This is one of the teachings. But whether one learns by confusion, humiliation, or illumination, it amounts to the same lesson. All things are the Great Gift and must be received accordingly. Even the most painful addictions and humiliations must be received as a gift from Great Spirit.

How did it begin? A single breath. The first deliberate breath, inhaling with intention, if only to resist the forceful smoke collapsing the chest. The plant needs a moment, Eva said. Then attending quietly to what emerges, deep in the darkness of being.

How did it begin? An Indian curse, said the woman waking up, what else could it be. The work of distant elders, medicine carriers, setting the ground for judgment. They gathered the burned bones of a murdered child, offered prayers and tobacco, and buried the remains deep in the earth beneath the ghosts of her razed village. These bones have now entered every clump of earth, every animal, every plant, every drop of water, from one end of the land to the other. The earth rumbles with prophecy. May the child return as pestilence, scorched fields, the white horse of vengeance. May her resurrected blood mark the enemy with a thousand pus-filled wounds. May you be ravaged by the evil you have committed—but all at once, your centuries of violence concentrated into one venom-tipped arrowhead tearing through your heart. May the smoke of burned leaves confuse your minds, poison your blood, crack your heads open. May your offspring fall into madness and sterility. May the earth bury you under the offal of your own corruption.

How did it begin? Before names and forms, there was ( ). It remains, an abiding presence. But we cannot say "it." We cannot say anything. A nonbinary resurrection awaits everyone. Silent as roots. The plants invite and deepen the decomposition of every form, being, and name. The dirt stirs with worms feeding on what remains. Ascending green stalks rise from the rich earth, inviting us to their deathly embrace, their silent dreams, their promise of renewed abundance. Jamie returns, with each deep inhale, to the formless everything.

How did it begin? There is no beginning. Qarrtsiluni: sitting together in the darkness, expectantly. Something is emerging, but we don't know what. A presence, an offering, a question. This abundance is now ours. We struggle to respond. A movement, like a snake through the grass.

. . .

Drug science is about neither drugs nor science. It is more properly, as we've seen, a collection of moral fantasies loosely backed by experiment: drug-war politics, neuro-materialism, prefrontal morality, pharmacological determinism. This may be inevitable given the moral and fictional underpinnings of addiction. So if myth is needed to encompass the fullness of it, we might as well sift through the options. Perhaps some amalgam of Inuit ritual, existential psychology, neuroscience, Taoist mysticism, and Lakota prophecy will do.

Myths are often denigrated as the *logos* of closed minds. But this is only true if the person is held captive to the story, as in addiction or scientism, without recognizing the creativity and ambiguity at play. Myth might even release us from our captivity, offering us the freedom to practice an entirely untethered recognition, liberated from any obligations to facticity. The fiction is obvious. And the truth is accordingly intuited not by recourse to some factual "reality" but by its concordance, as in contemplative or imaginative pursuits, with the wakeful silence of attention. Does it resonate with ( ) or not? There is no "real world" at question here. Instead, there is a window into vaster possibilities of being and imagination.

This window extends to the forgotten firmament beneath us. One need not deliberately subscribe to some mythology to be shaped by it. We often inherit our myths along with our other words, like the rich ground in which we take root. And we may have forgotten they are myths because we live in them: the dark substratum of reality. What is the genesis story that has brought our world into becoming? How did it begin? Our waking dream state might be a confluence of many fables, but the vision we share most clearly is a state with a common language, common borders.

Once upon a time. A blank slate, awaiting civilization. The promised land. A brave people, crossing seas into the unknown. Land of the free, of possibility, of upward mobility and equal opportunity. Fleeing the yoke of oppression. We hold these truths to be self-evident. Crushed by the crucifixion, austere in remembrance of the wounds of our Lord. In remembrance of the fallen soldier. In remembrance of the pilgrims, founders, workers. A harassed people, proud under the strain of church and crown. Converting the lost with the good word. A hardworking and rugged people, stewarding the land according to divine decree. A haven, a sanctuary, a marketplace. Freedom of expression and consumption. The servants of reason and justice shepherding the world. Redeeming the enslaved and benighted of other nations. In God we trust. A pinnacle of enlightenment. Checks and balances, elections and taxation. An inventive people, a logical people, led by the torch of science. Pioneers of progress. Bombs bursting in air. A moral people, a voting people, a utopian people. A lawful people. Speaking softly, armed with a big stick. The self-made man. Light on the mountain, our manifest destiny. Giving proof through the night.

These myths have created a world. They are behind our Constitution and Republic, and they have also inspired, in the centuries since the birth of the nation, much of what we consider the hallmarks of human evolution: scientific discovery, technological progress, new heights of personal and creative expression, and the expansion of freedom and opportunity for citizens. But the myth has also been a rigid *logos* inseparable from the reality it has shaped, fracturing our minds with visions of peace and abundance while permitting the many horrors of empire. This begins with the genocide and oppression of Indigenous peoples, and continued with the enslavement of Africans, with Anglo-Protestant supremacy, hypocritical morality, misogyny and homophobia, achievement culture, with underground reserves of capital, of nuclear weapons, of secret laboratories, of oil, social engineering, poverty, techno-fetishism, environmental collapse, superpower policing, mass shootings, mass suicides, mass overdoses, mass incarceration, mass violence, wars of revolution, cold wars, civil wars, drone wars, wars on drugs, wars on terror, wars for democracy, and wars for peace.

These myths permeate the private moments of everyone just as profoundly. These may be detected in the patterns so familiar to us as to be invisible, beginning with how we approach what sustains us, whether we are a working person, an addicted person, obese, athletic, or anorexic. What might the dominant myth be behind our modes of consumption, of food, of drugs, of one another? Do we use these things for pleasure, for forgetting, for performance, for conformity, for our own narrow ends, or do we approach them as gifts, bending to receive their generosity, with respect and humility, on their own terms? It may be possible to be propelled by one myth—the fiction that we have the God-given right, for example, to pursue our ideas of happiness—only to land in another more primordial myth, with the Great Ignorance yawning beneath our feet.

●

How did it begin? A world dies, another is born. But our dead worlds needn't remain dead. They might endure like taxidermy, collecting in our libraries as dusty parchment, ancient literature, embalmed myths conveying truth from another time. And some dying worlds live on by disappearing entirely into the banality of established truth, structuring the shape-shifting immensity into the stable cosmos we insist on comprehending. We learn dead words, dead facts:

> The Learned, who strive to ascend into Heaven by means of learning, appear to Children like dead horses, when repelled by the celestial spheres.

We are free to begin again, bringing greater freedom and intuition to the living-dying cycles of imagination at the origin of things. This is how we ground more fruitfully in our dark foundations, and ascend to something like home.

A common dream is possessing a many-tongued fluency, the eloquent repose of the polyglot passing freely through diverse languages and worlds, making a home in whatever might be said. This dream of perpetual homecoming might be extended to our Babel of myths and realities too. We wind fork-tongued through the woven fictions brought to each moment, tending to the celestial silence on the other side of every word.

One must relinquish a certain familiarity to find this native fluency: the worlds that anchor us as well as our reflexive ways of telling them, entering them, inhabiting them. The vast wilderness invites our sacrifice. This is where it ends, where it begins. A babbling torrent washes over our heads like a baptism, unveiling the multivocal force of our most primal pharmakon. In the beginning, it is said, was the word.

PART III

ORIGINS

I.

It was a fateful introduction to the Amazonian brew most popularly called *ayahuasca,* the Quechua word widely interpreted to mean "vine of the dead." I was a restless and bookish adolescent in the early '90s catching up on mid-twentieth-century literature, reading everything I could find that was unusual and startling. I would descend on a writer and devour whatever I could find, move on to someone else in alphabetical order: Bataille, Beckett, Bernhard, Blanchot, Borges. It was a state of wild enthusiasm comparable perhaps to that of Don Quixote devouring his novels—but instead of coming to see the world as a knight might, I had imagined my way into a more modern character: hyperliterate madman wrangling with a postwar world in shambles.

I was blazing through the works of Burroughs, *Junkie, Naked Lunch,* and read through most of *The Yagé Letters* with the impression that it was another semiautobiographical tripped-out fantasy, complete with an exotic drug that was completely made up. The description of the substance was classic Burroughs: mysterious origins, telepathy, esoteric magic, access to strange and hyperreal worlds. If only such a drug was real, I mused naïvely. I had realized by the book's end that this strange tea did in fact exist. But it was too late: "yagé" or "ayahuasca" had been indelibly stamped with the magical patina of fiction. Decades later, I continue to regard the tea as uncanny and not entirely of this world, something like a creation of pure imagination that had snaked through the space-time continuum into our remote corner of reality.

There is now a great deal popularly known about this once mythical substance: its plant constituents, its psychopharmacology, how to brew it, where to find it—even which "shamans" and retreats come recommended. These matters will be given attention in due time. But for now let's forswear any claim on authoritative knowledge, and acknowledge that much of what is written in the pages ahead might very well be an elaboration of the fiction that began for me in the enchantments of adolescence.

There is benefit in allowing our imaginations to run wild for a time, beginning with restoring our freedom to behold a reality unrestrained by reality. We've had ample preparation for this leap. Awaiting us might be recognitions and correspondences beyond ordinary comprehension, a mysterious kinship with strange and unfamiliar worlds. May we attend closely now to these words as they lead us toward the threshold of reunion—*my sibling,* as Baudelaire addressed his own readers, *and my double.*

●

In his *Letters*, Burroughs chronicles his journey with Ginsberg through the upper Amazon to locate and experience the fabled substance, propelled by the same motivations that would, more than half a century later, continue to inspire tourism to the tea-drinking traditions of the region: curiosity, a desperate need for healing, the taste for unusual experiences, and vague spiritual yearnings. The book is more social critique and hallucinatory travelogue than it is informative or insightful about the tea itself. But it was a compelling and impactful read. Most fascinating was that Burroughs, a seasoned drug user who had seen it all and who struggled with addiction to heroin and cocaine, would describe this pungent hallucinogenic brew made of leaves and bark as the most powerful thing he had ever used. His intriguing descriptions of the experience stayed with me as well.

That this obscure tea would lodge itself in my mind was no small feat. There were many other substances competing for my attention. I came of age in the San Francisco Bay Area, where drug culture—primarily centered around cannabis and psychedelics—had deep roots. This was also the height of the DARE (Drug Abuse Resistance Education) program. There was moral panic everywhere. We were asked to choose a side: drug user or sane citizen? Police officers would routinely come to our classrooms to reinforce the dichotomy, plying us with scare stories about the worst drugs of the bunch: heroin, cocaine, special K, PCP, acid, and the "gateway drug" of pot. There was a yet more powerful substance, which might also be helpful, as Burroughs had hoped, for heroin addiction? I was captivated.

It seemed worlds different than the drugs we were warned about in the over-the-top stories that were repeated, to the letter, by each cop visiting our classrooms. The tea had somehow managed to evade the gossip and propaganda. I imagined it as something we should all experience before our twenties, like an entry point into adulthood: a magical rite of passage in a consumer wasteland lacking anything resembling real initiation. I began to research, pre-internet, how I might find it.

•

First, the question of what to even call it: yagé, ayahuasca, la medicina, the brew, the tea? Names are a problem in general in the world of these substances, whether we call them psychedelics, sacraments, hallucinogens, imaginants, oneirogens, or psychoplastogens. It makes sense that our nomenclature would break down into babble when attempting a single name to sum up their effects, which invariably touch on the incomprehensible.

There are the obvious problems with "hallucinogen," the most common term in medical and scientific circles. Pure etymology would have it as *generating mental wandering*, which is often true. But what hallucinogen is taken to mean more commonly is *generating hallucinations*, which is mostly false. These substances—including LSD, DMT, psilocybin—do not routinely cause hallucinations, which are, strictly speaking, sensory phenomena taken to be real without an intersubjective referent. Instead, they cause illusions or sensory experiences that are loosely related to "reality," though with the person's so-called reality testing, the capacity to remain adherent to consensus intersubjectivity, largely intact. The suggestion that what is happening is pathological is another problem with the name. Other names originating within the mainstream current of psychiatry—deliriant (eliciting delirium), psychotomimetic (simulating psychosis), dissociative (causing dissociation)—are also indicative of this negative bias.

Then there are the problems with *psychedelic*. As already mentioned, the term means mind (or soul) manifesting. This name goes the opposite direction than "hallucinogen," and focuses on the benevolent effects that might emerge, including a greater capacity for insight, heightened subjectivity, and mystical-type or transpersonal experiences beyond the confines of the apparent ego. Entheogen (generating the god within) or mysticomimetic (simulating mystical experience) are other examples of names focusing on the ("spiritual") good that might come. But to call these substances by these names is like calling a knife a surgical implement, neglecting that it might be used to wound or kill as much as to operate. The experiments with mind control and torture conducted under MK-ULTRA with LSD and psilocybin should give us pause before representing these substances in such a limited and naïve way. Even widely revered plant medicines, such as ayahuasca, are seen as clearly dangerous by experienced individuals in the hands of "sorcerers" or exploitative *curanderos*, with the transpersonal effects working not to illuminate or heal, but to enable financial, sexual, and psychological depredation.

With more data emerging on the neural effects of these substances, other terms oriented around the findings of neuroscience are likely on the horizon. These might be helpful at correcting the problems with the names above, especially if they neutrally capture the full spectrum of what these substances do, including giving appropriate attention to psychoactive effects. The neural mechanisms of these substances, mentioned in passing earlier, may have some bearing on the names we find. These include the promotion of dendritic growth, plasticity, and neural connections, as well as modulation of default-mode network activity and connectivity, with the usual neural constraints on information processing dismantled. It is hypothesized that this allows for potentially fruitful disruptions in the predictive map generated by the brain for organizing and making sense of experience. Non-ordinary modes of perception and representation emerge, along with a cascade of non-ordinary realities.

Future names might invoke the array of these biological and experiential effects. Perhaps the best term would be the most fluid one, capturing the watery essence of these disruptions (though as mentioned earlier, all substances, including tobacco or alcohol, can be just as fluid, ineffable, and "psychedelic"). Certain ambiguous terms (*pharmakon*, *aqua vitae*) are good but overused and now banal. We might also move away from our Greco-Roman constraints, collapsing our alphabets and merging disparate tributaries to coin the name. Ohumayae (Korean, Sanskrit, Arabic: evening-illusion-water)? Mmirirs (Igbo, Germanic: springwater-looking-glass)? Finneganics (Joycean)?

These names have an important advantage over existing ones. They communicate the nonsense implicit in any name, an absurdity especially conspicuous when attempting to name experiences beyond words. Contrast these playful exercises of pharmakolalia with the puffed-up nomenclature fetishizing these substances as soul manifesting or God generating, conferring on them a special provenance, uniquely divine purpose, or inherently theistic importance. Carl Hart has termed the idolization of these substances above others "psychedelic exceptionalism."

As for what is most popularly called ayahuasca, I have settled on "the tea" as the term that sits most comfortably with me. The definite article is sufficient to denote it; few other teas might be mistaken for *the* tea. The neutral and nonsensational term also avoids issues of appropriation, of dissipating the power of its traditional names, or of privileging one Indigenous tradition over others (e.g., ayahuasca vs. yagé vs. uni vs. natem, etc.).

Despite my better judgment, it was impossible for me to avoid imagining this tea as somehow special, even exceptional. The process of crystallization had already started. Reading everything I could find on the subject—Cesar Calvo, Richard Evans Schultes, the McKenna brothers, Michael Taussig—I found that Burroughs was far from alone in regarding the tea as sui generis among other substances. It was accorded, even in Western accounts, a respect more fitting to a sacrament or master-teacher than a drug or medicine. This was only partly attributable to these writers' deference to its origin in the rituals, healing ceremonies, and prayers of the diverse Amazonian groups that approach it reverently. The psychoactive powers of the tea clearly commanded their respect as well. It could go in many directions, often unexpectedly and jarringly, and many writers have described this breadth as an important part of its power: elaborate visions might give way to precise guidance on real-world decisions, followed by confusing visitations, the reliving of long-forgotten memories, and otherworldly insights, interrupted by terrible ordeals of gastrointestinal distress that ease, just as abruptly, into a gentle and serene introspection. This seemed a substance so uncompromising and intractable that it necessitated being approached like an alien being: with humility, formal preparation, a readiness for disorientation, as well as a certain fear and trembling.

●

Since I first began to reflect on drugs and alcohol as a child, I marveled at them, conferring on them a nearly magical status. That something so apparently slight—a breath of smoke, a sip of fluid, a single pill—could profoundly change our emotions, feelings, thoughts, and behavior was endlessly fascinating, raising questions about who we are and what our minds and identities might be. The fears, taboos, and restrictions that surrounded psychoactive substances seemed to come, in some measure, from collective recognition of this power.

But they were also approached and consumed too casually: too freely talked about, named, commodified, instrumentalized, criminalized, compartmentalized. LSD, cocaine, PCP, heroin, tobacco, alcohol, cannabis, mushrooms, mescaline—they had all lost a significant mystery in my eyes by virtue of the systems into which they so easily fit, systems of the drug war and addiction and recreational consumption and commerce and the medical establishment. The DARE program also underscored how psychoactive substances could be mobilized to categorize people from an early age, educating children to embrace an us-them worldview, shaping our thinking about one another and ourselves. I wanted something as far away from these broken systems as possible.

The tea had seemed to circumvent the reach of these regimes. Even now, despite efforts to create and bring to market a synthetic "pharmahuasca" analog, or to establish a pay-for-service network of "ayahuasca retreats," the tea seems to retain its enigmatic spirit, beyond all translation. Nor has it given itself away too easily: something about it remains savage and uncivilized, befitting its wild origins.

Its legal status is similarly liminal and elusive. Though it has been illegal for decades (because it generally contains the illegal DMT), it was not on anyone's radar when I was coming of age. The plants from which it is brewed have always been legal and freely available as well. To this day, the DEA has not regarded the tea as high-priority, and certain groups are granted religious protections for ceremonial use.

Then there was its tremendous power. This was not something that could be taken casually. That it required a respectful and mutual approach, as if it were a wild animal, seemed exactly as things should be. Our systems had failed to contain it in every possible way: the tea was beyond habit, law, representation, civilization. Beyond even history: equally modern and ancient, a timeless aporia emerging from some self-created alien wilderness.

The tea was beyond being a powerful drug. I imagined it, with all the philosophical gravity of adolescence, as an *absolute drug*, taking what drugs are to an apotheosis. A Platonic substance, undiminished by our filters and paradigms. To receive it, I would need to bow my head and play by its rules, accepting its overwhelming otherness.

●

These words present dangers. I have been appointed various names: professor, physician, scientist. With them have come financial security, authority, and prestige. They have also come with demands. I am expected to shun the relationships described here. Or at the very least I ought to hold my tongue. Illicit engagements can mark a scientific or medical reputation indelibly. But it is *illicit pharmakolalia* that presents the most serious dangers—speaking about drugs transgressively, mythically, unreasonably. And most dangerous of all is providing the pharmakon the space to speak for itself, writhing the world with its other-than-human tongues.

The reach of the regime extends far and wide. Its deceptions, including the war on *drugs*, the war on *them*, the war on *others* more generally, are not the business of only a few elite liars. They affect us all, whether they pertain to matters of shared knowledge or of personal meaning. And we each play a role in them, with near-unanimous participation. Our silent acquiescence only emboldens the regime further, while deepening our complicity and captivity.

I offer these words in a spirit of resistance. *Sous les pavés*, that famous slogan from May '68, *la plage*. Under the pavement, the beach. A powerful current might be glimpsed through the in-between spaces. We must allow ourselves to unearth it. The same mainspring that formed our myths and monuments also throbs and swells in the heart of every human being. Each of our moments, no matter how seemingly mundane or banal, might be an incarnation of Shiva sustaining the world, Ulysses wandering home, coyote presiding over creation, or Orpheus descending into the realm of the dead. We are far more than our names and forms.

The tea is one of many practices for cracking the concrete and revealing this ancient fluid firmament. The path, as we will find, can be crooked. I provide this account of my own intoxications to show what's possible. This might seem more personal than is customary for a scientist or physician. It may even seem indecent, like dark and mysterious stains marking a white coat.

The horizon of scientific inquiry is itself impolite, a rubble of broken conventions. The work ahead is not to fortify the regime but to unpave it, open it up, breach its walls. I offer my own barbarism in that spirit.

•

As in other acts of imagination, the tea became more than material. It had gone as far as my imagination could take it; it had become incomprehensible.

These are the intoxications I had allowed to compact around the tea, well before any actual engagement. I had decided, from the start, that I would never *consume* it, as I would some physical, digestible thing. Nor would I be able to characterize or even name it. An eternal stranger, evading all possible resemblance to anything. Any relationship would be two-sided, possibly many-sided.

I envisioned the tea as deeply nocturnal: a resident of the fertile darkness that births our visions, gives them breath, then swallows them up again. A lunar Dionysian tumult on the other side of day. And the hope was that it would guide me through this sacred profane night, allowing me access to the secret depths of the dark.

The tea was sacred to me; it was primal and profane. An apophatic aperture into what cannot be said or known. There was also something personal in it: a concerned stranger carrying messages unique to us, in unknown languages. But more than a stranger too. The stranger we are to ourselves, a stranger residing in our own homes, conveying secrets from the earth, the elements, the water.

I had imagined my way to some kind of truth. Perhaps the truth itself was imagined too. I was hesitant to speak about the tea in the same way a lover guards his tongue, lest I be negligent with my words or grow too casual. I may have also felt protective of my nascent crystallization, cupping it in my hands against the indelicate intrusions of the larger world—and probably, I would later realize, against the realities of the tea itself.

I sensed a wild power, in any case, that invited care. Even its names might be incantations. We should speak them quietly, gently, asking for permission with each word. Dense vegetation might burst every surface, thousands of eyes peering through the leaves. An alien presence breaking through the ground, green feathered vines twisting upward, offering to us the opaque blood-red milk pouring from its pores.

●

Imagination and fiction might have inspired me to look for the tea, but access to it would not come from mythmaking alone. I needed to act, to put in the time and effort for a proper search.

There was a single lead. I knew some old-timers in the Haight who mentioned a few active circles, but they disclosed terrible experiences as well as skepticism about whether it was possible to find good tea outside the Amazon. They promised they would inform me if someone they knew and trusted from the Santo Daime, a Christianity-based syncretic religion incorporating the tea, would agree to pour *daime* for me. But they never contacted me.

It was difficult to know where to begin, despite living in a mecca of drug culture. The tea was still in the shadows. But I kept my eyes open, entreating the world to grant opportunity. As is so often said of the tea, I didn't need to search it out for long before a series of synchronicities placed it directly before me.

This is how I have come to understand the tea, years later. My myth was not far from the truth. Or perhaps I have never moved beyond myth: so much about the tea might be entirely my imagination. In either case, I am grateful that my imagination has been awakened so profoundly.

It is difficult to describe engagement with the tea without succumbing to an intoxicated kind of poetry, to ecstatic utterances, to total silence. We receive the night, indeed, as we do a poem, a dream, a crisis. We are in something like an oneiric trance as the experience unfolds, with heightened sensitivity to the meaningfulness of things, even as we might be making it all up as we go along. Whatever transpires, no matter how apparently trivial, strikes us as necessary, purposeful, issuing from some secret design. We are also invited to suspend all expectation, embrace a radical openness. To think we know what's coming is to set ourselves up for an illuminating trick.

The dream may not be ours alone. Perhaps the tea is traditionally received at night so that we might dream its thousand forms into being. It might be the dead dreaming, the earth and water dreaming, the dream of the night itself. The purging, the fasting, the total darkness: our role is to hollow ourselves out, tending to the sanctum within ourselves, protecting its silence so that we might more fully receive the mysteries of even the most commonplace elements, fulfilling the promise of water, of breath, of our bones and blood.

The elaborate visions, the insights, the emotional intensity, the heightened perception: this is just the beginning. Or the middle, or the end. The tea seems to move within a greater flow, a deeper dream beyond place and history. It even seems to transcend the bounds of birth and death.

The tea holds the same promise as do other substances, yet with seemingly greater force: access to greater possibility, a glimpse of an abundance beyond everyday limits. The abundance might even become our own, in a transition abrupt, often perplexing, yet charged with necessity. Nothing left to find, no more dreams to pursue. Contentment ceases to be in the future tense, no longer *a moving toward* in the hope of imminent, immediate gratification. It is already here. Gratification is restored to its true immediacy: in this moment now, in *a moving with* that is the most immediate gratification of all.

We have little choice in the dreams offered us. But we might recognize our place in them, bending with whatever is offered, in some cases waking up with a start, a vivid reality, a remembrance. It is the same perilous passage that other potent substances provide, whether into addiction or out of it. We are exalted, disillusioned, wounded into a more vulnerable intimacy with things. There is a sense of coming full circle, from reality through unreality to reality again, as speechless and naked as the day we came.

•

Perhaps most perplexing is we might discern intimations of the tea's current as soon as we set a date, well before the actual communion. Some *curanderos* remark that working with the tea (re)activates a prior relationship, perhaps predating our own lifetime. The preparatory process of eating simply, quieting our nervous systems, offering sacrifices and gifts, and practicing humility permits greater attention to our growing relationship with this subtle, other-than-human being—and to the profound reunion that might be unfolding.

The common names of endearment people have given the tea reflect this intuition of primal kinship: Mother, Mama Aya, Grandmother. The tea might also be assigned a supernatural intelligence and otherworldly, even extraterrestrial magic. But I hesitate to say too much. There is no magic here or, rather, no exceptional magic. Of course the tea is aligned with the magical current of being. Everything is.

Some materials nonetheless provide a fuller taste than do others. There is a reason Burroughs and many others have placed the tea in its own category. I have encountered few substances offering a more expansive intimacy. The tea unveils the abundance of what is before us. Other less exalted possibilities are brought to light, too: our ephemeral finiteness, our fragility and mortality, the reality that everything we think is the case will, at any moment, transform beyond recognition.

I have come to appreciate this fluidity as key to its power. I have also come to respect the perilous sacrifice it involves. We are invited to throw ourselves into its wild waters, putting our head down beneath the surface. Disoriented beyond our landlocked familiarities, we may be permitted, for a moment, to reunite with the ancient ancestral presence breaking against the stones.

Awaiting recognition is the immensity of our relationship with this world. And from this wild recognition, all else ensues: care, tenderness, discernment, repose, everything we consider good and right. Making a proper home in the chaos. The entire world reciprocates this primordial intention. A sense of profound familiarity blooms the moment we allow ourselves to turn toward ( ) with homebound yearning, finally putting to rest the realities clattering in our skulls.

And there will be further disorientations, reunions. "You are being taught," the medicine man said, "with the sticks and carrots of your spirit." The most merciful teaching, Jermaine recognized, is to suffer without reprieve from the wounds that should be paining us. We recognize the agony of our self-deceptions, the madness of our certainties. We are not at home in our interpreted world.

Following the pain will lead to a homecoming. The tea might accompany us along the way, offering to interrupt our anguish and wandering for a twilight moment. All the gifts of fiction—the illuminations, confusions, and reckonings—distilled into a few teaspoons of Finneganic fluid. The tea tastes like earth if the earth could bleed.

●

These myths I have brought to the tea are not about the tea. They are about me, perhaps about all of us, as we share together this precious living-dying moment, boundless mystery between us and within us.

We have been thrown into ( ), or perhaps we came more superfluously, brimming over into existence from something like an overflowing cup. There is no apparent reason, no clear sense to it. We did not need to be, and yet we are. The meeting ground itself is more than we can imagine: a torrential surplus of being.

We engage the ineffable abundance; we receive it as an explicit gift. And this myth pertains to the tea, as well as to everything else. A mystery beyond comprehension, given generously and without end. The earth is as much an excess and overabundance as we are. It did not need to be, and yet it is given.

We practice attunement and presence; we give care and remembrance. The cup is presented so that we might learn to receive it. What passes through is as dark and limitless as the night itself: nameless, landless, timeless, ownerless, cultureless, even meaningless—free of whatever representations we conjure up. Neither medicine nor poison, neither a natural solution nor a supernatural wound. Yet everything at once. The tea is a gift that echoes the greater gift, the Great Gift, mythical, boundless, and inescapable.

We drink from the surplus until we burst at the seams, receiving and pouring forth the same overflow. The tea came to be through our participation: we had brought the plants together, orchestrated the conditions for their fruitful marriage. We create this meeting ground reciprocally from the same full cup. What flows forth is beyond understanding. What we might be is reflected at us in the gift's sacred darkness. We give and receive, without grasping or comprehending, in endless circularity.

●

I maintain a scientific understanding of the tea, and am well read on its ethnography, biology, and pharmacology. I have also engaged with the tea in various contexts, ranging from Indigenous ritual to more syncretic and gnostic productions. But I do not pretend a knowledge that is impossible. I do not anchor my understanding in these representations, in any representation. I have learned to maintain an alert perplexity before the tea, before the earth, before you, as I would before the luminous depths of my own being.

I recognize the strangeness of these words. I have endeavored to speak from the darkness so that you might make your own sacrifices and listen from your own. I recognize the strain, my sometimes purple-drunk ambiguity at the margins of meaning. How to talk about what is beyond telling?

We are bound to fail, even if we succeed. The simplest myth gesturing at not-knowing and ineffability—the story of Abraham, for example, commanded by his inscrutable God to sacrifice his firstborn son—remains a representation of "not-knowing" and "ineffability," with the usual apparatus of cognitive control poised to take over and demand obedience. We are at constant risk of falling, like Jermaine in his pursuit of "pure being," into a well-defined, dark arrow directing our experience, inseparable from the man-made mythic schemes creating our worlds, worsening our captivity, and killing our children.

The strain of these words, however, is also their truth. Under the stones, the beach. The cracks show the ancient beauty underneath. No system endures. There remains a deeper silence than our words, our thoughts, even our "being experience."

May our words remain grounded in the water, their meaning polymorphous as pharmakon. A silent reunion awaits us all. A leap and fall, then stuttering like a flame into the ( ) forever remaking the world.

●

The various challenges associated with the tea lend themselves to mythology too. This begins with its representations, with the menacing moat of legend that surrounds it. Losing one's mind, undergoing severe trauma, falling into a plant medicine cult, facing death: the stories that circulate around the tea in the Global North are forbidding, often overstating the risks. Yet these representations touch on a truth. This is not to be taken lightly.

We are compelled to pause at the threshold. Something perilous waits just ahead. The fallibility of being human, of both our certainties and confusions, will be heightened. We might stumble into recognition; we might stumble into more painful depths. There may be a reckoning every time.

We cannot contain the materials of earth in the forms we fancy for them. The tea, yes, and other plants, other substances, animals, water, one another: we might begin with humility and sensitivity, give recognition to their irreducible darkness, and be nourished accordingly, one being in relationship with others. Or we might require a teaching lasting the rest of our lives. The earth nourishes us; it disciplines us.

The tea doesn't solve anything. Pointing the way forward, as a good teacher might, instead of doing the work we must do ourselves. Neither weakening us by becoming a habitual consolation, nor by fitting neatly into our utilitarian schemes. This invites us to find greater liberation from our most recalcitrant, invisible regimes of thought and habit—to recognize how limited our actual sphere of control might truly be, even as we strive to wrestle the whole world into obedience.

The impact of the tea does not end come morning. There may be sustained improvements in serenity and intentionality, as well as greater capacity for attunement, for sometimes weeks to months afterward. But the aftereffects are not always an afterglow: there may also be heightened and uncomfortable vulnerability, with exquisite sensitivity to insidious ways of being, relationships, and perspectives ordinarily passed over with normalcy. The brain-based reasons for these persistent effects have elicited scientific interest, though it remains unclear whether they are fully attributable to neural plasticity, altered cognitive mapping, or other brain-based effects. It may never be clarified. But here we are, wrangling with ourselves while still working through the mysteries of the night. This is no different from what has always been the case. Now we might better recognize what is before us.

The days and weeks afterward are crucial for attending to any afterquakes and reverberations—though not always honored in the mad rush for the next thing. But the mad rush will also lay bare its madness. The reports of trauma, psychosis, severe anxiety, and nightmarish near annihilation are far outnumbered by stories of the good mother feeding, succoring, and instructing her children. Yet we will also learn that the sweet mother might turn her face, at any moment, to reveal the blood-smeared smile of Kali, wearing a necklace of skulls, flicking her serpent tongue, and destroying the shackles we hold dear to our hearts.

II.

If the earth could bleed, from what would it bleed? From what break in the earth, what wound, what opening, from what weakness, from what wilderness? From what people, what violence, what history, what silence?

•

Our disparate maps float on the tea's dark surface like flotsam, shifting and rearranging with the current to reveal new associations, affording opportunity for self-discovery and sometimes startling panoptic insights. We encounter personal revelations, intimate and secret reorientations. Paradigm shifts of a more communal sort, pertaining to our shared systems of knowledge, might also originate in this fluidity.

But this epistemic flux has its dangers. Different ways of knowing converge under the tea's spell, with cognitive systems both empirical and unempirical—Hegelian dialectics, pre-Socratic philosophy, geophysics, pre-Cambrian evolutionary biology, quantum entanglement, Mesoamerican myth, object-oriented ontology, Tibetan scripture, ad infinitum—collapsing into something like a living metaphysics. Our maps become even more imaginary, in other words, than maps ordinarily are, more spectral, mythical, and compacted. Sustaining the (un) reality is a recalcitrant noetic quality: neither provable nor disprovable, the fiction simply *feels true,* with all the persuasive force of revelation. Our capacity to find correspondences is accelerated beyond good sense, too, with everything becoming related to everything else in manic hyper-connected conceptual schemes. We might become blinded, as had Jermaine, by our own totalizing visions.

Such visions might implicate the tea itself. There may be the inclination to exalt the tea as a complete cure-all, fetishize it as a superior being, or surrender agency in deference to its commands. Such fictions might radically reorient our lives, compelling us to circle around the tea as if it were a golden calf. In recognition of this tendency, I suggest a fourth meaning for pharmakon, implicit in the other three. Before it might be castigated as scapegoat, the substance must be raised up beyond its apparent indeterminacy as poison/medicine. It must become *an idol.*

It cannot, however, remain an idol for long. Its own nature forbids it. A clash will occur between the graven image and its negation; the "paradise" of the drug will meet its "hell." This ambivalence is analogous to that of a very different, explicitly imagined window into ( ): the sacred paintings of Christendom, which are intended to convey an impression of holiness at the same that they repudiate themselves as artifice or mere material. The Christian image, in the words of art historian Joseph Koerner, is "self-negating from the start," with an in-built iconoclasm calling attention to its illusoriness and ephemerality. It is, like all creation, both "idol" and "anti-idol," a presence and a vanishing. One is idolatrous (or iconoclastic) of the sacred representation only if one fails to see it truly, ignoring in the vision its primal emptiness. Learning to appreciate a sacred object is akin, in this regard, to learning to hold one's liquor.

The tea might be met with a comparable failure in appreciation, and thus raised up (or cast down) as a transcendent reality or truth. There are bound to be reckonings, usually at the feet of the grandmother herself. And also, of course, opportunities for working through our confusions and better attending to the sacred-profane fullness of what is before us. This begins with cultivating our capacity for paradox and ambiguity—and learning to intuit our way through this imagined world without the winds of absolutism ruling the day.

The confusions also occur on a communal level, especially given that the tea is commonly administered in ceremonial group settings, where shared beliefs, sometimes peculiar, might take root. The tea has a long-standing association with New Age communities, neo-shamanic retreats organized around a central charismatic leader, Indigenous communities compelled because of globalist incursions to subsist on "plant medicine" tourism, as well as urban bubbles of psychoactive exploration. Wild ideas might proliferate, including tea worship, fetishism, cults of personality, and other varieties of spiritual materialism. Dreams of utopia are also common. The tea might be invested with a capacity to effect social change or healing single-handedly, for instance, while participants take a backseat. Similarly, people might believe that frequent communal ritual alone is sufficient to civilize them into love and wisdom, the more medicines and visions the better.

•

The potential for the tea to promote communal renewal is real, just as it is possible to initiate a lifetime of new perspectives and values after a single powerful night. Anthropologists have long recognized, for example, the tendency for cultural worlds to revitalize themselves by passing through rituals that dissolve or temporarily reorganize hierarchical and cultural norms, engendering liminal social roles for a time and allowing opportunity for more ecstatic modes of engagement: a cyclical return to chaos to renew the social order. These traditions—which may or may not involve psychoactive substances—constitute an integral aspect of maintaining community; shared cultural values and group engagement are crucial for these rituals to exert a collective impact.

The meteoric rise of "ayahuasca" to mainstream popularity in Western societies, along with that of other "psychedelics," has been understood in these terms—as reflecting a need for "ego dissolution" on a widespread level, galvanizing enthusiasts to proclaim that a great awakening is upon us, with our calcified civilizations poised to transform under the spell of these substances. Some have argued that this might be nature's way to steer us right: a natural, primitivist corrective to all that ails us in our deathbed convulsions of late-stage capitalism, including technological manias, materialism, environmental violation, social fragmentation, anomie, hyper-individualism, and disconnection.

This conception draws on a familiar fiction: the tea as one of nature's mightiest emissaries, communicating her truths and teaching us to harmonize with the earth. It is a compelling notion, if only by giving us the reassurance that we are not alone in this. Survey data provide some credence to it, too, with some studies reporting more ecological mindedness and less consumer-oriented lifestyles after engagement with the tea and comparable substances.

It is naïve to expect a collective cultural shift, however, in the absence of collective culture. We can dream of understanding, harmony, and abundance for our species. But putting this into practice would require a foundational and therefore deeply intimate reorientation of beings to one another and to the earth. This can only come from individuals and small communities doing their part, with any impact on the collective a downstream possibility. Imposing a monolithic culture and engineered collectivism on our plurality of languages, myths, (un)realities, and mysteries, on the other hand, is hardly what's needed. This is precisely how our dominant regime(s) have maintained their hegemony: diverse communities are maneuvered, often forcibly, to circle around a shared origin of meaning, identity, and power, whether it is a region ("the West"), a style of politics ("democracy"), or a creed ("enlightenment values").

Consumer culture has imposed itself with similar pageantry. Consumer *anti*-culture, however, may be the better designation, with everything "cultural" that doesn't serve the market, beginning with inconvenient worldviews and rights, skimmed away. And its systems of representation are already scrambling for a claim on "psychedelics," too, including the industries of biomedicine, wellness, and entertainment, all of which are practiced at repurposing "culture" or "tradition" for mass consumption. These approaches are obviously dead ends, shoehorning engagement with the tea into the same globalized consumer-oriented structures so inimical to what is possible. Yet these dead ends also constitute the taproots of current "psychedelic culture."

The myth of Indigenous and natural panacea falls into related problems. Reprising a common theme in depictions of Indigenous peoples, this narrative represents these traditions as more integrated into the cosmos/nature than are those of postindustrial societies. Indigenous practices are therefore presumed to be the ideal solution for an empire out of balance with the natural order.

Assuming this diagnosis is true, there is still a substantial problem: How does one transfer the wisdom of some Indigenous tradition to other contexts? Which tradition(s) do we choose? And what is transferred, specifically? The hope of importing a living wisdom and embedded perspective from one culture to another, worlds different, is naïve at best. It is also extractive and dehumanizing, as if Indigenous people are primarily rich repositories of precious information ready to be mined when needed.

There is undoubtedly much to learn from Indigenous worlds. But care is required. Any pursuit of what might be termed "Indigenous knowledge" might fall into familiar patterns of colonialist ignorance and erasure. This can be subtle and insidious. Popular representations of Indigenous people continue to peddle in cartoonish caricatures of the "noble savage" or "pure man"; such representations obscure their human complexity behind an idealized façade commensurate with how they might be useful. To romanticize is to objectify—which is a few steps away from consuming and erasing.

Similar problems emerge from characterizing the tea and "natural intelligence" as a catalyst to our evolution, with human social structures—and "Western" systems specifically—regarded as a special concern of the planet. Perhaps Mother Nature might indeed be troubled by her ill-behaved children. But is it an ecological step forward for the Global North to be extracting and importing untold liters of the tea annually from the Amazon for an emerging ceremony market?

The Global North has good reason for falling into this obvious dissonance between some noble "eco" ideal and the reality on the ground. A historical precedent is already in place. There are echoes of *manifest destiny* in the notion that nature has taken a special interest in catalyzing the evolution of the Global North, both for its own sake, and for the sake of the world it has a unique dispensation to steward. All is permitted as we pursue our higher destiny, an earth abundant with the fruits of our hand. Should we need to bleed the ground or other beings to get there, so be it. God works in mysterious ways.

If the tea has been given us by nature to evolve civilization, then we might turn to Brazil for an example of what progress looks like. The tea has been flowing there for centuries; Brazil has the highest number of Indigenous and syncretic tea traditions in the world and has several large state-sanctioned religions involved in administering the tea (one of which is the Santo Daime mentioned earlier). Yet this has not protected Brazil from authoritarian regimes, neocolonial policies that continue to rob Indigenous lands, or from a GDP-obsessed human rights nightmare that sees millions of acres of rainforest cut or burned each year as well as the murder of activists who endeavor to end this.

Nature itself presents yet another obstacle. There is nothing without nature, including ourselves. Yet the word suggests a distinct world: jungles and rainforest and other scenes of undefiled prelapsarian splendor. We cannot constrain the wilderness in our imaginations like a gated garden. Nor can we even identify it. The wilderness is inevitable and everywhere, even in the heart of the most densely crowded concrete metropolis—and even in the digital simulations on our screens.

The deeper confusion is presuming to understand "natural order" or natural teleology, and then wedding it to an idea of social progress or other anthropocentric concerns. This objectifies the ineffable wilderness into a mechanism with "civilization" its primary purpose, imposing a fiction called "nature" onto ( ) that is then put in the service of "humanity," with often disastrous consequences.

Consider the *Volksgemeinschaft* notions of human evolution in Nazi Germany. *Volksgemeinschaft* originated in a presumed alliance between "nature" and National Socialism, and sanctioned hostility toward Jews, Communists, Roma, and other out-groups because they lacked the historical relationship with the "blood and soil" unique to "true Germans." The belief was that only those with rootedness to European land, such as indigenous Germans with "natural soul," could enjoy proper harmony with its *natur*. It is worth wondering: Would this view strike us as so preposterous when applied, for example, to Amazonian ethnic/linguistic groups, presumed to be living harmoniously, simply because of their indigenous roots, with *natur*?

The Shipibo-Conibo of Peru and modern ethno-fascism are worlds apart, of course, but we should remain mindful of the representations we allow to captivate us. Idealizing a nation, or presuming it enjoys a privileged relationship to "nature," medicinal plants, or the tea simply because of ethnic, territorial, or historical claims is bound to create problems, starting with its nativist echoes of exceptionalism and tribalism. It also reduces Amazonian ontology to something like squatter rights and diminishes the significance of the multidimensional being-with-the-earth unique to Indigeneity, including intimate attunement with the ecology, long-standing carefully cultivated relationships with local flora and fauna, specialized topographical, meteorological, and astronomical knowledge, and a historical depth of engagement with the terrain approaching the mythical. A "privileged" relationship to "nature," on the other hand, is a postcolonial absurdity projected onto them.

No strategy should be off limits, however, to Indigenous people given their ongoing struggle—including invoking "privilege," "authenticity," "land rights," and other weighty words if these might confer power or protection. They may even benefit from reifying and hardening a traditional episteme to defend against continued erasure. Everything might have its place, including some Indigenous version of ideology. In the crowded "ayahuasca" marketplace, for example, certain Indigenous groups have claimed the final word on all matters "plant medicine," with a specific articulation of their ways codified into something like an authoritative dogma or trusted brand. Such strategies might be necessary for preserving an embattled cosmovision and, more broadly, safeguarding territory and preserving a linguistic and cultural heritage. But these should remain tactics as opposed to identifications. It is communal rootedness in being-with-the-earth, and in a fluid multidimensional epistemology, that represents the profoundest gift of Indigenous people—and that deserves protection and stewardship, by Indigenous and non-Indigenous alike, as our firmest, most ancient relationship with this abundance now ours. Such reciprocity may permit more expansive modes of Indigeneity as well: beyond history, geography, and tribal affiliation, with its origin not in our variations or territories but in what we share. A gift given, a gift received, in sacred circularity.

The psychedelic variation on the nature-as-redeemer myth, in any case, is imbued with fictions that should have been long discarded—colonialism, primitivism, imposed collectivism, anthropocentrism, tribalism, pharmacological determinism. It cannot be a fruitful lens by which to approach the tea—nor, really, anything else.

This myth of natural redemption is motivated, however, by an important intuition, even if it has lost its way. It is true that engaging the tea might be helpful at refreshing our fictions, including those inherited from the regime. Indigenous groups have "natural experience" and centuries of learning to offer too. But as in Marcus's case with ketamine, it is important that we foreground thoughtfulness and humility in any engagement with pharmakon—receiving its power as a perilous act of generosity, with the requisite reflection and respect. This attitude of care, before any actual communion, is bound to exert its own "redemptive" power, illuminating and softening our encrusted tendencies of thought and gesture as we ready ourselves, lighting a fire at the threshold that will welcome the tea, and which will be welcomed and nourished by the tea in turn. And when the hour comes that all excrescences have been burned away, we will know to expect neither redeemer nor even nature. What remains is an immense mirror, wiped clean to perfect clarity, our prismatic liquid depths reflected everywhere. "Redeemed by nature" maybe, though only if we take that to mean nothing special.

●

Certain lies have been indelibly stamped with a skull: expect poison inside. "Final solution" is a phrase that continues to make us shudder. Somehow it has found a renaissance with psychedelics. There may be a deeper layer of pharmakolalia feeding it, with an endless capacity to captivate.

Let's call this myth "The Return to a Golden Age." Awaiting resurrection is a natural utopia, dormant in our blood. The presumption is that at the origin of human suffering and injustice are oppressive social systems; collective healing and liberation will come from overthrowing these systems and installing in their place utopian structures conducive to human flourishing. This is a notion common to many cultures. At some point in the darkness of history, humans lapsed from an original state of purity, with responsibility resting squarely on our twisted acculturation.

This viewpoint has been most forcefully articulated by Rousseau, who believed that humans are mostly decent and good-natured, with bad civilization to blame for many of our ills. The place of a panacea in this worldview is clear: anything that dissolves the existing social fabric stands to restore humanity to its blessed, primal condition.

His contemporary the Marquis de Sade had a very different picture of unbridled human freedom, comparable to Hobbes's notion of the nasty, brutish, and short existence of "pre-civilized" humanity. He suggested that without societal constraints, we would descend into a frenzy of rape, mutilation, theft, bizarre sexual acts, slavery, murder—the seven deadly sins run amok. Sade reminds us, in pornographic excess, how vicious human nature can be and exposes the callowness of ascribing our violence and confusion to social conditioning alone.

Sade's misanthropy and Rousseau's hopeful humanism, however, are two sides of the same counterfeit coin. Social systems can neither civilize us, nor can they corrupt us. We will always have the vast wilderness of being to nourish and discipline us, and our own ignorance, suffering, and (un)realities to goad us toward evolution.

Rousseau's viewpoint undergirds much of the millenarian thinking surrounding the tea and comparable "revolutionary" materials. These substances are celebrated for their capacity to dismantle our constructs while guiding us toward building anew. But even this representation is unexceptional. We might call them catalysts, mirrors, or teachers, like any other material on earth—but they are neither answers nor solutions. Any dissolution and rebuilding invariably requires our participation, our clear thinking and hard work. Where psychedelic mythology falters further is in the suggestion that a "transformational" experience and a return to some Golden Age of consciousness are inherently beneficial and socially progressive.

Utopian variations on this theme take us even deeper into ignorance, further revealing our hopeful confusions. The primary aim ceases to be collective action or political engagement to change corrupt systems. Instead, social renewal becomes a downstream inevitability. The solution is to restore people to their primal condition; existence will figure out the rest.

The thorniest conflicts might dissolve, it is hoped, into love and light. The Israeli-Palestinian impasse, for example, will find its resolution, according to some psychedelic advocates, not principally through concessions, protection of basic human dignities and freedoms, and the hard work of systematic social change, but through "mutual healing." Bipartisan "ayahuasca" sessions have been a particular focus: an ancient solution, as some researchers have called it, to what is often characterized as an ancient problem.

None of these things—the Zionist ethnic-majoritarian state, the coupling of militant settler nationalism to the Jewish covenant, state-based Palestinian nationalism, the practice of serving the tea in a non-tribal manner—is in the least ancient. They are all twentieth-century inventions. The only ancient aspect of this conflict is the age-old human tendency to mythologize problems and solutions, while obscuring what requires attention, including the violence and suffering—the suffering imposed on suffering—our myths inflict. I propose calling this blinkered captivity *mythomyopia*.

The mythomyopia in Palestine/Israel works on many levels, with "psychedelic healing" only the most recent myth to join the morass. It is worth examining in some detail, with the same care we have given the regimes of prior addictions. The conflict's origin is often cast as a religious squabble dating back millennia, or, more generally, as the most recent manifestation of ancient antisemitism, with resistance to Zionism entirely attributable to archaic hatred. More psychologizing voices point to "generational trauma" as creating and perpetuating the enmity.

These myths, however, work to obscure the historical record, which locates the origin of the suffering in an all-too-common crime. Israel is at once an attempt at "a Jewish homeland, a sanctuary for this long exiled and embattled people," *and* an effort at total domination of one group over another, with a settler ethno-state created and sustained by Anglo-imperialist powers—and fed on myths of privileged Zionist indigeneity ("biblical right to the land"), cultural superiority ("an outpost of civilization against barbarism"), and eschatological necessity (Christian Zionists hastening the final solution of Revelation)—dispossessing, delimiting, and brutalizing the existing Indigenous population for generations with seemingly absolute impunity.

It is the vicious imaginary of *Volksgemeinschaft* laid bare. Here the racialized claims of "national soul" are taken even further into abstraction, reducing "blood and soil" territoriality to an explicitly book-bound landscape: what nineteenth-century proto-Zionist British imperialists called "the Book and the Land," with the earth essentialized into a map of sacred sites and signs—"the land of the Bible," a palimpsest of multiple cultures and epochs restored to some ancient "primary text," a mythic (sub)stratum erasing all other realities. Jewish identity is refashioned with the same severity, its rich strata of national, cultural, and genetic heterogeneity shorn away to "reveal" the essential Israelite origin. Non-Jewish natives, in turn, are defined (or disappeared) within this script, the reality-machine of Zionist/imperialist/biblical orientalism re-creating them as a nondescript crowd of side characters: initially as lapsed amnestic Jews, nomadic transients, and idle hangers-on who degrade the ancient kingdom's glory, and later, with more blatant bigotry, as antisemitic savages, death-obsessed terrorists, and wreckers of enlightenment values. What falls beyond the confines of this "Holy Land" might as well not exist: "a land without a people for a people without a land."

The non-Jewish Indigenous inhabitants—the unholy others—have responded to this erasure and subjugation in kind, bringing their own sacred imaginaries to bear on the territory, whether it is "Palestine," "justice," or "*waqf* [endowment] from God" serving to articulate their birthright. And predictably, dogmatic (un)realities, reminiscent of Israeli ideology itself, have calcified in some members of the Indigenous community, too, including religious extremism and racism, which have worked to elicit further assaults of wide-scale demonization, and further aggressive supremacy, with each "reality" hardening its counterpart in mirror-image schismogenesis.

This is the bifurcated world into which the tea is being poured. With care and humility, some good may come of it. Its fluidity might be helpful, for example, at disorienting the flawed fictions underfoot, perhaps liberating participants for the space of an evening from the war-locked narratives foisted on them on either side of the partition wall—an important reprieve from the spectacles of state-mandated racism, exclusivist (un)realities, and geopolitical machinations ravaging the region. Perhaps these engagements might also serve to guide the twin dream of return propelling the two peoples, whether the promised land is ancient "Israel" or pre-colonized "Palestine," with their mutual exile finding a truer home, beyond all maps and boundaries, in the Holy Land of ().

This opportunity to enjoy more expansive modes of being, deterritorialized into deeper attunement with (), is reason enough to respect the power of these circles—and it is the reason that participants themselves have given for engaging with the tea together, their intention being to deepen their relationships and understanding without a political agenda or two-state solution in mind.

Imposing our complacent fictions on the tea, on the other hand, is playing with fire. Calling the tea a plant medicine peace initiative, as some advocates have done, carries echoes of the self-deception mentioned earlier, with the presumption that engagement with plant medicines is sufficient to make loving siblings of everyone, or that at the heart of this injustice is "trauma." But this goes even further than glancing over the tremendous work required for an end to the suffering, beyond the therapeutic or "psychedelic." The state-based institutions, laws, myths, and values that perpetuate the anguish and injustice—rooted in what has been viewed by Israel's own human rights organization B'Tselem as "apartheid"—are untouched, not even mentioned. How to work toward reconciliation if we don't address the many walls, physical and otherwise, erected by one group to contain the other?

Even calling the problem "Palestinian/Israeli"—a designation so commonplace as to seem a matter of fact—deepens the distortion. In addition to eliding the power gradient of oppressor and oppressed, this maintains the lie of moral equivalence, effectively normalizing the iniquitous, supremacist systems that need to be dismantled for any meaningful resolution to the suffering.

This binary division also maintains another lie: that "the conflict" is between two peoples, essentializing it into a matter of ethnic or religious difference. This provides yet further cover for the subjugation, imperialist geopolitics, and brutality, this time beneath the fog of an intractable, "complicated" conflict reaching back countless genera-tions.

Desperate times, moreover, call for desperate measures. Perhaps the most one can do for a conflict so apparently ancestral, murky, and deeply imprinted is to provide a Hail Mary medicine alleged to alter our DNA (in a sanguine New Age inversion of the chromosomal risks once attributed to LSD) and hope for the best.

There is yet another way this framing precludes thoughtful engage-ment. This conflict is not primarily about human beings against one another. The real struggle is human beings against themselves: our regimes on one side, *all* human beings on the other. It might be em-pire, slavery, colonialism, fascism, racism, misogyny, anti-Semitism, homophobia, Islamophobia, or any of the other (un)realities empow-ering one person or group to subjugate another: Jermaine had called it a "mind-disease of pure evil," Robyn the "system that runs everything." And our shared struggle is to assert our humanity against these vicious regimes, whether we are objectified into dropping bombs or objectified into being incinerated by them, aggrandized by the dominant order or buried under its rubble.

All erasure, domination, and tyranny begin here, in our captivity within a luminous reality abstracted from the primal ground and raised to power. Every regime—even (or especially) the noble and lofty—will grow more supremacist, more violent and divisive, the closer it comes to realizing the despotic, fractured dream at its origin. And our col-lective future hangs in the balance. A group of visionaries from this long-embattled region once said: "For we wrestle not against flesh and blood, but against principalities, against powers, the forces and author-ities governing this darkness."

No amount of medicine will lead to peace in these circumstances. But expecting a substance to solve our problems is not, of course, a unique fiction. We have seen it with one addiction after another. And we have also seen it in the obverse, with urban blight and suffering in American inner cities ascribed to drug use while the structural issues, racism, dis-proportionate policing, and resource iniquities—the real contributors—remain neglected. A drug is mythologized into a magical fix or a magical problem, while the substantive issues remain unacknowledged.

The so-called peace process, ongoing since the 1970s yet with no end to the suffering in sight, reveals how anything might be put to perverse use, be it the tea, the Holy Land, or peace itself. Its most recent major developments, such as the Oslo and Abraham Accords, make explicit the objectives that have been guiding this process all along: pacifying the Indigenous population under deepening inequality, dispossession, and oppression, and side-stepping the question of Indigenous rights and self-determination in the service of regional normalization, respectively. The process is thus more aptly described as "peacewashing" than peacemaking, carried out by a retinue of characters whose careers, as overseers, accomplices, and quislings, have been oriented around maintaining the deception: a "peace" providing cover rather than real resolution. This is no different than what occurs with addiction: a contentment process, a happiness and pacification process, with seductive mirages in the distance creating a distraction from what should pain us. It is also the same destructive smoke screen, hiding what is most important. The deepening suffering, the propaganda and manipulations, the painful facts on the ground: these remain unaddressed. There may be little interest in addressing them. This is not the place to dissect the peace process, its two-state deceptions or its territorial machinations. The point is that the truth of things is being actively obscured. And we have seen what happens when we attempt to obscure suffering, our own or that of others, as we fall deeper into a dream, an ideal, a final solution. "The Holy Land" locked into a bloody impasse, one myth against another, "God" against "God," "home" against "home," with the earth and its beings torn apart between the gnashing teeth of these sanctities.

We pause at this threshold, the cup resting in our hands, its coiled dark fluid glinting in the depths. There can be only one conclusion, one lesson, whenever we endeavor to fragment the sacred-profane materials of earth into man-made forms, tasking them with proclaiming the nonsense we expect to hear—only one reality when our regime imposes its facts on the ground of (). Our violence toward the wilderness, even in word or thought, will accelerate the inevitable reckoning, the lunacy rebounding amplified on ourselves and others. These lessons might extend beyond a single night, a single cup, to destabilize an entire (un)reality. It is always the same teaching, from individuals to nations: revealing what is hidden, unmasking what requires recognition. I doubt the tea will lend a hand to a process of peace that is in truth a system of war without raising absolute hell.

Perhaps the tea may have an important role to play in bringing peace after all. But before peace, there might be apocalypse. We must be prepared to pass through whatever madness the tea unveils.

III.

If the earth could bleed, what do we do with the blood? Do we drink the blood as a medicine? Is the blood an exorcism or teacher? A sign or a warning? Do we stop the blood, tend to the wound? Or do we drink ourselves to healing and illumination, more blood for more healing, until the earth is drained?

•

Having prepared our imagination with a thousand myths and a thousand medicines, we might now turn to more material matters.

I am occasionally referred patients who need support, what might be called "integration," in the aftermath of a harrowing "psychedelic" experience with the tea or other substances. Usually, they are still struggling to make sense of what happened or are burdened by significant psychological distress, unable to return to their customary lives. Some of these cases can be quite severe, having exhausted the conventional set of resources: I have seen people with psychosis and mania resistant to medicines, as well as a case of severe PTSD. Most people, including the most shaken survivors, went on to find resolution in the end, even as it took months to years of self-work and guidance for them to find their way and fully incorporate the disruptions.

The major issues common to substance use, however, are thought to be nearly impossible with the tea: overdose, tolerance, recreational irresponsibility. And heading the list is addiction. Though I had seen cases of addictive behavior with other classical psychedelics (such as LSD and psilocybin), it was rare and highly atypical, with problematic use patterns generally resembling the quasi-psychotic fixation that Jermaine experienced while he was pursuing his extraterrestrial correspondence and consolidating his *Matrix*-esque cosmology. The tea seemed an even less likely candidate for addiction given that it cannot be as easily or irresponsibly consumed, nor with such little personal preparation or readiness, as might LSD or mushrooms.

The tea is not simply psychoactive. It also has potentially uncomfortable physical and purgative effects. Its main component is the *Banisteriopsis caapi* vine, which contains a number of alkaloids that inhibit the enzyme that breaks down monoamine neurotransmitters throughout the body, such as serotonin and dopamine. This monoamine oxidase inhibition (MAOI) activity begins at the gut before extending to the brain, and in addition to psychoactive effects, may stimulate intense nausea, vomiting, and diarrhea, especially if certain restrictions are not observed. These alkaloids have the propensity to react adversely with common foods and substances. Care with medications therefore needs to be observed to ward off the danger of cardiovascular and psychiatric reactions.

Other plants might be brewed with the vine, depending on regional practices. The most common admixtures are *Psychotria viridis*, *Diplopterys cabrerana*, and to a lesser extent *Mimosa hostilis*. They each contribute, among other alkaloids, the psychoactive tryptamine DMT, which is ordinarily degraded quickly by MAOI enzymes when it is imbibed. The MAOI activity produced by the vine's alkaloids prevents this from happening. This allows DMT to pass undegraded into the bloodstream, and on to the brain, where it contributes to the visionary effects of the brew, typically lasting four to six hours. DMT can cause its own share of gastrointestinal distress, as well.

The tea requires a great deal of care because of how punishing it could be if consumed without observing the appropriate precautions. In addition, there are several dietary and lifestyle practices that are encouraged for sometimes several weeks before and after work with the tea, including a plant-based, low-salt diet, abstinence from intoxicants, solitude, fasting, and celibacy. These are intended to help the person respect and incorporate "the spirit" of the tea.

The tea is not a drug in the usual sense. Indeed, it is rarely administered outside of ceremonial and sacramental settings. These various factors—along with its association with sorcery and its reputation for eliciting harrowing experiences—are recognized to protect the tea from being taken recklessly. I also had my own mythical reasons for viewing the tea as one of the few substances that does not lend itself to addiction or consistent misuse. My own flights of imagination have already been shared.

But the current sweeps up everything, every representation and crystallization. A mentor once told me: hang around a medicine long enough and you'll see it turn to poison.

●

"I'm calling about my cousin," she began the conversation abruptly. "He got into a lot of trouble in the Amazon. He has gone crazy, cut himself open, doesn't want anything to do with his family. He is now in the hospital getting medicated, but we need someone to see him when he gets out."

She was harried and disturbed. I asked her to slow down and start at the beginning, provide the details. She's calling because Carlos's mother and father are overseas: a Mexican family, she said, mostly based in the Czech Republic. He himself was born in Mexico City, raised in Prague, and has lived in the States since late adolescence. Still in his early thirties, he had been previously high-functioning, working as a consultant until a few years ago.

Carlos had been growing more distant over the last decade or so. He had always been the black sheep, kept to himself, had some resentments. She didn't understand it. But he had done well in school, graduated top of his class with an MBA, had found a good job with various start-ups in the psychedelic space. The family wasn't sure what he was up to; they would see one another a few times a year. He was keeping his cards to his chest more often. Then he disappeared, he was no longer at his apartment, he had abruptly quit his job. He emailed his parents that he had gone to Peru, was living with a shaman and his tribe in the rainforest. He had become addicted to a drug they called ayahuasca. They were drinking it regularly; he didn't want to stop.

What led her to say that Carlos was addicted? I asked.

It drove him totally crazy in the end, she said, but even before that he was clearly meeting all the criteria. "I mean, I diagnosed him myself."

Was she a doctor?

No, she was a legal analyst and lobbyist. She must have sensed my skepticism. She offered to go through her thinking for me. She took a moment to take out her laptop, look up the DSM-5, and run through all the criteria over the phone, checking off one after another. She was right. He met criteria for the diagnosis, with the primary issue being that he continued to drink the tea even though he was experiencing social and occupational issues, cutting off his family, quitting his job, moving to South America, perhaps permanently. He even continued to drink it, she said, when severe psychiatric problems developed.

"I think his psychiatric issues probably started in Seattle, before he moved, but they only got worse in Peru. It is that drug, I'm sure of it. There's information about it all over the internet. Stories of people losing their minds. Lots of culty types online gabbing on and on about how it will elevate your soul, blah blah blah. It sounds like hokum to me. The stuff makes you hallucinate and warps your mind. And now look at him. Case closed. I just know that he had some in Seattle, it's probably the reason he went down to the jungle to begin with, he wanted more, maybe he was already addicted by that point. But cutting contact off with his family, believing his twin had returned from the dead to take his place, believing everyone was in on it—that all picked up over the past year or so. And he continued drinking it, just like an addict, continued to receive it from his dealer the shaman, even though he was going more insane by the day, I think he was paying something like three grand a month for the stuff and for accommodations. Anyway, it all came crashing down a few months ago when he freaked out one night, cut himself, and the shaman kicked him out because he was too *borracho* and *loco*. So, he wandered around the jungle, completely alone, raving mad; I can't stop crying thinking about what's become of him. He was ultimately put into a hospital near Iquitos, we were contacted, and we had him transferred to a hospital here in the city, where I could keep an eye on him. His parents are now back in Prague, where they are based, and they left me in charge of everything."

How's he doing now?

"He is much calmer. He's back to his quiet and reserved self. But when he first got to the hospital here, he was super agitated, really suspicious of everyone. They've been giving him medications to calm him down, sedate him. I think he's doing better, but he continues to talk about drinking ayahuasca again someday. It's totally crazy that he would even consider that. I think he might also still think some of the crazier things, the demonic twin stuff, which you can talk with him about. It's all really weird, and the last thing I would have suspected would happen to him. I mean, I had my concerns about him, he had always been questioning everything and into some off-kilter ideas, but never to this level. You were recommended as someone who has experience with this drug, as well as with addiction, so I hope you can help him."

We scheduled him for an appointment the day following his discharge from the hospital. I received documentation from the hospital in the meantime: he had been diagnosed with schizoaffective disorder, a wastebasket diagnosis for combined psychotic and mood symptoms that don't fit neatly into separate diagnoses, and he was started on a few antipsychotic medications. He had been largely cooperative the entire time, barring an initial agitated reaction at being put in the hospital against his will. He was taken to court to maintain his involuntary psychiatric status, as often happens to psychotic patients, and seemed to have handled that well, without an uptick in his agitation. There were no expressed delusions or hallucinations for the duration of his hospitalization, though he was observed to appear depressed and internally preoccupied at various points. He was hospitalized for nearly a month and a half altogether.

I do not typically consider psychotic phenomena during or after a "psychedelic" experience as a reason to medicate, unless the person is at severe risk, in terrible distress, or dramatically disorganized weeks out. The disturbances might subside on their own. It is therefore most conservative to watch, wait, and provide nonpharmacological support before beginning powerful, potentially unnecessary, and sometimes harmful medications. It was not clear from his notes whether medicating him was deemed critical by the treatment team to address a persistent behavioral issue or if it was a lazy sort of pharmacotherapy as usual. He seemed to have been calm and stable throughout, though still preoccupied with unusual thoughts.

My hesitation to medicate "hallucinogen-induced psychosis" from the start is due to clinical experience, as well as to what I've observed outside of medical contexts. I have consistently found that it is best to err on the side of attentiveness, patience, and openness with whatever emerges around these substances, no matter how distressing or disruptive it might be. An entirely unworkable psychotic breakdown might happen, of course—some people are vulnerable to such things. The more general situation, however, is that something is being illuminated that requires our attention. Approaching it as a priori pathological and medicating the phenomena away only hinders the process.

This conclusion reached by Carlos's treatment team, in any case, was that he was experiencing a protracted and unstable psychotic process requiring medication. It was not clear from the medical records how well that description fit. Nor was it clear what might have contributed to the psychosis in the first place. It seemed most aspects of his experience in the Amazon were fine. He had been staying with an Indigenous group esteemed globally for its ayahuasca practices. According to his hospital notes, he had observed a proper *dieta* for the duration of his stay at the retreat, which refers to the regimen of food and medicinal plant consumption to ensure optimal healing. There were no known preexisting issues; Carlos was very high functioning, as his cousin indicated, prior to his psychiatric problems.

I had seen this before: healthy young people ending up in a hospital after a difficult experience in ceremonial or recreational contexts, heavily medicated for psychosis. Preexisting psychotic issues were absent in most cases. There had been other things in these cases to account for the deterioration: cultural and language barriers, irresponsibility on the part of facilitators, maybe a fixed perspective inflamed to grotesque proportions.

There were indications that a similar process was happening here. I was concerned about the apparent negligence in his being banished from the retreat to wander the jungle alone. If this was indeed what had happened, it was striking in its irresponsibility. It called into question the quality of the support he was receiving, despite the good reputation of the community, underscoring how deprived he must have been of the proper attention and guidance prior to his departure—with his unusual visions and distress cast away into the jungle when they could no longer be passed over with the customary explanations, breaking through the frame attempting to contain them.

•

Before I had even met with Carlos, I was contemplating his story deeply. Many aspects of his case were profoundly challenging and generative. Most compelling was his cousin's impression that he was dealing with an addiction.

It is easy to dismiss what she had said. Her thinking was fraught with reductive DARE-type tropes, such as all psychoactive substance users are potential drug addicts. It was colored by a great deal of ignorance regarding work with the tea too. The notion of an ayahuasca addiction struck me as wrongheaded, for the obvious reasons. No experienced clinician would consider a substance use disorder to be the primary problem here.

Yet there was something that stayed with me, deepening a revolution in my thinking. She was technically correct: he met DSM-5 criteria for a hallucinogen use disorder based on her account. One cannot argue with the precision with which she checked off the diagnostic criteria: he had oriented his life around drinking the tea in the face of negative consequences, as relationships fell apart, as his psychological health deteriorated, while giving up his occupation and social life—and what horrified her the most was that he wanted to return to it, "was craving it just like an alcoholic."

What was most revelatory was not that his case could be squeezed into the descriptive heuristic of the DSM-5 in some original way. Her "diagnosis" was not going to change the way I approached Carlos. Nor had it motivated me to write up the world's first known diagnosis of ayahuasca use disorder. In fact, I did not regard it as an addiction in the conventional way that one might be addicted to heroin or alcohol, for example.

What I found revelatory was the challenge to my categories. I recognized that a complacency with the pharmakolalia of "gift" and "ineffability" had crept up on me, leading to an overly mythical, discursive sense of what the tea might be. Among other things, this led to the presumption that approaching the tea ceremonially, as a sacrament, would protect against addiction.

Addiction, however, is a trajectory possible with anything. It may even be inevitable.

Every world emerges the same way. A dream is enacted in our relationship with the charged materials of ( ). The dream might fall into stasis, into "reality," with the vast wilderness imagined into a compulsory, canalized landscape: a system of signs imposed on what might as well be nothing at all. And this "reality" glows with the exuberant possibility at the heart of ( ), promising to relieve our suffering and to grant access to a world more golden than what is at hand. This possibility is so meaningful to us, in fact, that we resist letting it go, despite the agonizing, leaden (un)reality that emerges, always an eyeblink away from collapsing, imploding, burying us alive.

The materials may be nothing, transformed into something. But the ( ) they represent is not nothing. Nor can we call it something. A black sun or strange attractor may be nearer the truth, a charged emptiness compelling us into orbit while we trace patterns and order the world under its influence, our inchoate, muddy firmament coaxed into conjuring a daytime image of itself. Every dawn finds the possibility of a truer world breaking the dark horizon; every dawn another mimetic emergence crystallizes the fragments into something like our more perfect likeness.

We say drugs, gold, chemicals, plants, the tea, earth itself, and we are speaking about ourselves as much as anything. The forms we find are never the final appearance, nor the last word. There is always another possibility. But we speak and speak, neglecting to attend to our pharmakolalia, to what it reveals and obscures. Addiction is this clamorous conversation, carried to an excruciating pitch: screaming at our own screaming. And addiction is also when the earth adds to our screaming, further destabilizing reality by amplifying the violence and wounds that have given it form. The pharmakon receives our words and violence and returns them, with morning-light clarity.

The tea gives as generously as it receives. In Carlos's case, it seemed an *absolute* substance leading to an *absolute* addiction. It is meaningful that this least compromising of substances would reflect back at him the least compromising of waking dreams: psychosis.

Beneath every compulsive striving—at the bottom of every craving and addiction—is a homesick delusion. The earth beneath our feet is torn apart and replaced by a single-minded (un)reality: *this fragment will be my fulfillment*. Addiction might be considered a muddy kind of psychosis. It is muddy because the person is not so far gone as to have uprooted himself from the earth entirely. He continues to have earth on his hands, grasps at the earth, tries to feed on and tear at the earth, even as the earth breaks and bleeds.

Freud wrote: "Things that in the neuroses have to be laboriously fetched up from the depths are found in the psychoses on the surface, visible to every eye." The same could be said about addiction. But here the "thing" that surfaces is so primordial as to be visible and invisible at the same time: the seeking, the striving—Freud's act of cathexis itself—come to their earthbound crisis. The psychosis is so familiar it passes unnoticed: it is perhaps the psychosis of everyday life. We are convinced, as is the addict, that fulfillment is somewhere just ahead, or far behind, and dependent on *that*. The addict is not psychotic, we presume within our own reasonable and cognitively controlled psychoses, just wrong in his choice of objects. He should not want that, but this, or this. We break ourselves, others, and the world in insane pursuit. We do not see the mud and blood on his hands because ours are stained too.

●

The word is often thrown around as if its meaning were self-evident. Yet, what is psychosis, really? The usual definition is a disconnection from reality: our perceptions, modes of engagement, and beliefs veer from what is the case. We come to experience existence in a manner removed from how others do, espouse beliefs that are patently false, interpret things in fixed and unusual ways, and attach to our inflexible worldview with absolute certainty.

We have seen this before. Psychosis—alongside paranoia, megalomania, and other organized delusions—may be a universal condition elevated to a moment of crisis. "Unreality" is an inescapable aspect of being human: our representations, our simulations, our paradigms, our static dreams. What we perceive and know is riddled with intransigent illusion, despite what we might believe. And we hold fast to our beliefs with a conviction they rarely merit.

Psychosis may be distinct from the common condition in degree as opposed to an essential difference. The stumbles borne of representation and certainty become heightened in the disorder (or perhaps more accurately, hyper-order) to an inescapable extent. Fixed fictions lead to agitation, alarming behavior, and loss of freedom; our subjection to the regimes of the mind tightens into a seemingly granitic confinement. The daylight becomes blinding, the night and its mysteries paved over with a phantasmagoria of signs.

Despite a tendency to question psychiatric conventions, I have adhered like most of my colleagues to the century-old Kraepelinian taxonomy that places psychosis in its own pathological category. It is a system so inherent to psychiatry as to seem absolute. The conversation with Carlos's cousin, and my reflections afterward, exposed my blind spots. It was liberating, even intoxicating: an upheaval in assumptions I hadn't thought to question. I was learning, yet again, to embrace the fluidity of human experience; even conditions I had seen as worlds apart—addiction and psychosis—might stem from shared wounds. Carlos may be neither psychotic nor addicted; he may be both at once. These are wounds that are inescapable, whether or not we become "psychotic" or "addicted."

I met with Carlos within a week of the call from his cousin, within a day of discharge from the hospital. He was a lean, proper, well-dressed man. But he had the stiff carriage, blunted facial expressiveness, and tremulousness of someone on too many psychiatric medications. Seated, he would fidget, shaking his legs. This restlessness is called akathisia, a common side effect associated with antipsychotics. Psychotropics are powerful substances requiring judicious use to optimize benefit. But conventional psychiatry is more inclined to medicate "psychotic" people with antipsychotic medications, with all the harms involved, than to respect their occasionally incomprehensible subjectivities. This is particularly problematic when the person is not a danger to himself or others, or when he resides in a safe environment conducive to working through his challenging experience, like a comfortable hospital. The prejudice against non-ordinary modes of being, and the moral and pharmaceutical panic in response to them, persist in psychiatry to this day.

He was polite and kind, as he had been throughout his hospital stay, though his speech was halting and monotonous as if constrained by a vise compressing his brain: another common side effect of antipsychotics. I asked him to tell me about himself, how he wished to be called, and what he hoped to achieve in our work together.

"You can call me Carlos. My true name is something else," he said.

"I think you know about what happened to me in Peru. I had been working with medicines for a few years with a group down there, and I had some experiences that I'm still struggling to understand. There was one night that was the scariest night of my life. I saw terrifying things. It seemed that demons had possessed others in the group. I felt I was being attacked by people from my past. I became scared and agitated. I had brought a knife with me. I needed to cut myself to release something. The shaman asked a few people to escort me out. He said I had gone crazy. They drove me to the edge of town. I haven't been back there. I wandered the jungle for a while and made my way back to town. Then I was hospitalized for a week before my parents arranged a transfer to a hospital on the East Coast. Now I'm here, living with my cousin in New Jersey. She is not the easiest to live with, but that's okay. I want to get back to normal, get back to working."

It was reassuring to see that his thoughts were largely organized and coherent: this is a good indicator that he might tolerate a reduction or even discontinuation of his medicines. But it was apparent that his thoughts and emotions were as blunted and restricted as his body was. His words had a muzzled tone and cadence to them, what psychiatrists call aprosody: a blunting of the musicality and rhythm that typically animate speech. The notes were robotic, flat, and rigidly patterned. His communication style also seemed overcompressed, telegraphic. It was as if he were far away and beaming himself into this double that was clumsy and stiff and not entirely responsive to his commands.

This is an impression I often have with individuals who have been "neurolepticized" (overly medicated with neuroleptic antipsychotic medication): they seem to have been transformed into lumbering automatons, but fit for work or sitting still, obedient and unobtrusive, with any internal program dialed down. Language becomes reduced to what is most functional, the distinctive music and poetry that runs through all of us muted. If the tea is a watery medicine of the jungle, then neuroleptics are the hard medicines of the regime, constraining the mind so that it might better fit into the "objective" world: more obedient, more comprehensible, less chaotic and musical.

"I am unable to sleep at night because I cannot stop moving. My legs feel like they belong to someone else."

It was unsettling to consider how disorienting this must have been for Carlos. Cracked open in the wild Amazon darkness, ravished by the merciless earth—and just as abruptly cracked open against the concrete of the city, the harsh, sharp-edged surfaces of hospitals, the court system, family involvement, psychiatry, neuroleptics. A succession of tyrannies, one overthrowing another, with the regime of psychosis ceding to that of psychotropics. I asked him to describe the experience that led him to leave the retreat and end up in a hospital.

"It is not easy to talk about. I'm not convinced anymore that it was real. I'm not agitated by it like I used to be. But I don't want to say that nothing happened either. I'm shelving it for the time being. It was something I would see for a while. There were flashes of it from the first time I sat with the medicine. My twin was there. He died when we were born. But I saw that he wasn't really dead. I remembered things that happened when I was a child. It involved my dad, my uncles, maybe some other men. They were twins of themselves too. I saw that we all have a twin who dies at birth. It may not be always physical. But our dead twin tries to take our place. My ancestors were not really themselves. I remembered my family doing the ritual. I would sometimes see it from eyes that were not my own. It had been going on for a while, maybe generations. My energy was being drained to resurrect the dead. Our twins will take our place. There was a deal made with dark forces a long time ago. A ritual for boys when they reach a certain age. I remembered it happening to me. I saw that the demonic twins were coming to life. The evil was being introduced into me. The medicine showed me. It was telling me what happened.

"I would speak about it, the group would listen. I was learning their language to better communicate. They believed it happened too. They said I had a curse placed on me. There was something evil trying to come to life. They told me I needed to drink more medicine.

I was doing the work, and I learned a lot. I felt I was healing. The demon seemed to be leaving. I was cutting myself nightly to release the bad blood. But then something changed. That night the demons were in the room. The ritual was happening again. I saw them preparing me. It was like the beginning. I needed to protect myself. I started screaming. I took out the knife and cut into my arm. I may have hit a few people who tried to stop me or strangle me. I was escorted out, perhaps they tried to take me to the hospital. I ultimately ran away. I was scared for a while. I wandered for many hours. I saw that I was protected. There were serpents that led the way. I could see their scales shining in the dark. The police picked me up and took me to a hospital. My parents were contacted, you know the rest, and now I'm here."

Making sense of psychotic phenomena requires considering how they might be relevant to all of us. I therefore approach such visions as myths or parables, with the potential to speak to everyone. The dark double is an especially pregnant, archetypal image. We each have a twin who follows us: our shadows and secrets, our addictions, our shame. Our self-image and vison of what we might become. To others, we might be a negative, a photograph, a word. And finally the twin who threatens to take our place: the memories we leave, our bodies and remains, ultimately the corpse that survives us.

Regarding the twin as a demon in collusion with one's family imparts a unique and meaningful form to it. A sustained process of attention, inquiry, and interpretation is necessary for understanding it, as with any private vision. But this had not happened in the Amazon. Instead, the demonic form impressed on the murky night was allowed to congeal, its apparent specificity too readily accepted as fact.

Carlos seemed at ease moving through different worlds, having had considerable practice: a Mexican raised in Prague, educated in the States, living with an Indigenous community in the Amazon. He'd experienced his fair share of dislocations. But it can be disorienting. The prior world's rules may no longer apply. Carlos and his Amazonian hosts did not inhabit the same language: what he calls a demon may be entirely different than what they regard as one. Both sides might not have given sufficient attention to these issues of translation. And there were many other facts and meanings that differentiated their world from his.

Other cases of tea-related psychosis I've encountered have also occurred within such disjunctions, in that wilderness separating one system of meaning from another. Most Amazonian Indigenous groups embrace an animist worldview encompassing a sophisticated demonology, wherein suffering can be traced to possession by a demon, spirit, aggrieved ancestor, or sorcerer. The main purpose of the tea is to facilitate exorcism. Carlos's visions of demons were interpreted in this light by his guides. They therefore encouraged him to continue drinking the tea, as is their practice, in the hope that this would release the entity back into the night.

Certain shadows and reflections, however, grow stronger the more they are refused. The problem is that Carlos's world—with its emphasis on positivism, self-control, and individualism—is not the world of Amazonian tribes; Carlos may have denigrated certain dark aspects of himself as *other* in ways incomprehensible to them, deepening the discordance between his (un)reality and their own.

Carlos had fallen through the cracks between worlds. Many worlds played their part. In interpreting Carlos's experience through their lens, and understanding it too readily, the Native *curanderos*—a confluence of *mestizo*, capitalist-globalist, and neo-tribal worlds themselves—did not realize that Carlos needed additional support in navigating his visions. Carlos, for his part, could not venture further than the explanations he received, and he hit a wall experiencing and incorporating these experiences in a way that allowed for developing a personal understanding. Carlos had deferred, in his words, to the wisdom of the tribe, given their "deep and ancient knowledge of the medicine." The wild visions grew more inflamed as they remained unheeded and overinterpreted, the tea kept coming, until everything boiled over and the vision broke out into the open. Now his experience was being overinterpreted through yet another lens, as hallucination, delusion, schizoaffective disorder.

His experience need not fit into one language or the other. Nor does he need to feel lost in the fault lines between them. There may be another way to understand that is truer to him, that returns him to the truths of his own experience, with neither demonic possession nor psychosis providing the answer. It may permit him to take the vision to its proper conclusion.

•

Irrespective of how we understand what happened to him, Carlos developed a severe and debilitating condition that attracted, among other labels, the word *psychosis*. And yet his diagnosing psychiatrists had a difficult time making sense of the matter. Further, in employing the usual tools and categories, they may have made things worse.

The "anti-psychiatry" movement of the 1960s—represented most prominently by R. D. Laing, Thomas Szasz, and Félix Guattari—was a free-thinking iconoclastic group of physicians at the margins of medicine, with "psychosis" a special target of their heterodoxy. The anti-psychiatrists believed that treating psychosis as abnormal or pathological was bound to lead to problems. They viewed the condition a normal pole of human experience, perhaps more likely to affect people of a certain sensitivity: a reasonable response, in any case, to insane processes within families and societies. The clinician's proper role is to support the person through psychosis, as opposed to medicating away its manifestations. Laing further believed that psychosis served as a critical passage toward greater well-being.

This model has been eclipsed by the normative pathologizing framework and palliative pharmaceuticals of biological psychiatry. Anti-psychiatry is now considered by most clinicians a countercultural anachronism. Yet we shouldn't be too quick to forget its lessons. Despite a tendency toward social determinism, with family/social systems assigned a primary etiologic role, the anti-psychiatrists were humane in their understanding of unintelligible experiences beyond the pale of intersubjectivity, and imaginative in the treatments they devised to support people, which often involved rethinking the relationship between psychiatrist and patient to facilitate broader social realignment. Some of these approaches merit reexamination, such as the antihierarchical and collaborative milieu of Guattari's clinic La Borde. The clinic is most famous, perhaps, for the annual plays that patients and staff would stage together.

Anti-psychiatrists were also sensitive to the problems of subjectivity and power in psychiatric treatment. They recognized the dangers inherent to diagnosing someone—and diagnosing them with psychosis in particular—from an "objective" standpoint. "Psychosis" has become such a routine affair in modern psychiatry that its ontological significance often goes unappreciated. In effect, the person's "being in the world" is deemed less valid than that of the diagnosing doctor. The injury this causes can be profound.

The wound comes with the word itself. It is invariably spoken by another. Psychosis does not appear in isolation; it necessitates the involvement of other people with a shared worldview. Intersubjectivity is violated, and the consensus sense of reality reasserts itself, subjugating the violation as "psychotic." The person's (un)reality effectively becomes an aberration in the order of things.

A man occupies several worlds at once, with a single perception containing multitudes: a pet dog is simultaneously ancestor, automaton, and divine judgment. He communicates through bizarre hand gestures, having relinquished spoken language. Perhaps he is found roaming the woods haunted by Armageddon. He is malnourished and isolated, seemingly at odds with the world and himself. But it is usually intersubjectivity that raises the alarm: the person is designated "schizophrenic" and perhaps hospitalized and medicated, like Carlos, until he better inhabits the intersubjective space from which he had been expelled.

In conventional psychiatric settings, the person's private sense of reality becomes subordinated to the intersubjective world, if not removed from it entirely, as opposed to participating in and contributing to it. This is comparable to what might occur when a scientific paradigm is faced with incommensurable evidence: the data are overinterpreted or overlooked, forced to fit the scheme. The truth of these data goes recognized, and the errors of the paradigm are reinforced. The sanity of psychosis might go unrecognized in a similar way.

We arrive at a vexing riddle. How to ascertain sanity if our paradigm itself is insane? Consensus psychosis is nearly invisible because there is no intersubjective yardstick by which we might discern a problem—the yardstick itself being out of its mind. To extricate ourselves from such madness would require learning to intuit truths on our own. This might seem its own mode of madness.

A well-armed man perpetrates a mass shooting against strangers whom he has designated, with absolute certainty, as enemies. Topping the list of explanations for such violence is *insanity*. But if these killings occur within military operations orchestrated by his government: business as usual. It is psychotic to kill strangers en masse—unless one is doing so to enemies of the state. The sense of moral injury, and perhaps posttraumatic distress, that emerge are disorienting because it seems wrong and unhealthy—even mentally ill—to be so troubled by acts widely regarded as brave and patriotic. Similarly, it is not psychotic to exhaust oneself collecting valuable objects and possessions, sacrificing a great deal and crowding one's life with them. And it feels *wrong and unhealthy* to find oneself discontented and bereft surrounded by so much.

Clearly, a disjunction is possible between the truths of the individual and the confusions of the consensus. History abounds with visionaries who go against the grain. Their voices are dismissed as unhinged, their work censored and attacked. There might be worse. After proposing the possibility that our universe is infinite, with no absolute center, Giordano Bruno was decried a heretic and burned at the stake.

Luminaries possessed of earthshaking revelations aren't the only casualties. I worked with an outspoken soldier at the Chicago VA hospital diagnosed as psychotic because he refused deployment, claiming that war results from a bioengineered parasite (derived from *Toxoplasma gondii*) infecting our minds and directing our actions for its own murderous ends. I also treated an elderly gentleman more recently from the Upper East Side who believed that his possessions were anguished ghosts; he was brought in by his family because he was giving away his property to liberate the spirits residing in them. We should hesitate before dismissing such ideas as "psychotic"; they may contain more truths than do our sanities.

The problem in some cases might be one of translation. Every profound spirit, Nietzsche wrote, needs a mask. Would Carlos—with his devastating, alien subjectivity—still be considered psychotic if he had maintained his part in this masquerade of intersubjectivity, despite the smoldering dark depths of his spirit? The "psychotic" regains sanity by reentering this play. But he may also *transcend* sanity by speaking the words that need to be said, that might be understood, even as he doesn't fully believe them—translating his primal wilderness into lies we can all comprehend.

This is how we all might come to better understand ourselves: considering what we know as fictions and our apparent selves as masks. There may be a passage through something like psychosis to get there. Robyn/"Robyn" emerged through a similar apocalypse. We might learn, as I hoped she had, to don the masks that serve the occasion, with playfulness, poise, and honesty, much like actors playing their parts in the theater of La Borde. Beliefs come and go, roles change, every year offers a new stage. We play our part, always remembering what is coming. An unmasking awaits us in the final act.

●

"I was no different than most people," Carlos told me during his first visit. "I had gone to the jungle to find myself."

A typically throwaway phrase that took a sinister turn hearing Carlos say it: finding oneself. What is finding what? In this case, meeting his dead double, his replacement. *No different than most people.*

"I grew up with my family constantly on my back. I was a sick child growing up. I was born with some cardiac issues and needed surgery as a baby. My twin didn't make it. I was delicate until junior high. They were constantly tending to me to make sure that I didn't die too. I was the sick one, the one who needed to be taken care of. It was difficult to do things without asking permission. That stayed with me. I needed to be away from all that. That is why I remained in the States after graduating. I don't want to be near anyone from the past. Living with my cousin is worse than being with my parents. She controls me because that's what she thinks she is supposed to do. I also think she wants to feel better than me. But really she feels terrible about herself. She is a bit older, nearly fifty and unmarried, bored with her job. She knows it all and doesn't let you get in a word. She has no real friends. So, she focuses on me. The worst thing about all this is that I'm where they want me to be. I'm the sick one again. They need to take care of me again. They refuse to recognize the new symbol I want for myself. They think I'm crazy for adopting it. But it feels right for me. It feels like the name I want for my future. I'm the only child, the only son. They don't want to lose the family brand. But I don't want my son to go through what I've been through. It's all about control. They see everything as evidence that I should have listened. This is what happens when you don't do what you're told. They probably think I've been insane all along. Now they are justified in not taking me seriously. I want to be my own person. I'm back to being under the thumb of my family."

What is the new name he has adopted?

"It is my true self. It needs to be seen to be understood. It isn't words. I'll show it to you when I'm ready."

And how was his work and social life before he left for the Amazon?

"I had a good job. I was involved in getting various start-ups off the ground. It is the psychedelic renaissance business. It's what you do, too, I think. That's how I came to you. I think my cousin reached out to some people I knew and they referred you. I worked for a few companies trying to make new medications that build on psilocybin or ibogaine. I used my medical connections and business experience to create a niche for myself. It was satisfying work, thinking about how to get these technologies into the marketplace. Nothing has come of it yet. But I put in my time and made good money. I had a few good friends before I left for Peru. I stayed in touch with some of them. I also made friends in the Amazon. I don't really have too many people here, except for cousins and extended family."

I maintained my calm and stillness, despite a tendency to flinch whenever I hear "psychedelic renaissance." But I appreciated the way Carlos put it. The psychedelic renaissance *business* is a more apt phrase. These substances never died to need resurrecting. They have been making their way through the world for thousands of years. What has been resurrected is a willingness to integrate them into our industries of academic research, commerce, popular consumption, and perhaps big pharma—in other words, to commodify them and place them in our multi-aisle marketplace.

The "renaissance" acquired a particular heaviness, furthermore, being invoked by this man ravaged by the tea and deadened with antipsychotics. He seemed a dark mirror of the times, with the usual cadavers descending on the next living thing and creating their likeness: products, idols, taxidermy, madness. The most authentic way—the real renaissance—is to restore our engagement with $()$ to a vital fluidity, beyond the rigor mortis of our schemes. And this begins with not calling this powerful class of pharmakon "technologies"—as if they are inert machines engineered and well greased to serve our mundane interests.

I asked him about intimate relationships.

"I haven't been in a serious relationship since college. I've been working on myself. I want to get to a point where I'm more comfortable in myself first. I mean, there have been hookups occasionally. There was one person with whom I felt a soul connection in Peru. But nothing came of that. The girl in college was my longest relationship. It ended abruptly. She didn't want to see me anymore. It was difficult for me. I became depressed. I started seeing a psychiatrist but then lost interest. She was beautiful and kind. I don't know what I did wrong. I think I wasn't good enough. I sometimes have a hard time getting it up. I get nervous. I feel that there is something dangerous about women. They look at you as if they know you're not good enough. But they want something from you, so they stay around. At least that's how I think about it. I don't know what they want."

He had suspicions about me, especially given my background in addressing addiction.

"I don't know what good you can do for me. I don't have an ayahuasca problem. My cousin doesn't get it. She thinks ayahuasca is a drug like acid or coke. I have never had any addiction issues. The closest I felt to addicted was keeping a social media presence. This was part of my job. You need it for networking. But it took on a life of its own. Maybe I was checking it too much. I wanted the profile to be just right. It bothered me that people didn't respond to certain posts. I would keep looking. This is the worst it got for me. Never had a problem with drugs, with alcohol. Maybe I watch porn too much sometimes. The internet has a way of sucking you in. Most of my job is in front of screens. It's easy to get distracted. Then I would go back to my personal page and refresh it. I would wait for things to happen. There is always another article to read. I forgot for a while how to wait without doing anything. If there was a free moment I was online again. But I don't consider myself addicted or anything. I can be as distracted as anyone else. Time in the jungle has helped with that."

His first experience with the tea began well before the jungle, as is increasingly the case in the Global North. It occurred in Seattle with a middle-aged White healer who had apprenticed in the Peruvian Amazon. Carlos found it profound and healing. The experience revealed the person he should have been: "I saw for myself who I would be if I hadn't been brainwashed and manipulated." He continued engaging with the tea a few times a month, while also practicing yoga regularly. He had also embarked on a self-improvement journey that continues to this day, spending hours on the internet watching videos, reading blogs, researching new ways to be smarter, healthier, more efficient. Nootropics and other smart drugs, micro-dosing LSD, breathing techniques, intermittent fasting, cryotherapy—he tried them all. Archetypal tech-industry biohacking. He felt better, his depression lightened, but he hit a wall. He was offered an opportunity to spend some time in the Amazon at a retreat connected to his healer. The intention was two months, but he ended up staying nearly two years.

It was in the jungle that his visions began to intensify. I asked him to elaborate on what he saw. He said they felt like memories, though he doesn't want to be too certain about that: "A memory is what happened. But I don't want to say they happened. They may also be what could have happened. We have a chance sometimes to not be stuck in the past. Something that might have been a memory becomes something else." I would understand more fully what he meant later.

The visions were consistent. There were glimmers and fragments in Seattle, but they coalesced into clear form in the jungle. They would happen for a significant portion of each night he consumed the tea. His twin hovered over him with a demonic smile. He had died at birth, succumbing to the same cardiac defect with which Carlos was born. But he continued to sense a ghostly presence, as if his twin had grown up alongside him, watching him from the shadows. He remembered a bottle of unusual fluid that would be kept away from him: his parents said it was medicine, they would administer a teaspoon every other day, but there was something nefarious about its taste. They sometimes seemed to regret that he was the twin who made it. There may have been events he had repressed too. He would dimly remember every night being surrounded by family members who were not quite themselves: they would accost him and jeer at him. Perhaps they had been taken over by their twins too.

"I'm not sure when the conversion would be complete. It began when I was a kid. Some kind of seed had been set. I was being emptied out to make room. The twin would grow until I was no longer myself, and my brother would then take my place."

There were also strange happenings that involved outlandish costumes, bizarre hand movements, church-like dirges, and weird incantations. He believes these were elaborate ceremonies aimed at sacrificing him to demonic powers: dark forms took his energy and drew his blood, preparing his body for possession.

Over the course of his work with the tea, he realized the immense scope of this sorcery. He was not the first sacrifice. This has been going on for many generations. Firstborn boys had been chosen by their elders to be carriers of the demonic dead. His ancestors had started performing this "black magic" to appease evil forces and ensure that their bloodline would achieve earthly power and status. But Carlos recognized what the demons really wanted. Their aim was to populate the world with evil counterfeits. Many people have already been taken over, including his "father" and a distant "uncle," who might have been orchestrating everything.

The space in which these childhood rituals occurred was always the same. It was a dark windowless chamber, draped with thick, fleshy reams of crimson fabric, candles flickering, a cloud of incense smoke, and the fragrance of copal mixed with a stench viler and more putrid, perhaps of urine or vomit. The ground was ribbed with the thick bodies of interlocking serpents, slithering tightly against one another, glistening red and black in the darkness.

It was a diabolical contract from perhaps thousands of years ago. The only way out, Carlos came to realize, was death. He concluded that he might have to sacrifice himself if the exorcism fails. He considered ritual suicide or crucifixion. There were visions of himself as Jesus Christ, bleeding from every orifice, mutilated and taunted by hundreds of men, as well as visions of Jesus as intersex and sexless, as the true body of the world, with the earth itself punctured with stigmata and pouring forth rivers of blood. There were ancestral memories as well, other boys, perhaps his distant ancestors, being tortured and bled in the same manner, sodomized by demons, and subjected to Satanic ritual and blood sacrifice to satisfy the terms of the ancient contract.

The evening that everything broke apart, the demonic forces materialized in the ceremonial space itself, the same demonic twins that had drank his blood in childhood, the same Christ laid out and bleeding on a bed of serpents, serpents emerging from Christ's wounds, serpents also covering his body as if to protect him, while everyone else in the circle performed jerky shadow-puppet movements to a strange hum emanating from the ground. The drone grew louder until he saw the *ayahuascero* glowing with an intense power, and he heard from him the same abysmal incantation that coursed through his childhood rituals. He realized that his time had come: the forces of evil had won, the Antichrist was in the seat of power, and there was little he could do now but complete the catharsis.

"I saw that God was actually His evil twin. He had been dethroned and replaced. We were all praying to an imposter that had taken God's place."

He had been secretly cutting himself every night to release blood: a series of small incisions on his upper arm. There had been many purposes. He hoped this would facilitate exorcism. It was also a personal sacrifice to honor the plants and jungle.

There may have been a messianic dimension to it as well. He would compare himself to a saint laying down his life to redeem a fallen world. "I began to bring a knife with me into ceremony. I wanted to be ready in case I needed to release everything. I was even willing to sacrifice myself if that meant preventing another evil twin from entering the world. When I saw the demons organizing themselves, I panicked. I took out the knife, cut my arm, everyone flipped out."

In the jungle that night, wandering alone, he saw a vision he was not able to communicate to me just yet. He didn't feel he possessed sufficient fluency and clarity. But it had reassured him, sustaining him as he was put into one hospital after another.

Carlos had the general impression through the entire ordeal that one often hears from a psychotic person. He was the only sane one in a system gone completely insane. But he spoke about it in ways that led me to see that it might very well be true.

"I was being given these medicines as if I were mentally ill. They wouldn't give me a straight answer when I asked why they thought I was ill. They were blaming ayahuasca and also saying I was sick anyway. The real problem was obvious. They didn't know what to do with me. I wasn't doing what I was supposed to do. What I was saying made no sense. But I knew what I was going through made more sense than schizoaffective disorder."

His eyes filling with tears were especially poignant and affecting in a face otherwise flat, masklike, and nearly expressionless. "They did not care about me. Nobody wanted to listen to what I experienced. To them my story was another symptom. They said I was sick. But I wasn't sick. I was healing."

We ended that first session with an outline of the work ahead. I include it here because it reveals an important aspect of treatment: finding the proper mythology by which to enter into the mystery of suffering and to draw meaning from it.

"I respect the work you've been doing," I told Carlos. "I also recognize that the process is still happening. Important things are being revealed to you that require our full attention.

"There's a lot to unpack. I'm not just talking about the visions. Your entire life will need to be given attention: your reasons for going to the Amazon in the first place, your relationship with the community and your family, your relationship with yourself."

We sat for a moment in quiet reflection. I had been deliberately emphasizing the relational aspect of Carlos's challenges, the entire fabric of kinship in which he existed, while also emphasizing a kind of intimacy often obscured: our relationship to vulnerability, pain, and discontentment, and the clinging and grasping we carry into our relationship with a pharmakon, such as the tea, in our search for relief.

"Perhaps healing is the best word for this. But even healing begins with the recognition that we're sick. Then there is the tremendous effort and sometimes distress before we come to its other side. The tea sometimes comes as a purge. It may also come as confrontation.

"There has been a lot of pain, but we should remember: this experience has been given to you for some reason. It's still being given. The path ahead is to see through this process and its appearances—exorcism, medicine, psychosis, possession—so that you might understand whatever is at its source. I will help you come off these medications, which might be getting in the way."

We will be careful to open that door gently. Our role is to keep our eyes open, bend with whatever is shown, and work toward recognizing the generosity that has brought Carlos to his knees.

•

I had noted two types of fiction that might be brought to suffering. One fiction is generated from outside the person, generally in the minds of scientists or health workers, and comes from an intersubjective appraisal of his brain, words, behavior—the apparent facts. There is the brain model, the 12-step narrative, cognitive science, the fictionalization process I proposed. These frameworks indicate an origin for addiction, while proposing a solution. They each have their methods based on how they imagine the problems to emerge. And they each have their limitations.

The other type of fiction the person creates himself, such as imagining that loneliness is best addressed with vodka. This narrative of problem and solution works to maintain the addiction and can often break the person apart into a thousand quarrelling voices: *this fragment of earth will fulfill me.* And addiction is so insidious that it is compelled not only by these myths, but by a desperation to escape the cacophony they create as well.

Addiction and its possible treatments show very clearly how impactful our myths might be, how captivating and oppressive. Every route of healing has its own mode of reimagining things too. There is the myth that is imparted in the rituals of AA, that may be facilitated by psychotherapy or psychedelic therapy, that comes with a placebo, and that might emerge spontaneously. Even prescribing a medicine in a doctor's clinic involves the patient in a plot: "Addiction is a brain disease in need of interventions, and this medication might help." We have also considered the myth that signals the end of myth: embracing the ineffable silence, as had Marcus, and being guided by it.

The importance of myth is not limited to the treatment of addiction, psychosis, or other "psychiatric" challenges. We must be careful with how we understand ourselves more fundamentally. Not knowing enough, ignoring what needs to be known. And maybe more fundamentally, knowing ourselves too well.

An excess of knowledge, for example, is the problem with the brain model, or with materialism and other metaphysical systems more generally. The inconceivable nature of things becomes too easily named and identified. The wilderness of experience is covered and pruned; we disregard the limitations of our comprehension in the face of the fundamental mysteries, starting with the primordial mystery of being.

Contemplative practices, such as meditation, can help with keeping in abeyance any hard conclusions. They come with their own notions of the world, their own soft myths, implicit in the practice. And if more explicit mythopoesis is needed, it is most helpful when the myths are neither too mysterious nor too knowing: they gesture at the mystery, and suggest what our relationship to it might be, without fossilizing existence into too many words, rules, and explanations. Myths resonate with us most deeply when they propose a way of experiencing things that is just beyond the reach of our minds but which we intimately understand with the wakefulness of being.

I suggested to Carlos that he receive the tea and its workings as a gift: the cup offering an inarticulable abundance. This is the myth that came to orchestrate our conversations. It guided us to receive the mysteries of the tea, and by extension everything else, including his psychosis.

Carlos had moved from "possession" to "psychosis" to "gift"—but we cannot stop there. "Addict" and "patient" were only meant to be temporary identifications for Steve, as well. There is a creative indeterminacy that must not be fixed into place, with a myth or incarnation only useful if it allows access to that fluent possibility.

Nor do we need our imagined cast of characters, not Being nor the tea. There is already more than enough, a soft murmur below the usual chatter. An inescapable myth, constantly mutating, as creation, The Great Gift, Zion, Israel, samsara—even the *more, more, more* of our insatiability. But saying the words risks obscuring them. They are so banal as to be vacant, like anything else repeated to the point of overfamiliarity.

This abundance is now ours. Let us be careful to not say this too loudly. We pour the surplus forth and then receive it in greater fullness, giving, receiving, and giving again, in silent reciprocity.

•

Carlos is not just Carlos. We begin with him but invariably return to ourselves.

French offers the same word for recognition and gratefulness: *reconnaissance*. Giving attention, full and undistracted attention, we recognize the generosity. The primordial surplus, beyond all names or forms. And yet *reconnaissance* also reflects the primordial virtue, the most attentive response to this abundance now ours. Recognition and gratefulness may be the only gift originating in us, the only gift ours to give. Everything else is circulated.

You are reading now—stories of suffering and confusion, freedom and understanding—because you have a moment to attend to this surplus of words. Your basic needs are likely met for the moment, your immediate survival assured. But watch your step. We are not yet out of the woods. The danger at present is far trickier than losing life or limb. It is losing attention, losing recognition, losing ourselves.

There are distractions at every turn. The practice of *reconnaissance* is perpetually embattled, our minds forging one mutilated image of the world after another. Carlos is not the only casualty of this, of course, not the only "addict" or "psychotic" invited to recognize the generosity in things unraveling. We each have our own confusions with which to contend. Carlos will for the moment lead the way.

Attend closely to our procession of words. Feel the pain of every apparent reality, the suffering concealed by each sign. Each recognition creates a strain in the stone. It need not be ours. It is through receiving the profound gift of Carlos's suffering, for instance, that we might better engage with our own.

The focus of our sessions, as in most psychotherapy, was the word. Words were exchanged, emphasized, edited, clarified, retracted, whispered, heard, ignored, repeated. Our conversations were intended to extricate Carlos from his strictures, evacuating his dead words like held breath. It is through language that we might save ourselves from language. Every word both scalpel and abscess, opportunity and trap.

Reading offers similar possibilities. Attend silently. Maintain fluidity of meaning without raising idols. A wild pharmakolalia to resist the fossilization—engaging the fearful symmetry of language to break through its symmetries.

We return for the moment to ( ). An overflow of being, a charged emptiness. Words rush in to reclaim meaning. We speak toward the immensity: *This abundance is now ours*. And watch, once again, as even a single word curdles and rots, like standing water, to poison the rest.

The abundance is *ours*, as in possessive grasping. The abundance is *ours*, only ours, with solipsistic entitlement. It is *this* abundance I crave, with the single-minded focus of addiction on that one thing. This being is *ours*, with a narrow notion of who we are; this being is *ours* to do with as we wish, colonizing the world and remaking it in our image; and wanting it *now*, scrambling for what seems the most immediate gratification. Even *abundance* might become some obsession, an idol towering over our heads and casting shadows.

Inherent to language, or at least this language, is its capacity for fragmentation. Each word carving the emptiness into fixed form, every moment of meaning isolated to its own corner. Our worlds will follow suit. Lurking within each word is this possibility of disunity and breakdown: the earthbound psychosis of *this fragment will be my fulfillment*. Remember Ahmed's words: "I would like to go home today so I can get started on the rest of my life." This abundance is now ours but fractured, muddied up. Home is elsewhere; life has yet to be lived.

We yearn for the same recognition, no matter how perverse our fixations. Beneath our words the same silent current, churning and babbling into our glistening worlds, our screams, our psychoses. Carlos came with his mind scrambled and overmedicated, his social standing in uncertainty, his family in anguished, overprotective disbelief. Yet he recognized that something momentous had been given, something also abundant and generous and obscure. He yearned to receive it, make sense of it. But he also yearned to refuse it, let it all go—restoring everything to its proper place.

The opportunities ahead were clear. Perhaps Carlos might learn to dispel the deceptions obscuring the boundless immensity presented to him. Maybe he might also engage with that generosity more deeply:

learning to recognize, learning to live. And then the final inescapable
lesson: learning to give, surrendering even his most cherished incarnation. Living, loving, dying—passing all at once through the same overflowing cup.

●

Carlos seemed willing to do whatever it takes. His main challenge was
not shirking the process or failing to rise to the challenges ahead. Nor
was it psychosis, depression, even trauma: he did well discontinuing his
psychiatric medications, becoming progressively more articulate and
lucid as their effects subsided. He cheerfully engaged in a variety of
different treatments, including somatic therapies and group therapy,
and was diligent about taking care of himself: eating well, meditating,
sleeping, exercising. It took years for the circle to close on the most
acute issue. It had come to its crisis in the jungle but it continued to
exert a persistent and insidious influence, even in the space of our psychotherapy.

Carlos viewed the process of addressing his suffering, echoing Jermaine, as "the work." He applied himself with vigor and tenacity to
it: journaling constantly, writing down realizations, aiming to find the
right rules to live by. Commitment to personal evolution is important
and to be encouraged. I admired his energy and resolve.

But *the work* had a dark side too. It seemed an agonized scramble to
run away from what he was. There was a sense of being on the cusp of
the revelation that would finally save him. He wrote down everything
just to make sure, waiting for the right words to come. He had to be
prepared or he would miss it. He worried that he was missing it repeatedly.

He aimed to systematize himself. He was working toward an exact
regimen of thinking and acting that would serve as the total design for
his future. A variety of books, online courses, and podcasts laid the
groundwork. But there was always a new book to read, a new diet or
exercise routine to take up. The entrepreneurship of the self, as Byung-
Chul Han called it, with identity our contender in some secret rat race.

Scribbling and reading were important parts of it. He would embark
on marathon sessions of automatic writing intended to excavate his inner demons, his neuroses, his traumatic memories—always something

else poisoning the well that needed to be expelled. He feared he was an inexhaustible toxic cesspool of traumas, memories, and "stories no longer serving me."

Purity in all things was the purpose. He would meditate, keeping a timer to ensure that each session was a bit longer than the last and would takes notes to identify and correct not sitting still enough, not cultivating sufficient silence. He saw himself as a nobody unless he made himself into a somebody. Who that somebody is he couldn't say. But he knew that it wasn't who he was currently.

Carlos regarded himself as "traumatized": an increasingly common description for the many varieties of suffering, particularly among those doing "the work." He had been under assault, he said, from day zero: born into a frail and precarious body, raised by despotic, overprotective parents, and haunted by the twin he might have been. Carlos depicted his parents as controlling and belittling: holding up an idea of him that did not give him the space to develop himself. He remembered his childhood as hampered by the cautious care his parents meted out to him; he described it as the kind of support reserved for invalids, hands-on and vigilant, compromising his capacity to assert himself and make his own mistakes. The rule was become what they say, or be ill, be dead, be nothing at all. He despised them for putting a mask on him. His role in the larger world he saw as a sham as well: his career and social life another charade, hemmed in by oppressive expectations and dehumanizing abuses.

His solution, understandably, was to work toward finding himself, in progressively more ambitious ways. His fulfillment was just ahead in the guise of a new name, new identity, new life. He turned to the tea to heal his traumas and facilitate self-determination; maybe it might "purge" any hurdles and entanglements interfering with his evolution.

Carlos found himself, however, faced with psychosis, disintegration, and loss of autonomy by the end. What went wrong?

Perhaps whatever happened in that wilderness was already the case, awaiting fruition. We tend to organize the inscrutable night into what feels familiar, even if it is suffocating, broken, something we want to leave far behind. We know it, we understand it. We want to awaken from it: a childhood bed. The night grows more calcified the more certain we become. In Carlos's case, it was the urgent, wounded dream of a clear-cut self that came to harden his eyes, insisting he is this, denying he is that. Traumatized, yes. Masked by the family name: never again. *We want to be more, better than this, but find ourselves immensely less.*

A vision emerged cup after cup that rendered into violent form the confusions and certainties motivating his transformation: *this will be my fulfillment.* It doesn't conclude with fixation on a single fragment. There is the fragment that fulfills; inextricably linked to it are the many fragments that do not. A mysterious twin—long-dead, insatiable— threatened to replace who Carlos believed himself to be. He may have been half-possessed already. His family had not simply delivered him into a broken body only to raise and treat him as if he were someone dead. They may have also been aligned with malevolent forces bent on the destruction of him and of the world: an ancient demonic pact aimed at doing violence to us from infancy and replacing us with dead doubles.

"Every night I would pray that trauma and darkness would leave me," he said. "I could feel it inside me, around me, ready to pounce. I'd stay awake for fear that I would drop my guard. But I had protectors too. The medicine was weakening one side, strengthening the other."

Carlos engaged with the tea to purge the ancestors and ghosts haunting him, and he had carved into his arm to complete the catharsis. But his deepest wound was a fissure created within himself. His dead twin, his family, his origins: there are some things that can never be purged. They are as much ourselves as our own beings. Fleeing them is like running from our shadows, trailed at every step by swarms of reflections. Carlos was duplicating, like Jamie, like Marcus and Robyn, like so many of us, the process of narrowing ourselves down, identifying with a still-born notion of self, with neither this, nor that, but only *this* capturing the fullness and truth of ourselves. First, his parents did it to him, then the larger world, and now he was doing it to himself: one fiction after another. He was finding himself, and therefore losing himself.

Carlos would vacillate between trauma as identity—"I am traumatized"—and trauma as a circumscribed wound that might be vanquished, without any lasting impact on who he is. The number of selves would ramify to accommodate this contradiction.

"There's this idea we can heal our past," Carlos said. "I don't mean healing ourselves right now from the traumas of the past. We heal now, and we also go back to the person we were, giving healing to that person too. We heal that person's trauma directly, and maybe the pain of other ancestors, too, right when everything was happening.

"I know that I don't have to be damaged. But it's there, my trauma, I can feel it beneath everything. I want to return to the source and heal the ancestors who made me what I am."

His visions of Satanic trauma might be memory. But they might also be tricks we play on ourselves to bring our fictions into the light. This is no different from addiction or any other blinkered engagement with the earth's mysterious materials. The good-evil fictions had encroached on the material of ancestry, origin, and self, on the most intimate material of all. Involving the tea and jungle had only accelerated the reckoning. He could not escape what returned to torment him: grotesque, wrathful demons that mirrored the repudiations leveled at his origins, at himself. The depths of things were reclaiming themselves, agitating the two-headed dream imposed on their surfaces.

We can imagine the addiction that might result if other materials were involved. Fred was beset by similar resentments toward his family and the life he led. He too had assigned a clear role to his substance: a device by which he might find sanctuary. The alcohol ultimately brought not peace, but a sword. He was wounded with each cup, the jagged edges of his own violence drawing blood every night until it became impossible to sleep.

The tea, unlike OJ and vodka, was not intended to quiet the demons, but to invoke them and restore them to the night. Carlos knew that suffering might come as part of the process, had welcomed it as an important dimension of his "transformation." But we must be prepared and watchful at every threshold, as if for death itself. Carlos had gone further than Fred in this regard, but perhaps not far enough. There was a complacent violence that he had not yet claimed as his own, a wound growing more inflamed with each overinterpreted vision. Few could have predicted the apocalyptic enormity of what would come. The earth can touch us in ways not easily forgotten; it might create moments that can last a lifetime.

•

The visions would yield new meanings every session. A compacted dream: a thousand dreams. We continued to explore the personal sense of inadequacy, the challenges with being the only child of a demanding family. The sorrow of losing a brother in the womb, growing up alone. There was the lifelong struggle with asserting himself, finding his way to self-expression despite the resistance of others. Turning to the tea as if it would complete him, make something of him.

We would also venture beyond his private challenges to more universal realities. Carlos revealed afflictions similar to those that Jamie had expressed. The birth trauma of falling into a form that limits and sullies us. The risk of dying at birth, left behind like our stillborn twin. It happens at every fork in the road. Systems of organization that cleave us into two, one half against the other. The millions of possibilities never realized and left behind.

We explored his sense of being mired and corrupted, his need for purity. Entangled at birth. The strangeness of flesh, its occult desires, processes, appendages. We hesitate to remember because it is nearly unspeakable. These are words we would rather not say. We are born, wrote Augustine, between shit and urine. The violence at the beginning of the world. The pubis ripped open to make way for the human crown. Going further back we find the abscess that infected our mothers: a flesh sac of mucus, piss, reptile. The serpent decapitated in the egg, discharging its venom into the yolk. A frothy confluence of two halves in a single bloodbath. The church father saw in this history a shameful reminder of our filth. The exalted shall be humbled. Carlos saw it in his own history too. He could not accept it. He had a habit of wiping his rear until the tissue paper was pristine white, skin rubbed red and raw.

Filthiness is just the start. We also inherit sickness and decay, some of us from conception. "I was literally born with a broken heart," Carlos would say, with a hint of maudlin self-pity. He would come to another, more complete view with time. The birth defect was his first initiation into how to live. The psychosis and disintegration driving home the same lesson. Death and loss are all around. The passage of all things must be felt. To break a heart is to create it.

"I look at a beautiful woman," he said, "and I'm terrified. I see my own death and destruction in her: the exhaustion of spurting out all my cum, numb and sticky with sleep, the whole thing against my will."

These are our origins. We began in a moment of violent beauty. We began as a spasm of love. We began as an amoeba, a worm, a heart defect. A strange accident of lizard and chimp, stitched together into a series of compulsions and names: Mexican, Carlos, only son, schizoaffective disorder . . .

Awaiting us is a wilderness of such immense and bewitching grandeur we fear losing our heads. The force might be feminine: an ancient mother, a ravishing seductress. She suckles and nurtures us; she cuts out and consumes our hearts. A family affair, children, mother, somewhere a father. His phallic violence wrestling everything into submission. There may also be nothing familiar about it. A surrender to the chthonic, beyond all binaries. Mud and worms working their way into the hollows of our bones. Earth covering earth.

A kinship we cannot easily forget or renounce. We are inseparable from the ground at our feet: we are also visitors and strangers to this ground. Recognizing this renders us mute. There is nothing to say. We call anything filthy, demonic, or shameful, and it is like sneering into the pudenda of our own grandmothers.

"This is what made life unbearable. I could have been anything. But I was worse than nothing, barely keeping it together. I sometimes seem to barely exist."

The tea itself might have conspired to that end: "dissolving his ego" in the most terrifying manner. An attempt to take him over, if not with a dark double than with an obedient slave doing its bidding:

"Anyone who has sat with ayahuasca knows how spooky it can be. We are basically letting this other thing into our lives, which may not care about us at all. We think it's for healing or whatever, but it may be serving nothing but itself. I've met tons of ayahuasca puppets, people whose entire identity is ayahuasca. These are the people who make it obvious, who have clearly given themselves over. But the possession might be totally subconscious and invisible. Once we let it inside, anything goes. We think we know what's going on, but what's actually in charge might be this other, more powerful force, pulling the strings for who knows what reason."

The alienness of the tea an implacable occupier, with designs of its own. The dark arts of ceremony and plant magick, inviting us to a new birth, while setting seeds for an insidious takeover.

Even the facts of birth, death, and otherness were not the end of it. Nor our identifications with the earth's materials, the body dissolving into the sublime and the excremental within the same moment. Buried in his visions was something more personal and yet more ancient. He was haunted by a past beyond his own. We inherit innumerable years of history as much as we do our bodies and minds.

"Recently I've been reflecting a lot on my origins. There is so much I don't know. I say I'm Mexican, without thinking twice. I speak Spanish, I look Latino. But I say it because that is what is easiest. I am not really Mexican. I was raised to see myself as different. My parents identified as Sephardic Jews more than they did *mestizos*. Not really a secret, but the closest to it we had, how we talked about ourselves at home and nowhere else. I had assumed growing up that they kept it quiet so as to not alert anyone that they were something special. Ancient Israel might have been another planet. There was mysterious pride in tracing their ancestry back thousands of years, maybe to Egypt. Disguising themselves wherever they are. I could pass for Mexican because passing is in our DNA."

It wasn't until a year into treatment that he revealed this. He had been in a slowly subsiding panic until then to ensure the visions didn't take more than they had. His belief was that there was something cursed about him, that he needed to change himself entirely. He wasn't haunted by his twin in a concrete sense any longer, but there was a lurking sense of sinfulness: what he felt as a propensity to aggression and impurity. He was learning to be gentler, no longer fleeing himself toward some other golden state of being.

This disclosure occurred as his intense self-work was easing up. He was practicing greater attentiveness and stillness, sitting with whatever rears its head. Perhaps being Jewish had been such a family secret he had become habituated to keeping silent about it. More likely it was a fraught aspect of his complicated history difficult to discuss. It might have been his inheritance, but where did he stand? Did he consider himself Jewish?

"That's the issue. I had told you I'm not religious. Being Jewish is different. It's more than faith. There is blood and history. And we aren't just Jews: we have Spanish and Indigenous blood as well. I'm Jewish, I'm not Jewish. Though that is not the way it works. It has to be one or the other.

"This always bothered me. There was something unsettling about emphasizing my Jewishness more than the other races flowing in my veins, even amongst ourselves. Why have we held on to it and secretly declared it? It's not like we were observant. There was no Bar Mitzvah, I never went to synagogue or celebrated the high holidays. In fact, I'm more comfortable in church, having learned Catholic prayers and attended obligatory Mass from my private school days in Mexico City.

"But I also feel pride, I can't deny that. The little I know about my lineage is very complicated. They were chased out of Spain, lived in Italy for a while, made their way to the Americas, lots of persecution, concealment, assimilation. But my ancestors stayed true to themselves, preserving the line despite centuries of wandering.

"There were some illustrious relatives, though some of them seemed too wild to be real. Christopher Columbus, my father would boast about him the most, the secret Jew who led the Christian charge into the new world. He would talk about some of them as if they were still alive. Hiding themselves and outshining everyone else. That is how we survived."

Maintaining a double life is an art that touches on more universal truths. We are secrets to ourselves, to one another, whether or not we put a name to this difference. There is a world within each of us that is impenetrably private and timeless. It deserves to be protected and respected; perhaps we might also learn to share it and offer it.

"In hindsight, my parents kept private for complicated reasons. It was probably fear, most of all. They didn't want to attract any hostile attention, especially with their success. You can't just forget what happened. The pogroms, the racism, the Holocaust.

"But I keep returning to that proud look in my father's eyes as he talked about Columbus or Spinoza. I went to the Amazon knowing that nothing disappears. I wanted to reawaken my Jewish blood, to rise to the burden it placed on me. It's always been about doing better, being better, earning my keep as one of the chosen. I wanted to understand the trauma, as well as the specialness.

"In the jungle, they call everyone family. I felt the truth of it. Their blood is my blood. These aren't just words. But they might as well be. Where is the memory, the recognition? Think about these continents, the countless killed and erased. The secret genocide that isn't so secret. Everybody knows, everybody forgets.

"Maybe it's too close to home. We walk all over their graves without even flinching. Countless tribes erased, some probably my ancestors, mixed-blood great-grandfathers, great-grandmothers. I saw that my native blood needed real understanding too. The people lost, forgotten. They live on in me, I know it. I can feel it."

He spoke about his stay in the Amazon as I had heard some speaking about making aliyah to Israel. There was a need for remembrance, for reconnecting to an ancient wound and home.

"I had a vision sitting with the medicine that a true family doesn't need to protect its bloodline. It knows that nothing is lost. Their life is the river itself. No secrecy, no superiority. No pretense of blending in. Everyone is family. Living as they had lived for thousands of years, surviving without shame or fear in the heart of the jungle. They don't need to write anything down. They trust that the earth will remember everything.

"I grew up hearing about another kind of history. Our history. A people of the book, nearly erased. All sides keeping a record. What the conquerors remember and write down. The words that console the defeated, the exiled, remembering whatever they could. There is also what goes silent, the histories and holocausts that disappear entirely, never preserved by anyone.

"But it's all white noise. The history books are just words anyway. Nothing really disappears. Even a totally exterminated people will make itself known one day."

He was entering into a history that could not be recorded, that might never be. We don't have the words for it. Intuition and dreams are its ground. We feel its echoes in the quiet corners of our beings, shadows of it when we suffer inexplicably, seeing through eyes not quite our own.

"I had cut into my arm to protect myself, to release the possessed blood. It was also to release and sacrifice my own blood. I want to honor what I've been given." He rolled up his sleeve and showed me his upper arm: the scars had organized into a ● several centimeters in diameter. "This is who I am. It is truer to me than any name: a mark of what I've been through. When I think of myself, this is what comes to mind."

I noted that ● looked like a portal or doorway.

"That's one way of looking at it. Things pass through me I don't expect. I need some protection."

He traced the circumference of the circle with his finger before rolling down his sleeve, like a private ritual.

"I'm not sure what I would have done without my cousin. Despite the issues, she was there for me. But living with her brought home what I've been dealing with my whole life. Where were my parents? They could have been completely missing, and it would have been the same. This had been my entire life. Burdened with an ancient secret, burdened with their pain. And left alone with it all, in the jungle, in one facility after another. Mexico City and London and Prague, rootless and nowhere, with only this burden to give me my bearings."

He paused. Then he proceeded haltingly, in fragments, as if musing to himself.

"I knew my place. All was fine so long as I performed my part. The rule was silence. The past concealed. The secret genocides, the blood denied and ignored. Jewish and everyone else. Forget what doesn't serve you. Forests mowed down to make way for cattle. Civilizations dying out, people wiped off the map. And my parents are looking back secretly, remembering some ancient kingdom. They didn't recognize the hypocrisy. Being ancient is not the exception. They ignored everything but that one name. I thought the power and pain we felt within ourselves was being Jewish, being chosen. Chosen by whom? This might have come from any other tribe in our blood, or no tribe at all."

The work was to go back to the moment, he said, before the irreversible erasure, when some defining history or identity had not yet congealed. He came to recognize his complicity in the madness. He had named himself, forgotten himself. He was both conqueror and conquered, ancestor killing ancestor: the violence we perpetrate on ourselves, in thrall to our apparent origins. It need not be so cinematic as ritual sacrifice or demonic possession. The reality is both more banal and more terrible. It has been happening for thousands of years, people bleeding and preying on one another, purifying the land of one another, and consigning the dead to oblivion.

The jungle threw his story into disarray, crystallizing the confusion at its heart. Good side, bad side, working to become who he really was, to exorcise who he was not. It was inevitable that the lines would cross, short-circuit. The tribe he had hoped would heal him had abandoned him. The world he had attempted to purge was now supporting him back to health. He had lost himself further in the doubling: an inversion of the system that had led him to the medicine. He wanted to know what was true and real, what wasn't. But it was all the same generosity, the same origins. Shit on one side, piss on the other. Darkness adjacent to darkness. His visions stemmed from seeds set at the beginning: the ancient conflict of family turning against itself, against the earth, against being itself. This might have been a dream that was not his own, passed down from time immemorial. We heal in reverse, Carlos had said, as much as we do in the present. He was returning to a time before the lines were defined, Jew or not, drug user or not, human or not, with history moving in a circle that includes every birth and every death of every being in its orbit.

"I was not alone in these circles. My ancestors were there. I could see what happened to them, what they had done, I remembered their memories as if they were my own. They suffered just as I did, over and over. It was now my turn to do the work, doing my part to make everything right."

To be human is to be born into a lie: the myths of our parents, then those of our civilizations and realities, extending to the confusions we share with everyone. One family torn apart by a thousand names and forms. The blood spilled to sustain a dream might reach back generations. We have a choice to maintain our psychosis or surrender it. A more luminous vision awaits. But the sacrifice may not be easy. Seeing through the nightmare, and awakening from it, might release sorrows and violence that have been building for millennia. The fallout might be so cataclysmic as to span continents, from Treblinka to Pucallpa to New York. It may come to engulf the entire earth.

•

Carlos's situation improved when he moved out to live on his own, a few years into our work together. He was doing consultant work for a few start-ups in the tristate area, largely making his own way with only minor financial support from his family. He had recognized that he was hard on himself and was learning to be gentler.

"I know I need to be more accepting. I know it, trust me. It can be so strangely hard sometimes: simply accepting. But I have my moments when things click. I'm learning to find that stillness and peace while meditating. Breathing exercises help. There was a time when I couldn't sit still, I was so impatient with myself, when my mind was so active it wouldn't leave me alone.

"I'm getting better. It's good to have the space to do it, without my cousin lording it over me. I'm learning to quiet myself, to recognize what agitates me and stay away from those things. I've been refining my day-to-day to make everything as serene as possible: no coffee, staying away from sugar, meditation twice a day, learning to forgive myself when I make mistakes. The exercise is good at keeping me limber and active. I have a routine with push-ups, jump rope, and yoga that is perfect for me.

"Things are better with my parents. The best thing is the self-awareness, being able to let go of patterns. I notice the thoughts now, just as we practiced, especially the ones that take me down rabbit holes. I let them pass. But I still find myself stumbling and beating myself up sometimes, wanting to be anywhere but here."

Months passed. The pandemic hit, conversations moved online, the city shut down. There were riots, political problems, social distancing. Carlos maintained his momentum and created a regimen that was less punishing, to which he was adhering with less agitation and more self-acceptance. He was deepening his compassion and serenity, finding greater freedom from self-loathing. I commented on his poise and equanimity in the midst of all the changes that were occurring worldwide, as well as the rifts and challenges closer to home. He seemed to be handling the uncertainty, navigating the grim realities of life under COVID better than a lot of people I knew, including some of my own friends and family members.

"I've been here before. Those first months putting the shards of my life together. The world is now going through the same panic, the same experts with their bullshit, maybe even the same will to evolve. It has never been so obvious how much we need it.

"Peru has prepared me for anything. Everything getting jumbled. Skeletons coming out of the closet. Broken stuff breaking for good. Insane stuff happening everywhere. Been through it before. And it'll happen again. The only thing unprecedented about this is that we're now going through it together."

Has COVID deepened his sense of community?

"Of course. But it's not a community with a flag. The link is death and disease. Everyone focused on breathing right, not getting sick, surviving. Imagine if that's how it will be, people focused on what's real.

"It's like a ceremony. Showing up for our own reasons, we are where we need to be, everything will make sense come morning. Waiting together for whatever is coming. Second cup, third cup, night after night, the body falling apart, our frailty no longer possible to ignore. But being real together, deep in the night together, there is a tenderness in it, some of the people I've sat with are now close as family . . .

"You told me when we first met that I would come to see the generosity of everything. I definitely see it now. The chance to build again, this time hopefully better. It's what I've been asking for from my first ceremony, when I really think about it. COVID is another opportunity. I'm not sure that we will come to find gratitude in this. But here we are, still learning. The universe could just blink and all life as we know it would be wiped out."

We sat in silence for a moment.

"I have been remembering the vision in the jungle very clearly recently. It might still be premature to put it to words. But I feel more ready than ever to tell you what happened."

Carlos was referring to his visions prior to being hospitalized. They sustained him, he had said, even as he couldn't relate them to me when we first met.

"It was after everything happened. My arm cut open bleeding, wandering the jungle in total darkness. The medicine still strong, flashes of fractals everywhere. Repeating my *icaros* to myself, praying I'd find my way to safety.

"Something caught my foot, then just air. Falling face forward. I thought it was the end, lost in a ravine with a broken back and nobody around for miles."

He took a deep breath; his image seemed to freeze on the screen.

"It was nothing, stumbled into some bushes. But it shocked me. It shocked everything. Pitch-black night to dawn in seconds. I looked up to see a gigantic serpent moving through the leaves, brightly pixelated like a cartoon. Baby snakes scrambling around it. All with rainbow-colored skin, reflective and luminescent, slithering with thousands of wide-open eyes."

Serpents are a common sight with the tea, and he had reported similar visions to me before. But this time, he said, it was profoundly different.

"The serpent was familiar, too familiar, like some storybook version of serpents. The jungle was familiar too, archetypal. Paradise, or something like it. Perfect, new, and I was the first person to see it.

"I thought of the story. Genesis. But in reverse. This time falling into the garden, coming full circle. Kicked out of the sacred space for breaking the rules, falling right through the jungle back to the beginning."

The fearful symmetry of the tea. Mirror-image clarity. Everything perfectly arranged, the first fall giving way to the grace of the other.

"But there was something off. A strange dread in my bones. God had been evil, replaced by demons. Now the serpent was beautiful, angelic. This all might have been an insane trick, luring me deeper into hell. Isn't that the story of the snake too?

"The medicine was building, throbbing. Maybe it was messing with me, maybe it was helping. Undoing one story, throwing me into another, everything against my will. Thousands of serpents, braids of them, coursing through all my vessels, through my blood, as if they were taking over. Glowing striated skin, intricate patterns enfolding everything.

"A screen of snakeskin, covering the jungle. Then mirror eyes opening. I saw them like I see you now, my twin and me. We were rising from the mud, but half-finished, still being formed, all our muscles and tissues exposed.

"Around us were mounds of the same raw flesh, stitched-up, packed together, molded into the world. Trees, rocks, ground, all the same shimmering flesh.

"I watched as we began to stuff our faces, grabbing at whatever we could find. Snakes lashing at us, biting us. I grew sicker with every mouthful. We couldn't stop, even as vomit surged up my throat. Meat mixing with bile. Our hands sick, too, restless. Stealing from the earth, the plants and animals, the dirt. We stole from one another. Brothers fighting: an old story too."

Silence, a held breath, his image glitching into apparent freeze-frame before returning to life.

"I saw the sickness, the crime, whatever you want to call it. Paradise is here. Nobody has banished us. But we take the goodness and evil takes its place. We have locked ourselves up with a goodness that has put us in hell."

An astonishing vision of earth. Endless paradise, abundant with generosity and goodness, and yet inspiring us to love the goodness so deeply that we gorge ourselves on hell, our heaven-intoxicated hearts breaking with nausea and venom at every fulfillment.

"Everything must be turned on its head. It's the only way. Brought low just like the snake, belly to the ground, down to the level of the most despised and evil creature on earth. No more evil, no more good. Simply this garden, and the serpent poisoning us to help us and teach us. I laughed so much I could taste my tears."

His eyes glistened in remembrance. I felt inexplicable emotion well up in me too.

"Everything was radiant. The earth itself seemed to be the sun, blinding fire at its center. An ancient incinerating love, so intense I needed to protect my eyes.

"We are not human. I mean, not only human. Everything is something else. We are every animal, every animal is us. Serpents too. We might have been serpents, maybe we remain serpents, trying to straighten our backs into the sky. Our backs will be broken. There is no other way. Everything will fall back down to earth.

"I felt an intense energy flowing through my spine, bending me in every direction, opening me up to everything. I just let it happen, let myself break, feeling intense waves of tenderness and freedom and love. The serpent had released me. We had released one another."

He paused for a moment.

"I will never forget this. And I will never forget the hell that followed. Hospitals, courts, the pills. Losing my reputation, my freedom, my rights. It had happened to my ancestors, the system eating away their humanity. Now something similar was happening to me.

"Remembering the protection helped. Remembering the truth. I knew what would happen if I forgot. I saw it happen a thousand times. The serpent striking my neck and eyes, tormenting and teaching me, reminding me to give everything back, that it belonged to nobody and nothing. Just get through it, pass through it. The serpent protects everything, it protects us, connecting us with the good in the bad, the bad in the good. Moving beyond both standing and falling to find the garden as it has always been.

"You learn to listen to what things are telling you. Seeing myself in the dirt, freeing myself from the goodness that stiffens my spine. I'm in no position to judge anything. Every day I try to see the generosity we talked about; I remember there is nothing to hold on to. It will keep coming. I return to this vision and remember so as to not be reminded. I don't want to be reminded again."

One myth or a thousand myths: the generosity and abundance can be shaped into whatever form might best nourish and sustain us. We might be raised. We might be brought low. Seeing ourselves in the most despised animal, in the dirt at our feet, in the addict and the thief, recognizing ourselves in the most ignorant and fallen among us. The earth and all its beings are charged with the grandeur of what we might call God.

It is always remarkable to receive an original vision, neither unreal nor real, but speaking to our depths as the most complete dreams might. We can imagine dreaming it ourselves.

●

Carlos might lead the way. But Carlos is not even Carlos.

As with prior addicts, Carlos or ● had been written as an anonymized stand-in for a real patient. In his case, a composite was assembled that retained the bones of what had happened, fleshed out with details from life or imagination. And as with other addicts, he was a recognizable simulacrum. Intimate friends or family would be able to delineate traces of the person, though there was little that would allow for discerning the facts of biography from complete fiction.

This is not, however, the story included here.

There are many reasons why people might decline permission to appear in print. They may want to keep every biographical detail secret, however disguised it might be. There may be a concern, perhaps, that close acquaintances reading it might sense some resemblance and confuse fiction for fact, assuming certain details to be true. It can also be disconcerting to have any of our intimate truths out in the world, rendered into words not our own.

It may also be jarring to be *translated*. It has been recognized since Freud that we must be careful with the process of interpretation in psychotherapy; offering a formulation too early, or in too many words, can be damaging or counterproductive. There is a related concern. It has to do with the act of storytelling itself—with capturing a person's experience in words. It is natural to recoil from attempts to put our experience into language; we resist having our lives taken from us, turned into a public representation. This is especially the case in writings of this sort, which delve deeply into our private worlds, touching the most mysterious dimensions of ourselves.

The patient on whom this section was based asked me to remove their story for these various reasons. And they also gestured at a deeper untranslatability. They did not agree to being captured in words, full stop, neither those of others nor their own. The original version has been accordingly rewritten. It goes further into fiction than previous case studies; the person has been reproduced as a stranger, someone mythical called Carlos or ●, even as the overall arc remains recognizable.

● provides a fitting counterpart, in this sense, to the knight of *Don Quixote* at the origin of our story. Bookending this narrative are two complete fictions wrangling with reality, each the mirror image of the other. At the heart of their struggle, from first to last, is the question of self-determination: Who decides our story? Who tells our truth?

Quixote had been made of words and had also been unmade by them. Knighted by fables, he would go on to be rearticulated by others in more sobering terms. A summary was rendered to him of his adventures, less ennobling and more diagnostic, aligned with what the crowd decrees to be true. The turn to "reality" is depicted in the novel as a terrible disillusionment—the humiliation of surrendering our ecstatic affirmations and fantastical subjectivity for a cruder, though saner existence.

Quixote's struggle is poignant and enduring because it is our own. Our shared path is to liberate ourselves from stultifying representation. We yearn to be free, exalted, boundless—an ecstatic secret, above all to ourselves. Yet others might presume to interpret us, sit in judgment on us. Psychosis heightens the tension of the situation: what we think we know is at loggerheads with what others think they know. Addiction is another way our subjectivity comes to feel embattled. It is understandable why we might double down, protecting our ideas, yearnings, and joys from the tyranny of more conventional appetites—from the tyranny of reality itself.

I respect the patient who inspired ● for refusing to lend their experience to this narrative. They might flourish where Quixote foundered. Sanity need not be a matter of fitting into the "reality" fashioned for us by others. There is another truer way, beyond surrendering to consensus incarnations and fictions. We might make our own ineffable path, demanding silence where silence must be observed.

The words of others, devastating as they might be, are not the most poisonous. The most potent incarnations are ultimately our own, the conclusions populating the privacy of our own minds. This is the opportunity before us, with clamorous encroachments arriving from all sides. We learn to deepen our silence in response to the incessant chatter, whether the voice is our own, another's, a nightingale's.

These mind-forged manacles, as Blake described them, may be overlooked in romantic notions of the unconstrained and primal individual: Rousseau's fantasy of the original man, for example, liberated from societal strictures. Psychosis and addiction are sometimes valorized as revolts against the regime's monopoly on knowledge or happiness, with affected people depicted as courageously sacrificing everything to incarnate their private absolutes. This narrative of heroism is yet another restrictive idealization, no different in its rigid reimagining from the demonization more often directed at these conditions.

The psychotic or addict is no closer to liberation than is the conformist. We remain oppressed so long as we allow our systems of knowledge or happiness, whether blandly conventional or unintelligibly strange, to determine who and what we are. Quixote was not simply unmade by words. He was constructed of them in the first place. His tragedy began the moment he identified with the grand fictions of knighthood borrowed from his libraries.

We are more than what can be known. There is an inexhaustible mystery to us eluding total identification. Self-determination, as the story of ● suggests, might lead to madness if we pretend otherwise. It is the deepest ignorance to know things too well: we become imprisoned within a simulation of the world, fitting within the narrow absolutes of our comprehension. We are bound to wither under such constraints. Even representing our beings as "selves" or "ours" is placing what we are into a cage. We flourish most fully in an open, incomplete expanse, with the freedom for anything—self, others, the body, poisons, medicines, animals, plants, addiction, recovery, being, emptiness, even death itself—to be incorporated into our unveiling. And at the heart of our hearts: ( ).

What we are is entirely relational. We might be nothing at all without the abundance of everything with which we are in constant relationship. We are that as much as we are this. Even defining ourselves in opposition to something else, such as unhappiness, does not free us from it, but instead binds us to it more tightly.

The process of self-determination is therefore paradoxical. We are beyond what can be identified, possessed, or completed. Yet we are each responsible for attending to our being. *Self-stewardship* might be a more fruitful fiction—or better yet, ()-*stewardship*. We serve as keepers to this moment, bending with the forces impacting on us, relinquishing our fixations and deliberately finding our place within the confluence of currents brimming over into existence. We disappear into this meeting ground so that we might appear more truly: a perfect reflection of innumerable other incarnations and confluence points, all existing concurrently in all places and all times. The skeptic and dreamer, darkness and dream, come to their reconciliation in a primal vision untethered to any reality yet beyond all doubt.

There is no "lower" self to subdue or master: no dark double to flee, overpower, or purge. And there is no final identity to carve into indelible creation on the skin of the earth. Every animal is us; we are every animal. We are a particular surplus of being, and we are also inseparable from the multidimensional weave of relationships that embodies us in one apparent specificity after another. We know ourselves; we don't know ourselves. The ceaseless current, beyond our facts and forms, is what we are.

Names and identities are provisional, the "sense of self" as fluid and multiform as any fact. Yet ● overthrew nearly everything for "his truth." Telling our own story, pursuing self-determination, is often seen in this light: speaking and acting with sufficient certainty and even force to deflect those who might silence us. But it is hardly evolution to fall into the same strident loudmouthed ignorance as do our naysayers. We must watch for falling into that familiar trap of knowing too much. No certainty is worth losing the vastness of being.

"Reality" is only valuable insofar as it aligns with our truest possibility. A simple question to ask at every turn: How do we relate to what we know? Are we supported by it, or suffering in its coils? Knowledge is not a conclusion. It is a makeshift myth, forever being redrawn into more perfect translucence and emptiness.

The representations imposed on us by others require comparable discernment. We might work toward approaching their judgments as we should all fictions, including our own, and pass through them freely, seeing through any distortions that obscure what we are.

As with the half-imagined case of ●, all words will wind their way to total fiction by the end. There is no sense pretending that what we are speaking about is real. Yet we shouldn't pretend it is unreal either. What is reflected back at us and revealed is a dark double we might be too knowing about ourselves to recognize: a luminous darkness within darkness.

●

A vision ends this story. It began as an act of imagination; I had written it as one of a few ways to close the case of ●. Then, as if by magic, it was

reported to me. The same situation, the same circle. A moment of reality converging with fiction. Perhaps we all might come to experience
such reunions.

● had been concerned from the start of our work together that the
circle during his final ceremony had not closed properly. The night felt
unfinished, an open breach. It was important for him, he said, to honor
his work in the Amazon by finding a respectful way to conclude things.
This was the reason he had told his cousin that he needed to resume
work with it. The cup was still half-empty, he had told her while still in
the hospital, and it needs to be completely drained. He could not rule
out returning to conclude the work. She did not respond well, heard in
his words craving and madness. He learned to stay quiet about this. A
few years later, he had found an opening.

"My parents were visiting this past week from Europe. We had a nice
dinner, my parents, my cousin, and I. My mother said something that
nearly led to an argument. I kept my cool and composure, didn't react.
It was clear that I was hurt, though, I'm sure everyone noticed. I saw
that she backed off, was a little quieter and gentler. I felt something
release within me. While we were still around the table, I decided to
bring it up. I told them that I know it was painful to talk about and yet it
was necessary. We had never really discussed as a family what had happened to me. I told them about the pain I went through, the confusions,
the sense of being manipulated by the courts, my anger at everyone,
my fear that my life was over. I told them about how the medications
messed me up, how lucky I have been to finally find treatment with
people who understand. I was not being judgmental or angry, just telling them what was in my heart. They listened quietly. I saw my parents
tear up, I even saw my cousin affected and getting emotional. I could
feel myself tearing up too. I also told them about all the healing I've
received, starting with the jungle itself, that it was far from all bad.
I told them about how much better I'm doing now, the progress I've
made, how thankful I was for their support, how much I've learned to
be a better person over the course of all this. I apologized for anything
that I might have done to hurt them, acknowledged how painful this
must have been for everyone. Everything was coming out. I reassured
them that I adopted the symbol not to bother them. They could still

call me whatever they wanted. But I also hoped they could accept me as whoever I am. They apologized, too, they expressed their gratitude and happiness that I'm better. The energy in that room was intense. It was like the spirit was right there with us. I felt it, I'm sure they felt it too. I suggested we stand up and link hands. Standing there in silence, seeing my father tear up for the first time in my life, feeling my family around me, I felt the circle come to a close. It was exactly as it should be."

I think of that final circle often. There were many variations the circle took over the course of our work together: cup, ceremony, ●, COVID, the serpent closing on itself. A family brought together, origins linked together in the form of the earth. That night had come to a close, exactly as it should, exactly as his dark visions from the deep Amazon had deemed impossible. We must be ready for the illuminating trick. Everything is possible. Something ends, another begins. We will fall, we will rise, a mysterious current creates and dissolves all we know. The emptier and more silent we keep the center of things, the greater the tenderness and understanding we will receive from what passes through us and between us, the silence that is not quite silent, the emptiness that is inexhaustible, this abundance that is now ours.

We have neared the end. The door that had once been wide open has almost closed. Only a paper-thin sliver of space remains. We gather here to give recognition to what has passed.

People begin and end with words, often the same words at every meeting, bringing their words to me above all else. They voice their hopes, memories, fears. I listen closely. I heed their stories and attend to the striving and anguish caught in their throats. I give their words the same solemn respect I generally reserve for the dead.

I also respect their words for having tried and failed. No word is final; no moment is finished. We draw conclusions, and yet nothing concludes. There is always more to recognize: all we have struggled to remember, everything we have endeavored to forget. I respond to their words with only a few of my own, principally intended to resurrect some of these unquiet moments to awareness. We return to what needs our attention: our dreams, wants, and wounds. We return to ourselves.

The passage before us is unfamiliar and difficult. The end of our words is imminent: a mute darkness awaits, beyond all coordinates and maps. Yet there is no other way. The same fall, the same ground. An inevitable homecoming. Any disorientation yields in the end to the serene expanse within which our words erupt, repeat, disappear. A more complete moment haunts our depths, awaiting its turn, and awaiting its silence.

We pause together at this perilous threshold. A moment of silence for this dying world that had been brought to life. A few words in remembrance as we throw earth over it. The ground comes to a gentle stillness with time, the earth settling over and swallowing up everything. Thoughts quiet, everything quiets, and we grow suppler and more wakeful, threading a serpentine path through the open eye of each instant.

PART IV: CONCLUSIONS

I have learned and dismantled all the words in order to draw
from them a single word: home.

—MAHMOUD DARWISH

BREAKING EARTH

Every conclusion is unfinished.

We attend to these words straining to speak louder than the emptiness. And we recognize the silence that entombs every attempt at a last word.

We receive this effort at reality and presence. We give remembrance as it flashes for an instant before it fades away.

We honor the yearning and striving. We honor the failure.

We stand in silence as the dead are presented and recognized. We bear witness as their forms are restored to the earth. And we begin again.

We conclude again, fail again, begin again.

A conclusion is a death never to be complete.

Every conclusion offers guidance. Every dead end is a path. We learn how we might begin again, this time beyond our conclusions.

At the threshold of receiving these conclusions, we return to the beginning, the beginningless beginning, before names and beliefs, before even ourselves.

We find a person coming to his conclusions, a person dwelling in possibility. We find maybe nothing, perhaps something.

There are many possibilities, realities, and conclusions; each might come to be called addiction. Addiction itself might come to be called many words.

Addiction is being human. All our conclusions begin in this one. Every conclusion begins and ends with being human.

Addiction is a crisis. Addiction is being human brought to a moment of crisis.

Addiction is dreaming into deeper sleep. It is an interrupted sleep. Addiction is the dream ending in failure.

Addiction is a refusal to fail.

Addiction is the threat of silence.

Addiction is a face frozen into a careless expression.

Addiction is a mirror.

Addiction is a trick, a mask.

Addiction is grasping a gift, refusing a gift. Addiction is the gift unveiling its immensity.

Addiction is a ruthless instruction.

Addiction is a teaching that has not concluded. Addiction is a teacher unrecognized.

Addiction is an aborted passage. Addiction is an endless ritual.

Addiction is a religion praying to broken fragments.

Addiction is a God grounded in the word.

Addiction is a phantasmagoria of made-up materials. Addiction is the collapse to ground zero.

Addiction is losing ourselves. Addiction is finding ourselves.

Addiction is a crucified dream.

Addiction is God's plan for the world.

Addiction is nostalgia for a swaddled past.

Addiction is the trauma haunting our lullabies.

Addiction is a thousand voices quarreling.

Addiction is the scream of the earth as it is torn into good and evil.

Addiction is all the nightingales in the garden howling for more.

Addiction is wanting everything.

Addiction is believing beyond our capacity; addiction is an excrescence of words.

Addiction is a phantom limb. Addiction is the mutilated emptiness.

Addiction is a simulation.

Addiction is the system behind everything.

Addiction is violence visited upon violence. Addiction is war, its mad scream for silence and peace.

Addiction is the regime clearing the land.

Addiction is the blank slate on which we inscribe our words.

Addiction is the same word repeated.

Addiction is the amnesia upon awakening.

Addiction is taking a dream to its breaking point.

Addiction is an earthbound psychosis.

Addiction is a dark double agitating for the throne.

Addiction is a misdirected prayer.

Addiction is haunted by hell, haunted by heaven. Addiction is haunted by the promise of marriage between the two.

Addiction is an entanglement with a dream of earth.

Addiction is the earth refusing to cooperate.

Addiction is placing our joys and sorrows into captivity.

Addiction is the golden crown we place on our own cracked skulls.

Addiction is seeding the earth with plundered jewels.

Addiction is reaping the fruit of our harvest.

Addiction is agitating the surface of things with our reflections.

Addiction is wanting to stop, refusing to stop.

Addiction is the secret worm. Addiction is the hunger kept out of sight.

Addiction is the creditor. It is the debt to be paid.

Addiction is a vision of conquest foundering in the jungle.

Addiction is exaltation followed by humiliation.

Addiction is the teetering of empire.

Addiction is the clamor of too many minds.

Addiction is the wilderness snaking its way into our skulls.

Addiction is a myth clotted with an abundance of words; addiction is a vessel compacted.

Addiction is the cup from which nothing pours.

Addiction is the dream of water that suffocates and drowns.

Addiction is the mud filling our mouth and eyes.

Addiction is love gasping for breath.

Addiction is a flight through the darkness. Addiction is the light that blinds.

Addiction is the venom of the snake of Eden.

Addiction is a stasis of possibility; addiction is the impossible promise.

Addiction is an implacable contract, a single transaction.

Addiction is a gift promised. Addiction is a promise that cannot be fulfilled.

Addiction is an incessant promise.

Addiction is the gift that we refuse.

Addiction is clinging to life; addiction is clinging to death. Addiction is the shackles we hold dear to our hearts.

Addiction is Kali flicking her serpent tongue.

Addiction is the bruise of morning. Addiction is an abrupt awakening.

Addiction is an ending.

Addiction begins in conclusions; addiction begins in what cannot be concluded.

Addiction is a cycle of conclusions, repeating without relief.

Addiction is the truth inflaming our conclusions. Addiction is the truth breaking us apart.

Addiction is a death unfinished.

Addiction concludes in paying the debt. Addiction concludes in returning what has been taken.

Addiction concludes when we emerge from the dreams that enclose us; addiction concludes when the night runs its course.

Addiction concludes when we surrender what is meaningful.

Addiction concludes when we feel our death.

Addiction begins and ends in a circle.

Addiction begins and ends with a single breath; addiction begins and ends, breath after breath, in absolute silence. Addiction concludes in beginning again. Addiction concludes in beginning, again and again, in the open eye of silence.

The earth breaks under the weight of our dreams. We break the earth in hunger, in mad pursuit, in respectful remembrance. The earth breaks at sunrise. It breaks under the plow of morning; it breaks to invite the golden seed.

We begin, dream, and fail again, begin and dream again, until we awaken to the earth breaking; we dream until we enter, beyond our dawns, beyond our dreams, into a perpetual sunrise of awakening.

ACKNOWLEDGMENTS

I am grateful for the patients and participants who have provided their stories; for my parents and family; for my teachers and students; for my editors Karen Rinaldi at Harper US and Laura Stickney at Penguin UK, as well as their respective teams; for my agent Georgia Bodnar; for my colleagues at Columbia University and New York State Psychiatric Institute; for the support of NIH; and for the generous readers, listeners, and companions who have engaged with the many variations of these words over the years, offering their encouragement, criticisms, and suggestions: for Rozita Alaluf, Alex Aliume, Stephen Apkon, Kevin Balktick, asha bandele, Michael Baretz, Dilara Bugdayci, Sita Ram Chaitanya, Priscilla Duggan, Carl Erik Fisher, Ryan Fox, Kade Friedman, Tiokasin Ghosthorse, Alex and Allyson Grey, Roland Griffiths, Marcina Hale, Carl and Robin Hart, Kristin Hayter, Garrett Hedlund, Ben Hoffman, Dan Hunt, Jamie Kaufmann, Helen Kongsgaard, Mitch and Karen Kuflik, Chara Malapani, Anna-Louise Malfilatre, Olivia Marcus, Michelle Yi Martin, Duff McDonald, Joseph McElroy, Bethany McLean, Dara Mitchell, Elizabeth Montgomery, Don Morris, Vivian Nixon, Kate O'Malley, Esther Perel, Genesis P-Orridge, Moksha Priya, Coco Qvortrup, Deborah Roth, Jack Saul, Lance Sheldon, Andrew Solomon, Srinivasan, Saleena Subaiya, Susan Tusa, Chris Wink, and Paxton Winters; for my quiet comrades; and for those who fed the fire.

This book is dedicated to the struggle of Indigenous, occupied, and exiled peoples, and with special recognition to the Lenape and Palestinians, on whose haunted land this book was largely written.

NOTES

Preface

ix *the buzz phrase*: Pollan, *How to Change Your Mind*.

 x *a paradigm-shifting Prozac*: Piore, "Magic Mushrooms May Be the Biggest Advance in Treating Depression Since Prozac."

xi Integration *is another word*: Geoff et al., *Psychedelic Integration: An Analysis of the Concept and Its Practice*.

Words at the Threshold

 1 *"global mental health crisis"*: WHO, "COVID-19 Pandemic Triggers 35% increase in Prevalence of Anxiety and Depression Worldwide."

 1 *Increased rates*: Panchal & Saunders, "The Implications of COVID-19 for Mental Health and Substance Use."

 2 eudaemonia: Aristotle, *Aristotle's Nicomachean Ethics*.

 2 *happiness* reward: Burke et al., "The Role of the Orbitofrontal Cortex in the Pursuit of Happiness and More Specific Rewards."

 2 *happiness . . . the basis for ethical conduct*: Bentham, *An Introduction to the Principles of Morals and Legislation*.

 2 *The US tops the world*: On mental health issues: SAMHSA, "SAMHSA Announces National Survey on Drug Use and Health (NSDUH) Results Detailing Mental Illness and Substance Use Levels in 2021." On opioid consumption: Salmond and Allread, "A Population Health Approach to America's Opioid Epidemic." On incarceration rates: Lee, "Does the United States Really Have 5 Percent of the World's Population and One Quarter of the World's Prisoners?" On military spending domestically and abroad: SIPRI, "Sipri Military Expenditure Database."

 4 *According to this [brain disease] model*: Leshner, "Addiction Is a Brain Disease, and It Matters."

 6 scientism: Hayek, *The Counter-Revolution of Science: Studies on the Abuse of Reason*.

 6 *the thoughtful reflections of a sixteenth-century French nobleman*: Montaigne, *The Complete Essays*.

Chapter 1: Drugs and Other Fictions

12 *Zhuangzi*: Zhuangzi, *The Essential Writings with Selections from Traditional Commentaries*.

13 *Beckett's picture of progress*: Beckett, *Worstward Ho*.

14 *worst of it has passed*: Elopement patterns during opioid detox: Kim and Nelson, "Reducing the Harm of Opioid Overdose with the Safe Use of Naloxone: A Pharmacologic Review."

17 *drugs "hardwire" the brain*: Ersche et al., "Abnormal Brain Structure Implicated in Stimulant Drug Addiction." NIH, *NIH News in Health.*

17 *"abuse liability"*: FDA, "Guidance for Industry. Assessment of Abuse Potential of Drugs. Draft Guidance."

17 *most people who use drugs don't develop a problem with them*: United Nations, "United Nations Office on Drugs and Crime: Drugs Statistics and Trends."

18 *"self-sabotage"*: For an example of this language: Rounds, "3 Ways We Self-Sabotage During Recovery."

20 *the entire universe would die with him*: Shiva and the demon: Chaturvedi, *Shiv Purana.*

20 *"there is no crime I cannot imagine committing"*: Goethe, *Maxims and Reflections.*

21 *broken and burned, and blown anew*: Donne, *John Donne Holy Sonnets.*

22 *the spacious moorings for beginning again*: Ashbery, *The Mooring of Starting Out.*

23 *Relics and residues . . . of alcohol and cannabis*: Pain, "A Potted History."

23 *Dionysian rites of ancient Greece*: McGovern, *Ancient Wine: The Search for the Origins of Viniculture.*

24 *mostly harmless and often beneficial*: The majority of adults who use substances do so unproblematically: United Nations Office on Drugs and Crime: Drugs Statistics and Trends.

25 *Our desires overreach our capacity*: Montale, *The Collected Poems of Eugenio Montale.*

25 *Lucifer . . . in* Paradise Lost: Milton, *Paradise Lost.*

27 *We cannot step, Heraclitus*: "We cannot step into the same river twice": Heraclitus, *Fragments.*

27 *perceptions are private, perhaps relational*: Sensory perception: Granit, *Receptors and Sensory Perception: A Discussion of Aims, Means, and Results of Electrophysiological Research into the Process of Reception.*

28 phenomena *and* noumena: Kant, *Critique of Pure Reason.*

28 *Phenomena are the limits*: Schopenhauer, *The World as Will and Representation.*

29 *Descartes*: Descartes, *Meditations on First Philosophy.*

29 *Studies have shown*: King et al., "Rewarding, Stimulant, and Sedative Alcohol Responses and Relationship to Future Binge Drinking."

30 *Frederick Douglass*: Douglass, *Narrative of the Life of Frederick Douglass.*

30 *To make a paradise of bread*: Porchia, *Voices.*

30 *diagnose language as a virus*: Burroughs, *The Ticket That Exploded.*

32 *Don Quixote*: Cervantes, *Don Quixote.*

33 *Cervantes began* Quixote: Byron, *Cervantes, A Biography.*

33 *The rise of addiction*: Rates during the pandemic: Chacon, "Substance Use During COVID-19 Pandemic."

34 *addiction has been estimated to affect only 3.9 percent*: Grant, "Epidemiology of DSM-5 Drug Use Disorder."

34 *Substance use disorders: Diagnostic and Statistical Manual of Mental Disorders*, 5th ed.

34 *variety of vulnerabilities*: Contributing factors to addiction: *Principles of Addiction.*

35 *"process" or behavioral addictions*: Robbins and Clark, "Behavioral Addictions."

35 *A recent meta-analysis*: Alimoradi et al., "Estimation of Behavioral Addiction Prevalence During COVID-19 Pandemic."

35 *nearly half of adults*: Hasin and Grant, "The National Epidemiologic Survey on Alcohol and Related Conditions (NESARC) Waves 1 and 2."

35 *problem gambling*: Recognition of gambling as a behavioral addiction: *Diagnostic and Statistical Manual of Mental Disorders*, 5th ed.

39 *decision making oriented around drug use*: Shaham and Hope, "The Role of Neuroadaptations in Relapse to Drug Seeking."

39 *"hardwire" the seat of consciousness*: Ersche et al., *Abnormal Brain Structure Implicated in Stimulant Drug Addiction.* NIH, *NIH News in Health.*

39 *"Hijacked" is the common metaphor*: NIH News in Health.

40 *pharmakon has three meanings*: Derrida, *Dissemination*. See also: Pendell, *Pharmako/poiea*.

40 *suicides inspired by* The Sorrows of Young Werther: Jack, "Goethe's *Werther* and Its Effects."

Chapter 2: The Pursuit of Knowledge

45 *Lichtenberg*: Lichtenberg, *The Waste Books*.

49 *the psychiatrist Kenneth Kendler*: Kendler, "Toward a Philosophical Structure for Psychiatry."

50 *annual budget in excess of $1 billion*: NIDA, "Fiscal Year 2024 Budget Information."

51 *"the war on drugs"*: NIDA's emergence: NIDA, *National Institute on Drug Abuse (NIDA)*.

51 *primarily of African American men*: Disproportionate effects of the war on drugs' cost: ACLU, "The Drug War Is the New Jim Crow."

51 *President Barack Obama*: Obama's refusal to end the war on drugs: McWhorter, "The Root; Why Won't Obama End the War on Drugs?"

51 *Dr. Nora Volkow*: Zuger, "A General in the Drug War."

52 *only interpretations*: Nietzsche, *The Will to Power*.

52 *every word is a lie*: Khouzani et al., *Discourse of Shams Tabrizi*.

52 *putting Nature on the rack*: Bacon, *The Essays, or Counsels Civil and Moral*.

52 *Discoveries don't occur*: Bird and Sherwin, *American Prometheus*.

53 *Kuhn called this framework a* paradigm: Kuhn, *The Structure of Scientific Revolutions*.

53 *not the territory*: Korzybski, *A Non-Aristotelian System and Its Necessity for Rigour in Mathematics and Physics*.

53 *rhizomic immensity*: Deleuze and Guattari, *A Thousand Plateaus*.

53 *like Babel*: Borges, *Ficciones*.

54 *"defines the conditions of possibility of all knowledge"*: Foucault, *The Order of Things*.

54 *the parable of the blind men*: Several blind men inquiring into the nature of an elephant come to disparate conclusions about its identity based on which part of the animal they touch: wall, rope, fan, spear, etc. From: Ireland, *Udana and the Itvuttaka*.

54 *every fact also fiction*: Einstein, "Physics and Reality."

54 *"There are more things in heaven and earth"*: Shakespeare, *Hamlet*.

54 *"reality"*: Nabokov's "reality": Nabokov, *Lolita*: "On a book entitled Lolita (afterword)."

56 *We come to see . . . what we know*: Schopenhauer, *The World as Will and Representation*.

57 *conducted a small study*: Mindfulness study: Dakwar et al., "Individual Mindfulness-Based Psychotherapy for Cannabis or Cocaine Dependence: A Pilot Feasibility Trial."

60 *We join the laughing animals*: Rilke, *Selected Poems*.

60 *The most minor observations that pass through the chinks of our interpretive filters*: Vallery-Radot, *The Life of Pasteur*.

61 *Theory is gray*: Goethe, *Faust: A Tragedy*.

66 *an empirical elaboration of imaginaries*: Whitehead, *Process and Reality*.

66 *The traps of language*: Wittgenstein, *Philosophical Investigations*.

66 *We can't say we know*: Nikhilananda, *The Upanishads*.

67 *An understanding . . . outside the rules of understanding*: Gödel, "On Formally Undecidable Propositions of Principia Mathematica and Related Systems I."

67 *the "hard" problem*: Chalmers, "Facing Up to the Problem of Consciousness."

69 *predictive map of the world*: Friston and Kiebel, "Predictive Coding Under the Free-Energy Principle."

70 *should be passed over in silence*: Wittgenstein, *Tractatus Logica Philosophicus*.

70 *"yet it was believed that the thundering sky was Jove"*: Vico, *The New Science*.

71 *buzzing clamorously against its walls*: Wittgenstein, *Philosophical Investigations*.

72 *"The wind blows where it wills"*: Michaels, *The Gospel of John*.

72 Cogito, ergo sum: Descartes, *Meditations on First Philosophy*.

72 *language-games*: For an exploration of what he coined language-games, see: Wittgenstein, *Philosophical Investigations*.

Chapter 3: Darkness Within Darkness

75 *"For technicians, nothing is possible"*: Bajac, Ray, and Chéroux, *Man Ray: Portraits: Paris, Hollywood, Paris*.

80 an excrescence of words: Emerson, *Self-Reliance*.

80 *Behaviorism*: Skinner, *The Behavior of Organisms: An Experimental Analysis*; Watson, *Behaviorism*.

81 *The brain becomes programmed*: For an example of data indicating the preferential salience a drug cue (cocaine) acquires relative to other natural reward cues (food) as encoded in the brain activity of addicts, see Tomasi et al., "Overlapping Patterns of Brain Activation to Food and Cocaine Cues in Cocaine Abusers."

82 *guide his decision making*: Attentional biases and decision making: Liu et al., "Relationship Between Attentional Bias to Cocaine-Related Stimuli and Impulsivity in Cocaine-Dependent Subjects."

82 *"disease of free will"*: Volkow, "Addiction Is a Disease of Free Will."

83 *freedom and behaviorism*: Compatibilism: *Stanford Encyclopedia of Philosophy*, *Compatibilism*.

83 Cognitive control: Posner and Snyder, "Attention and Cognitive Control."

84 *"underlying mechanism"*: Craver, *Explaining the Brain: Mechanisms and the Mosaic Unity of Neuroscience*.

84 *It has been recognized and critiqued*: Field et al., "Indeed, Not Really a Brain Disorder: Implications for Reductionist Accounts of Addiction." Hart, "Viewing Addiction as a Brain Disease Promotes Social Injustice." Hart et al., "Is Cognitive Functioning Impaired in Methamphetamine Users?"

84 *cue reactivity*: Courtney et al., "Neural Substrates of Cue Reactivity: Association with Treatment Outcomes and Relapse."

85 *This has been demonstrated*: Tang et al., "Food and Drug Cues Activate Similar Brain Regions: A Meta-analysis of Functional MRI Studies."

86 *"Behaviorism is thus right insofar"*: Cassin et al., *Dictionary of Untranslatables*, "Behavior."

86 *"the reason of Ulysses or the fox"*: Whitehead, *The Function of Reason*.

87 *a great majority of people who use drugs*: Schlag, "Percentages of Problem Drug Use and Their Implications for Policy Making: A Review of the Literature."

87 *self-administration studies*: Panlilio & Goldberg, "Self-Administration of Drugs in Animals and Humans as a Model and an Investigative Tool." Jones & Comer, "A Review of Human Drug Self-Administration Procedures." MacKillop & Murphy, "Drug Self-Administration Paradigms."

88 *"alternative or secondary reinforcers"*: Hart et al., "Alternative Reinforcers Differentially Modify Cocaine Self-Administration by Humans." Skinner, *The Behavior of Organisms: An Experimental Analysis*.

88 *cost threshold*: Hart et al., "Alternative Reinforcers Differentially Modify Cocaine Self-Administration by Humans."

88 *contingency management strategies*: Benishek et al., "Prize-Based Contingency Management for the Treatment of Substance Abusers: A Meta-analysis."

88 *disrupt a long-standing addiction*: Barker et al., "Natural Recovery: A Cross-Cultural Perspective."

89 *mongrel concept*: Block, "On a Confusion About a Function of Consciousness."

90   *Whitehead's distinction*: Whitehead, *The Function of Reason*.

93   *Sifted science*: Joyce, *Finnegans Wake*.

93   *brain disease model*: Leshner, "Addiction Is a Brain Disease, and It Matters."

94   *faith-based healing programs*: Fisher, *The Urge: Our History of Addiction*.

95   *If history gives any indication*: Foucault, *Madness and Civilization*. Scull, *Madness in Civilization*.

99   *hyper-refined and insular, endless, ultimately inconsequential*: Mann, *The Magic Mountain*.

99   *overdoses increasing in incidence*: Hedegaard et al., "Drug Overdose Deaths in the United States."

99   *barely effective*: Treatment failures and lack of access: Pullen and Oser, "Barriers to Substance Abuse Treatment in Rural and Urban Communities: Counselor Perspectives." Rapp et al., "Treatment Barriers Identified by Substance Abusers Assessed at a Centralized Intake Unit." Greenfield et al., "Substance Abuse Treatment Entry, Retention, and Outcome in Women: A Review of the Literature."

99   *Seeing the lie*: Emerson, *Self-Reliance*.

101   *darkness within darkness—the gateway to all understanding*: Lao Tsu, *Tao Te Ching*.

101   *All that I know*: Plato, *Apology*.

102   *regime of signs*: Deleuze and Guattari, *A Thousand Plateaus*.

Chapter 4: Addiction/Freedom

103   *"Acting as both poison and remedy"*: Derrida, *Dissemination*.

104   *"Before Zen"*: Tanahashi and Leavitt, *Essential Dōgen*.

113   *an escape from the same oppressive premises*: Bateson, "The Cybernetics of 'Self.'"

114   *to find solutions . . . when there isn't a problem*: Janis and Janis, *Marcel Duchamp, Anti-Artist*.

118   *"developing discrepancy"*: Miller and Skolnick, *Motivational Interviewing*.

118   *man's search for meaning*: Frankl, *Man's Search for Meaning*.

119   *"And they do not fall"*: Anonymous, *Meditations on the Tarot*.

122   *A recent study found that when addicted individuals approach a drug*: Westbrook et al., "Mindful Attention Reduces Neural and Self-Reported Cue-Induced Craving in Smokers."

124   *reimagines his beloved into a perfect fiction: crystallization*: Stendhal, *Love*.

125   *heavy drinkers remain inattentive*: Mollaahmetoglu et al., "The Acute Effects of Alcohol on State Rumination in the Laboratory."

126   *The success rates of AA are low*: Chappel, "Long-Term Recovery from Alcoholism."

130   Abandon all hope: Alighieri, *The Divine Comedy*.

Chapter 5: The Return to Silence

131   *"charged with the grandeur of God"*: Hopkins, *Gerard Manley Hopkins: The Major Works*.

135   *that there is* this *where there might be nothing*: Heidegger, *What Is Metaphysics?*

135   *in the philosophies of Empedocles and Parmenides*: Various, *Early Greek Philosophy*.

135   *Vedanta*: Torwesten and Rosset, *Vedants: Heart of Hinduism*.

136   *Even licentious beds . . . are touched by dawn and its Absolute*: Baudelaire, *Les Fleurs Du Mal: The Complete Text of The Flowers of Evil*.

137   *like the system of yoga articulated by Patanjali: The Yoga Sutras of Patanjali*.

140   *we step onto air as if it were earth*: "The real miracle is not to walk either on water or in on thin air but to walk on earth.": Hanh, *Thich Nhat Hanh: Essential Writings*.

140   *Lovers, poets, and madmen*: Shakespeare, *A Midsummer Night's Dream*.

140   *this vegetable universe is just a faint shadow*: Blake, *Jerusalem, the Emanation of the Giant Albion*.

140 *a gift from the gods*: Plato, *Phaedrus*.
140 *Cocaine was considered a wonder drug*: Das, "Cocaine Abuse in North America: A Milestone in History."
142 *"rearranging their prejudices"*: Interestingly, the author of this quote remains under dispute, with the attribution to James perhaps a matter of prejudice.
142 *Beginning in 1890, cocaine was blamed*: Hart, "How the Myth of the 'Negro Cocaine Fiend' Helped Shape American Drug Policy."
142 *crack epidemic of the 1980s*: Covington et al., "Crack in America: Demon Drugs and Social Justice."
146 *controllable administration*: Ketamine's mechanism: Zhang et al., "Structural Basis of Ketamine Action on Human NMDA Receptors." Krystal et al., "Subanesthetic Effects of the Noncompetitive NMDA Antagonist, Ketamine, in Humans."
146 *recognized . . . as one of the world's essential medicines*: McQueen, "Table 15.3, World Health Organization's List of Essential Medicines for Anesthesia and Pain Management."
146 *Perhaps the benefits of ketamine*: Hart, *Drug Use for Grown-Ups*. Saadi et al., "End the Use of 'Excited Delirium' as a Cause of Death in Police Custody."
146 *it functions as an anesthetic*: Domino et al., "Pharmacologic Effects of CI 581, a New Dissociative Anesthetic, in Man."
146 *Ketamine is dissociative*: Ketamine's subjective effects: Erowid, "Erowid Ketamine Vault: Effects." Ghoneim, *Ketamine: Behavioral Effects of Subanesthetic Doses*.
147 *It is thought to work by*: Ketamine neuroimaging studies: Dawson et al., "Subanaesthetic Ketamine Treatment Alters Prefrontal Cortex Connectivity with Thalamus and Ascending Subcortical Systems."
147 *[John Lilly] called ECCO*: Lilly, *The Center of the Cyclone: An Autobiography of Inner Space*.
147 *P-Orridge*: Leland, "Genesis P-Orridge Has Always Been a Provocateur of the Body. Now She's at Its Mercy." P-Orridge, private correspondence.
148 *Both models emerged in the 1950s*: Bakalar and Grinspoon, *Psychedelic Drugs Reconsidered*.
148 *The antiwar, anticonformist counterculture was*: Stevens, *Storming Heaven: LSD and the American Dream*.
148 *Starting in the early 1950s*: Kinzer, *Poisoner in Chief: Sidney Gottlieb and the CIA Search for Mind Control*.
150 *Suggestogen has been proposed*: Irvin, *God's Flesh: Teonanácatl: The True History of the Sacred Mushroom*.
151 *Research had even been conducted in the 1990s in St. Petersburg, Russia*: Krupitsky, "Ketamine Psychotherapy for Heroin Addiction: Immediate Effects and Two-Year Follow-Up." Krupitsky, "Ketamine psychedelic therapy (KPT): a review of the results of ten years of research." Krupitsky, private correspondence.
151 *In 2000, researchers at Yale discovered*: Krystal et al., "Subanesthetic Effects of the Noncompetitive NMDA Antagonist, Ketamine, in Humans."
151 *This finding has been replicated in depressed people*: Coyle et al., "The Use of Ketamine as an Antidepressant: A Systematic Review and Meta-analysis."
152 *Hundreds of studies have been conducted*: Zanos and Gould, "Mechanisms of Ketamine Action as an Antidepressant."
152 *Janssen, for example, has patented s-ketamine*: Garber, "Esketamine Nears FDA Approval, Prompting Both Excitement and Concern."
152 *"tame the ketamine tiger"*: Domino, "Taming the Ketamine Tiger."
153 *my team had already completed a few laboratory studies*: Dakwar et al., "The Effects of Subanesthetic Ketamine Infusions on Motivation to Quit and Cue-Induced Craving in Cocaine-Dependent Research Volunteers." Dakwar et al., "Cocaine

Self-Administration Disrupted by the N-Methyl-D-Aspartate Receptor Antagonist Ketamine: A Randomized, Crossover Trial."

153 *trial combining a ketamine infusion with mindfulness training*: Dakwar et al., "A Single Ketamine Infusion Combined with Mindfulness-Based Behavioral Modification to Treat Cocaine Dependence: A Randomized Clinical Trial."

154 *"learned helplessness"*: Seligman, "Failure to Escape Traumatic Shock."

154 *This might be due to the effects of ketamine on glutamate-related learning*: Kang et al.,
"The Mechanisms Behind Rapid Antidepressant Effects of Ketamine: A Systematic Review with a Focus on Molecular Neuroplasticity."

155 *the "gold standard" for studying clinical efficacy*: Hariton et al., "Randomised Controlled Trials—the Gold Standard for Effectiveness Research."

155 *a single forty-minute ketamine infusion*: Dakwar et al., "A Single Ketamine Infusion
Combined with Motivational Enhancement Therapy for Alcohol Use Disorder: A
Randomized Midazolam-Controlled Pilot Trial."

155 *despite a variety of pharmacological and behavioral options*: Fuller, "Alcoholism
Treatment in the United States. An Overview."

156 *we observed that "mystical-type" experiences during the infusion*: Dakwar et al., "A
Sub-Set of Psychoactive Effects May Be Critical to the Behavioral Impact of Ketamine on Cocaine Use Disorder: Results from a Randomized, Controlled Laboratory Study."

156 *replicated by other groups*: Barrett et al., "Classic Hallucinogens and Mystical Experiences: Phenomenology and Neural Correlates." James et al., "Psilocybin Occasioned Mystical-type Experiences." Mollaahmetoglu et al., "This is something
that changed my life."

156 The Varieties of Religious Experience: James, *The Varieties of Religious Experience:
A Study in Human Nature.*

157 *psychologists have analyzed the different components of a mystical experience*: Streib
et al., "The Mysticism Scale as a Measure for Subjective Spirituality: New Results
with Hood's M-Scale and the Development of a Short Form."

157 *There is a robust literature on alcoholics and other addicted individuals*: Galanter,
"Spiritual Awakening in Alcoholics Anonymous: Empirical Findings."

157 *brought on by belladonna treatment*: Brooks, "Bill Wilson's Gospel."

157 *Research with classical psychedelics*: The impact of mystical-type experiences on
healthy volunteers: Griffiths et al., "Psilocybin Can Occasion Mystical-Type Experiences Having Substantial and Sustained Personal Meaning and Spiritual Significance." On tobacco addiction: Garcia-Romeu et al., "Psilocybin-Occasioned
Mystical Experiences in the Treatment of Tobacco Addiction." On end-of-life
anxiety: Griffiths et al., "Psilocybin Produces Substantial and Sustained Decreases
in Depression and Anxiety in Patients with Life-Threatening Cancer." On alcohol
use disorder: Bogenschutz et al., "Clinical Interpretation of Patient Experience in
a Trial of Psilocybin-Assisted Psychotherapy for Alcohol Use Disorder."

157 *the brain enters into a heightened state of entropy*: Carhart-Harris et al., "REBUS and
the Anarchic Brain: Toward a Unified Model of the Brain Action of Psychedelics."

158 *We found that one aspect of the experience*: Rothberg et al., "Mystical-Type Experiences Occasioned by Ketamine Mediate Its Impact on at-Risk Drinking: Results
from a Randomized, Controlled Trial."

158 *the Alone . . . to which we come alone*: Corbin, *Alone with the Alone.*

159 *deterritorialized vantage point*: Deleuze and Guattari, *Anti-Oedipus.*

159 *Neuroimaging data on neural correlates*: Ching et al., "Safety, Tolerability, and
Clinical and Neural Effects of Single-Dose Psilocybin in Obsessive-Compulsive
Disorder: Protocol for a Randomized, Double-Blind, Placebo-Controlled, Non-
Crossover Trial."

162 *"I wanted something in the here and now"*: Nádas, *A Book of Memories.*

165 *The placebo response*: Kirsch, "Placebo Effect in the Treatment of Depression and Anxiety."

167 *a recent report found that half of German doctors prescribe deliberate placebos*: Meissner et al., "Widespread Use of Pure and Impure Placebo Interventions by GPs in Germany."

169 *the tiger's fearful symmetry*: Blake, *Blake's Songs of Innocence and Experience.*

170 *Another viewpoint, also supported by biomedicine*: Prossin et al., Wager, Tor D., and Lauren Y. Atlas, "The Neuroscience of Placebo Effects."

170 *This will invariably change the way*: Olson et al., "Tripping on Nothing."

Part II: Into the Wilderness

178 *This is the compassionate truth of harm reduction strategies*: Tatarsky, *Harm Reduction Psychotherapy.*

180 *And so, we return*: Joyce, *Finnegans Wake.*

Chapter 6: Crucifixion Dream

205 *Whoever aspires ever upwards*: Goethe, *Faust: A Tragedy.*

205 *The serenity prayer*: "The AA Prayer."

207 *most people who recover from an addiction do so on their own*: Tucker et al., "Epidemiology of Recovery from Alcohol Use Disorder."

209 *Each incarnation suffering the dreary ooze of being into doing*: Beckett, *Molloy.*

209 *the Great Doubt*: Nishitani, *Religion and Nothingness.*

Chapter 9: Qarrtsiluni

256 *"The Learned"*: Blake, *A Descriptive Catalogue.*

Part III: Origins

261 *the Quechua word widely interpreted to mean "vine of the dead"*: McKenna et al., "The Scientific Investigation of Ayahuasca: A Review of Past and Current Research."

261 *The Yage Letters*: Burroughs, Ginsberg, *The Yage Letters.*

262 *my sibling . . . and my double*: Baudelaire, *Charles Baudelaire: Complete Poems.*

262 *In his* Letters: Burroughs, Ginsberg, *The Yage Letters.*

263 *sensory phenomena taken to be real*: Leptourgos et al., "Hallucinations Under Psychedelics and in the Schizophrenia Spectrum: An Interdisciplinary and Multiscale Comparison."

264 *with the usual neural constraints on information processing dismantled*: Carhart-Harris et al., "REBUS and the Anarchic Brain: Toward a Unified Model of the Brain Action of Psychedelics."

264 *It is hypothesized that this allows for potentially fruitful disruptions*: Carhart-Harris et al., "REBUS and the Anarchic Brain: Toward a Unified Model of the Brain Action of Psychedelics."

265 *"psychedelic exceptionalism"*: Lawlor, "Psychedelic Exceptionalism and Reframing Drug Narratives: An Interview with Dr. Carl Hart."

266 *"pharmahuasca" analog*: "Ayahuasca Pill Is Officially Here, Filament CEO Discusses Future Plans."

267 *certain groups are granted religious protections for ceremonial use*: Labate and Cavnar, *Religious Freedom and the Global Regulation of Ayahuasca.*

267 Sous les pavés . . . la plage: Cousin, *Pourquoi J'ai Écrit : Sous Les Pavés La Plage.*

276 *The Christian image*: Koerner, *The Reformation of the Image.*

277   *Anthropologists have long recognized:* Turner, *Liminality and Communitas.* Van Gennep, *The Rites of Passage.*

277   *this might be nature's way to steer us right:* For one person's psychedelic mythologizing in this regard, see: Pinchbeck, *The Return of Quetzalcoatl.*

278   *with some studies reporting more ecological mindedness:* Irvine et al., "Transpersonal Ecodelia: Surveying Psychedelically Induced Biophilia."

278   *This is precisely how our dominant regime(s) have maintained their hegemony:* Hamm and Smandych, *Cultural Imperialism: Essays on the Political Economy of Cultural Domination.*

279   *Popular representations of Indigenous people:* Ellingson, *The Myth of the Noble Savage;* Deloria, *Playing Indian.*

280   *Yet this has not protected Brazil:* Raftopoulos and Morley, "Ecocide in the Amazon: The Contested Politics of Environmental Rights in Brazil."

280   *Volksgemeinschaft:* Welch, "Nazi Propaganda and the *Volksgemeinschaft*: Constructing a People's Community."

281   *codified into something like an authoritative dogma:* Halley, "The Colonization of the Ayahuasca Experience."

282   *"Final solution":* Bloxham, "The Final Solution: A Genocide."

283   *This viewpoint has been most forcefully articulated:* Rousseau, *Émile: Or, Concerning Education.* Rousseau, *A Discourse on Inequality.*

283   *picture of unbridled human freedom:* Thomas, *The Marquis de Sade.* For a forceful positioning of Sade's viewpoint contra Rousseau, see: Paglia, *Sexual Personae: Art and Decadence from Nefertiti to Emily Dickinson.*

283   *two sides of the same counterfeit coin:* For an examination of how this fiction has informed culture and anthropology, see Graeber, *The Dawn of Everything: A New History of Humanity.*

284   *"mutual healing":* Holland, *Good Chemistry: The Science of Connection from Soul to Psychedelics.* Psychedelic Chronicles, "A Plant for Peace? The Role of Ayahuasca Ceremonies in the Israel-Palestine Conflict."

284   *an ancient solution:* George et al., "Ancient Roots of Today's Emerging Renaissance in Psychedelic Medicine."

284   *an ancient problem:* Dowty, *Israel / Palestine.*

285   *Israel is at once an attempt:* Chomsky and Pappé, *On Palestine.* Finkelstein, *Beyond Chutzpah: On the Misuse of Anti-Semitism and the Abuse of History.* Mayer, *Plowshares into Swords.* Pappé, *The Ethnic Cleansing of Palestine.* Khalidi, *The Hundred Years' War on Palestine.* Said, *The Question of Palestine.*

285   *proto-Zionist British imperialists:* Talbot et al., "Perceiving Palestine: British Visions of the Holy Land." Kamel, *Imperial Perceptions of Palestine.*

285   *Jewish identity is refashioned:* For more on the construction of a national and genetic origin of otherwise heterogenous and transnational groups, see Sand, *The Invention of the Jewish People.*

285   *erasing all others:* For an examination of how this occurred in Israeli archaeological practices explicitly, see: Abu el Haj, *Facts on the Ground.*

285   *Zionist/imperial/biblical orientalism:* For more on what he termed biblical orientalism, see: Kamel, *Imperial Perceptions of Palestine.*

285   *"a land without a people":* Garfinkle, "On the Origin, Meaning, Use and Abuse of a Phrase."

285   *"Palestine," "justice," or "waqf [endowment] from God":* For an examination of how the Indigenous people of the region forged a sense of collective identity, see: Khalidi, *Palestinian Identity.*

286   *This opportunity to enjoy more expansive modes:* Roseman et al., "Relational Processes in Ayahuasca Groups of Palestinians and Israelis."

286   *plant medicine peace initiative*: Psychedelic Chronicles, "A Plant for Peace? The Role of Ayahuasca Ceremonies in the Israel-Palestine Conflict."

286   *B'Tselem*: B'Tselem, "Un Régime de Suprématie Juive de La Méditerranée Au Jourdain : C'est Un Apartheid."

287   *"For we wrestle not against flesh and blood"*: Ephesians 6:12

287   *And we have also seen it in the obverse*: Covington, "Crack in America: Demon Drugs and Social Justice."

289   *But before peace*: These words were written before Israel began its most recent assault on the Palestinians, primarily in Gaza but also in the West Bank, with the unprecedented Hamas attack on October 7, 2023, serving as the pretext. The scale of Israeli destruction in Gaza has been catastrophic: massive displacement, forced starvation, daily atrocities, destroyed civilian infrastructure, and the large-scale killing of civilians, mostly women and children. An incremental genocide, as historian Ilan Pappé called the Israeli suffocation and destruction of Gaza presciently in 2006, has now intensified into what the ICJ has deemed a plausible genocide, with the mendacity, brutality, and criminality of the regime on full display—despite censorship, the killing of journalists, and legacy media collusion. If this unveiling doesn't bring us to our senses and compel action, what will? How much more bloodshed, deception, and dehumanizing cruelty before our eyes open and hearts awaken, finally, to *never again*?

290   *This monoamine oxidase inhibition (MAOI) activity begins*: Ruffell et al., "The Pharmacological Interaction of Compounds in Ayahuasca: A Systematic Review."

290   *Other plants might be brewed with the vine*: For a considerable survey of DMT-containing plants and ayahuasca admixtures see Ott, *Pharmacotheon*; Shulgin, TIHKAL.

290   *This allows DMT to pass undegraded into the bloodstream*: Erowid, "Erowid DMT Vault: Effects."

297   *"Things that in the neuroses"*: Freud, *An Autobiographical Study*.

298   *the century-old Kraepelinian taxonomy*: Kraepelin, *Psychiatrie: Ein Lehrbuch für Studierende und Ärzte*.

302   *a confluence*: Halley, "The Colonization of the Ayahuasca Experience."

303   *The "anti-psychiatry" movement*: Important texts include Deleuze and Guattari, *Anti-Oedipus*. Szasz, *The Myth of Mental Illness: Foundations of a Theory of Personal Conduct*. Laing, *The Politics of Experience and The Bird of Paradise*. Guattari, *Molecular Revolution: Psychiatry and Politics*.

303   *La Borde*: Guattari, *Molecular Revolution: Psychiatry and Politics*. For a film on the staging of one such play: Philibert, *Every Little Thing*.

305   *Every profound spirit . . . needs a mask*: Nietzsche, *Beyond Good and Evil*.

317   *The entrepreneurship of the self*: Han, *Capitalism and the Death Drive*.

321   *We are born . . . between shit and urine*: Augustine, *The Confessions*.

334   *These mind-forged manacles*: Blake, *Songs of Experience*.

334   *Rousseau's fantasy of the original man*: Rousseau, *Émile: Or, Concerning Education*.

Part IV: Conclusions

341   *"I have learned and dismantled"*: Darwish, *Unfortunately, It Was Paradise: Selected Poems*.

BIBLIOGRAPHY

B'Tselem. "Un Régime de Suprématie Juive de La Méditerranée Au Jourdain : C'est Un Apartheid." n.d.

"Compatibilism (*Stanford Encyclopedia of Philosophy*)." 2019. November 26, 2019. https://plato.stanford.edu/entries/compatibilism/.

"Erowid DMT Vault : Effects." n.d. https://erowid.org/chemicals/dmt/dmt_effects.shtml.

"Erowid Ketamine Vault : Effects." n.d. https://erowid.org/chemicals/ketamine/ketamine_effects.shtml.

"Fiscal Year 2024 Budget Information—Congressional Justification for National Institute on Drugs and Addiction | National Institute on Drug Abuse." 2023. National Institute on Drug Abuse. April 3, 2023. https://nida.nih.gov/about-nida/legislative-activities/budget-information/fiscal-year-2024-budget-information-congressional-justification-national-institute-drug-abuse.

"National Institute on Drug Abuse (NIDA): What We Do." 2022. National Institutes of Health (NIH). March 3, 2022. https://www.nih.gov/about-nih/what-we-do/nih-almanac/national-institute-drug-abuse-nida.

"The AA Prayer—Alcoholics Anonymous Serenity Prayer." 2023. *Alcoholics Anonymous.*

"The Drug War Is the New Jim Crow." 2005. American Civil Liberties Union. September 14, 2005. https://www.aclu.org/documents/drug-war-new-jim-crow.

Alighieri, Dante. 2014. *The Divine Comedy: Inferno, Purgatorio, Paradiso.* Penguin.

Alimoradi, Zainab, Aida Lotfi, Chung-Ying Lin, Mark D. Griffiths, and Amir H. Pakpour. 2022. "Estimation of Behavioral Addiction Prevalence During COVID-19 Pandemic: A Systematic Review and Meta-analysis." *Current Addiction Reports* 9 (4): 486–517.

Anonymous. 2002. *Meditations on the Tarot: A Journey into Christian Hermeticism.* TarcherPerigee.

Aristotle. 2012. *Aristotle's Nicomachean Ethics.* University of Chicago Press.

Ashbery, John. 1998. *The Mooring of Starting Out.* HarperCollins.

Augustine, Saint. 2008. *The Confessions.* Oxford Paperbacks.

Bacon, Francis. 1883. *The Essays, or Counsels Civil and Moral.*

Bajac, Quentin, Man Ray, and Clément Chéroux. 2010. *Man Ray: Portraits: Paris, Hollywood, Paris.* Editions du Centre Pompidou.

Bakalar, James, and Lester Grinspoon. 1997. *Psychedelic Drugs Reconsidered.* The Lindesmith Center.

Barker, Judith C., and Geoffrey Hunt. 2007. "Natural Recovery: A Cross-Cultural Perspective." In Springer eBooks, 213–37.

Barrett, Frederick S., and Roland R. Griffiths. 2017. "Classic Hallucinogens and Mystical Experiences: Phenomenology and Neural Correlates." In *Current Topics in Behavioral Neurosciences*, 393–430.

Bateson, Gregory. 1971. "The Cybernetics of 'Self': A Theory of Alcoholism." *Psychiatry MMC* 34 (1): 1–18.

Bathje, Geoff J., Eric Majeski, and Mesphina Kudowor. 2022. "Psychedelic Integration: An Analysis of the Concept and Its Practice." *Frontiers in Psychology* 13 (August).

Baudelaire, Charles. 1982. *Les Fleurs Du Mal: The Complete Text of The Flowers of Evil.* David R. Godine.

Baudelaire, Charles. 2007. *Charles Baudelaire: Complete Poems.* Fyfield Books.

Beckett, Samuel. 2012. *Molloy.* Faber & Faber.

Beckett, Samuel, et al. 1994. *Worstward Ho.* Brøndum.

Benishek, Lois A., Karen L. Dugosh, Kimberly C. Kirby, Jason Matejkowski, Nicolle Clements, Brittany L. Seymour, and David S. Festinger. 2014. "Prize-Based Contingency Management for the Treatment of Substance Abusers: A Meta-analysis." *Addiction* 109 (9): 1426–36.

Bentham, Jeremy. 1876. *An Introduction to the Principles of Morals and Legislation.*

Bird, Kai, and Martin J. Sherwin. 2007. *American Prometheus: The Inspiration for the Major Motion Picture* Oppenheimer. Vintage.

Blake, William. 1974. *Jerusalem, the Emanation of the Giant Albion.*

Blake, William. 2007. *Blake's Songs of Innocence and Experience.* Tate.

Blake, William. 1990. *A Descriptive Catalogue.* Woodstock Books.

Block, Ned. 1995. "On a Confusion About a Function of Consciousness." *Behavioral and Brain Sciences* 18, 227–287.

Block, Ned Joel. 2000. *Consciousness, Function, and Representation.* MIT Press.

Bloxham, Donald. "The Final Solution: A Genocide." 2010. Choice Reviews Online 48 (01): 48–0494.

Bogenschutz, Michael P., et al. 2018. "Clinical Interpretations of Patient Experience in a Trial of Psilocybin-Assisted Psychotherapy for Alcohol Use Disorder." *Frontiers in Pharmacology.*

Borges, Jorge Luis. 1962. *Ficciones.* Grove Press.

Brooks, David. 2010. "Bill Wilson's Gospel." *New York Times,* June 29, 2010.

Burke, Kathryn A., Theresa M. Franz, Danielle N. Miller, and Geoffrey Schoenbaum. 2008. "The Role of the Orbitofrontal Cortex in the Pursuit of Happiness and More Specific Rewards." *Nature* 454 (7202): 340–44.

Burroughs, William S. 1962. *The Ticket That Exploded.* Olympia Press.

Burroughs, William S., and Allen Ginsberg. 1963. *The Yage Letters.* San Francisco: City Lights.

Byron, William. 1978. *Cervantes, A Biography.* Garden City, NY: Doubleday.

Carhart-Harris, Robin, and Karl J. Friston. 2019. "REBUS and the Anarchic Brain: Toward a Unified Model of the Brain Action of Psychedelics." *Pharmacological Reviews* 71 (3): 316–44.

Cassin, Barbara, Christian Hubert Steven Rendall, Michael Syrotinski, Jacques Lezra; translation edited by Emily Apter and Michael Wood. 2014. *Dictionary of Untranslatables.* Princeton, NJ: Princeton University Press eBooks.

Cervantes Saavedra, Miguel de. 1998. *Don Quixote.* New York: Oxford University Press.

Chacon, Natalia C., Namrata Walia, Abigail A. Allen, Anthony Sciancalepore, Joyce Tiong, Rachel Quick et al. 2021. "Substance Use During COVID-19 Pandemic: Impact on the Underserved Communities." *Discoveries* 9 (4): e141.

Chalmers, David J. 1998. "Facing Up to the Problem of Consciousness." In Routledge eBooks, 207–28.

Chappel, John N. 1993. "Long-term Recovery from Alcoholism." *Psychiatric Clinics of North America* 16 (1): 177–87.

Chaturvedi, B. K. 2004. *Shiv Purana.* Diamond Pocket Books (P) Ltd.

Cheung, Yee Tak Derek, Man Ping Wang, William Li, Antonio Kwong, Vienna Lai, Sophia Siu Chee Chan, and Tai Hing Lam. 2017. "Effectiveness of a Small Cash Incentive on Abstinence and Use of Cessation Aids for Adult Smokers: A Randomized Controlled Trial." *Addictive Behaviors* 66 (March): 17–25.

Ching, Terence H. W., Rachael Grazioplene, Calvin Bohner, Stephen A. Kichuk, Giuliana DePalmer, Elizabeth J. D'Amico, Jeffrey Eilbott et al. 2023. "Safety, Tolerability, and Clinical and Neural Effects of Single-Dose Psilocybin in Obsessive-Compulsive Disorder: Protocol for a Randomized, Double-Blind, Placebo-Controlled, Non-Crossover Trial." *Frontiers in Psychiatry* 14 (April).

Chomsky, Noam, and Ilan Pappé. 2015. *On Palestine*. Penguin UK.

Courtney, Kelly E., Joseph P. Schacht, Kent E. Hutchison, Daniel Roche, and Lara A. Ray. 2015. "Neural Substrates of Cue Reactivity: Association with Treatment Outcomes and Relapse." *Addiction Biology* 21 (1): 3–22.

Cousin, Bernard. 2008. *Pourquoi j'ai Écrit: Sous Les Pavés La Plage.*

Corbin, Henri. 1998. *Alone With the Alone*. Princeton University Press.

Covington, Jeanette, Craig Reinarman, and Harry G. Levine. 1998. "Crack in America: Demon Drugs and Social Justice." *Contemporary Sociology* 27 (3): 310.

Coyle, Caoimhe M., and Keith R. Laws. 2015. "The Use of Ketamine as an Antidepressant: A Systematic Review and Meta-analysis." *Human Psychopharmacology: Clinical and Experimental* 30 (3): 152–63.

Craver, Carl F. 2007. *Explaining the Brain: Mechanisms and the Mosaic Unity of Neuroscience*. New York: Oxford University Press.

Dakwar, Elias, and Frances R. Levin. 2013. "Individual Mindfulness-Based Psychotherapy for Cannabis or Cocaine Dependence: A Pilot Feasibility Trial." *American Journal on Addictions* 22 (6): 521–26.

Dakwar, Elias, Carl L. Hart, Frances R. Levin, Edward V. Nunes, and Richard W. Foltin. 2016. "Cocaine Self-Administration Disrupted by the N-Methyl-D-Aspartate Receptor Antagonist Ketamine: A Randomized, Crossover Trial." *Molecular Psychiatry* 22 (1): 76–81.

Dakwar, Elias, Edward V. Nunes, Carl L. Hart, Mei-Chen Hu, Richard W. Foltin, and Frances R. Levin. 2018. "A Sub-Set of Psychoactive Effects May Be Critical to the Behavioral Impact of Ketamine on Cocaine Use Disorder: Results from a Randomized, Controlled Laboratory Study." *Neuropharmacology* 142 (November): 270–76.

Dakwar, Elias, Edward V. Nunes, Carl L. Hart, Richard W. Foltin, Sanjay J. Mathew, Kenneth M. Carpenter, C. Jean Choi, Cale Basaraba, Martina Pavlicová, and Frances R. Levin. 2019. "A Single Ketamine Infusion Combined with Mindfulness-Based Behavioral Modification to Treat Cocaine Dependence: A Randomized Clinical Trial." *American Journal of Psychiatry* 176 (11): 923–30.

Dakwar, Elias, Frances R. Levin, Carl L. Hart, Cale Basaraba, Jean C. Choi, Martina Pavlicová, and Edward V. Nunes. 2020. "A Single Ketamine Infusion Combined with Motivational Enhancement Therapy for Alcohol Use Disorder: A Randomized Midazolam-Controlled Pilot Trial." *American Journal of Psychiatry* 177 (2): 125–33.

Dakwar, Elias, Frances R. Levin, Richard W. Foltin, Edward V. Nunes, and Carl L. Hart. 2014. "The Effects of Subanesthetic Ketamine Infusions on Motivation to Quit and Cue-Induced Craving in Cocaine-Dependent Research Volunteers." *Biological Psychiatry* 76 (1): 40–46.

Dakwar, Elias, John J. Mariani, and Frances R. Levin. 2011. "Mindfulness Impairments in Individuals Seeking Treatment for Substance Use Disorders." *American Journal of Drug and Alcohol Abuse* 37 (3): 165–69.

Darwish, Mahmoud. 2013. *Unfortunately, It Was Paradise: Selected Poems*. University of California Press.

Das, Gopal. 1993. "Cocaine Abuse in North America: A Milestone in History." *Journal of Clinical Pharmacology* 33 (4): 296–310.

Dawson, Neil, Brian J. Morris, and Judith A. Pratt. 2011. "Subanaesthetic Ketamine Treatment Alters Prefrontal Cortex Connectivity with Thalamus and Ascending Subcortical Systems." *Schizophrenia Bulletin* 39 (2): 366–77.

Deleuze, Gilles, and Félix Guattari. 2004. *Anti-Oedipus*. A&C Black.

Deleuze, Gilles, and Félix Guattari. 1987. *A Thousand Plateaus: Capitalism and Schizo-phrenia*. University of Minnesota Press.

Deloria, Philip J. 2022. *Playing Indian*. Yale University Press.

Derrida, Jacques. 2021. *Dissemination*. University of Chicago Press.

Descartes, René. 2013. *Meditations on First Philosophy*. Broadview Press.

Diagnostic and Statistical Manual of Mental Disorders, 5th ed. 2013.

Domino, Edward F. 2010. "Taming the Ketamine Tiger." *Anesthesiology* 113 (3): 678–84.

Domino, Edward F., Peter Chodoff, and Guenter Corssen. 1965. "Pharmacologic Effects of CI-581, a New Dissociative Anesthetic, in Man." *Clinical Pharmacology & Therapeutics* 6 (3): 279–91.

Donne, John, and John Daniel Thieme. 2014. *John Donne Holy Sonnets: With an Introduction by John Daniel Thieme*. Vicarage Hill Press.

Douglass, Frederick. 2016. *Narrative of the Life of Frederick Douglass*. Dover.

Dowty, A. 2012. *Israel / Palestine*, 3rd ed., fully revised and updated. Cambridge, MA: Polity Press.

Einstein, Albert. 1936. "Physics and Reality." *Journal of the Franklin Institute* 221 (3): 349–82. https://doi.org/10.1016/s0016-0032(36)91047-5.

El-Haj, Nadia Abu. 2001. *Facts on the Ground: Archaeological Practice and Territorial Self-Fashioning in Israeli Society*. The University of Chicago Press.

Ellingson, Ter. 2001. *The Myth of the Noble Savage*.

Emerson, Ralph Waldo. 2014. *Self-Reliance*. FV Éditions.

Ersche, Karen D., P. Simon Jones, Guy B. Williams, Abigail J. Turton, Trevor W. Robbins, and Edward T. Bullmore. 2012. "Abnormal Brain Structure Implicated in Stimulant Drug Addiction." *Science* 335 (6068): 601–4.

Field, Matt, Nick Heather, and Reínout W. Wiers. 2019. "Indeed, Not Really a Brain Disorder: Implications for Reductionist Accounts of Addiction." *Behavioral and Brain Sciences* 42 (January).

Finkelstein, Norman G. 2020. *Beyond Chutzpah: On the Misuse of Anti-Semitism and the Abuse of History*. Verso Books.

Fisher, Carl Erik. 2022. *The Urge: Our History of Addiction*. Scribe Publications.

Food and Drug Administration. 2010. "Guidance for Industry. Assessment of Abuse Potential of Drugs. Draft Guidance." US Food and Drug Administration (FDA) Center for Drug Evaluation and Research (CDER).

Foucault, Michel. 1988. *Madness and Civilization: A History of Insanity in the Age of Reason*. Vintage.

Foucault, Michel. 2018. *The Order of Things*. Routledge.

Frankl, Viktor E. 2014. *Man's Search for Meaning*, Gift Edition. Beacon Press.

Freud, Sigmund. 1925. *An Autobiographical Study*. The Hogarth Press.

Friston, Karl J., and Stefan J. Kiebel. 2009. "Predictive Coding Under the Free-Energy Principle." *Philosophical Transactions of the Royal Society* B 364 (1521): 1211–21.

Fuller, Richard K., and Susanne Hiller-Sturmhöfel. 1999. "Alcoholism Treatment in the United States. An Overview." *Alcohol Research & Health* 23, 2: 69–77.

Galanter, Marc, Helen Dermatis, and Cristal Sampson. 2014. "Spiritual Awakening in Alcoholics Anonymous: Empirical Findings." *Alcoholism Treatment Quarterly* 32 (2–3): 319–34.

Garber, Judith. 2019. "Esketamine Nears FDA Approval, Prompting Both Excitement and Concern." Lown Institute. August 16, 2019. https://lowninstitute.org /esketamine-nears-fda-approval-prompting-both-excitement-and-concern/.

Garcia-Romeu, Albert, et al. 2015. "Psilocybin-occasioned mystical experiences in the treatment of tobacco addiction." *Current Drug Abuse Reviews*.

Garfinkle, Adam M. 1991. "On the Origin, Meaning, Use and Abuse of a Phrase." *Middle Eastern Studies*.

George, Daniel R., Ryan Hanson, Darryl Wilkinson, and Albert Garcia-Romeu. 2021. "Ancient Roots of Today's Emerging Renaissance in Psychedelic Medicine." *Culture, Medicine and Psychiatry* 46 (4): 890–903. https://doi.org/10.1007/s11013-021 -09749-y.

Ghoneim, M. M., et al. 1969. "Ketamine: Behavioral Effects of Subanesthetic Doses." *Journal of Clinical Psychopharmacology* 5 (2).

Gödel, Kurt. 1930. "On Formally Undecidable Propositions of Principia Mathematica and Related Systems I," January. https://patterns.architexturez.net/doc /az-cf-177058.

Goldstein, Lara. "Ayahuasca Pill Is Officially Here, Filament CEO Discusses Future Plans." n.d. https://www.filament.health/news/ayahuasca-pill-is-officially-here-filament-ceo-discusses-future-plans.

Graeber, David, and David Wengrow. 2021. *The Dawn of Everything: A New History of Humanity*. Penguin UK.

Granit, Ragnar. 1967. *Receptors and Sensory Perception: A Discussion of Aims, Means, and Results of Electrophysiological Research into the Process of Reception*.

Grant, Bridget F., Tulshi D. Saha, W. June Ruan, Risë B. Goldstein, S. Patricia Chou, Jeesun Jung, Haitao Zhang et al. 2016. "Epidemiology of DSM-5 Drug Use Disorder." *JAMA Psychiatry* 73 (1): 39.

Greenfield, Shelly F., Audrey J. Brooks, Susan M. Gordon, Carla A. Green, Frankie Kropp, R. Kathryn McHugh, Melissa Lincoln, Denise A. Hien, and Gloria M. Miele. 2007. "Substance Abuse Treatment Entry, Retention, and Outcome in Women: A Review of the Literature." *Drug and Alcohol Dependence* 86 (1): 1–21.

Griffiths, Roland R., William A. Richards, Una D. McCann, and Robert L. Jesse. 2006. "Psilocybin Can Occasion Mystical-Type Experiences Having Substantial and Sustained Personal Meaning and Spiritual Significance." *Psychopharmacology* 187 (3): 268–83.

Griffiths, Roland R., et al. 2016. "Psilocybin Produces Substantial and Sustained Decreases in Depression and Anxiety in Patients with Life-Threatening Cancer: A Randomized Double-Blind Trial." *Journal of Psychopharmacology*.

Guattari, Félix. 1984. *Molecular Revolution: Psychiatry and Politics*. Puffin Books.

Halley, Catherine. 2021. "The Colonization of the Ayahuasca Experience." *JSTOR Daily*. September 29, 2021. https://daily.jstor.org/the-colonization-of-the-ayahuasca-experience/.

Hamm, Bernd, and Russell Charles Smandych. 2005. *Cultural Imperialism: Essays on the Political Economy of Cultural Domination*. Broadview Press.

Han, Byung-Chul. 2021. *Capitalism and the Death Drive*. John Wiley & Sons.

Hanh, Thich Nhat. 2001. *Thich Nhat Hanh: Essential Writings*. Orbis Books.

Hariton, Eduardo, and Joseph J. Locascio. 2018. "Randomised Controlled Trials—the Gold Standard for Effectiveness Research." *BJOG: An International Journal of Obstetrics and Gynaecology* 125 (13): 1716.

Hart, Carl. 2015. "How the Myth of the 'Negro Cocaine Fiend' Helped Shape American Drug Policy." *The Nation*, June 29, 2015. https://www.thenation.com/article /archive/how-myth-negro-cocaine-fiend-helped-shape-american-drug-policy/.

Hart, Carl L. 2017. "Viewing Addiction as a Brain Disease Promotes Social Injustice." *Nature Human Behaviour* 1 (3).

Hart, Carl L., Margaret Haney, Richard W. Foltin, and Marian W. Fischman. 2000. "Alternative Reinforcers Differentially Modify Cocaine Self-Administration by Humans." *Behavioural Pharmacology* 11 (1): 87–91.

Hart, Carl. 2021. *Drug Use for Grown-Ups: Chasing Liberty in the Land of Fear*. Penguin.

Hart, Carl, Caroline Marvin, Rae Silver, and Edward Smith. 2012. "Is Cognitive Functioning Impaired in Methamphetamine Users? A Critical Review." *Neuropsychopharmacology*.

Hasin, Deborah S., and Bridget F. Grant. 2015. "The National Epidemiologic Survey on Alcohol and Related Conditions (NESARC) Waves 1 and 2: Review and Summary of Findings." *Social Psychiatry and Psychiatric Epidemiology* 50 (11): 1609–40.

Hayek, Friedrich August. 1979. *The Counter-Revolution of Science: Studies on the Abuse of Reason.* Indianapolis: Liberty Press.

Hedegaard, Holly, Arialdi M Miniño, and Margaret Warner. 2022. "Drug Overdose Deaths in the United States, 2001–2021."

Heidegger, Martín. 2018. *What Is Metaphysics?* Jovian Press.

Heraclitus. 2003. *Fragments.* Penguin.

Holland, Julie. 2022. *Good Chemistry: The Science of Connection from Soul to Psychedelics.* Harper Wave.

Hopkins, Gerard Manley. 2009. *Gerard Manley Hopkins: The Major Works.* Oxford: Oxford University Press.

Ireland, John D. 2007. *Udana and the Itivuttaka: Two Classics from the Pali Canon.* Buddhist Publication Society.

Irvin, J. R. 2022. *God's Flesh: Teonanácatl: The True History of the Sacred Mushroom.* Logos Media.

Irvine, Alexander, David Luke, Freya Harrild, Sam Gandy, and Rosalind Watts. 2023. "Transpersonal Ecodelia: Surveying Psychedelically Induced Biophilia." *Psychoactives* 2 (2): 174–93.

Jack, Belinda. 2014. "Goethe's *Werther* and Its Effects." *Lancet Psychiatry* 1 (1): 18–19.

James, Edward, Thomas L. Robertshaw, Mathew Hoskins, and Ben Sessa. 2020. "Psilocybin Occasioned Mystical-type Experiences." *Human Psychopharmacology: Clinical and Experimental* 35 (5).

James, William H. 1902. *The Varieties of Religious Experience: A Study in Human Nature.* Longmans, Green and Co. eBooks.

James, William. 1907. *Pragmatism: A New Name for Some Old Ways of Thinking.* Longmans, Green and Co. eBooks.

Janis, Harriet, and Sidney Janis. 1945. *Marcel Duchamp, Anti-Artist.* Vol. XII. Horizon.

Jones, Jermaine, and Sandra Comer. 2014. "A Review of Human Drug Self-Administration Procedures." *Behavioral Pharmacology.*

Joyce, James. 1997. *Finnegans Wake.* Editions Gallimard.

Kamel, Lorenzo. 2020. *Imperial Perceptions of Palestine: British Influence and Power in Late Ottoman Times.* I.B. TAURIS.

Kang, Melody J. Y., Emily R. Hawken, and Gustavo Vázquez. 2022. "The Mechanisms Behind Rapid Antidepressant Effects of Ketamine: A Systematic Review with a Focus on Molecular Neuroplasticity." *Frontiers in Psychiatry* 13 (April).

Kant, Immanuel. 2007. *Critique of Pure Reason.* Penguin Classics.

Kendler, Kenneth S. 2005. "Toward a Philosophical Structure for Psychiatry." *American Journal of Psychiatry* 162 (3): 433–40.

Khalidi, Rashid. 2022. *The Hundred Years' War on Palestine: A History of Settler Colonialism and Resistance, 1917-2017.* Metropolitan Books, Henry Holt and Company.

Khalidi, Rashid. 2010. *Palestinian Identity: The Construction of Modern National Consciousness.* Columbia University Press.

Khouzani, Ehsan Ashrafi, and Majid JamalPour NikSirat. 2022. Maqalat Shams Tabrizi: Vol. 1: Discourse of Shams Tabrizi: Vol. 1.

Kim, Hong, and Lewis S. Nelson. 2015. "Reducing the Harm of Opioid Overdose with the Safe Use of Naloxone: A Pharmacologic Review." *Expert Opinion on Drug Safety* 14 (7): 1137–46.

King, Andrea C., Harriet De Wit, Patrick McNamara, and Dingcai Cao. 2011. "Rewarding, Stimulant, and Sedative Alcohol Responses and Relationship to Future Binge Drinking." *Archives of General Psychiatry* 68 (4): 389.

Kinzer, Stephen. 2019. *Poisoner in Chief: Sidney Gottlieb and the CIA Search for Mind Control.* Henry Holt and Company.

Kirsch, Irving. 2019. "Placebo Effect in the Treatment of Depression and Anxiety." *Frontiers in Psychiatry* 10 (June). https://doi.org/10.3389/fpsyt.2019.00407.

Koerner, Joseph Leo. 2004. *Reformation of the Image.* Reaktion Books.

Korzybski, Alfred. 1958. *Science and Sanity: An Introduction to Non-Aristotelian Systems and General Semantics.* Institute of GS.

Kraepelin, Emil. 1915. *Psychiatrie: ein Lehrbuch für Studierende und Ärzte.*

Krupitsky, Evgeny, et al. 2002. "Ketamine Psychotherapy for Heroin Addiction: Immediate Effects and Two-Year Follow-Up." *Journal of Substance Abuse Treatment* 23 (4): 273–83.

Krupitsky, E. M., and A. Y. Grinenko. 1997. "Ketamine Psychedelic Therapy (KPT): A Review of the Results of Ten Years of Research." *Journal of Psychoactive Drugs.*

Krystal, John H., Laurence P. Karper, John Seibyl, Glenna K. Freeman, Richard Delaney, J. Douglas Bremner, George R. Heninger, Malcolm B. Bowers, and Dennis S. Charney. 1994. "Subanesthetic Effects of the Noncompetitive NMDA Antagonist, Ketamine, in Humans." *Archives of General Psychiatry* 51 (3): 199.

Kuhn, Thomas S. 2012. *The Structure of Scientific Revolutions: 50th Anniversary Edition.* University of Chicago Press.

Labate, Beatriz Caiuby, and Clancy Cavnar. 2023. *Religious Freedom and the Global Regulation of Ayahuasca.* Taylor & Francis.

Laing, R. D. 1990. *The Politics of Experience and The Bird of Paradise.* Penguin UK.

Lawlor, Sean. 2022. "Psychedelic Exceptionalism and Reframing Drug Narratives: An Interview with Dr. Carl Hart." *Psychedelics Today*, October 4, 2022. https://psychedelicstoday.com/2020/02/18/psychedelic-exceptionalism-and-reframing-drug-narratives-an-interview-with-dr-carl-hart/.

Lee, Michelle Ye Hee. 2021. "Does the United States Really Have 5 Percent of the World's Population and One Quarter of the World's Prisoners?" *Washington Post*, December 7, 2021. https://www.washingtonpost.com/news/fact-checker/wp/2015/04/30/does-the-united-states-really-have-five-percent-of-worlds-population-and-one-quarter-of-the-worlds-prisoners/.

Leland, John. 2018. "Genesis P-Orridge Has Always Been a Provocateur of the Body. Now She's at Its Mercy." *New York Times*, 2018.

Leptourgos, Pantelis, Martin Fortier-Davy, Robin Carhart-Harris, Philip R. Corlett, David Dupuis, Adam L. Halberstadt, Michael Kometer et al. 2020. "Hallucinations Under Psychedelics and in the Schizophrenia Spectrum: An Interdisciplinary and Multiscale Comparison." *Schizophrenia Bulletin* 46 (6): 1396–1408.

Leshner, Alan I. 1997. "Addiction Is a Brain Disease, and It Matters." *Science* 278 (5335): 45–47.

Lichtenberg, Georg Christoph. 2000. *The Waste Books.* New York Review Books.

Lilly, John C. 1972. *The Center of the Cyclone: An Autobiography of Inner Space.*

Liu, Shijing, Scott D. Lane, Joy M. Schmitz, Andrew J. Waters, Kathryn A. Cunningham, and F. Gerard Moeller. 2011. "Relationship Between Attentional Bias to Cocaine-Related Stimuli and Impulsivity in Cocaine-Dependent Subjects." *American Journal of Drug and Alcohol Abuse* 37 (2): 117–22.

MacKillop, James, and Cara Murphy. 1994. "Drug Self-Administration Paradigms: Methods for Quantifying Motivation in Experimental Research." *The Wiley-Blackwell Handbook of Addiction Psychopharmacology.*

Mann, Thomas. 2018. *The Magic Mountain.* Random House.

Mayer, Arno J. 2021. *Plowshares into Swords: From Zionism to Israel.* Verso Books.

McGovern, Patrick E. 2003. *Ancient Wine: The Search for the Origins of Viniculture.*

McKenna, D. J., C. S. Grob, and J. C. Callaway. 1982. "The Scientific Investigation of Ayahuasca: A Review of Past and Current Research." Erowid. 1982. https://www.erowid.org/chemicals/ayahuasca/ayahuasca_journal3.shtml.

McQueen, Kelly. n.d. "Table 15.3, World Health Organization's List of Essential Medicines for Anesthesia and Pain Management, 2013—Essential Surgery—NCBI Bookshelf." https://www.ncbi.nlm.nih.gov/books/NBK333510/table/ch15.sec4.table3/.

McWhorter, John. 2011. "The Root: Why Won't Obama End the War on Drugs?" NPR, June 17, 2011. https://www.npr.org/2011/06/17/137243512/the-root-why-wont-obama-end-the-war-on-drugs.

Meisnner et al., 2011. "Widespread Use of Pure and Impure Placebo Interventions by GPs in Germany." *Family Practice* 29 (1): 79–85.

Michaels, J. Ramsey. 2010. *The Gospel of John*. Wm. B. Eerdmans Publishing.

Miller, William, and Rollnick, Stephen. 2023. *Motivational Interviewing: How to Help People Change and Grow*. The Guilford Press.

Milton, John. 1750. *Paradise Lost: A Poem in Twelve Books*.

Mollaahmetoglu, O. Merve, Edward Palmer, Emily L. Maschauer, Melissa C. Nolan, Tobias Stevens, Molly Carlyle, Lorna Hardy, Edward Watkins, and Philip G. Morgan. 2021. "The Acute Effects of Alcohol on State Rumination in the Laboratory." *Psychopharmacology* 238 (6): 1671–86.

Mollaahmetoglu, O. Merve, et al. 2021. "'This Is Something That Changed My Life': A Qualitative Study of Patients' Experiences in a Clinical Trial of Ketamine Treatment for Alcohol Use Disorders." *Frontiers in Psychiatry*.

Montaigne, Michel. 2004. *The Complete Essays*. Penguin UK.

Montale, Eugenio. 2011. *The Collected Poems of Eugenio Montale: 1925–1977*. National Geographic Books.

Nabokov, Vladimir. 1955. *Lolita*. Olympia Press.

Nádas, Péter. 2008. *A Book of Memories: A Novel*. Macmillan.

Nietzsche, Friedrich Wilhelm. 2006. *Beyond Good and Evil*.

Nietzsche, Friedrich Wilhelm. 2017. *The Will to Power*. Penguin UK.

NIH. 2017. *NIH News in Health*. September 8, 2017. https://newsinhealth.nih.gov/2015/10/biology-addiction.

Nikhilananda, Swami. 1990. *The Upanishads*.

Nishitani, Keiji. 1992. *Religion and Nothingness*. University of California Press.

Olson, Jay A., Léah Suissa-Rocheleau, Michael Lifshitz, Amir Raz, and Samuel P. L. Veissière. 2020. "Tripping on Nothing: Placebo Psychedelics and Contextual Factors." *Psychopharmacology* 237 (5): 1371–82.

Panchal, Nirmita, and Heather Saunders. 2023. "The Implications of COVID-19 for Mental Health and Substance Use." *KFF*, www.kff.org/mental-health/issue-brief/the-implications-of-covid-19-for-mental-health-and-substance-use/.

Panlilio, Leigh V., and Steven R. Goldberg. 2007. "Self-Administration of Drugs in Animals and Humans as a Model and an Investigative Tool." *Addiction* 102, no. 12.

Paglia, Camille. 1990. *Sexual Personae: Art and Decadence from Nefertiti to Emily Dickinson*. New Haven, CT: Yale University Press.

Pain, Stéphanie. 2015. "A Potted History." *Nature* 525 (7570): S10–11.

Pappé, Ilan. 2007. *The Ethnic Cleansing of Palestine*. Simon & Schuster.

Pendell, Dale, and Gary Snyder. 2010. *Pharmako/poeia: Plant Powers, Poisons, and Herbcraft*. North Atlantic Books.

Philibert, Nicolas. 1998. *Every Little Thing*.

Pinchbeck, Daniel. 2007. *2012: The Return of Quetzalcoatl*. Penguin.

Piore, Adam. 2021. "Magic Mushrooms May Be the Biggest Advance in Treating Depression Since Prozac." *Newsweek*, September 29, 2021. https://www.newsweek.com/2021/10/01/magic-mushrooms-may-biggest-advance-treating-depression-since-prozac-1631225.html.

Plato. 2016. *Apology*. Xist Publishing.

Plato. 2005. *Phaedrus*. Penguin UK.

Pollan, Michael. 2018. *How to Change Your Mind: What the New Science of Psychedelics Teaches Us About Consciousness, Dying, Addiction, Depression, and Transcendence*. Penguin.

Porchia. 2003. *Voices*.

Posner, Michael I., and C. R. Snyder. 1975. "Attention and Cognitive Control." The Loyola Symposium, January, 55–85.

Principles of Addiction: Comprehensive Addictive Behaviors and Disorders. 2013. Academic Press.

Prossin, Alan R., Alisa E. Koch, Phillip L. Campbell, Geoffroy Laumet, Christian S. Stohler, Robert Dantzer, and Jon-Kar Zubieta. 2021. "Effects of Placebo Administration on Immune Mechanisms and Relationships with Central Endogenous Opioid Neurotransmission." *Molecular Psychiatry* 27 (2): 831–39.

Psychedelic Chronicles. 2022. "A Plant for Peace? The Role of Ayahuasca Ceremonies in the Israel-Palestine Conflict," December 20, 2022.

Pullen, Erin, and Carrie B. Oser. 2014. "Barriers to Substance Abuse Treatment in Rural and Urban Communities: Counselor Perspectives." *Substance Use & Misuse* 49 (7): 891–901.

Ott, Jonathan. 1993. *Pharmacotheon*. Natural Products Co.

Raftopoulos, Malayna, and Joanna Morley. 2020. "Ecocide in the Amazon: The Contested Politics of Environmental Rights in Brazil." *International Journal of Human Rights* 24 (10): 1616–41.

Rapp, Richard C., Jiangmin Xu, Carey J. A. Carr, D. Timothy Lane, Jichuan Wang, and Robert G. Carlson. 2006. "Treatment Barriers Identified by Substance Abusers Assessed at a Centralized Intake Unit." *Journal of Substance Abuse Treatment* 30 (3): 227–35.

Rilke, Rainer Maria. 2011. *Selected Poems: With Parallel German Text*. Oxford University Press.

Robbins, Trevor W., and Luke Clark. 2015. "Behavioral Addictions." Current Opinion in Neurobiology 30 (February): 66–72.

Roseman, Leor, et al. 2021. "Relational Processes in Ayahuasca Groups of Palestinians and Israelis." *Frontiers in Pharmacology* 12 (May).

Roseman, Leor, and Nadeem Karkabi. 2021. "On Revelations and Revolutions: Drinking Ayahuasca Among Palestinians Under Israeli Occupation." *Frontiers in Psychology* 12 (August).

Rothberg, Rebecca L., Nour Azhari, Nancy A. Haug, and Elias Dakwar. 2020. "Mystical-Type Experiences Occasioned by Ketamine Mediate Its Impact on At-Risk Drinking: Results from a Randomized, Controlled Trial." *Journal of Psychopharmacology* 35 (2): 150–58.

Rounds, Michael. 2020. "3 Ways We Self-Sabotage During Recovery." *Psychology Today*, October 14, 2020. https://www.psychologytoday.com/us/blog/10000-days-sober/202010/3-ways-we-self-sabotage-during-recovery.

Rousseau, Jean-Jacques. 1985. A *Discourse on Inequality*. Penguin Classics.

Rousseau, Jean-Jacques. 1888. *Émile: Or, Concerning Education*. Penguin Classics.

Ruffell, Simon, Nige Netzband, Catherine Bird, Allan H. Young, and Mário F. Juruena. 2020. "The Pharmacological Interaction of Compounds in Ayahuasca: A Systematic Review." *Revista Brasileira de Psiquiatria* 42 (6): 646–56.

Saadi, Altaf, Joanna Naples-Mitchell, Brianna Da Silva Bhatia, and Michele Heisler. 2022. "End the Use of 'Excited Delirium' as a Cause of Death in Police Custody." *Lancet* 399 (10329): 1028–30.

Said, Edward W. 1992. *The Question of Palestine*. Vintage.

Salmond, Susan, and Virginia Allread. 2019. "A Population Health Approach to America's Opioid Epidemic." *Orthopaedic Nursing* 38 (2): 95–108.

Sand, Shlomo. 2009. *The Invention of the Jewish People*. Verso.

Schlag, Anne Katrin. 2020. "Percentages of Problem Drug Use and Their Implications for Policy Making: A Review of the Literature." *Drug Science, Policy and Law* 6 (January): 205032452090454.

Schopenhauer, Arthur, and E. F. J. Payne. 1966. *The World as Will and Representation.* Courier Corporation.

Science of Addiction: *Drugs, Brains, and Behavior* (rev. ed.). 2009. DIANE Publishing.

Scull, Andrew. 2015. *Madness in Civilization.* https://doi.org/10.2307/j.ctvc77hvc.

Seligman, Martin E. P., and Steven F. Maier. 1967. "Failure to Escape Traumatic Shock." *Journal of Experimental Psychology* 74 (1): 1–9. https://doi.org/10.1037/h0024514.

Shaham, Yavin, and Bruce T. Hope. 2005. "The Role of Neuroadaptations in Relapse to Drug Seeking." *Nature Neuroscience* 8 (11): 1437–39.

Shakespeare, William. 2022. *A Midsummer Night's Dream.* D.C. Books.

Shakespeare, William. 1954. *Hamlet.* The Folio Society.

Shulgin, Alexander T. 1997. *TIHKAL: A Continuation.* Transform Press.

SIPRI. "Sipri Military Expenditure Database." www.sipri.org/databases/milex.

Skinner, B. F. 1991. *The Behavior of Organisms: An Experimental Analysis.* Copley Publishing Group.

Sobell, Linda C., Timothy P. Ellingstad, and Mark B. Sobell. 2000. "Natural Recovery from Alcohol and Drug Problems: Methodological Review of the Research with Suggestions for Future Directions." *Addiction* 95 (5): 749–64.

Stendhal. 1975. *Love.* Penguin UK.

Stevens, Jay. 1987. *Storming Heaven: LSD and the American Dream.* http://ci.nii.ac.jp/ncid/BA20361570.

Streib, Heinz, Constantin Klein, Barbara Keller, and Ralph W. Hood. 2020. "The Mysticism Scale as a Measure for Subjective Spirituality: New Results with Hood's M-Scale and the Development of a Short Form." In Springer eBooks, 467–91.

Substance Abuse and Mental Health Services Administration (SAMHSA). 2023. "SAMHSA Announces National Survey on Drug Use and Health (NSDUH) Results Detailing Mental Illness and Substance Use Levels in 2021." HHS.Gov, January 4, 2023. https://www.hhs.gov/about/news/2023/01/04/samhsa-announces-national-survey-drug-use-health-results-detailing-mental-illness-substance-use-levels-2021.html.

Szasz, Thomas S. 1988. *The Myth of Mental Illness: Foundations of a Theory of Personal Conduct.*

Talbot et al. "Perceiving Palestine: British Visions of the Holy Land." *Institute for Palestine Studies.*

Tang, Deborah, Lesley K. Fellows, Dana M. Small, and Alain Dagher. 2012. "Food and Drug Cues Activate Similar Brain Regions: A Meta-analysis of Functional MRI Studies." *Physiology & Behavior* 106 (3): 317–24.

Tanahashi, Kazuaki, and Peter Levitt. 2013. *The Essential Dogen: Writings of the Great Zen Master.* Shambhala Publications.

Tatarsky, Andrew. 2007. *Harm Reduction Psychotherapy: A New Treatment for Drug and Alcohol Problems.* Jason Aronson.

The Yoga Sutras of Patanjali. 1990.

Thomas, Donald. 1992. *The Marquis de Sade.* Kensington Publishing Corporation.

Tomasi, Dardo, Gene Jack Wang, Ruiliang Wang, Elisabeth C. Caparelli, Jean Logan, and Nora D. Volkow. 2014. "Overlapping Patterns of Brain Activation to Food and Cocaine Cues in Cocaine Abusers." *Human Brain Mapping* 36 (1): 120–36.

Torwesten, Hans, and Loly Rosset. 1994. *Vedanta: Heart of Hinduism.* Grove Press.

Tucker, Jalie A., Susan D. Chandler, and Katie Witkiewitz. 2020. "Epidemiology of Recovery from Alcohol Use Disorder." *Alcohol Research* 40 (3).

Turner, Victor. 2017. "Liminality and Communitas." In Routledge eBooks, 94–130.

Tzu, Lao. 2012. *Tao Te Ching*: Text Only Edition. Vintage.

United Nations. 2010. "United Nations Office on Drugs and Crime: Drugs Statistics and Trends." UNODC. 2010. https://www.unodc.org/documents/wdr/WDR_2010/2.0 _Drug_statistics_and_Trends.pdf.

Vallery-Radot, René. 1975. *The Life of Pasteur*.

Van Gennep, A. 2013. *The Rites of Passage*. Routledge.

Various. 2002. *Early Greek Philosophy*. Penguin.

Vico, Giambattista. 1999. *New Science*. Penguin UK.

Volkow, Nora. "Addiction Is a Disease of Free Will." Addiction Education Society. n.d. https://addictioneducationsociety.org/addiction-is-a-disease-of-free-will/.

Von Goethe, Johann Wolfgang. 1882. *Faust: A Tragedy*.

Von Goethe, Johann Wolfgang. 1893. *Maxims and Reflections*. Library of Alexandria.

Wager, Tor D., and Lauren Y. Atlas. 2015. "The Neuroscience of Placebo Effects: Connecting Context, Learning and Health." *Nature Reviews Neuroscience*.

Watson, John B. 1924. *Behaviorism*. Norton & Company, Inc.

Welch, David. 2004. "Nazi Propaganda and the *Volksgemeinschaft*: Constructing a People's Community." *Journal of Contemporary History* 39 (2): 213–38.

Westbrook, Cecilia, J. David Creswell, Golnaz Tabibnia, Erica Julson, Hedy Kober, and Hilary A. Tindle. 2011. "Mindful Attention Reduces Neural and Self-Reported Cue-Induced Craving in Smokers." *Social Cognitive and Affective Neuroscience* 8 (1): 73–84.

Whitehead, Alfred North. 1929. *The Function of Reason*. Beacon Press.

Whitehead, Alfred North. 1929. *Process and Reality: An Essay in Cosmology*.

Wittgenstein, Ludwig. 2010. *Philosophical Investigations*. Wiley-Blackwell.

Wittgenstein, Ludwig. 2012. *Tractatus Logico Philosophicus*. Simon & Schuster.

World Health Organization: WHO. 2022. "COVID-19 Pandemic Triggers 25% Increase in Prevalence of Anxiety and Depression Worldwide." World Health Organization, March 2, 2022. https://www.who.int/news/item/02-03-2022-covid-19 -pandemic-triggers-25-increase-in-prevalence-of-anxiety-and-depression -worldwide#:~:text=In%20the%20first%20year%20of,Health%20Organization %20(WHO)%20today.

Zanos, Panos, and Todd D. Gould. 2018. "Mechanisms of Ketamine Action as an Antidepressant." *Molecular Psychiatry* 23 (4): 801–11.

Zhang, Youyi, Fei Ye, Tongtong Zhang, Shiyun Lv, Liping Zhou, Daohai Du, Lin He, Fei Guo, Cheng Luo, and Shujia Zhu. 2021. "Structural Basis of Ketamine Action on Human NMDA Receptors." *Nature* 596 (7871): 301–5.

Zhuangzi, and Brook Ziporyn. 2009. *Zhuangzi: The Essential Writings with Selections from Traditional Commentaries*. Hackett Publishing.

Zuger, Abigail. 2011. "A General in the Drug War." *New York Times*, June 13, 2011. https:// www.nytimes.com/2011/06/14/science/14volkow.html.

INDEX

ABOUT THE AUTHOR

ELIAS DAKWAR is an associate professor of psychiatry at Columbia University and a practicing psychiatrist, working primarily with people suffering from addiction. He has been investigating novel treatments for addiction for nearly two decades, with a focus on combining contemplative practices, medicines, and psychotherapy to disrupt substance use disorders. His work has been published in numerous medical and academic journals, and he has spoken at conferences around the world.